On
Economics
and
Society

Harry G.
Johnson

On
Economics
and
Society

The University of Chicago Press
Chicago and London

The University of Chicago Press
Chicago 60637
The University of Chicago Press, Ltd.,
London

Published 1975
Printed in the
United States of America

**Library of Congress Cataloging in
Publication Data**
Johnson, Harry Gordon, 1923-
  On economics and society.
  Includes index.
  1. Economics—Addresses, essays, lectures.
2. Economic policy—Addresses, essays, lec-
tures.   I. Title.
HB71.J59   1975   330   74-11625
ISBN 0-226-40162-6

HARRY G. JOHNSON is Charles F. Grey
Distinguished Service Professor of Economics
at the University of Chicago. He has published
more than four hundred articles in scholarly
journals, and he is the author of many books,
including *Macroeconomics and Monetary
Theory, Inflation and the Monetarist Controversy, The Theory of Income Distribution,*
and *Essays in Monetary Economics.*

Contents

Introduction   ix

Part 1.
The Relevance of Economics

1. Economic Theory and Contemporary Society   3
2. The Economics Approach to Social Questions   15
3. The Political Economy of Opulence   32
4. The Social Policy of an Opulent Society   45

Part 2.
The Keynesian Revolution, for Good or Ill

5. The General Theory After Twenty-five Years   61
6. Keynes and British Economics   77
7. The Keynesian Revolution and the Monetarist Counter-revolution   91
8. Cambridge in the 1950s   107

Part 3.
Economics and the Universities

9. National Styles in Economic Research: The United States, the United Kingdom, Canada, and Various European Countries   129
10. Scholars as Public Adversaries: The Case of Economics   140
11. The University and Social Welfare   153
12. Some Political and Ideological Influences on Contemporary Economics   176

Part 4.
Economics and Contemporary Problems: Inflation and Inequality

13. The Problem of Inflation   197
14. Some Microeconomic Observations on Income and Wealth Inequalities   212

15. Inequality of Income
    Distribution and the Poverty
    Problem   220

Part 5
Economics and Contemporary
Problems: World Inflation, Money,
Trade, Growth, and Investment

16. World Inflation: A Monetarist
    View   239
17. Political Economy Aspects of
    International Monetary
    Reform   248
18. Mercantilism: Past, Present, and
    Future   267
19. The Problem of Economic
    Development   282
    I. Social, Political, and Economic
       Problems of Development   282
    II. Commercial Policy and
        Industrialization   291
20. Direct Foreign Investment:
    A Survey of the Issues   303

Part 6.
Economics and the Environment

21. Man and His
    Environment   317

Notes   341
Index   353

In gratitude to my secretaries in
Chicago and London:

Billie Blackhurst	*Susi Conti*
Judy Kidd	*Sherry Hamilton*
Elaine Goldstein	*Clare Moore*
Lillian Rochon	*Nancy Bergh*
	Lois Rodgers

Introduction

One of the penalties—or privileges, as the case may be—of advancing age and professional maturation in an academic career in the social sciences is that one is forced to think in terms of progressively broadening frames of institutional and cultural reference. The young economist, whatever may have been his original motivations for becoming an academic, comes out of the graduate student mill with a narrow range of specialized skills and the stamp of his teachers' ideas heavy upon him. He makes his way initially by applying his skills—and attempting to get them over-valued by society and his employers—in an institutional and social context taken as an immutable part of his environment. Only as he acquires self-confidence, on the one hand, and abrasive experience of the larger extra-departmental and extra-academic world, on the other, can he afford again to accord himself the liberty to question society's institutions that he enjoyed as a carefree undergraduate. And only then can his questions, and the answers at which he arrives, be of potential serious interest to his fellow citizens; for only then are his thoughts informed and authoritative enough to be worthy of their serious consideration, and his formulations and solutions of questions well enough connected with the general culture of his society to be communicable and comprehensible to their understanding.

All being well, that is! For it is one of the vices of the social sciences to safeguard spurious pretensions to academic superiority by "talking down" to the public—either by insisting on adherence to a professional jargon that, like the drunkard's lamp-post, provides more support than illumination, or by insultingly oversimplifying one's conclusions to a level deemed appropriate to a presumedly cretinous audience.

The essays collected in this volume all represent, though in various ways, efforts to explain economics or the application of economics to audiences assumed to be literate, mature, and intelligent, though amateur in relation to the standards of the best professional work on the subjects under discussion. The justification for publishing them in collected form is that together they constitute—or so I hope—a rounded and consistent position on a range of issues of a broadly economic kind that have been and continue to be matters of serious discussion in circles of intelligent opinion formation.

Part 1 is concerned with expounding what contemporary economics is all about, and what it, as a social science, has to say about contemporary society.

Much of what the layman thinks of as economics, especially on the basis of a fragmentary memory of an introductory college course refreshed by reading an occasional newspaper editorial derived from the same source, is concerned with an artificial and highly abstract imaginary world difficult to relate to the real world of observation and experience. By comparison, the slogans and stereotypes of John Kenneth Galbraith and less gifted armchair critics of the modern economy possess at least a welcome air of no-nonsense realism. These essays attempt to show how serious economics copes with the same phenomena as do popular social commentators, how it has been attempting to extend its understanding of them into the comprehension of political as well as economic processes, and what it has to say about why the world of affluence is still not fit for idealists to live in and what can be done to improve it.

The economics of part 1 is technically described as microeconomics, which for present purposes can be understood as the detailed workings of the economic machine. The kind of economic issue that is most in the public eye, however, is concerned with such issues as inflation, unemployment, and economic growth—technically, with macroeconomics, or how the machine works overall in delivering the goods. Every layman is aware that prevailing modern ideas on these matters are the result of a major change in economic theory—the so-called Keynesian revolution that occurred in the 1930s—and are generally categorized as "Keynesian economics." Some are also aware that in recent years a counterrevolution has been going on—"the monetarist counterrevolution"—the focus of controversy being the importance of the quantity of money, and more specifically of changes in the rate of growth of the quantity of money as determined by the central bank (the Federal Reserve), or "monetary policy," in governing the rates of unemployment and inflation.

Part 2 is concerned with the Keynesian revolution and the monetarist counterrevolution. One of the two major essays attempts to describe the enduring changes in economic theory that have followed from the Keynesian revolution, and relate them to the longer perspective of theoretical development; the other attempts to account for the speed of propagation of both the revolution and the counterrevolution.

One aspect of a system of thought that makes it an orthodoxy ripe for revolutionary or counterrevolutionary attack is its crystallization into a rigid and self-satisfied orthodoxy. That happened very quickly to the Keynesian revolution, and accounts for the rapid subsequent decline of the two major revolutionary centers—Cambridge, England (and indeed English economics generally), and Cambridge, Massachusetts, more specifically Harvard University and its American intellectual satellites (with the honorable exception of Yale). The two other essays in this part describe the decline of English Keynesianism into orthodoxy. (The American story is too complex to recapitulate here.) One presents a personal assessment of the long-run impact of the Keynesian revolution on contemporary British economics; the other, a professional-biographical sketch, describes what it was like to teach in Cambridge, England, in the immediate postrevolutionary phase when the new orthodoxy was still mopping up the last remnants of the old guard. The latter serves in a way as a bridge to the subsequent essays on economists and their universities.

Part 3 turns from the inner to the outer aspects of academic economics. The first two essays deal with economists in their roles as researchers, and as consultants and advisers on economic policy (sometimes the two are hard to distinguish). These essays are an indirect response to the recent malaise of the universities, as reflected indirectly in questioning of the social usefulness and efficiency of scientific research, on the one hand, and doubts about the potentially corruptive effects of participation of social scientists in public decision-making, on the other. The second two essays deal with aspects of the university as the institution within which economics functions as an academic discipline. One is concerned with the functions of the university and the question of whether and to what extent it can be considered a purposive social institution—a question prompted by the growing public concern about how well universities do their job and justify the public money needed to support them. The other analyzes the broadly political forces that have been operating on the development of academic economics in recent years, and ends with some on-the-whole gloomy predictions about future prospects.

The remaining three parts turn back to the detailed pursuit of themes and problems sketched broadly in part 1. Part 4 deals with what may be termed domestic problems of modern industrial society. The first essay is concerned with the problem of inflation and attempts a scholarly debunking of popular alarmism about inflation. Inflation, like sex, raises to the serious mind the question "if it is such a terrible thing, why are we all here?" The last two essays deal, at different levels, with the problems of inequality and poverty, which *are* serious social problems but for which the solutions generally proposed are about as superficial as popular remedies for inflation and promiscuity.

Part 5 is concerned with problems of the international economy. The view expressed here that inflation is a world phenomenon is to be contrasted with the more popular view that inflation is the sum of a series of national accidents, to be solved by finding who is to blame and punishing him. Similarly, the view that it is world inflation that has, for the time being at least, wrecked the international monetary system, and that it is international politics that stand in the way of fundamental reform, is contrasted with the official view that reform is a technical problem to be solved by committees of experts. The remaining essays call attention to the dangers of a deterioration of the world trading order into mercantilist rivalries among trading blocs, to some of the problems of promoting the development of the less developed countries that have been obscured until recently by a mythology of painless development derived from the 1930s and the Keynesian revolution, and to the issues really at stake in current alarmism about the emergence of the multinational corporation.

Part 6 gives solitary pride of place to an essay on ecological doomsterism, or more neutrally to the economics of the relationship between man and his environment. One of the most serious faults of the natural sciences, to which social science properly grounded in historical knowledge should serve as a corrective, is the propensity of their practitioners to believe that because man needs their help to predict eclipses of the sun or the approach of comets, he also needs their help to tell him to take off his coat and loosen his tie on a hot summer's day. Another is their propensity to believe that because they can predict that the sun will turn nova some day, millions of years from now, they owe it to their fellow citizens to warn them to prepare to meet their doom now. The economy provides its own system of signaling approaching change and its own warnings and indicators of how to react to it. And the time between prediction and its fulfillment is also the time available for taking evasive action (if evasion is possible; if not, brooding on fate does not add to happiness).

My late great teacher Harold Adams Innis (now unfortunately famous more as the progenitor of the ideas of Marshall McLuhan than as one of the few original economic historians the world has ever produced) used to counter the demands of those anxious to mobilize the social sciences to the single purpose of defeating Hitler with the remark "the answer to those who demand answers is that there are no answers." In similar vein, the answer to those who cry "wolf!" is, "why do you think we hire shepherds?" "Intolerable complacency!" comes the shriek of scientific rebuttal of reasoned argument. But surely it makes no sense to be stampeded into turning vegetarian today because the wolves might come, baying loudly as they approach, tomorrow, or next week, or next year, or next century, or during the next millennium!

Acknowledgments

I should like to thank Jacob Frenkel, who assisted with suggestions for the selection of the contents and in particular emphasized the desirability of including the part on the universities, and Elizabeth Johnson, whose prolonged immersion in the work and personality of John Maynard Keynes has provided invaluable insights into the character of the man and his approach to economics that I have used shamelessly in my own writings on the subject.

Part 1

The
Relevance of
Economics

1. Economic Theory and Contemporary Society

To anyone who has been exposed to it casually—as most people in this day and age must have been—economic theory appears to be an extremely abstruse and complex subject, with little direct bearing on the real world of observation and experience. It has, indeed, been the endeavor of a generation of mathematicians manqués to make it appear so, even to the majority of work-a-day professional economists themselves. Yet economics is a social science, concerned with the study of one important aspect of human society, and economic theory is the theory of how the economic mechanism of society works, and in addition a theory of how it ought to be made to work— so that economic theory should be able to contribute to our understanding of contemporary society and of contemporary social problems. In this essay I shall attempt to summarize some of the more important things that economic theory has to say about contemporary society. In so doing I hope to demonstrate, incidentally, both that the central corpus of economic theory is rather easier to understand—though not necessarily to apply—than it often appears to be, and that its range over social phenomena and problems is considerably broader than even most economists appreciate.

To begin with, it is necessary to define more precisely the scope of economic theory. From the standpoint of social relevance, economic theory can be described most succinctly as the theory of the laws of demand and supply. But to leave this definition at that would be both arrogant, in implying that these laws transcend human volition, and unsatisfactory, in leaving the provenance and nature of these laws unexplained. More fundamentally, economic theory is concerned with the nature of choice between alternatives ("the allocation of scarce means between competing ends"), the consequences of choice-making in particular systems for giving expression to choice, and the responses of the choices so made to changes in the alternatives available. Traditionally, economic theory has been concerned with the study of choice-making by individual consuming households and producing firms in a system of interconnected markets for goods and services, because it has been through the competitive market system that the organization of production, consumption, distribution, and exchange has

This essay was delivered as a Centennial Lecture in Convention Hall, University of Toronto, November 1967.

3

largely been effected in the economies in which the study of economic science has been most vigorously pursued; hence the analysis of choice has found its expression in the market concepts of demand and supply. But the logic of economic choice is equally applicable to other types of economic systems—and to other categories of choices than economics choices, such as political decisions, and to other kinds of decision-taking units than the household and firm operating in a competitive market environment, such as the administrative decisions of governments, nonprofit institutions such as universities, and other bureaucratic institutions. The essence of economic theory in all these contexts is the assumption that, in choosing among the available alternatives, the choice-maker will attempt to arrive at the choice yielding the best possible outcome in terms of achieving his objectives, subject to the restraints on his capacity to do so, and that consequently changes in these restraints will alter the choices that eventuate. Economic theory is, further, concerned with the conditions under which the environment of choice confronting the choice-taker will be such as to lead him to reach an optimal choice from the social point of view, and with the circumstances in which his choice will have adverse social consequences.

Let me illustrate these general remarks on the nature of economic theory by some concrete examples drawn from both economics and other fields. First, suppose that some technological improvement or scientific discovery reduces the cost of producing a commodity needed to satisfy a certain want, either by reducing the cost of an existing product—for example soap—or by developing a cheaper substitute—for example detergent. Economic theory would predict that the producer would have a profit incentive to cut the price, or to spend more on bringing the product to the attention of potential users, in order to increase sales; and that consumers would respond by using more of the commodity. In general, there would be a presumption that human welfare would be improved, because society would be satisfying its desire for cleanliness at lower cost and would have more resources available to satisfy its other wants. But this would only be the case if the cost of production to the producer and the price to the consumer fully reflected the social cost of the new product. If the cost of production were artificially low because the producer was allowed to make free use of a depleting natural resource, or if the use of the product by the consumer had undesirable side-effects for which he did not have to pay—as, in the case of detergents, the gradual pollution of water supplies—then the free competitive market would not produce socially optimal results. An even better example than detergents perhaps is the automobile, which both pollutes the air, increases the risk of death or injury, and imposes an aesthetically and socially displeasing pattern on the architecture of our cities. Such problems of disparity of private and social costs are becoming increasingly important with the growth of wealth and population, and especially the concentration of population in large metropolitan areas, that is associated with the rising productivity made possible by the development and application of modern technology. It is important to note, at this stage, that these problems are ultimately attributable to the failure of our system of property rights to capture the economic and social consequences of private decisions; no one would cavalierly pollute his own water-well, or poison his own air. From this point of view, governmental corrective action is typically aimed at compensation for the defects of the private property system.

Problems of the same sort, however, arise under other systems of decision-making. Governmental decisions, for example, are supposed to be taken for the general good of the community. The politicians who govern, however, have to win election by pleasing the electorate, and it can therefore be predicted that their decisions will be biased toward preserving the population in its existing locations and existing activities, whereas the common interest might better be served by developing new activities in new locations. Also, since established industries and enterprises usually stand to benefit commercially from population growth, governments will have a bias toward encouraging population growth, especially by immigration, in disregard for the social and economic problems that may result from increasing population density and congestion. Similarly, bureaucratic decision-taking systems such as govern both large corporations and nonprofit institutions like universities and foundations will predictably have built-in biases associated with the ways in which the alternatives for and the payoffs from decisions present themselves in such systems. For example, there is usually a personal payoff to the bureaucratic decision-taker, in the form of enlarged responsibilities and correspondingly increased emoluments, from decisions that will increase the size of the bureaucracy's operations, and hence a tendency for bureaucratically organized institutions to grow too large for efficient performance of function. There is also a tendency for the flow of information upward through the various layers of decision-taking to be biased toward the suppression of information unfavorable to, and the exaggeration of information favorable to, the objectives of the organization as established by those at the top, with predictable consequences in inefficient decision-taking: universities, for example, rarely discontinue courses or close down departments. Finally, bureaucracies establish their own internal standards of successful performance, which may depart widely from the social objectives for which they have been established; educational institutions, for example, almost invariably measure their performance by the examination results of their students, which are a by-product rather than the end product of good education, while foundations for the support of research pride themselves on the promotion of new research projects, which may be far less useful to society than the completion, continuation, or confirmation of previous research endeavors.

Economic theory, then, is concerned with the logic of choice, the consequences of choices arrived at in systems of decision-taking, and the effects on choices of changes in the available alternatives. Formally, economic theory has found it convenient to divide its subject matter into two levels of analysis: macroeconomics, which is concerned with the overall behavior of the economy—the determination of the level of output, the level of unemployment, the state of inflation or deflation, and the rate of economic growth; and microeconomics, which is concerned with the allocation of the economy's resources among various particular uses—production, consumption, distribution, and exchange. Macroeconomics is of relatively recent origin, dating from the Keynesian revolution of the 1930s; microeconomics, on the other hand, has constituted the core of economic science since its inception in the writings of the English "classical" economists in the late eighteenth and early nineteenth centuries.

The central message of macroeconomics is extremely simple: it is that the level of economic activity in an economy, and the level of unemployment, are determined by the aggregate demand for the economy's output of goods and services; and that the government can exercise a controlling influence over aggregate demand, and hence over economic activity, by proper use of its fiscal policy (policy with respect to the levels of taxation and expenditure), monetary policy (policy with respect to the quantity of money and/or level of interest rates), and exchange rate policy (policy with respect to fixing the value of the national currency in terms of other nations' currencies). Conversely, government policy can itself create problems of depression and unemployment on the one hand, or of unhealthy boom and price inflation on the other, by failure to make appropriate use of its powers of budgetary, monetary, and exchange rate control. This message is obviously of fundamental importance for contemporary economic society, which achieves its high productivity by means of an extreme specialization and division of labor within an interdependent system of markets, the smooth functioning of which requires confidence both in the stability of the overall demand for output and in the stability of the value of the money for which goods and services are sold. Yet it is a message that seems extraordinarily difficult for public opinion to grasp and to apply. There seem to be two major reasons for this. One is that we are accustomed to think of the budget of the government as exactly analogous to the private budgets of households and firms, and to believe erroneously that the same criteria of financial probity should apply to the former as to the latter. The other is that most people have difficulty in seeing beyond the proximate causes of economic disturbances to the macroeconomic forces that are ultimately responsible for them. Thus, for example, when aggregate demand is permitted to slacken off and unemployment rises significantly, as happened toward the end of the 1950s, it seems more plausible to blame the unemployment on automation, or on the inadequate education of parts of the labor force, than on the underlying inadequacy of aggregate demand that allows these factors to produce unemployment. And conversely, when the pressure of demand is permitted to become excessive, and prices rise appreciably, it is more plausible to blame the inflation on the exercise of monopoly power by unions and large corporations than to blame it on the laxness of monetary and fiscal policy that has created a demand situation in which wages and prices can safely be increased—and, indeed, have to be increased in response to economic pressures. The result is that society wastes much effort—and considerable moral indignation—in attacking the symptoms rather than the causes of its macroeconomic diseases. The moral is that a better public understanding of the basic principles of macroeconomics could contribute importantly to the improved functioning of our economy and society.

The central message of microeconomics is equally simple: it is that the economy is organized by the choices of households and firms, expressed primarily through the market, and that this system of organization is a rational one (that is, a system with a logic behind it) which responds rationally to changes in the alternatives of choice. Unlike the message of macroeconomics, however, the message of microeconomics points not to a few simple concrete propositions about society but to an infinite range of applications. It is this that makes microeconomic theory more difficult than macroeconomic theory, but at the same time makes it more immediately relevant to problems of everyday life. This relevance I shall demonstrate in the remainder of this lecture.

Contemporary society, whether it describes its economics system as a "free-enterprise," a "mixed," or a "centrally planned" economy, is based on an industrial system that is governed by the corporate form of organization. This form of organization of industry has proven itself remarkably skillful in mobilizing and pooling the productive talents of large numbers of individuals and in mobilizing the capital and technical knowledge required for efficient production. Through an increasingly fine specialization and division of labor, coordinated by an essentially bureaucratic system of decision-taking within the enterprise, it has institutionalized steadily rising productivity and a steadily rising standard of living for society as a whole. In the process, as J. K. Galbraith has argued in his book *The New Industrial State*, the basis of economic power in society has shifted from the ownership of land (where it lay in precapitalist times) and the ownership of capital (where it lay in the traditional capitalism analyzed by Marx) to the managerial team—the "technostructure," as Galbraith calls it. I shall not pursue further the political implications of that theme but would instead emphasize the social aspect of it, the changed basis of participation by the bulk of the population in the productive process. Whereas in the past the few owned and controlled and the majority worked for wages, in the modern industrial economy participation in production has increasingly been based on personal knowledge, training, and education rather than on property ownership or the supply of labor time. Moreover, industrial progress has fed on itself in this respect, steadily increasing the system's capacity to utilize educated skills and thus to provide substantial economic returns to the acquisition of education. Among the more important consequences have been a significant reduction in the proportion of the population normally classifiable as poor, the easing of discrimination based on race and religion, and the emancipation of women. That emancipation has had two facets, both the consequence of industrial progress: the progressive opening of job opportunities to women as brains and manual dexterity have replaced brute force as the characteristically human contribution to production; and the freeing of women from household labor through the substitution of labor-saving household capital equipment for female labor time. (The emancipation of women does mean, however, that part of the recorded increase in the standard of living is illusory, since by statistical convention a housewife's labor in the home is not counted as part of the national income, whereas a woman's work for wages outside the home is so counted.)

The evolution of the basis of human participation in the productive process away from brute force toward education and knowledge has been recognized in economic theory by the increasing use of the concept of "human capital" in the analysis of the economic role of the individual both as a supplier of labor and as a consumer. As a supplier of labor, the individual is the owner of a productive asset—his skills and knowledge—that has been created by past investment of his time and of real resources in the acquisition of his training, and that yields its returns in a flow of income over time. In this aspect of his life, he is confronted with the same problems of how much to invest, and in what to invest, as confront the owner of material property; and he has, incidentally, the same incentives to try to increase the value of his property by monopolistic practices—the formation of unions, or the establishment of professional associations with licensing rights—as does the owner of a business. As a consumer the individual is equally the owner of a productive asset—his capacity to earn an income by supplying labor—and it is perfectly natural for him not only to insure this asset by life and health insurance, but to use it as a collateral for the purchase of household goods on the installment plan: the growth of installment buying, far from being evidence of the improvidence of wage-earners, is evidence of their economic intelligence. It is also rational for the consumer, in certain circumstances, to attempt to increase the value of his asset by investing in further education, or in moving his labor-supply capacity to a more favorable location or occupation.

The fact that in contemporary society the worker, broadly defined, is typically a capitalist on a substantial scale has some important political and social implications. The most obvious and most fundamental is that, contrary to the analysis of Marx, which was based on nineteenth-century capitalist industry, twentieth-century industry contains no internal contradictions likely to lead to revolution and the transformation of the system. In place of a polarization of society into a small class of capitalist owners and a growing class of propertyless workers, modern industrial organization imposes a pluralistic hierarchy of capitalists of varying degrees—and, moreover, a hierarchy whose rationale is explicitly provided by the industrial system itself rather than by the arbitrariness of property rights and inheritance. Not only does the system not generate a potentially revolutionary class; it also ensures that the poor will be the obviously incompetent, and so undeserving of the sympathy of the equally obviously competent rich. In the modern world, the seeds of revolution are to be found, not within the industrial system itself, but in preindustrial economies envious of the wealth which the industrial system generates, or among minority ethnic or cultural groups within the industrial society that consider themselves to be debarred by discrimination from full participation in the benefits of the system.

Apart from guaranteeing political stability, the increasing prevalence of capitalists in contemporary society has significant implications for the quality of political and social life. The management of capital, whether human or otherwise, requires rational calculation, and this in turn requires the assembly and evaluation of relevant information. In modern industry and other administrative structures, this activity is generally entrusted to committees, supported by the research of experts. Both the habit of rational evaluation of alternatives, and the resort to reliance on expert committees for advice and policy proposals, have been spreading from private economic decision-taking to the consideration of political and social issues. The result has been to remove much of the excitement from political activity—both politicians and political scientists complain of the decline of Parliament as an institution of power—but to improve the quality of political decision-taking in matters affecting everyday life. The underlying tendency is, however, obscured by the facts that most of the political decisions that are important to people in their everyday lives fall to be taken at the provincial or municipal level of government, or are taken routinely and quietly at the federal level, and that political debate tends to be most intense over the issues that are least within the control of the politicians. But there is one important real issue that contemporary politics has yet to resolve: where to draw the line between public and private responsibility for individual welfare. As people become more substantial and more capable capitalists, it becomes increasingly possible for them to rely on market institutions—insurance, mutual funds, and so forth—to protect themselves against the various risks of life; and such institutions will develop, under the profit incentive, to meet the need. But both the long tradition of socialist thought, and the experience of the Great Depression of the 1930s and the postwar inflation, have implanted the belief that these risks should be assumed collectively through the state. This belief obviously needs to be re-thought, in the light of experience of the evolution of contemporary economic society.

In their personal and social lives also, the practice of capitalism has been leading people toward more rational decision-taking based on more adequate knowledge of alternatives. Much of the relevant knowledge is provided in the form of commercial advertising, which has become one of the favorite whipping-boys of the critics of contemporary society. From the point of view of economic theory, however, advertising is not just a vulgar excrescence of the competitive system that should be deplored and restrained, but an integral and rational part of the contemporary system of production and distribution. The key points in understanding the role of advertising are two. The first is that in a society which is steadily raising its standard of living by the application of science and technology to the discovery of new and better or cheaper ways of doing things, the dissemination of information about such discoveries is important both to the producers of innovations and to the potentially beneficiary consumers. In a static society everyone knows both what he wants and what is available; in a dynamic society information on these matters becomes a valuable commodity, worth providing in its own right. But for many items of consumer expenditure, the value of information on the relative merits of alternative commodities to the consumer is too small to warrant his paying the money and time costs of acquiring it, whereas it is to the producer's advantage to disseminate information in the hope of attracting purchases of his product. Naturally, the information so disseminated will be somewhat biased; but the consumer will not be oblivious to this fact. The second point is that modern technology offers an infinite variety of ways in which producers may disseminate information, ranging from personal contact, as in door-to-door selling, to newspaper and radio and television broadcast messages. Each has its own costs, and its own degree of effectiveness, with respect to any product; and the producer may be expected to choose the method that promises to be most profitable for his product. The media used by advertising communicate messages cheaply in vast quantities, at the expense of subtlety and specificity of the messages communicated. This last characteristic is the focal point of social criticism of advertising; but one might on the contrary argue that the crudeness of its messages is a social virtue of advertising—by comparison, say, with what an unscrupulous used-car salesman is capable of accomplishing. One could go even further, and argue that the very impersonality of advertising exercises a democratizing influence on society, by enabling consumers to make purchasing decisions without having to rely on personal relationships with shopkeepers. In any case, it is always possible for consumers who are willing to take the trouble to acquire information through routes other than advertising; and in fact they have increasingly been resorting to two quite feasible alternatives, the legislation of labeling requirements and other standards for producers, and the financing of consumer research on a subscription basis.

The increasing rationality of decision-taking, based on better knowledge of alternatives, is evident not only in the economic choices that people make, but in other areas of personal and social life as well—where it frequently appears to social observers as evidence of social breakdown or decay. The economic emancipation of women already referred to was bound to increase the freedom of relations between the sexes, though a probably far more powerful force has been the improvement of the technology of birth control, culminating in the pill. The increasing frequency of resort to divorce, and the associated pressure for the liberalization of the divorce laws, reflects both the improvement of the economic alternatives to marriage now available to women, and the fact that more reliable control over procreation has tended to standardize the time profile of the marriage experience. It also reflects what might be termed an increasing standardization of the role of the housewife as manageress of a domestic factory, and increasing opportunity for the comparative reevaluation of the human capital value of the spouse by the other partner. Increasing social tolerance of male homosexuality, and perhaps an increasing practice of it, reflect both the emancipation of women and a change in the role of children from productive family assets to utility-yielding parental consumption goods, with consequential de-emphasis of the responsibility of males to beget children. Finally, in an increasingly opulent society, certain kinds of petty crime, such as shoplifting and other petty thievery, cease to be regarded—at least by their perpetrators—as serious infringements of the rights of private property and hence become a part of the costs of doing business for the enterprises affected. At the same time, with mounting affluence, the imposition of fines becomes less effective and the imposition of prison sentences more effective, as a deterrent to wrongdoing. One of the most difficult legal problems of contemporary society, however, is to devise effective methods of detecting and penalizing crimes of fraud implemented through the corporation.

By and large, the ever-rising standard of living generated for the majority by the modern industrial system implies not merely improvement in national standards of consumption, but greater personal freedom and broader opportunities for self-fulfillment. A rich, technologically progressive economy affords its citizens not only rising incomes to spend at their discretion— and increasing leisure time in which to spend those incomes—but wider opportunities for interesting careers and more satisfying rewards for the development of personal talents. The resulting improvement in the general quality of civilization is evident in the increasing numbers of people who have traveled widely, or who can afford to take a serious interest in the performing arts or in artistic endeavor on their own, or whose careers enable them to display their artistic or scientific creativity. It is true that we still have a long way to go to the millennium when the distinction between work and play will have disappeared, and all of everyone's waking hours will be devoted simply to living; but our typical ways of life are moving in that direction.

In a paper read to the recent University of Windsor Seminar on Canadian-American Relations, Professor H. Scott Gordon has disputed this point, predicting that automation will tend to eliminate the white-collar jobs in the middle salary ranges which corporate enterprise has thus far created in such cast numbers, polarizing society once more into a privileged few who possess a monopoly of the intelligence and the high-powered education in depth required to design and install automated production systems, and the many who will have to be content with serving as relatively low-paid meter-watchers and machine-minders. While every man has the right to be his own social soothsayer, I do not find this prediction at all convincing, for two reasons: first, it seems to me that automation, like assembly-line production and the use of mechanical and then electrical power at earlier stages of industrial history, is in large part a response to rising labor costs rather than an independent and exogenous force tending to push wages down; second, over the longer run and in the aggregate these apparently labor-saving inventions— which have invariably been resisted and decried at the time of innovation— seem to have operated both to free men from routine toil and to release their energies for more productive and rewarding economic activities. There is, in my judgment, ample opportunity for those released by automation from routine clerical work in factories and offices to be more gainfully and interestingly employed in the service and research and development sectors of the economy. I therefore expect that the evolution of the modern economic system will continue to offer broadening opportunities for the gainful employment of trained skills at rising standards of living.

I have said that the modern industrial system offers broadening economic and occupational opportunities for individual self-development. This, however, is not an unmixed blessing; indeed, it is precisely in this connection that the major social problems of contemporary society are to be found. I shall conclude by discussing three of these problems.

In the first place, the fact that contemporary society offers to the typical individual expanding opportunities for choice and self-expression implies as a corollary that it imposes on him the necessity of taking decisions, of learning new standards of choice as his opportunities broaden, and of adapting to continual economic and social change. Not everyone is equal to the challenge; many are unable to cope effectively with the various problems of interpersonal relations, sex, alcohol, automobility, budgeting, management of personal debt, and legal rights and obligations in which members of a mobile and progressing society necessarily become involved. In consequence, the social worker is inevitably one of the chief luxury goods on which an affluent society is forced to spend its money; the lawyer is a close second.

Secondly, as I have already mentioned, the rising affluence of modern industrial society promotes and in some ways requires both the growth of the population, and the concentration of population in densely populated metropolitan areas. This gives rise to a number of problems of conflict between individual and collective self-interest, which economists lump together in the general category of "external economies" and have recently come to analyze more positively under the title of "the theory of public goods;" the outstanding examples are urban congestion, the slum problem, "urban sprawl," and the pollution of air and water by the discharge into them of private wastes. Quite a lot has been said in recent years about these problems—perhaps too much, in view of the fact that the damage one man can do another can generally undo by spending enough money, and will be motivated to undo if the damage makes him uncomfortable enough. As previously mentioned, externalities are associated with the inappropriate definition of property rights; and such rights can be reshuffled by market transactions, or counteracted by expenditure on mitigation of the damage, as well as altered by legislation. For example, if I want to be able to swim in clean water in natural surroundings I can form a club and buy a lake; if I want to drink clean water I can buy it by the bottle; and if I want to breath clean air I can build a house, or club together to build an apartment building, with an air filtration system. These are rather drastic remedies, however, which ignore the common democratic presumption that every citizen regardless of income has a right to share in the original beauties of the natural environment, and that it is one of the functions of government to maintain and preserve that right. The problem is that as the pressure of population on space and natural resources grows, this presumed right becomes an increasingly important element in the social welfare; yet we have still to work out effective means of implementing it, in rivalry with the claims of the rights of private property.

Thirdly, while it is true that by and large the progress of industrial society enlarges freedom and the opportunity for self-expression, there is one vital area in which it has been severely constricting freedom, with visible results in generating social unrest. This is the area of secondary and higher education, which has increasingly become the exclusive filter for the entry of the individual into the higher reaches of the industrial system. To gain such entry the individual must remain in tutelage up to an age well past that of biological maturity, and also well past that conventionally recognized as the age of social maturity. In medieval, and even into comparatively recent modern times, an individual so continuing his education did so at his private expense, and hence controlled his own destiny—or, if his education were paid for by charity, this was sufficient of a rarity to keep him properly grateful for the opportunity. In contemporary times, however, education is largely paid for through the state; correspondingly, it is administered by bureaucratic methods, not by the market principle of giving the customer what he wants to buy, or selling him what he ought to have. Yet the customer is otherwise an economic, social and political adult, at least by the time of university admission. It is small wonder that he frequently seeks to escape from the rat race into hippiedom and drugs; or that if he perseveres he feels that he ought to have some right to a voice in the management of the bureaucracy that controls his fate.

2. The Economics Approach to Social Questions

Once upon a time—long ago now—it was possible to refer anyone who thought that economic theory had something to say about society and its problems, and wanted to find out what it was, to Marshall's classic *Principles of Economics*, wherein he could find the structure of economic theory spelled out in literary terms intended to be comprehensible to the businessman of average intelligence. (Even when I went up to Cambridge in 1945 the myth still prevailed that "it is all [mercifully] in Marshall.") That situation has been revolutionized as a result of the introduction of geometrical and mathematical methods of theoretical investigation in the 1930s, and the postwar emphasis on the empirical testing of hypotheses and measurement of economic relationships. Economic theory is now written in set theory, mathematical models, and regression results, with the consequence that it seems to be too abstruse and remote from reality, as well as too technical, to be of any interest or use to the non-specialist concerned with understanding and improving the world in which he lives. This impression, unfortunately, is all too often shared by the professional economists themselves, who frequently confine the use of their scientific tools to technical and academic problems, while relying on intuition, emotion, or political ideology to form their attitudes on social questions. Yet economics is essentially a *social* science, concerned to further understanding of society by the application of scientific methods of analysis and research to the economic aspects of society's activities, and the great advance of the science that has occurred in the past thirty-odd years has made it more and not less capable of illuminating social questions. This, at least, is what I hope to demonstrate—necessarily in very broad and sketchy terms—in this paper.

Economists have, of course, always expressed themselves freely on social questions, though their views have rarely been popular among the rest of the educated elite. It was, indeed, the insistence of the classical economists and their followers on the inevitability of the consequences of Malthus's

An inaugural lecture delivered at the London School of Economics and Political Science, October 12, 1967. Reprinted with permission from *Economica* 25, no. 137 (February 1968): 1–21. Some of the ideas presented have been developed in earlier writings by the author, notably *The Canadian Quandary* (Toronto: McGraw-Hill of Canada, 1963), part four, and "The Economics and Politics of Opulence," *University of Toronto Quarterly* 34 (1965): 313–31. The lecture was abridged for oral delivery.

(fallacious) theory of population growth that earned the discipline in the nineteenth century the description of "the dismal science"; while their general endorsement of laissez-faire, though seriously qualified by John Stuart Mill and later by the welfare economics of A. C. Pigou, remains to this day an active source of intellectual suspicion of economists' views on economic and social policy. The conservative and negativistic role of economists in public discussion of economic policy was sharply reversed by the Keynesian revolution, which put the economist in the unaccustomed position of arguing, not that economic choices were constrained by limitation of resources, but that the resource constraints believed to exist by the politicians and the public did not in fact hold, so that it was possible to have more of every good thing simultaneously. This reversal of roles was, however, necessarily transitory: once the Keynesian lessons about how to maintain full employment had been learned, economics had to become once again, in the classic statement of my predecessor in this Chair, "the science which studies human behavior as a relationship between ends and scarce means which have alternative uses"[1]; for in a fully employed economy total productive capacity again becomes a binding constraint on economic choice. In other words, the problems of predominant concern in contemporary economic and social policy are those that preoccupied Pigou—economic welfare and public finance—rather than the problem of unemployment that proccupied Keynes.

It is, in fact, arguable that British economics has suffered from basking too long in the reflected glory of Keynes's great intellectual achievement, in two major ways. First, economic theorizing, research, and policy discussion in this country have been excessively concerned with macroeconomic problems—theoretical models of economic growth, empirical studies of general price and wage-level behavior, prescriptions for speeding growth without encountering balance-of-payments problems—to the neglect of the microeconomic problems of efficient resource allocation whose solutions are likely over the long run to be more important to the achievement of a highly productive and rapidly growing economy. Second, Keynes's phenomenal success in overthrowing orthodoxy in one major area has fostered among many British economists the conviction that orthodox theory is wrong in every other context—which was certainly not Keynes's view—and the belief that if one is only clever enough in disputing orthodoxy one can come up with a similarly revolutionary advance in economic knowledge—which overlooks the fact that Keynes evolved the *General Theory* after many years of immersion in and contribution to the orthodox tradition in monetary theory. The unfortunate result of this attitude is that, instead of the tools of theory being improved by experience in using them, they tend to become rusty from disuse; and it becomes more important to be unorthodox than to be right, which is the antithesis of scientific criteria of judgment. Meanwhile, of course, traditional economics has not stood still, but has evolved more sophisticated and useful concepts for the analysis and investigation of contemporary economic phenomena.

In a fully employed economy, the main concern of economic theory is with the microeconomic problems of allocation of scarce resources among competing uses, these uses being defined to include provision for the satisfaction of future needs. What does the apparatus of thought that economists have developed for this purpose have to contribute to the understanding and resolution of broader social questions? I shall develop my answer in three stages: first, a brief general statement; second, a discussion of some of the new concepts and approaches that economic theorists have found useful in their own work, and which have a more general application; and third, examination of some examples drawn from recent experience and public debate in this country.

The general statement can most conveniently begin with Robbins's definition of economics as the study of the allocation of scarce means among given ends. Following Robbins further, one can distinguish between *positive* economics, which is concerned with how the economy actually works, and *normative* economics, which is concerned with how the economy should be made to work to maximize the social welfare.

On the positive side, the central concept of economics is that of a system by which the resources of the economy are allocated in production, distribution, and exchange by the interactions of the decisions of individual economic units in an interrelated network of markets. In formal theory the economic units are usually identified as households, which demand goods and supply factors of production, and firms, which supply goods and demand factors of production, though there is no difficulty for the analysis in introducing government into the model of the economy. The essence of the concept of an allocative system is the interdependence of the separate parts of the economy, which implies that a change in conditions in any part of the system—whether occurring autonomously or resulting from changes in governmental policy—will set up repercussions that will reverberate to a greater or lesser extent throughout the whole system. Thus, for example, the British policy of protecting coal from the competition of rival fuels not only imposes an international competitve disadvantage on energy-intensive British industries, but it accounts in part for the inadequate standards of heating and lighting to be found in many British homes, and contributes marginally to the misery of the aged poor.

The concept of an interdependent system, in which the quantities and prices reflect a balancing of opposing forces, is a powerful engine of clarification and understanding of economic relationships and phenomena, and its usefulness extends well beyond the confines of economics proper. In relation to social questions, it has two important implications: that things are the way they are for some powerful reason or reasons, which have to be understood if effective social solutions are to be devised; and that any solutions so devised and applied will have repercussions elsewhere, which will have to be faced and which ought to be taken into account.

On the normative side, the more generally applicable concepts of economic theory are associated with the distinction between means and ends, and the problem of choice implicit in the concept of allocation of scarce resources. The distinction between means and ends is of course relative to circumstances—what are means in one context may be ends in another, and vice versa—but it is nevertheless an important distinction for clarity of thought. Much of the work of economists concerned with policy issues is devoted to sorting out the true ends of policy from the means intended to achieve these ends, and to assessing the relevance and relative efficiencies of the various means proposed—in short, to determining what the problem really is, and attempting to evaluate the various ways of solving it. This sort of clarification is even more necessary, and useful, with respect to broader social questions, where means all too frequently become mistaken for ends and are defended (or attacked) with hot emotion on that basis. For example, no one would dispute that the application of the so-called Means Test in the 1930s to deprive individuals of their presumed legal rights to social assistance was infamous; but it is the height of emotional irrationality to oppose, on the basis of that deplorable piece of history alone, the application of a fairly designed Means Test in order to ensure that the limited amount of money that Parliament is able and willing to make available for the relief of distress is allocated to those with the strongest claims on it—especially as a "Means Test" in the reverse direction, in the form of income tax, is applied to those who furnish the money in the first place. For another example, most people would accept the general proposition that anyone who is qualified and willing to go to a university should have the opportunity to do so; but to insist, as many do, that to this end university education should be provided free of charge is to guarantee that, given the limited public funds available to be spent on university education facilities, the number trained at this level and the quality of the training they receive will both be lower than could be achieved by alternative means of financing higher education.

These examples already introduce the second relevant concept, the concept of choice. This concept has two major facets. The first is the *fact* of choice, or more precisely of the availability of choice between alternatives. There are almost invariably a number of alternative ways of achieving a given end, and efficient decision-making requires consideration of their relative advantages and disadvantages. The second facet is the *process* of choice, which involves the concept of differing costs and returns attaching to alternative courses of action, and of choice as the process of weighing up returns against costs and selecting the alternative with the largest net benefit or highest benefit-cost ratio. The notions that there are always alternatives, that they have costs as well as benefits, and that there are scientific procedures available to assist the making of choices, are extremely important guides to any rational discussion of social questions.

After this very general preliminary statement, I turn to recent developments in economic theory that have significant implications for broader social questions. Six such developments seem to me of outstanding importance; the first two relate to the "robustness"—as the jargon now has it—of fundamental theoretical principles, and the treatment of values in operational economics; the other four involve new approaches to the economics of labor, of time, of information, and of government.

The "robustness" of a theory means the extent to which its conclusions survive under changes in the assumptions from which it is derived. In the 1930s, in the heyday of the imperfect-monopolistic competition revolution, it came to be widely believed that the conclusions of neoclassical economic analysis were crucially dependent on a long list of "unrealistic" abstractions, such as perfect knowledge, perfect competition, and rational utility or profit maximization on the part of economic decision-takers; and it became quite a popular professional sport to belabor economists working in the neoclassical tradition for the lack of realism of their assumptions. The subsequent rise of "positive" economics[2] has shifted the emphasis from testing the reality or plausibility of the assumptions to testing the robustness of the conclusions of a theory, a test which may be conducted either by empirical estimation or by theoretical investigation: and the results have almost invariably been to confirm and strengthen the main propositions of abstract theory. Thus it has been shown, for example, that imperfect competition theory yields virtually no testable positive predictions that might be inconsistent with the theory of pure competition[3]; that whether firms consciously seek to maximize profits and minimize costs or not, competition will eliminate the inefficient firms[4]; and that whether consumer behavior is rational or purely random, the demand curves for products will tend to slope downward as in the Marshallian analysis.[5] In consequence, it is possible for economists to treat the economy as an interdependent system responding to change according to certain general principles of a rational kind, with considerably more confidence than appeared justifiable thirty years ago.

With regard to the treatment of values and value judgments in economics, the neoclassical tradition, as already mentioned, carried a strong presumption in favor of laissez-faire as the policy required to maximize economic welfare. That presumption was destroyed by Lionel Robbins's *The Nature and Significance of Economic Science*, which denied the very possibility of handling value judgments scientifically. The "new welfare economics," which emerged rapidly in response to Robbins's challenge, has made economists much more aware of the pervasiveness and relevance of value judgments in economic analysis and prescription, and much more careful about treating them explicitly. It is true that in the hands of some practitioners the new welfare economics amounts to no more than the unhelpful insistence that nothing can be said about the welfare effects of economic changes except under extremely stringent conditions never fulfilled in practical situations. But among more work-a-day economists, the practical impact has been recognition of the legitimacy of alternative systems of values, and willingness to analyze economic problems and make policy prescriptions in terms of these values. This replacement of dogmatism by pragmatism in the treatment of values in economic analysis has been further encouraged by the development of the "economics of second-best"—largely the creation of James Meade, Richard Lipsey, and Kelvin Lancaster at this School[6]—which starts from the recognition that the world is an imperfect place, and that most policy problems concern changes that will leave it an imperfect place, and which has established the central proposition that whether such changes are for the better or for the worse depends on the detailed circumstances of the individual case and cannot be settled on a priori grounds.

The two developments just described, which may for short be summarized as increased professional confidence and increased ethical pragmatism, pertain to the general approach of economists toward the problems that confront them. I turn now to new developments and insights of analytical economics that have made it a more useful and illuminating guide to the understanding of contemporary society. As already mentioned, I consider four such developments to be of particular importance.

The first of these is the development of a new approach to the economics of labor—more broadly, the economics of the role of human beings in the productive process—based on the concept of "human capital."[7] According to this concept, the skilled (or even the so-called unskilled) worker, and the academically or professionally trained executive, are envisaged as particular types of capital equipment employed in the production process, in the sense that their capacity to make a contribution to the productive process is developed by a process of investment (which means simply the sacrifice of current resources for future returns) incurred in the formal education system and through on-the-job training, and that this investment yields its returns over the lifetime of the individual concerned. It should be noted that the concept of investment in the formation of human capital extends readily beyond the education system, into the economics of such apparently unrelated phenomena as immigration and emigration and the social value of medical care, though I shall not develop any of the implications of that fact here.

The concept of human capital has tremendous integrative power, in that it provides a unifying principle for the consistent explanation of many phenomena of the labor market. Perhaps its most fundamental implication, from the point of view of social thought, is that the worker in an advanced industrial economy is typically a very considerable capitalist, though that fact is usually not apparent to social philosophers accustomed to think of a capitalist as the cigar-smoking owner-manager of a big business. (This is the major reason why Marx's prediction of social revolution has failed to come true.) The capitalist character of labor in a modern economy is reflected on the side of consumption behavior in the widespread resort to hire-purchase, which amounts to borrowing on the security of human capital. On the side of participation in production, it is reflected in many aspects of union behavior and policy, which can be explained as efforts to increase the returns on past investments in human capital or to protect such investments against the inroads of competition; even the commitment of labor to the nationalization of certain industries can be interpreted as reflecting the desire to bring additional coercive power over the rest of society to bear in defense of the returns to investment in certain kinds of human capital. It should be added that the motive of protecting past educational investments also explains many of the restrictive practices of professional bodies and associations, which frequently serve either to restrict entry, or to prevent competition among qualified practitioners from reducing the price of professional services.

A second implication, which is extremely relevant to the broad question of social and economic inequality, is that the economic rewards for alternative occupations and careers need to be compared in terms of lifetime income profiles, and not in terms of the highest annual income earned in the course of the career. Typically, careers with a low education-intensity yield earnings that begin at a relatively high level early in adult life and rise slowly to a peak somewhere in the middle age, whereas careers with a high education-intensity yield earnings that begin at a relatively lower level rather later in adult life but rise much more rapidly to a much later peak, the contrasting nature of the two profiled reflecting the economics of investment. To measure the inequality of incomes by reference to peak incomes only may give a quite misleading picture of the relative lifetime income streams offered by the two careers—though this is the practice of most political radicals and the basis of most income tax systems. As concrete examples, university students like to think of themselves, and to have public policy consider them, as a subdivision of the deserving poor, whereas in terms of lifetime income prospects they are, by the very fact of having reached university, destined almost inevitably to earn incomes well in excess of the national average; on the other hand, there is a pronounced general tendency to regard medical practitioners as being grossly overpaid, though the exceptional length of their training period both entails extra investment (largely in the form of foregone income) and shortens the working life during which that investment can be recouped.

A third implication, also relevant to the question of inequality, is that in their choices among alternative possible careers, new entrants to the labor force face the same problems of assembling information, assessing risks, evaluating returns, and obtaining the resources for investment, as do prospective investors in material capital equipment or in stocks and shares. The main focus of social policy in this connection has been the last of these problems, that is, the limitation of educational opportunity for the children of the poorer classes; but even given adequate opportunity, children (or their parents) may arrive at different educational decisions as a result of differences in the information available on the returns to education, differing preferences for immediate as compared with future income and consumption, or differing willingness to undertake investments with a risky future outcome. Differences in educational decisions due to differences in information constitute a social problem; but differences due to differences in time preference or willingness to undertake risks, though they may produce similar variations in the distribution of income, do not constitute a problem of inequality in any comparable sense.

The second important new development in economic analysis is the treatment of time as the fundamental unit of cost in individual allocative decisions with respect to both labor and consumption.[8] This conception is to be distinguished sharply from the classical treatment of labor time used up in production as the determinant of economic value; and its usefulness derives from the characteristics of the affluent modern economy, in which the typical consumer has a standard of living stratospherically above mere subsistence and is constantly required to choose among competing consumer goods. The central principle of the analysis is that in reality each consumer good has two prices attached to it—a money price, as in the traditional theory of consumer choice, and a time cost of acquiring and consuming the commodity. The money price is, however, resolvable into the work-time required to earn it, so that consumption and labor-supply decisions are both facets of the allocation of time, the individual's basic resource. To complete the concept, it is necessary to recognize that work-time may itself be a form of consumption, in the sense that the individual may derive enjoyment from the exercise of his skills and knowledge.

The most interesting implications of this approach to consumption and labor-supply theory relate to the effects of technical improvements that raise the potential standard of living. Such improvements will tend to reduce the supply of labor, and the measured growth rate of the economy, if their predominant effect is to lower the cost of equipment for time-intensive leisure activities; television is probably an outstanding case in point. Over the long run of industrial history, technical progress has been predominantly of this type, as reflected in the shortening of working hours and lengthening of holidays; but it is an interesting fact that the rapid economic growth of Japan in the postwar period has apparently been accompanied by no reduction in working hours, the Japanese thus far preferring to spend their rising potential incomes on commodities rather than leisure.[9] This illustrates the alternative possibility, that technical improvements will tend to increase the supply of labor if they reduce the leisure-time-intensity of consumption by substituting manufactured equipment—consumers' capital goods—for human labor time. While it is stretching a point to classify housewifery as a leisure activity, there is no doubt that the increasing participation of women in the labor force has been greatly facilitated by the increasing availability of time-and-labor-saving electrical and gas-powered equipment; certainly it would be excessively naïve to attribute this trend to the decay of British family standards under the pressure of materialism.

The time-allocation approach to the theory of consumption and labor supply also suggests some intriguing speculations—I would call them no more than that—about a problem that has concerned many people in this country for many years, namely the reasons for the country's relatively slow rate of economic growth and general lack of "economic dynamism." Given the great gap that exists between the standard of living in the United States and that of the rest of the world, one might suppose that the problem of raising the standard of living in the rest of the world is mainly one of imitation and emulation—which has in fact been the Japanese solution. What has impeded Britain from adopting that solution? Economic analysis suggests that the answer is to be looked for in two factors: household preferences, and household opportunities. As regards preferences, there is deeply ingrained in the culture of the country, largely as a consequence of the experience of the Second World War, a certain contempt for material comfort, and a propensity to regard austerity as desirable and to take pride in the practice of "make do and mend," which have great survival value but provide little encouragement to deliberate striving for material improvement. As regards opportunities, the structure of incentives created by income and excise taxation on the one hand and the social services on the other undoubtedly biases the choices of British consumers toward leisure-time-intensive activities. The difference is exemplified by two generalizations drawn from personal observation: whereas North Americans are happy to tell you about the efficient gadgetry or the high cost of their housing, Britons bask in the age or the cheapness of theirs; and whereas North Americans will tell you in detail why they bought one brand of household equipment rather than another, Britons will explain precisely why they chose one continental country rather than another to spend their vacation in.

The third important new development in economics is the recognition that the information required for the making of choices is not a free good, but has a cost of acquisition that may not be work paying.[10] In view of the cost of acquiring the requisite information, relative to its value in improving the outcome of the decision-making process, it is natural to expect that many decisions, even some quite important ones, will be taken on the basis of extremely fragmentary information or by rules of thumb, or on the basis of information provided in persuasive capsule form by parties interested in influencing the outcome of decisions. I use the term parties advisedly, since the practice of economizing on the acquisition and dissemination of relevant information is at least as characteristic of political as it is of economic activity. The fact that decisions are so frequently taken in this sort of way is generally regarded in the neoclassical tradition of economic theory, in which knowledge is assumed to be costless, as a reflection of the irrationality, or gullibility-cum-rapacity, of man in a capitalist economic system: it is on the contrary a manifestation of rationality in a situation in which the decisions that have to be taken are increasingly numerous, multiplying as incomes rise, while time is short and increasingly valuable. Two important implications for social questions are that the production and distribution of information relevant to consumption choices is a necessary part of the activities of the economic system, not merely a wasteful excrescence of it; and that the economizing process will ensure that information is provided and acted on in a form falling far short of the standard that would be exacted by academic scholarship.

The fourth important new development in economic analysis is the emergence of an economic theory of political democracy.[11] Following Bentham, the neoclassical tradition of economic theory—and, indeed, the heretical tradition also, for the most part—has tended to look on government as the impartial servant of the public good. This is a necessary assumption of political debate, but it leaves unexplained much of the actual activity and policy of government, as well as generating endless frustration among social scientists interested in public policy who take the assumption seriously. The economic theory of democracy regards the election process as one in which policies are exchanged for votes, with parties attempting to maximize their chances of reelection by appropriate choice of policies in an environment in which information about the consequences of alternative policies is highly imperfect and the average voter has little economic incentive to acquire the amount of information necessary for intelligent voting, because his indi-vidual vote will make a negligible difference to the outcome of elections. This theory explains not only the tendency of the programs of the parties in a two-party democracy to become virtually indistinguishable—which is a long-recognized implication of the theory of duopoly—but also such phenomena as the role of stereotypes in political ideology, the influence of pressure groups, and the dominance of producer over consumer interests in the actual formation of public policy.

This last point is one of the important general findings of the economic theory of democracy. Political representation is based on residence; and producer interests are far more concentrated, and hence worth spending time and money to protect, than consumer interests. Hence the political process is inherently conservative, in the sense that it is strongly biased toward the preservation of what currently exists rather than the promotion of change and development. This proposition can be documented without limit from the history of postwar British economic and social policy, illustrative examples ranging from the subordination of macroeconomic policy to the defense of the exchange rate for sterling, through the special favors accorded to coal and the cotton textiles and aircraft industries, to regional employment policy.

One of the outstanding unresolved issues in the economic theory of democracy is whether the political process tends to under-allocate or to over-allocate resources to governmental activities. John Kenneth Galbraith is characteristically in no doubt on this matter: he contrasts the private affluence with the public squalor of contemporary society.[12] This alleged tendency toward under-spending on public goods can easily be rationalized by reference to the aversion of the public toward paying higher taxes, and the difficulty of persuading it that increased public spending on social amenities and social services will yield a longer-run pay-off in terms of a more pleasant and comfortable social life and a reduced necessity for social expenditure on preventative and salvage operations. On the other hand, the theory of coalitions in game theory suggests a tendency toward over-allocation to governmental activities, on the grounds that a majority agreed on a particular item of social expenditure can by coalitions force the minority to bear part of the cost of that expenditure.[13] My own view, which I have not the time to develop in full, is that neither general proposition is correct, but that instead the governmental process tends to under-allocate resources in some directions and over-allocate them in others. Specifically, government tends to over-allocate resources to activities that can be justified by a vague but persuasive national purpose, and with respect to which it can plausibly rely on the advice of its own experts, such as national defense, the support of investment and research and development activities in established national industries, and the promotion of prestigious "basic scientific research"; but that it tends to under-allocate resources to public amenities, the social services and the relief of poverty, because for such items of public expenditure the social return is nebulous and problematical to the average citizen while the private cost to the taxpayer, and especially the fact that that cost is incurred largely for the benefit of others, is all too clear.

I now turn to the application of economic principles to social questions. For this purpose I have selected three examples drawn from public discussion during the past year or so, with which to illustrate what economics has to contribute to the understanding of social questions.

. . . .

My first example is the alleged problem of "brain drain" from Britain. It may be remarked at the outset that seldom has so much unreasoning emotion been ventilated on the basis of so few hard facts: as Professor Brinley Thomas pointed out in a lecture here last year,[14] the data required to determine whether Britain is a net loser or a net gainer of brains, and the magnitudes of the relevant flows, just do not exist. Economic analysis does suggest, however, that the so-called "brain drain" is part of a more general international circulation of human capital in search of better opportunities, one aspect of the mobility of labor, and from a cosmopolitan point of view presumably contributes to a more efficient allocation of world economic resources.[15] The common assumption that "brain drain" involves a loss to the country of emigration must therefore rest on a particular, nationalistic, definition of economic welfare in terms of the income generated within a politically delineated geographical area, rather than in terms of the economic welfare of individuals born in that area, who presumably emigrate in order to improve their standards of living. Recent analysis of the economics of "brain drain" by Professor Thomas and others does, however, indicate one possible source of loss when economic welfare is measured on an individualistic basis, which is particularly relevant to the British case; this possibility is especially interesting because it entails one of the fine points of the economics of investment in the formation of human capital. The economic theory of on-the-job training[16] distinguishes between two types of skills that may be so acquired: general skills, which are transferable to other firms or industries in the economy, and skills which are specific to the individual firm providing the training. For the former, general, type of training, the competitive economics of the situation will necessitate apprenticeship or other arrangements under which the worker will pay the cost of the training, since if the employer bore the cost he could not be sure of recouping his expense by paying the fully trained worker less than the value of his contribution to production. For the latter, specific, type of training, either the worker may pay the costs of training and later receive the full value of his contribution to production, or the employer may pay the costs and recoup the expense subsequently out of an excess of the worker's productive contribution over his wage, the outcome depending on the relative certainty of the commitment of the employer and the employee respectively to the contract for future employment. The relevance of this piece of labor market analysis to the "brain drain" problem is that in the modern world a university education is an internationally transferable item of human capital; but in Britain educational policy makes the state bear the cost of it, while the country relies on a combination of state administration of low salary scales for educated people, and steeply progressive income taxation, to recoup the cost. The implication of this inconsistency of policy is that either public opinion in this country will have to become accustomed to a steady outflow of native talent, compensated to a greater or lesser extent by an inflow of talent from poorer countries, as part of the cost of current education and income-determination policies, or else policy will have to be changed so as to increase the share of the cost of education that is borne by the student, and to decrease the share of the higher productive capacity created by education that is absorbed by the community through the fixing of low salary scales and the imposition of heavily progressive income taxation.[17] The latter alternative has the more to recommend it, from the point of view of the long-run objective of reducing inequality by increasing the proportion of the population that receives higher education.

My second example departs from the field of specific academic interest: it is the question of advertising, which has long been the subject of intense social criticism.[18] As already mentioned, traditional economic theory, in common with much other social thought, assumes that information is costless and that everyone really knows what he wants, or would if he were not hectored by the hucksters; on this assumption, advertising easily appears both economically wasteful and socially undesirable. Once it is recognized, however, that consumption choices require information that is not available as a free good, and that in particular in a growing economy people want information about the expanding alternative opportunities for consumption that a rising standard of living opens up to them, advertising appears as an economically necessary and socially valuable activity; moreover, the major criticisms of it turn out to be directed at the fact that it is economically efficient in achieving its purpose. That it is paid for by the producer and biased in his interests is due to the fact that it is worth the while of the producer, but not of the individual consumers, to disseminate information about his particular product; and that advertising messages are frequently tasteless, meaningless, or grammarless is due to the fact that the technology of the media employed by advertising permits cheap communication of messages in quantity at the expense of quality. This is not to say that the independent provision of the same or similar information on the basis of collective financing by consumers or the state, or the establishment of public standards for the types of information that may be disseminated by commercial producers, might not make for a better society; but the endeavor might turn out to be more difficult than it appears at first sight, since the criteria that motivate the mass of consumers' decisions are obviously very different from those that are assumed to motivate the educated bourgeois readers of *Which?* (or, in the United States, *Consumer Reports*).

My final example is the problem of poverty.[19] Poverty, meaning the lack of sufficient resources to maintain an adequate standard of living for the individual or family, is to be distinguished from inequality, though the two are frequently confused in public discussion: a society could be poor while yet equalitarian, or its distribution of income could be highly unequal without anyone being poor. Since the level of resources that constitutes the dividing line between poverty and adequacy is determined by social judgment, and likely to be shifted upward as the standard of living rises, it can be reliably predicted that there will always be a poverty problem, though public awareness of it will be more or less acute at different points of time. Given the poverty standard, however, the proportion of the population classed as poor will depend on the social factors governing the division of the society into consuming units and the economic factors governing the distribution of income among such units. I shall conclude this lecture with an economic-theoretic formulation of the determinants of poverty.

In most economies of interest to the social scientist, the consuming units are individuals or households, which obtain the resources to finance their consumption by the sale of the labor services of their members and/or the services of their property to productive enterprises. Conceptually, therefore, the sources of poverty may be divided into two groups of factors—those which make the number of individual consumers in the household unit large relative to the amount of productive services the household is able to supply, and those which make the value of the productive services the household can supply low relative to the household's needs.

With respect to the first group of factors, excessive family size in relation to income, it should be observed that the general tendency of modern society toward the narrowing down of the family unit to the nuclear family—the young and the old couple, and the couple rearing children—has the incidental effect of increasing the apparent prevalence of poverty, by separating into discrete households consuming units prone to poverty— notably young couples, fatherless families, and retired persons—that in a more extended family system would be living on a pooled income averaging out above the poverty level. Apart from this influence, the main source of poverty under this head is family size excessive in relation to family income. In a fully rational capitalistic system of family support, both birth control and abortion techniques would be generally accessible and freely advertised, and families would be planned in relation to the budget constraint of prospective family resources, so that variations in income per person associated with variations in family size could be assumed to reflect voluntary choices between material consumers' goods and the intangible benefits of family life, not calling for measures of poverty relief. Our society is moving rapidly in that direction, but it still has a long way to go, so that measures such as family allowances and income tax relief for dependents aimed at subsidizing the larger families have a rationale in the imperfect availability and utilization of knowledge in this area of consumer decision-making. A more sophisticated philosophy of capitalism might go further, and regard the rearing of children as an investment industry producing human capital for the future, and deserving of financial support by society on purely economic grounds.

Turning to the second group of factors determining poverty, those that make the value of the services the household can supply too low to afford an adequate standard of living, one can distinguish a variety of causal factors, implying rather different approaches to the relief of poverty.

One major factor—which has not been of general importance in this country in the postwar period, though it was of great importance in the interwar period, operates now in certain regions of the country, and may become of general importance again as a consequence of the recent change in governmental policy—is the maintenance of less than "full" employment. Mass unemployment has not only a direct and immediate effect in creating poverty among those unable to get employment, or employment of the kind for which they were trained, but also an indirect and persistent effect in eliminating the pressure created by a high demand for labor on employers to upgrade labor skills. There is a strong case for generous compensation of those rendered unemployed by deliberate governmental policies of deflation; but even such compensation would not remove the indirect poverty-promoting consequences of general unemployment.

A second important factor is the chronic obsolescence of acquired human skills resulting from persistent trends in technical change.[20] The agricultural worker, the cotton textile worker, and the coal miner are the standard examples in advanced countries like Britain, though the category extends to include other regionally specialized skills. Major problems here are the limitation of social knowledge of technological trends and alternative opportunities, which lead children to follow their parents' occupations into perpetual pockets of poverty, and the bias of the political process toward the conservative defense of existing populations in existing locations, which results in efforts to preserve people in economically decadent communities rather than disperse them to nascent centers of economic growth. This tendency, in combination with the tendency toward under-spending on social services, tends to perpetuate sore spots of regional and occupational distress, whereas what is required is a much greater investment in the augmentation of the value of human capital through geographical and occupational mobility of labor.

A third important factor is mental or physical incapacity of the individual to render productive services of sufficient value to raise him or his household above the poverty line. This factor in poverty is interrelated with the level of unemployment, in the sense that the scarcer is labor in general, the more economic incentive there is to devise square holes in the economic system to accommodate the square pegs available. The alleviation of poverty attributable to this source requires the assistance of social workers, the maintenance of an adequate health service, and, probably most important, the provision of adequate social assistance transfers.

A number of other causal factors in poverty can be grouped under the general heading of discrimination, which denies particular groups the opportunity to acquire or to use the capacity to make valuable productive contributions. From the economic point of view, discrimination is equivalent to the imposition of a special tax on those discriminated against. The denial or restriction of educational opportunities to the children of the lower income groups, and the use of educational qualifications to restrict entry to particular occupations or careers, are probably the most obvious examples to a British audience; but there are important other forms of discrimination that promote poverty. Discrimination on grounds of color is a far less important source of poverty in this country than in the United States, partly because colored people are, as a result of Britain's deliberately discriminatory immigration policy, a far smaller proportion of the population; but it is by no means a negligible influence. Discrimination by age and by sex are also important, though their presence and effects are disguised by moral and emotional rationalizations. Discrimination by age operates at both ends of the spectrum, severely restricting the ability of the young to take gainful employment, and forcing the old to retire from employment whether they so desire or not; if society believes that children should be in school and the elderly in the limbo of retirement, it has an obligation to provide family allowances and old age pensions on a scale generous enough to allow them to dwell there in adequate comfort. Discrimination against the female sex runs through both the education system and the labor market, and is rationalized by the conventional assignment of females to the role of housekeeper for the family; an important consequence is a high incidence of poverty among unmarried, separated, divorced, or prematurely widowed mothers of families, whose capacity to render productive services is too low, as a result of systematic discrimination, to sustain the responsibilities of head of a household unexpectedly thrust on them: again, if society wishes to push women into housekeeping, it has a responsibility to shield that role against the risks of poverty. Finally, considerable discrimination of a poverty-promoting kind is exercised by trade unions, which in their efforts to improve their members' wages and working conditions restrict the demand for skilled labor and force nonmembers to resort to lower-paid employment elsewhere in the economy.

The eonomic analysis of poverty indicates—as is indeed implied by the fact that poverty, being defined simply as an insufficiency of income to meet expenses, has innumerable causes—that the social attack on the poverty problem should take a variety of forms. To the pure theorist of the classical tradition, the problem is of course incalculably simpler: if some people have more and others less money than they are deemed to need, take money away from the former and give it to the latter. Unfortunately, this simple prescription has left its mark on those of the other social sciences that pride themselves on the directness of their concern with the poverty issue, and assume that enonomics (or the economic system) has solved the problem of generating enough money income so that no one need be poor. But neither the economic system nor the political is so simple: economically, poverty has deep social roots; and the political system is constrained by the same social foundations to limit the degree of rectification of poverty by income transfers that it will tolerate. That being so, the most promising—though also the most difficult—cures for poverty lie in the direction of providing increased opportunity to earn adequate incomes, rather than in the direction of recapturing and redistributing incomes after they have been earned. The cures are difficult both because they involve sacrificing many of our conventional notions of what is good and what is bad for social equality, and because they require serious thought about social causation; but they are promising because they seek to remedy poverty not by transferring income between individuals in society, but by making such transfers no longer necessary, except in cases where the justice of transfers is clearly evident to all as a matter of social conscience.

In this paper, I have attempted to explain and illustrate the approach of economic theory to social questions. The central concepts of the relevant economic theory are, I believe, relatively simple and easy to grasp; the hard task, as every economist knows, is to recognize their relevance to particular problems and apply them to finding the solutions. I hope that I have succeeded in conveying some appreciation of the process of using economic theory to illuminate social questions in the particular cases I have examined.

3. The Political Economy of Opulence

"Economics is the science which studies human behaviour as a relationship between ends and scarce means which have alternative uses."[1] Lionel Robbins's well-known definition of their subject is one which most economists would probably accept, at least as a description of their workaday activities. The definition allows—and it was specifically framed by its author to allow—for the pursuit of other ends than purely material ends; but in practice economists devote themselves predominantly to the study of the allocation of material means between ends conceived and defined in material terms. Inherent in the way economists set about their task is the implicit assumption that material means are scarce and material wants are pressing —in short that economic society is materially poor, and resources must not be wasted.

This assumption permeates the theoretical apparatus of the subject; it also directs what economists have to say about enonomic policy. In the debate which has been going on over the general problem of inflation, for example, economists have been divided between those who stress the loss of production and potential growth of output that results from anything less than full employment of labor, and those who stress the loss of production and potential growth of output that results from the misallocation of resources brought about by inflation. Again, in making comparisons between the Russian and Western economic systems, economists have generally tended to accept as their standard of performance the rate of growth of output per head, a standard which gives away most of the positive points on the Western side. In both cases, the adoption of the output standard implicitly assumes that the economic problem is of prime importance.

The assumption that the economic problem is of prime importance is obviously gratifying to the self-esteem of the economics profession; but that does not necessarily make it valid. It has in fact been powerfully challenged in Professor J. K. Galbraith's book of some years ago, *The Affluent Society* (London, 1958). No doubt many of you have read this book; at the very least you must have heard it mentioned in the cocktail-party conversation of those

This paper was presented at the annual meeting of the Canadian Political Science Association in Kingston, 10 June 1960. Reprinted with permission from *Canadian Journal of Economics and Political Science* 26, no. 4 (November 1960): 552-64.

people who can afford to read only one book a month. Nevertheless, I shall summarize it briefly, since it forms the starting point of this paper.

Galbraith argues that classical economics was formed in and shaped by an atmosphere of grinding poverty for the mass of the population. In that environment, the economic problem appeared as a tripartite one: the inadequacy of production, which expressed the prevalence of poverty and the grimness of the human lot; the inequality of distribution, which accentuated the insufficiency of production to provide more than a miserable standard of living for the masses; and the insecurity of income, which reinforced the misery of inadequacy. Accordingly, the problem of economic policy was to increase production and mitigate inequality and insecurity; and since scarcity of resources was the apparent cause of poverty, and the more efficient use of these resources the way to increase production, the need to increase production placed severe limits on the pursuit of policies aimed directly at overcoming inequality and insecurity.

Production, inequality, and insecurity were the economic problems of the nineteenth century. But, Galbraith argues, these problems are no longer with us. Technological progress on the one hand, and the modern corporation on the other, have solved the problem of production. At the same time, the rising trend of average income has both rendered inequality of income less blatantly obvious and removed its social and political sting; while the expansion of production, together with the development of the social conscience, has pretty well solved the problem of insecurity.

But the solution of the economic problems of the nineteenth century through expansion of production raises new problems, because this solution involves our economic society in a rat-race in which people have to be persuaded by high-powered advertising and hidden persuasion to buy the goods which the business men think up to produce. Real scarcity has been succeeded by contrived scarcity, and the successful functioning of the economy depends on reiterating the contrivance. One consequence is the growth of consumption financed on the installment plan, and the associated increase in potential instability of the economy. Another is the problem of chronic inflation, which is associated with the fact that the solution of all three nineteenth-century problems is tied to keeping individuals employed at high pay. Most important, the necessity of, and insistence on, sustained expansion of production carries with it a number of attitudes inimical to sensible economic policy. The old emphasis on efficiency leads to bitter opposition to efforts by entrepreneurs, farmers, and workers to increase their security of income by price agreements, government subsidies, and restrictive practices of various kinds. Luxurious living, which drives the whole machine, becomes the necessary cost of production, so that the margin of resources available for social uses such as defense is unduly small in relation to national income. In particular, the assumption that it is private consumption that counts, together with the emphasis on the scarcity of resources and the need for efficiency, creates strong resistance to the provision of public services and collective consumption goods by tax-financed governmental activity.

Thus Galbraith's argument; and I must say that I find it extremely convincing, at least in its broad outline. It is, I believe, important to recognize that, judged by any reasonable historical or comparative standard, the citizens of the Western industrial countries are in fact very well off, that the economic problem is not all that pressing, and that the belief that it is leads economists (and the general public, in its views on economic matters) into inconsistencies and false positions on economic policy. In insisting on these points, Galbraith is performing an important service—regardless of what one thinks of his choice of audience to which to address himself, and the tone in which he writes. Nor can his argument be dismissed by pointing out what is true, that the force of his reasoning assumes the continuation of an unequal distribution of income, a relatively low level of social services and public investment in education, a limited defense effort, and a limited contribution to the assistance of underdeveloped economies. All of these are things which important sections of public opinion—including Galbraith himself (see chaps. 18-25 of *Affluent Society*)—would like to see changed, and the changing of which could make the growth of production of pressing importance; but as there seems little prospect that they will be changed at all radically, to make a point of them is to miss the point. The point is that we live in a rich society, which nevertheless in many respects insists on thinking and acting as if it were a poor society.

Not only do I believe that Galbraith is right in emphasizing the fact of affluence; I also think there is much justice in his claim that economics is not adjusted to this central fact of modern life. But—and this "but" is not, I hope, entirely due to my inability to multiply my academic income by writing a best-selling denunciation of my profession—I think he goes much too far in asserting that marginal production is of no real use to people, so that economics is of no importance. Moreover, he lets himself off much too easily by contenting himself with satirizing demand theory; indeed, he makes a serious error in contending that the indifference curve technique precludes the notion of a hierarchy of more and less essential wants (see his chap. 10, sec. 4, pp. 115-18)—though it is, I suppose, barely conceivable that Harvard has not yet heard of the Engel curve. And he offers no suggestions on what economists might usefully occupy themselves with, in the affluent society.

This brings me to the subject of this paper. Suppose we start from the Galbraith view of the economy, as one which is well off and tending to grow progressively more so, more or less automatically, through the institutionalization of capital accumulation and technical progress in the modern corporation. (If the idea of starting from Galbraith is distasteful, one can start equally well from W. W. Rostow's recent book, *The Stages of Economic Growth* [Cambridge, 1960],[2] according to which the United States and other advanced countries have embarked on the historical phase of high mass consumption, in which compound-interest growth is built into the structure of the economy.) Then how should economic doctrine be formulated, to be as illuminating as possible a guide to the economic system of such an economy?

Economics so formulated I call "the political economy of opulence." The term "opulence" goes back at least as far as Adam Smith, who uses it occasionally as a synonym for wealth; this brings the subject into the grand tradition of English classical economics. I use the term "political economy," instead of the more recent "economics" or the more technical "economic theory," as an excuse for a broad, discursive political-philosophical approach, and a willingness to deal with difficult theoretical questions by sage circumlocution; this brings the subject still more into the grand tradition of English classical economics. I am not, however, prepared to follow that tradition all the way into the adumbration of a complete system of thought, suitable for entombment in an 871–page volume, the sapience of whose footnotes could only be fully appreciated after two generations of careful study.[3] Instead, I shall skim through the main branches of an elementary course in economic principles, suggesting ways of looking at various problems which seem to me more fruitful and enlightening than the ways in which these problems are generally treated. Much of what I shall say, however, is merely a restatement of approaches which can already be found in the literature.

The logical place to begin is with the theory of consumption and demand. This is also the most interesting place to begin, since it is on the consumption side that the phenomena and special problems of opulence appear most clearly, and economic theory seems most remote from reality.

The theory of demand is a johnny-come-lately in economic analysis. Its master-creator, Alfred Marshall (hallowed be his name), approached it from a broadly sociological, if somewhat stuffily Victorian, point of view. Since his time, however, the trend has been to reduce the theory of demand to the bare logic of choice. We assume an individual of given preferences, or at least of a given consistency, choosing between different given commodities, endowed with a given income and facing given prices. The main conclusion to which the theory leads is that the demand curve slopes downward—except that it may not.

I submit that the juice has long since been squeezed from this particular lemma, and that there is a great deal to be gained in the way of understanding how the economy works by turning from sharpening our axioms to developing the implications of the generalization laid down by Marshall (in book III, chapter 2, of the *Principles*, before the marginal utility and the tea-drinking set in): "although it is man's wants in the earliest stages of his development that give rise to his activities, yet afterwards each new step upwards is to be regarded as the development of new activities giving rise to new wants, rather than of new wants giving rise to new activities" (p. 89). In other words, the purpose of economic organization is not merely to satisfy wants, but to create wants. Further, in assessing the nature of the system from the point of view of welfare, it is I think important to keep in mind a notion which has been stressed for many years by F. H. Knight, that one of the basic human social characteristics is a continuing desire to improve and educate one's tastes.[4]

Progress takes the form both of satisfying wants more fully and of raising the standard of wants. In technical jargon, it is expressed both in improvements in the production function, and in improvements in the consumption function. A natural corollary is that, just as it pays the entrepreneur to invest in improving the technique of production in order to adjust the product more profitably to the want, so it pays him to invest in improving the technique of consumption in order to adjust the want more profitably to the product; in short, it pays to advertise. In both cases, "improvement" from the standpoint of the producer's profit may consist in adulteration as judged by some objective standard of performance.

The fact that wants are created, and not original with the individual, raises a fundamental philosophical problem whether the satisfaction of wants created by those who satisfy them can be regarded as a social gain. This is a question which is ignored, and hence implicitly answered in the affirmative, by welfare economics of both the older "superiority of the competitive system" and the newer "subsidy, tax, and lump sum redistribution" varieties, both of which assume stable and independently given consumer preferences. Yet it is a question which has persistently troubled observers of the influence of advertising; and it is a crucial question for the age of opulence, one of whose chief characteristics is the promotion of wants by advertising.

To begin with, it must, I think, be recognized that the creation of wants by advertising does not by itself justify dismissing these particular wants as inferior to others, or the resources required to gratify them as wasted. All economically relevant wants are learned, and, what is more important, all better taste has to be acquired by study and practice. Even the presumption that one knows better than other people what is good for them, which underlies a large part of the argument of Galbraith and other critics of advertising and is formalized in the distinction drawn by the Cambridge school between rational and irrational preferences,[5] is acquired by education—the best education, of course. Thus the problem of whether the creation and satisfaction of wants by advertised production constitutes a genuine increase in welfare cannot be settled simply by distinguishing base material from elevated spiritual types of wants, and asserting the priority of the latter over the former. Rather, the answer depends in both cases on whether there exist generally accepted standards for distinguishing better from worse taste, standards which can themselves be learned, and a social process by which such standards are in fact learned and enforced. I am myself inclined to the view that the creation and satisfaction of wants by advertised production does result in social gain, on the grounds that there are generally accepted standards for distinguishing meretriciously from genuinely superior products, and, equally important, that there are social and governmental processes which set to work when the exploitation of helpless consumers becomes flagrant. If this be denied for commercial products, I do not see how it can be asserted for educational, cultural, and artistic activities.

The creation of wants raises serious problems for welfare economics and for any theory of economic policy. It also raises problems for positive economics, by making it difficult to predict the direction of evolution of demand.[6] This difficulty is aggravated by the tautological fact that increasing income implies the gratification of less and less essential wants. In particular, the margin of want-satisfaction tends to move from the physiological to the psychological and sociological: the physiological needs are satiated, the psychological and sociological become necessities, while the luxuries are psychiatric—hence the Hidden Persuaders and Motivational Research.[7] The sociological emphasis inherent in a high-consumption economy is further reinforced by the hierarchical nature of the bureaucratic production unit which makes opulence possible—to the Organization Man, goods are status symbols, to be bought and used as such.[8]

The consequence of these characteristics of opulence is that the most interesting (and commercially valuable) problems of demand analysis may well lie outside the present static and physiologically orientated concepts of consumer theory. Nevertheless, it seems to me that more can be done with the existing tools of economic analysis in analyzing demand in the age of opulence than is usually done. Notably, a great deal more understanding can be derived by regarding consumption typically as the process of enjoying the services of consumer capital, rather than as the consumption of a flow of perishable goods. Not tea, but T.V., is the exemplary commodity of the age of opulence.

To conceive of the typical consumer good as an item of consumer capital equipment requires a number of significant changes in the analysis of consumer choices. In the first place, as Boulding emphasized in his *Reconstruction of Economics*,[9] it is necessary to distinguish between purchases and consumption, the two being separated by a stock of consumer capital. This distinction leads in a number of directions. In cycle theory, it points to the possibility of consumer inventory cycles, and to the possible importance of consumers' price expectations in the mechanism of con-

ventional business cycles. In national income theory, it raises the fundamental question of what the national income as conventionally calculated
really means: a country which is producing a stable output a substantial
proportion of which consists of new consumer durables is really enjoying a
rising standard of living; and a country which has a large stock of consumer
durables has a war potential greater than its national income figures would
indicate, since consumer capital permits both goods and labor time to be
diverted from household consumption in time of emergency.

In the second place, the existence of consumer capital makes it necessary
to distinguish in conventional demand theory between short-run and
long-run adjustment, thus reintroducing a distinction between the short-run
and long-run demand curve which was rejected by Marshall in spite of the
attractive parallel with his treatment of supply.[10] The distinction between the
short-run and long-run demand curve is necessary in two connections. First,
the use of consumer durables involves a lumpy investment expenditure
followed by a flow of maintenance expenditure which is determined by the
durable's length of life, which is itself dependent on the price of the
commodity. Consequently a change in the price of the good will have both a
short-run effect on demand through altering the optimal length of life of the
existing stock, and a long-run effect on demand through altering the stock of
capital of this type that is desired. Second, the use of services of consumer
durables in the consumer's consumption pattern implies that the consumer
has the same problem of short-run fixity of capital equipment as the
producer, so that the response of demand to a fall in the price of a currently
consumed good (which may be either complementary with the services of
consumer capital or an input into the capital-using consumption process,
such as fuel or power) will not be complete until the capital stock is adjusted
to permit full advantage to be taken of the price reduction.[11]

In the third place, the prevalence of consumer capital makes the rate of
interest, and the terms of credit which surround it, a much more significant
determinant of consumer purchases, both in pattern and in total, than it is
conventionally considered to be—the rate of interest may well be more
important, as a determinant of the relative costs of substitutes and
complements, than the prices of the goods themselves. In this connection,
incidentally, the conception of consumption as using the services of capital
goods provides a rationale for installment buying, a practice often still
condemned as mortgaging the future: there is no reason why a rational
consumer should pay for his consumption in advance, by paying cash for
capital goods, rather than concurrently, as he enjoys the services of those
capital goods.

As I have already mentioned, the more interesting problems of demand in
the age of opulence are concerned with the evolution of demand as wealth
increases. Here the assumption that consumption is typically the con-

sumption of the services of capital seems particularly illuminating. Progress, whether the result of capital accumulation or of technical progress, tends to cheapen commodities, and particularly the more durable commodities, in terms of labor, and consequently to encourage the substitution of capital-intensive for labor-intensive methods of satisfying consumer wants. The technique of consumption consequently tends to become progressively more capital-intensive. This increase in capital-intensity of consumption manifests itself in two contrasting ways.[12] On the one hand, there is the shift of labor services out of the household into the factory or service enterprise, where they can be more efficiently armed with capital. The most outstanding example of this is probably the development of the preparation and cooking, and even service, of food outside the home. On the other hand, there is the replacement of labor service inside and outside the home by capital equipment in the home operated by the consumer. The most outstanding examples of this are entertainment devices, cleaning equipment, and do-it-yourself repair and maintenance equipment. The household thus tends to become a fully automated utility factory (apart from the managerial services of the householders themselves), a tendency which is undoubtedly fostered by the influence of high-income-taxation and the special tax advantages enjoyed by householders.

The tendency of the household to become an automated utility factory through the substitution of capital for labor is associated with, and reinforces, two other features of the modern consumption pattern—the suburbanization of living, and the tendency to earlier marriages and larger families. Suburbanization is dependent on private transport facilities, convenient domestic storage capacity, and the conversion of electricity into power inside the home, all of which assume substantial capital investment; the familial trend, in addition, exploits economies of scale in the use of household capital.

So far, I have been suggesting the desirability of treating consumption as typically meaning consumption of the services of durable equipment, rather than of perishable commodities. To do so, however, is to stick to the classical view of consumer's choice as being mostly concerned with choices among commodities and labor services. I would now like to suggest that an increasingly important consumption good in the age of opulence is not a commodity or a labor service, but the use of one's own time, which opulence makes increasingly valuable by comparison with commodities. Choice of the use of one's time has three aspects. The first is the choice of how to employ one's working time. Here increasing opulence tends to make the non-pecuniary aspects of employment—working conditions and social considerations—more important as compared with the monetary rewards, a tendency which affects the supply of labor services from the household. The second is the division of time between working and leisure time, which includes length of working life as well as days and hours per week. Here the fact that the enjoyment of commodities and the availability of leisure in which to enjoy them are complementary, once basic physical maintenance is assured, implies a relative reduction in working as contrasted with leisure time as opulence progresses. The third is the choice of leisure-time activities. Here, the cheapening of commodities in terms of labor which I have already mentioned implies an increasingly capital-intensive use of leisure; this trend is exemplified in the growth of domestic and foreign travel, holiday resorts, and sports requiring expensive capital equipment.[13]

Let me now turn from the theory of demand to another branch of economic principles, the theory of production and the firm. Despite the rise to dominance of the corporate form of enterprise, the theory of production still generally takes as its central unit of analysis the Marshallian firm. This is a small and essentially anonymous enterprise in which decisions are centralized in the hands of an "entrepreneur"; and its main problem is conceived to be the choice of the optimum combination of factors to insert into a given production function to produce a given product. This conception is not fundamentally altered by Chamberlin's extension of it to include choice of the most profitable combination of product quality and advertising expenditure,[14] and more recent elaborations of the theory of multiple production. I suggest that both the unit of analysis and the conception of the decision-problem it faces need to be adapted to conform more closely to the facts of the corporation economy.

As to the unit of analysis: the Marshallian firm, it will be recalled, was likened by its author to a tree in the forest, each tree growing and dying in due course while the forest—which represented the industry in the analogy—retained its same outline.[15] The forest analogy will still serve for the corporation economy, provided, first, that the analogy is drawn for the economy as a whole and not the industry; and, second, that one thinks, not of a deciduous English forest, but of a California redwood forest, in which each tree is an individual distinct from the others, survives unless some disaster befalls it or the forest, and so long as it survives continues to grow in a competitive struggle to survive among its growing fellows. To drop the analogy, the corporation is not mortal, with a life cycle of vigor and senility which passes through a phase of maturity, but immortal and continually growing, provided that no disasters occur and its organization remains efficient.

This last proviso points to one of the key differences between the problems facing the corporation and those facing the firm as theoretically conceived. The corporation, in contrast to the single-minded Marshallian entrepreneur, is a large organization with a hierarchical administrative and decision-taking structure. One of its most important problems is to achieve and maintain an effective internal organization, which will secure both coordination and flexibility.[16] A second key difference is that, in contrast to the entrepreneur, who is assumed to be financially self-sufficient, the corporation is dependent on the capital market for finance, and this dependence imposes on it a built-in obligation to grow: as W. J. Baumol has argued in his recent book *Business Behavior, Value and Growth*, the fact that success is immediately capitalized in a rise in the market value of a company's shares means that the company's executives cannot be content with one successful decision, but must go on making successful decisions to please the stockholders.[17] The need to grow points to a third key characteristic of the corporation as contrasted with the conceptual firm: in order to continue to grow, the corporation must both foster and adapt itself to the growth of the market, through the introduction of new products, the improvement of old products, and the extension of the range of products its offers; thus research, including both technological and marketing research, and selling activities, rather than physical production per se, are the vital activities of the corporation. Effective organization, satisfactory growth, and profitable change, rather than minimization of cost for a given production function and maximization of profit for a given demand, are the key problems of the productive unit in the opulent society. Correspondingly, the technique of organization it adopts in the pursuit of satisfactory growth through profitable change, rather than the technological or market characteristics of the products it produces, is the fundamental distinguishing characteristic of the corporate enterprise.

Let me now turn from the theory of value to the theory of distribution. The classical theory of distribution originated by Ricardo ran in terms of categories of income earned by factors which contributed recognizably distinct types of service to the production process and shared in the output in proportion to the values of their contributions to it, factors which, moreover, could be identified in the real world with definite social groups.[18] Initially three factors were distinguished, land, labor, and capital, receiving for their services incomes in the form of rent, wages, and profits; later, the capital factor was separated into two components, pure capital and entrepreneurship (the management of capital embodied in specific real form), a corresponding distinction being drawn between interest and profits. The resulting picture of distribution was logical, simple, and conformable to common-sense observation; but it began to dissolve under closer theoretical scrutiny even as it was being perfected. Marshall began the rot, and inaugurated neoclassical distribution theory, by elaborating the principle that rent is not peculiar to land, but is the ubiquitous consequence of specificity and immobility of factors of production.[19] Fisher showed that interest, properly considered, is not a category of income but a means of relating the time-stream of income earned by a factor's services to the capital value of the factor, which is applicable to all factors and not simply to capital as generally understood.[20] Schumpeter and Knight showed that true profit is not an income earned by rendering productive services, but a capital gain resulting from the successful undertaking of contractual obligations in the face of uncertainty about the future.[21] Thus three of the four concepts of income distribution theory no longer match the categories of income distribution; and consequently the theory of distribution is, to put it mildly, in a rather unsatisfactory state.

Apart from the force of intellectual tradition, the main reason why the classical categories remain embedded in the theory of distribution seems to be that economists accept the classical notion of labor as a unique original factor of production, distinct on the one hand from other original factors in the shape of natural resources, and on the other hand from produced means of production in the shape of capital goods. This acceptance is explainable by the institutional fact that democracies expressly prohibit markets in human capital (so that only the services of labor are marketed, whereas capital goods themselves rather than their services are typically bought and sold) and also by the liberal anthropocentricity of social science and the stereotyped concept of "labor" employed in socialist political philosophy. But the notion of labor as an original factor of production is not necessarily economically sensible; on the contrary, the progress of opulence makes the concept less and less acceptable as a reasonable theoretical approximation. In the England of the Industrial Revolution, as in the underdeveloped countries today, labor could reasonably be thought of predominantly as the application of crude force, with which individual laborers could be assumed to be roughly equally endowed, together with some decision-taking of a rather trivial kind. But in an advancing industrial society both the provision of force and the elementary decision-taking are increasingly taken over by machinery, while what the worker brings to this task are the knowledge and skill required to use machinery effectively. His knowledge and skill in turn are the product of a capital investment in his education in the general capacities of communication and calculation required for participation in the productive process, and the specific capacities required for the individual job, a capital investment which is variously financed by the state, the worker himself, and the employer. Thus the laborer is himself a produced means of production, an item of capital equipment. As capital equipment, labor differs from nonhuman capital in that a human being is necessarily present when his services are used in production; this means, on the one hand, that labor is inherently a more flexible instrument of production than machinery, on the other that its supply to particular employments is influenced significantly—and likely to be increasingly influenced as opulence progresses—by nonpecuniary considerations.

I suggest, therefore, that the time has come to sever the link with the classical attempt to identify categories of income with distinctly different kinds of productive factors; and that a more useful approach would be to lump all factors together as items of capital equipment, created by past investment and rendering current services to production. The exceptions are not important: "the original and indestructible properties of the soil"[22] are now a threadbare unscientific myth, and human genius is rare enough to be ignored in the broad picture. Such an approach does not require the sacrifice of the concepts of classical income-distribution theory; on the contrary, these concepts appear as illuminating ways of looking at the price of factor services. The current price of a factor's services can be divided conceptually into two elements: the payment necessary to keep the factor in existence (or in a particular employment[23]) corresponding to the classical notion of "wages"; and a surplus above that necessary payment, arising from scarcity of the factor and corresponding to the classical notion of "rent." Considered as a return on the capital investment incurred in creating the factor, the current price can be resolved analytically into interest on the capital invested, and a residual corresponding to the profit or loss resulting from the entrepreneurial decision to invest capital in the specific form represented by the factor. This formulation, incidentally, clarifies the difference between wages and rent, which are income concepts, and interest and profits, which are capital concepts.

The revised approach to the theory of distribution which I am suggesting has the advantages of greater generality and logical simplicity; it also has important substantive implications. In particular, the conception of labor as a produced rather than an original factor implies that much of modern macroeconomic theory has been concerned with problems that are wrongly formulated, if not entirely spurious. I refer especially to the theory of economic growth, where a great deal of intellectual effort has been devoted to exploring the difficulties of reconciling the accumulation of capital with the growth of the labor force at a different, autonomously determined rate,[24] and explaining the constancy of the share of labor which apparently results from the growth process.[25] These problems are in large part created by the classical apparatus itself, with its treatment of labor as an original factor and its identification of capital with the stock of capital equipment;[26] they present an altogether different appearance once labor as well as capital equipment is recognized as a medium of investment.[27] A similar criticism applies to the prevailing economists' conception of the problem of promoting the economic development of underdeveloped countries, which rests on an extremely questionable identification of development with the accumulation of physical, and primarily industrial, capital.[28]

In this paper I have been concerned with the question of how economic principles can most usefully be formulated to fit the facts of economic life in the age of opulence. The main suggestions I have made call for explicit recognition of the role of capital in two contexts—consumption, and the nature of labor—where its importance is growing in fact but tends to be ignored in contemporary theory. In concluding, I should like to comment briefly on a subject which lies outside the range of economic principles but still within the scope of political economy as I conceive it, the implications of the economic system of opulence for the political and social life of the opulent society. Application of Marx's general analytical method to the system of corporate industrial production suggests, not the polarization and eventual breakdown of capitalist society that he predicted, but the consolidation of a highly differentiated hierarchical society in which status is determined ultimately by educational attainment. The gloomier implications of this form of social organization have been elaborated in a number of contemporary works, ranging from Burnham's *Managerial Revolution* through Riesman's *Lonely Crowd* and Whyte's *Organization Man* to Young's *Rise of the Meritocracy*.[29] But it is possible to take a more favorable view. While it is not true, despite the efforts of the apologists of corporate enterprise to persuade us to the contrary by adroit use of stock ownership statistics, that the masses are becoming capitalists in the sense of owning and controlling the means of production they use, it is true that they are becoming capitalists on an increasing scale in two other ways—as owners of consumption capital, and as possessors of educated skills. Thus, though the productive structure remains hierarchical, the political and social systems may nevertheless move in the direction of the ideal democratic free society.[30]

4. The Social Policy of an Opulent Society

In the past ten years or so our ideas about the nature of the society in which we live have been changing rapidly. We have become aware that we are an opulent society, by any comparative or historical standard, and that we are becoming progressively more opulent as time goes on, as a more or less automatic consequence of the way our economic institutions function. At the same time, we have become aware that the ultimate sources of our large and growing wealth are very different from what the conventional wisdom of our times would have us believe; that they are to be found not in the individual parsimony and hard labor of our public imagery but in the accumulation of capital and application of technical progress by corporate enterprises and the acquisition of increasing skill and knowledge by individuals—the accumulation of human capital.

Our ideas about social policy have not been adapted to the facts of life in the opulent society. In saying this I am not simply referring to the point made by J. K. Galbraith in his powerful and provocative book *The Affluent Society* (London, 1958), that an opulent society can afford to spend liberally on social security and collective consumption, and to tolerate any inefficiencies that result from such liberality, though that is true enough. I want to make the more fundamental point that our approach to social policy is still dominated by an individualistic conception of our society that might have been

A speech delivered at the opening plenary session of the Forty-first Annual Meeting and Conference of the Canadian Welfare Council, Ottawa, 29 May 1961, and published in my *Money, Trade and Economic Growth* (London, Allen & Unwin, 1962); reprinted with permission. This essay is dated, inasmuch as it was written early in 1961, before the upsurge of publich concern about poverty, inequality, the environment, and the quality of life; and many of the ideas in it are expressed better and more appositely in other later essays. But I have chosen to include it partly for that reason. It represents an attempt, at a time when economics still prided itself on its "hard science" character and concern with great statistical aggregates like employment, output, and economic growth to the virtual exclusion of concern with problems of common humanity, to show both that economics is a humane subject and that it has some important things to say both about what aspects of the harsher side of human life cannot and should not be insisted on as necessary to the functioning of the economic system, and what types of social policy are likely to prove futile and what effective in securing commonly accepted humanitarian objectives. These ideas have since become generally acceptable and familiar to economists; but it is, I think, worth remembering that they have a long-standing and reputable place in the historical development and central philosophical core of the subject.

appropriate, or at least the best that could be managed, in the early stages of development of modern industrial society, but is certainly not appropriate now. This individualistic conception of society is most in evidence in the opposition of various sections of public opinion, notably business groups, to the spending of public money for almost any social purpose—what one might call the rugged individualism of the directors' dining room, the prestige advertisement, and the expense-account business convention. But it also permeates the social security and welfare services that have been built up in spite of the rugged individualists. It is implicit in the two main concepts of our social security system, the insurance principle and the social minimum— as is evident from the most elaborate rationalization of these concepts available, that contained in the Beveridge Report.[1] The insurance principle seeks to disguise something that is not insurance, but the imposition of a special kind of income tax earmarked to finance special kinds of income transfers, in words acceptable to an individualistic philosophy. Insofar as true insurance principles are applied, by proportioning benefits drawn to contributions made, the result is inadequate provision of social security, and a need for supplementary social assistance. The social minimum principle conforms to individualism in its implication that the minimum is the maximum the state should provide, the individual being responsible for anything above it. Both principles, and indeed the prevalent philosophy of social policy, see the role of social policy essentially as that of mopping up the milk spilt by the system of private decision-taking. In that respect, our philosophy of social policy is the same as that of the nineteenth century; the principal difference, and it is an important one, is that in this century we have become much more critical in deciding how much spilt milk it takes to make a mess.

Now, I want to make it perfectly clear at the outset that I am not arguing in any sense against the liberal democratic ideal of individual self-development in a free society. On the contrary, my arguments will rest on that ideal. What I am arguing against is the naïve and unrealistic view of the relation of the individual to society on which we attempt to base the expression of that ideal in our social policy. We assume, in effect, that ours is a simple, stable, and relatively unchanging society, in which the normal individual arrives at maturity equipped with the capacity and knowledge to make the most of himself. We do assist him to take a place in society by providing a free education up to the secondary level and forcing him to accept it up to a certain age; we have been forced grudgingly to recognize contingencies— unemployment, old age, large family size and most recently hospital expenses—for which the individual may be unable or unwilling to provide; and we recognize that some individuals may be incompetent or unlucky enough to need help. But we assume that, by and large, the individual can and should be expected to cope with the society in which he lives; and that the society will operate efficiently if he is left, and preferably forced, to do so.

The realities of life in the opulent society are, I suggest, far different from the simple model on which our social philosophy is based. Far from being simple and easily comprehensible to the average person, our society is one of tremendously complex interdependence between people each of whom is specialized on a small part of the process of production, distribution and exchange. It is this specialization that provides our high standard of living. Far from being stable and relatively unchanging, our society is characterized by irregular, unpredictable growth and change; indeed, its basic dynamic principle is growth through change, change introduced by any person or firm that sees a profit in it. It is this freedom to introduce change that keeps our standard of living rising.

Complexity and dynamic change are the characteristics of the opulent society and the source of its opulence. But it takes only a little thought to realize how seriously these characteristics undermine the assumption of individual responsibility and capacity to cope with society. At this point I should stop talking about the individual, who is a nineteenth-century political fiction elaborated when only *men* counted for anything in society, and start talking about the family, which is really our basic social unit. Now the family in our society originates as a biological unit and not an economic one; and the more opulent we have become, the more personal preferences and social considerations rather than economic calculation have come to determine the selection of marriage partners, and the more too has the family been stripped down to its central core of parents and children. Yet in our individualistic system the family is entrusted with economic responsibilities that are of crucial importance to the welfare and progress of the opulent society. It is the basic spending unit, whose decisions determine whether increasing opulence will raise the quality of life or debase it; the income it has to spend is obtained by selling the services of its members and their property, so that its decisions in this regard determine both its income and the efficiency with which its human and nonhuman capital is used; and it determines the amount and type of education acquired by its children, so that collectively it determines the size and quality of the stock of human capital bequeathed to the next generation.

In a complex, rich, growing and changing society these are all difficult decisions requiring a high degree of knowledge, intelligence and foresight, and also the ability to command capital. The capacity of the family to undertake these responsibilities effectively is limited to start with by its small size as an economic unit and its mode of formation. Its capacity is further limited by the fact that our free society prohibits it from dealing in what is usually its most important asset, human capital, with the same freedom as it can deal in nonhuman capital: you cannot sell your daughter into slavery to keep the family from starving, and you cannot sell your son to someone who will invest in his education. The small economic size of the family also makes its welfare dependent to an important extent on the physical and social environment in which it lives, and over which it has little control. Finally, the narrow economic base of the family, its dependence for income on the sale of the services of its head or heads, renders its income and welfare extremely vulnerable to the human risks of illness, accident, and death, and the economic risks resulting from either the freedom for change that the opulent society allows, or the inability or incompetence of the government to stabilize the economic system.

Let me elaborate on these points. First, consider the family in its role as a consuming unit, adjusting to a high and rising standard of living. It is not all that easy to grow rich successfully; it requires a continual process of learning to improve one's tastes and standards, to budget one's income, to invest wisely in the complex consumer capital goods that constitute a modern high standard of living, and to manage one's property and oneself efficiently. The possibilities of failure are amply illustrated by the financial problems of spendthriftiness and personal bankruptcy, the medical problems of over-indulgence in food, drink, and tobacco, and the social problems of irresponsible parenthood, lax morality, and broken homes. Much of the criticism of the opulent society is concerned with the foolish things on which people spend their money, and the susceptibility of the public to the appeal of gadgetry and meretricious advertising. As a believer in a free society one must have faith that all these things are part of the process by which people learn eventually to manage wealth successfully. But there can be no doubt that the family needs, and can profit by, a great deal of expert help.

Now consider the family as an income-earning unit, selling the services of its human and nonhuman capital. To make the most of the opportunities of the opulent society requires knowledge of the opportunities and the capacity to move resources to the most profitable opportunity. Knowledge and movement both cost money—in the case of geographical or occupational movement of human resources, often a great deal of money, more than the family with its limited borrowing power can raise. Now knowledge has the peculiarity that once it is there any number of people can use it; for that reason it can be profitable for society to collect it and place it at the disposal of families, even though no individual family would find it worthwhile to collect it. Again, the limitation of family borrowing power may mean that people do not move to higher-paying employment, even though the higher earnings would pay an ample return on the cost of movement. In both respects, the capacity of the family to exploit its opportunities may be seriously restricted by its small economic size.

Now consider the family as the source of the future stock of human capital. In the opulent society, the family typically does not provide on-the-job training for children destined to inherit a family craft, business or profession. Instead, it must prepare its children to seek employment in a specialized economy where their value will depend on the skills and talents they have to offer—which in turn depends on their education. Now, education entails an investment of family resources, even when schools and tuition are provided free, because it requires the family to support the child and forego the money it could earn for the family if it did not go to school. The ways in which the character and attitudes of the family can affect the use the child makes of its educational opportunities are well known, and I need not elaborate on them. Instead, I want to make two points about the economics of investment in human capital. The first is that even for the best-intentioned and most thoughtful family the planning of a child's education is a terribly difficult problem which can only be solved by the most rudimentary kind of guesswork or rule of thumb. The product of this kind of investment is a more or less specific item of human capital, the returns on which will be realized by the owner by selling his services in the market over the next forty or fifty years. How much information would a professional investor want before he invested the cost of an education in a plant lasting fifty years? By contrast, how much relevant information does the typical parent acquire—and how much could be obtained if he tried—before he decides how much to invest in educating his children and what type of education to invest in? How can anyone—except a college president beating the bushes for endowments—be sure that "an education," of any kind for any person, is a good investment? My second point is that because our laws prohibit slavery, even if voluntarily entered into, investment in human capital tends to be very inefficient by comparison with investment in nonhuman capital. On the one hand, the bright child of poor parents cannot be sold to a capitalist who wants to invest in his talents, nor can his future earning capacity be tied up as security for a loan; the result is that his talents must go undeveloped unless a university or the state is willing to make him a present of an education. On the other hand, family pride coupled with money can result in expenditure on education yielding a low or negative rate of return— especially as education is a consumption good as well as a production good, and educational investment is a foolproof way of beating the inheritance tax.

I have been discussing the difficulties under which the family labors in carrying out the economic functions assigned to it by an individualistic economic system in the opulent society. I want now to discuss the ways in which the limited economic size of the family unit restricts its power to assume full responsibility for providing for its own welfare.

As a consuming unit, the power of the family to govern its own welfare is limited by the fact that, to participate in the benefits of the opulent society, it must live in a community, and its welfare and the quality of its life must accordingly depend in part on the nature of its community environment. One of the demographic effects of the progress of opulence is the concentration of the human population in metropolitan agglomerations of urban and suburban communities. Efficient living in such agglomerations demands the collective provision of a wide variety of services and amenities—water, roads, sewage and garbage disposal, parks et cetera—and the quality of life depends on the quality of these services. But the family cannot itself choose the level and quality of the collective services it enjoys, except to the very limited extent that income and occupation permit it to choose between rival communities providing such services to different extents. Within the community, the level of collective services provided depends on the willingness of families collectively to finance such services by taxation. And there is an inherent tendency in an individualistic and mobile society for such services to be underprovided, because the sacrifice of family income entailed in paying taxes is direct and easily appreciated, while the contribution to family welfare of better community services is indirect, and generally not closely related to the family's tax contribution or proportioned to its current desires for such services. Aside from collective services, the welfare of a family living in a community inevitably depends in countless ways on how the other members of the community—families and business enterprises—conduct their affairs. Such dependence ranges from trivial matters like the irritation of having noisy and untidy neighbors to such serious matters as the threat to health from the pollution of air by smoke and chemicals and of water by sewage and industrial waste, and the threat to security of person and property from the existence of slum neighborhoods. The welfare of the family is influenced by such things, but the family itself cannot control them—it can only move away if it can afford to. Like the provision of collective services, control of these things requires collective action. And as opulence progresses, it seems likely both that it will appear efficient to undertake the provision of more services collectively, and that increased scientific and social knowledge will reveal more and more cases in which the activities of some members of the community have adverse effects on others requiring social control.

The most serious limitations on the power of the family to support itself, however, result from the narrowness of its economic base—its dependence on the sale of the services of its human capital—and the personal and economic risks to which this subjects it. The personal risks—sickness, accident, incapacitation or death, and survival of self or dependents beyond the end of working life—can in principle be covered by private insurance, annuities or pension plans; the need for social provision for these contingencies arises from lack of sufficient family earning power or foresight to provide for them, or from the inability of commercial insurance to provide adequate coverage of the risks at a profit. The economic risks are uninsurable, because their incidence is unpredictable. They are especially serious for the family in the opulent society, both because its high income is obtained by specializing on a tiny part of the economic process, and because to enjoy that income to the full it must plan its expenditures on the expectation that income will continue to be earned. And these risks are an integral part of the opulent society itself, built into its structure.

There are in fact two sorts of economic risk to family income inherent in the structure of the opulent society. The first is due to the fact I have already noted, that the opulent society is built on the principle of freedom to introduce change if it seems profitable to do so, regardless of the effect on the value of other people's sources of income. The second arises from the fact that such a system is subject to fluctuations in aggregate income, prices, and employment that are difficult for the government to manage, and that may be aggravated by incompetence or wrong-headedness on the part of the managers. It seems to be asking a great deal too much to expect the family to bear the consequences of these kinds of risks, and to assume that it is capable of guessing when it selects occupations for its children what the probability is that twenty or thirty years later automation will be invented, the Japanese will learn to use modern technology, or the governor of the central bank will decide that it is more important to stop inflation than to maintain an adequate level of employment. Nor is unemployment insurance by itself an adequate form of protection of family income against these risks, since it amounts to little more than forcing the worker to save a part of his income to fall back on when he becomes unemployed.

I have spent a considerable amount ot time on the problems of the family in the opulent society, because I think it is necessary to appreciate these problems in designing an appropriate social policy. My main point can be summarized in the following very over-simplified model of the opulent economy. In this society there are two basic economic units. On the production side there is the big, well-financed, scientifically managed corporate enterprise; on the consumption side there is the little, precariously financed, not scientifically managed household. The enterprise is responsible for introducing the new, improved, or cheapened products and services that raise the standard of living; the household has to learn how to use them. The corporation is responsible for the replacement, accumulation and improvement of nonhuman capital; the household is responsible for the replacement, accumulation and improvement of human capital. The corporate enterprise has come to dominate the productive processes of our economy because it is peculiarly efficient in handling the problems of growth through technical change and capital accumulation; exactly parallel problems arise in the consumption processes of the economy, but our culture confines us to the family partnership. The household and not the corporation is supposed to be the beneficiary of the system; but the knowledge, intelligence and resources it can itself muster to the task of making the most of its opportunities are grossly inadequate by comparison with those of the corporation. The starting point of social policy in an opulent society should be to recognize these limitations and their sources; its objective should be to overcome them by social action consistent with the ideals of a free democratic society.

Before I go on to discuss what I think social policy in the opulent society should be, I want to say more about the notion of human beings as capital, which I have touched on at various points in my argument. The general idea is familiar enough, if only because politicians are so fond of declaiming to labor audiences that "our greatest natural resource is the skill and adaptability of our people." But we rarely carry it any further, because in a democratic society our thoughts—even those of economists—rebel at the idea of seriously considering people as pieces of capital equipment equivalent to inanimate objects. It is only recently that economists have begun to appreciate the importance of human skill and training as a cause of opulence, and to work seriously on the value of human capital and the returns to investment in it. There is, I think, nothing inhuman or undemocratic in looking at human ability and skill in this way, providing one knows where to stop. And serious application of the idea could provide a very useful guide to social policy and a yardstick for assessing its efficiency. By serious application I mean that we do not simply say "education is an investment in human capital" or "human beings are valuable assets" and conclude that any expenditure on education or conserving human life must be worthwhile. I mean instead that having recognized that various private activities in our society are concerned with investment in increasing the value of human capital or preventing loss of it—education, medical care, mobility of labor and so forth—we should, first, think seriously about the efficiency of these activities and whether it can be improved by social action; and secondly, calculate whether the investment of public money in carrying these activities further would pay a worthwhile rate of return or not. Similarly, one could check the return on activities now being undertaken, to see if the money could be better spent.

I have suggested the calculation of rates of return on investments in human capital as a guide to social policy; but I would point out that they could never be the final arbiter of our social policy, given our political and social attitudes and our legal restrictions on the sale or pledging of human capital. For one thing, our social and religious beliefs do not permit us to contemplate the scrapping of human capital; yet is evident that some people, such as the mentally subnormal or ill and the old age pensioners, are economic liabilities, whose value as liabilities we in fact do much to increase by caring for them—in the interests of common humanity we are prepared to make investments with negative yields. For another thing, though this is something on which we might change our minds, our legal and political tradition is against the state charging interest or taking the profits on its investments in human capital; thus the returns on such investment accrue to the person invested in, and the question may legitimately be raised why the taxpayer should be burdened for such investments. This is an important source of discord over educational policy; for example, it is one thing to argue that poor bright boys ought to be invested in, and quite another to insist that this be done by free scholarships, so that the boy and not the taxpayer who pays for it gets the return on the investment. Thirdly, the rates of return on investments in human capital can only serve as guides because both the costs and the returns are extremely difficult to measure, and once you have measured them you still have to decide what rate of return makes a profitable investment.

Before I leave the subject of human beings as capital, I should say something about the orders of magnitude involved. I have no figures for Canada, though one can obtain a rough idea of the importance of human capital in this country from the fact that about three quarters of Canadian national income is earned by work and only one quarter by property. For the United States, Dr. Burton Weisbrod has calculated the value of the average male at $17,000, if one discounts his prospective earnings at a 10 percent rate of interest, or $33,000, if one discounts them at a 4 percent interest rate. He estimates the aggregate value of the male population in 1950 at $1,335 billions (using the 10 percent rate); this figure may be compared with an estimate of $881 billion for the aggregate value of tangible nonhuman assets. Dr. Weisbrod reckons, incidentally, that the social profit from preventing the death from tuberculosis of a man as old as fifty is in excess of 700 percent.[2] My senior colleague at the University of Chicago, Professor T. W. Schultz, who is interested in the economics of education, has calculated that the value of the stock of education embodied in the United States labor force in 1957 was $535 billion, equal to 42 percent of the stock of reproducible wealth (that is, tangible nonhuman wealth excluding natural resources). Professor Schultz has also calculated the ratio of additional lifetime earnings associated with education to the costs of the education (including both the cost of schools and teachers and the earnings foregone by students); for 1958 his ratios work out at 11 for a college education, 12 for high school, and 40 for a completed elementary school education.[3] These results, however, do not necessarily mean that investment in education is more profitable than other investment. Dr. Gary Becker, who has carried out a major study of the economics of education for the National Bureau of Economic Research, has concluded that the rate of return on college education is about the same as that on business capital.[4]

After this digression on human beings as capital, I return to the question of social policy in the opulent society. The argument I have been presenting seems to me to lead to some general principles of social policy. Let me state these principles, and to elaborate a little—I have no time for more than a few suggestions—on what concrete measures they might lead to.

The first principle is that the complexity and changefulness of the opulent society are such that the individual citizen may need, and ought to be provided with, assistance of a variety of kinds if he is to make the most of the opportunities it provides him. The first need is for as good an elementary and secondary education as the individual can absorb. The free provision of such education is our accepted way both of equipping the child to take a place in our complex economic system and of compensating, in part at least, for the inequalities of family circumstance into which children are born. But it needs to be recognized that in the opulent society an increasing part of the real cost of education is the earnings foregone by going to school instead of to work, a cost which may put severe pressure on poor children to drop out of school even though the advantages to themselves and society of further education are great; accordingly society should be ready to assume the financial burden of maintaining schoolchildren, as well as of paying the costs of teaching them. The second need is for social provision of a wide variety of expert informational, welfare, and counseling services to help the individual and family to manage their affairs as intelligently and successfully as possible; in this connection it needs to be recognized that a rising standard of living entails increasing use of consumer durables, and demands increasingly the ability to understand and manage credit. A third need is for appreciation of the severity of the demands that life in the opulent society makes on those who participate in it, and recognition that those who for one reason or another are unable to meet these demands ought not to be treated simply as contemptible failures, but should instead be treated as casualties of the struggle for progress.

The second principle is that in an urbanized industrial society an important part of the process of raising the standard of living consists in the progressive improvement of the standards of services and amenities provided collectively, and of the quality of the environment. A community in which the schools look like factories used to look and the factories like schools ought to look, in which the decay and squalor of city centers forces people to risk their lives and blood pressures commuting miles from and to cosy homes in cheerlessly regimented suburbs, and in which the pollution of local beaches forces them to drive hundreds of miles in search of water fit for people and fish to swim in, can hardly be said to be employing its opulence wisely. Nor can anyone seriously believe that urban and rural slums are an appropriate training ground for responsible citizens of the opulent society. The opulent economy concentrates people in metropolitan agglomerations and gives them increasing leisure for enjoyment. The welfare of the opulent society requires the social provision of the collective requirements of decent living, restraint on the private propensity to poison one's neighbor's pleasure, and progressive improvement of the social environment of private living through town planning, slum clearance, and imaginative public works.

The third principle is that since the society is founded on the belief that individual freedom to introduce change serves the social good, the society and not the individual member should assume the costs that this freedom may impose on other members when these costs become unreasonably high. Beyond a certain point, the society collectively should bear the economic risks imposed on the family by dependence on the sale of its services, because society itself creates those risks. The same principle should extend to the personal risks, though there the reason is that these risks are the only major remaining risks to family welfare in a properly functioning opulent society. What I am arguing for here is the reversal of the social insurance principle. In the opulent society, the average family should be able to bear the costs of short-term unemployment or minor illness and accident, by drawing on family savings or borrowing against future earning power. It is the prolonged loss of earnings from technological or structural unemployment or unemployment due to depressed business conditions, and the combined high expense and loss of earnings from severe illness or accident, that is disastrous to family finance. And these are precisely the contingencies that cannot be covered by insurance, whether private or social. Instead of providing unemployment benefits for a limited period after the individual has become unemployed, and eventually casting him off to depend on his own resources and public assistance, social policy should provide benefits beginning after the individual has been unemployed for some time, and increasing in amount toward the level of his normal income in employment as he remains unemployed. At some stage it should be recognized that the unemployed individual is a victim of anti-inflationary policy or of economic change; in the former case he should be supported until the government is prepared to restore full employment, in the latter he should be compensated by being retrained or provided with an adequate pension on which to retire. Instead of leaving the individual to bear the risks of unlimited medical expenses, social policy should hold him responsible for a first slice of the costs proportioned to his ability to pay, and bear the remaining costs of providing the medical care he needs up to a socially determined standard. In addition, social provision should extend to replacing the income lost by prolonged illness or incapacitation, on the same plan as I have suggested for loss of income by unemployment.

The fourth principle is that the opulent society ought to apply to its social policy the same principles of rational calculation, innovation and exploitation of technical progress as it applies in its productive system. Let me illustrate what I mean by three examples. First, take education: this is by far our most important capital-goods-producing industry, yet it is very doubtful that it is carried on with anything like the efficiency of a commercial enterprise. Its selection of material for processing is strongly influenced by the irrelevant consideration of family capacity to pay, though it should be possible to design some form of enforceable long-term education loan to support poor but promising students, or at least to take some notice of the fact than an educated man generally will produce substantially more future tax revenue for the state than an uneducated man. Its standards of pay are set by political decision, its methods of teaching by academic tradition, and the proportion of the student's year devoted to it is an inheritance from our agricultural past; very little attention is paid to the fact that an opulent society progressively raises the value of labor—including students' time—and cheapens the cost of capital equipment. And it is very doubtful indeed that it allocates its output among products on the basis of sufficiently detailed and long-range forecasts of demand for them, or builds enough flexibility into its products to make them as adaptable to an uncertain future as they should be.[5]

Second, take medical care. The rising cost of medical care has created the chief threat to family security in the opulent society, and constitutes one of the main obstacles to generous social provision of medical care. One cause of the high cost of medical care is the high cost of doctors' services. This in turn is the consequence of allowing the medical profession to govern the standards and duration of medical training. The progressive raising of standards has had the effect of greatly increasing the investment of money and foregone earnings required by a medical education, an investment the returns on which must be recouped from the fees the doctor charges his patients; further, the great cost of the investment and the uncertainty of the returns has restricted the supply of doctors, so that the average rate of return on a medical education is appreciably higher than that on almost any other comparable educational investment.[6] A rational approach to investment in medical training would aim at reducing the cost of the investment by specializing doctors at an earlier stage and fixing the standard of basic training at what society could afford to pay for, and by carrying investment in medical educations to the point at which the rate of return was brought down to the average for the economy. It would also remove the conflict between the doctor's professional responsibility and his private interest inherent in the fee system, by putting doctors on salary or fixing standard prices for standard treatments.[7]

Third, take the problem of relief of depressed areas, an activity Canada has been engaged in, one way or another, since Confederation. Sentiment strongly favors methods that leave the people in the area, and that aim at creating employment opportunities that otherwise would not exist there, to avoid the social and human problems of moving the people elsewhere and to reconcile aid with the ethic of self-respecting independence. The trouble with this type of policy is that it generally results in creating self-perpetuating pockets of low-quality living that continue to require public support. It would frequently be much cheaper over the long run to invest very large sums in moving people out of such areas and establishing them in more prosperous areas where they, or at least their children, could become full participants in the opulent society.

Those are the principles that I believe should govern social policy in the opulent society. Before concluding, I should comment briefly on two objections that will doubtless be raised to any and all applications of them.

The first objection is that such a policy costs money, and taxes are too high already. High taxes are often blamed on social security and welfare expenditure, though in fact the present level of taxes is accounted for to a great extent by defense expenditure and by our habit of financing wars by borrowing rather than by taxation—two activities that probably contribute more to the security of the upper classes than they cost them in taxes. But more expenditure on social policy would undoubtedly require more tax revenue.

The main economic objection to high taxes is the incentive they give to tax avoidance. This problem and the revenue problem could to a significant extent be solved simultaneously by tightening up on business expense allowances and treating capital gains as income subject to tax; and additional taxes, including a tax on advertising and heavier taxes on gifts and inheritances between generations, could be easily justified. But the dilemma that more extensive social measures require more taxation is fundamentally a consequence of our antiquated way of financing governmental activity. Though government plays an important role in creating and maintaining the conditions under which wealth is created and income is earned, we allow the wealth and income to accrue as private property, and finance the government by taxing back the money after it has passed into private hands. I suggest that a more sensible way of conducting public finance in an opulent society would be to give the government a direct participation in the income of the economy, rather than a tax claim on it. One way of moving in this direction would be to accumulate the proceeds of inheritance taxes in the form of a government portfolio of ordinary shares and industrial bonds, instead of spending them as current income.

The second objection is the allegation that any extension of social security will sap the initiative and enterprise on which the competitive system depends. To that there are two answers. One is that an opulent society can afford to tolerate some inefficiency and waste in its social policy just as it does in its household consumption. The other is that there are good reasons for thinking that increased social security will increase and not reduce the initiative and enterprise of the individual in our society. One such reason is the characteristic ethos of the opulent society itself—an ethos of professional expertise and responsibility, of pride in applying intelligence and ingenuity to the solution of problems, of doing one's job well, of looking for opportunities to assume more responsibility. Educated people are driven not by the fear of failure but by the challenge of accomplishment, and they work best when they have the security to concentrate on the job they are qualified to do. Another, and to me more cogent, reason is that if social policy does not provide people with the security they want, they will not simply do without it. They will try to provide it by whatever means they can, and usually the means they choose reduce the efficiency, flexibility, and progressiveness of the economy. Trade unions enforce restrictive practices; companies form price agreements; workers and executives alike demand that their company provide health and pension plans, thus tying themselves to that company; industries unable to meet foreign competition demand tariff protection; depressed areas demand discriminatory treatment. The result is an inefficient social security system and an inefficient economy. And whatever one thinks of an inefficient social security system, an inefficient economy is undesirable. In the first place, we face a challenge to our high standard of living from the spread of industrialization and modern technology around the world. In the second place, we have an obligation to share the fruits and techniques of our opulence with the underdeveloped nations. And finally, we are nowhere near the point of satiation with the good things that enrich and civilize life.

Part 2

The Keynesian Revolution, for Good or Ill

5. The General Theory after Twenty-five Years

What should one say in commemorating the twenty-fifth anniversary of a book? Normally one thinks of the publication of a book as a birth of new ideas; and the appropriate occasion for a speech is either the day the youth attains his majority, when he is congratulated on the achievement of adult status and a brilliant future is predicted for him, or the day the old man retires, when he is congratulated on a lifetime of productive labor and wished a peaceful old age. A twenty-fifth anniversary suggests a marriage—a union of ideas with literary expression, so to speak—and the appropriate speech is one which compliments the couple on their success in solving the problem of marital adjustment and congratulates them on the number and promise of their progeny, while tactfully refraining from mentioning that in its early years the marriage was judged by many to be a mistake and doomed to failure. It is in this spirit that I wish to commemorate the silver anniversary of the *General Theory*. We have had the coming-of-age party in the revolutionary days of the late thirties and the pension presentation ceremony in the obituary assessments of the late forties. We are now well into the post-Keynesian era; and it seems more appropriate at this point to take stock of the intellectual capital embodied in the *General Theory* than to debate whether the investment should be considered the foundation of our fortune or written off as a dead loss.

To keep the subject within bounds, I propose to concentrate on the *General Theory* and to use it as a basis for discussion. I shall first discuss the book as economic literature. My excuse for doing so is that the book long ago attained the status of a classic—meaning a book that everyone has heard of and no one has read—and the translation of its untidy construction into neat models suitable for geometic and mathematical manipulation, effective as it proved in converting economists to the Keynesian school, has obscured some characteristics of Keynes's methods of analysis which are relevant to the evaluation of his theory. From the book I shall proceed to the theory presented in it, considering it first as monetary theory and then as a theory of income and employment. I shall then comment, more briefly, on the policy

The Invited Lecture to the 1960 Annual Meetings of the American Economic Association, reprinted with permission from *American Economic Review* 51, no. 2 (May 1961); copyright 1961 by the American Economic Association.

implications of the theory. In each case I shall be concerned to assess Keynes's ideas in the context of subsequent developments; and I shall conclude with a summary assessment of the contributions of the *General Theory* to modern economics.

The *General Theory* as Economic Literature

Not even the most ardent admirer of Keynes's powers as an expositor of economic ideas and a literary stylist would wish to have his reputation in these respects judged solely by the *General Theory*. Arresting phrases and brilliant passages there are, as everyone who has read it remembers, but the book as a whole is not easy to read and master, and it has not become easier with the passage of time. In support of this judgment one need only refer to the fact that no less than three successful books aimed at guiding the reader through the *General Theory* have appeared at intervals in the past twenty-five years—those of Joan Robinson, Dudley Dillard, and Alvin Hansen—not to speak of less well-known monographs and the countless interpretative articles which still continue to appear.

For the difficulty of the *General Theory* there are a variety of reasons. At the literary and expository level, there is the evident strain of the "long struggle of escape ... from habitual modes of thought and expression" mentioned by Keynes in his Preface. There is also the nonrigorous Cambridge style of theorizing, the didactic Marshallian style, in which awkward complications are hidden in plain view and common sense is allowed to run away with the argument—a style which Keynes defended in his critical remarks on mathematical economics. There is the intrusiveness of Keynes the philosopher, interrupting the argument to muse on the social virtues and vices of the organized speculative markets on which he had made his own and his College's fortune, or to dilate rather pretentiously on the essential properties of interest and money. And above all there is the pervading influence of Keynes the born propagandist, with his instinct for dramatizing his ideas, and his Cassandra complex, fortified as polemicists often are by a certain obtuseness in understanding the arguments of his adversaries.

In directing his attack at the neoclassical concept of an economic system equilibrating at full employment and presenting a general theory of underemployment equilibrium of which the neoclassical theory was a special case, Keynes's polemical instinct was surely right, both because neoclassical ways of thinking were then a major obstacle to sensible antidepression policy and because, for professional economists, the concept of equilibrium has always had far more intellectual sex appeal as an analytical companion than its opposite, disequilibrium. But his concentration on equilibrium was in the longer run inimical to his purpose, since his central theoretical contribution—that in a monetary economy the stability of employment in the face of changes in aggregate demand for output depends on the uncertain monetary effects of changes in money wage levels, which changes may themselves be slow—could be and was easily converted into a demonstration that his underemployment equilibrium depended on wage rigidity or on special empirical assumptions about the monetary consequences of wage changes. I shall return to this point later; for the present, let me merely remark that the polemical spirit impedes the argument.

These are idiosyncrasies of method of presentation; more fundamental difficulties for the reader are inherent in the analytical content of the book. In the first place, it is difficult for a modern reader to appreciate, after twenty-five years of rapid theoretical development, the extreme limitations of the concepts then available for dealing with economic aggregates and economic dynamics. Keynes tells us that "the three perplexities which most impeded my progress in writing this book, so that I could not express myself conveniently until I had found some solution for them, are: firstly, the choice of units of quantity appropriate to the problems of the economic system as a whole; secondly, the part played by expectations in economic analysis; and thirdly, the definition of income." These perplexities reflect the absence, in the Marshallian partial-equilibrium tradition, of a clear notion of real income; the lack of a technique of dynamic analysis in the Hicksian sense, explicitly incorporating expectations; and the fact that national income accounting was in its infancy. In resolving these perplexities, Keynes was thrown strongly back on the very classical tradition he was seeking to attack. His choice of the wage unit depended on the extremely questionable classical view that labor is a uniquely homogeneous aggregate. His treatment of expectations in terms of states of expectation, and especially his distinction between short-term and long-term expectations, incorporated the pseudo-dynamics of the Marshallian distinction between short-period and long-period analysis. And his laborious discussion of the definition of income was essentially an elaboration of the Marshallian short-period theory of the firm. More fundamentally, the theory of the book is constructed on the model of Marshallian short-period equilibrium; it incorporates the same assumptions of fixity of capital stock and increasing costs and the same vagueness as to the time-period for which the analysis is relevant. This vagueness is an especially serious weakness in the *General Theory*, which attempts to bring markets with widely different speeds of adjustment—the goods market, the money market, and the labor market—into one short-period equilibrium analysis; and much of the subsequent criticism of the *General Theory* is essentially an iteration of the inadequacies of Marshallian short-period equilibrium as a technique of aggregative dynamic analysis.

A second source of difficulty for the reader is the fact that, as Keynes noted in his Preface, the ideas of the *General Theory* evolved from those presented in the *Treatise on Money*. The *Treatise* received rather rough treatment from its critics, and the tendency among both Keynesians and anti-Keynesians has been to forget it. But the *Treatise* contains important clues to Keynes's methods of reasoning, and also an extensive analysis of various problems which he consequently dealt with only sketchily in the *General Theory*. The presence of the *Treatise* in the background accounts for the gap left in the *General Theory* between the marginal efficiency of capital, as the prospective rate of return on new investment goods, and the pure rate of interest, as determined by liquidity preference and the quantity of money—a gap very inadequately bridged by the concepts of lender's and borrower's risk and the later addition of the concept of finance. It also accounts for the rather cursory treatment in the *General Theory* of the theory and practice of monetary policy—a subject dealt with at length in the *Treatise*.

A third source of difficulty is Keynes's clumsy and misleading way of presenting what is essentially a general equilibrium model as a system of unidirectional causation. I refer to the order of analysis of the *General Theory*, in which income is defined as the sum of consumption and investment; consumption is determined by investment through the multiplier; investment is determined by the marginal efficiency of capital and the rate of interest; and the rate of interest is determined by liquidity preference and the quantity of money; but at the very last stage of the argument the level of income re-enters as a determinant of liquidity preference, so that the apparently simple line of causation from the demand for and supply of money to the interest rate to investment to consumption to income vanishes completely. Keynes's method, carried over from the *Treatise*, of placing the saving-investment relation in the center of the picture and working backward to the demand and supply of money is admirably adapted to concentrating attention on effective demand and diverting it from monetary complications; but it is also apt to be misleading. It misled Keynes himself into important errors of statement, of which the most serious is the doctrine that the rate of interest is nothing more than the price for surrendering liquidity; and it has misled both critics and disciples into numerous misinterpretations of Keynes's theory. At one time it even led so great an authority as Alvin Hansen into the belief that Keynes's interest theory is indeterminate.

A fourth difficulty, especially troublesome to anyone who comes to the *General Theory* after being introduced to Keynesian ideas at the textbook level, arises from Keynes's attempt to apply the Marshallian short-period model to the analysis of an economy in which behavior is governed by expectations about the future. There are really two theories in the *General Theory*. One is the theory that, given the money wage rate, the equilibrium levels of aggregate income and the rate of interest are determined by the

propensity to consume, the investment demand schedule, liquidity preference, and the quantity of money, the first three being stable functions in
the short run. The other, which finds its fullest expression in the "Notes on
the Trade Cycle," is that all three of the fundamental propensities are highly
unstable, under the influence of changing expectations about the future. It is
the first theory, of course, which has become *the* Keynesian theory—
inevitably so because it alone offers a system of relationships amenable to
theoretical manipulation and empirical application. The second theory,
carried to its logical extreme, would amount to a negation of the first theory.
This was clearly not Keynes's intention; but he offered no formal analysis of
the formation of expectations, and it was left to later writers to develop his
short-period analysis into theoretical and econometric models of cycles
and growth.

I have dwelt on the difficulty of the *General Theory* as a book, not with the
intention of leading up to the remark that in the thirties the effort required
to open the oyster led those who were successful to overvalue the intellectual
pearl within—which is true but trite—but to emphasize the necessity of
distinguishing between the *General Theory* as one of the great books in our
literature and the general theory as a system of analysis, and to enable me to
place the book conveniently in its historical setting. In so doing, I have
stressed the extremely Marshallian character of Keynes's theory, which I
regard not as a qualification of his achievement but as a measure of the
limitations which his powers of original thinking enabled him to transcend.
The *General Theory* is built on Marshallian concepts. In the light of
subsequent developments, it is also possible to detect Marshallian influences
at a more subtle level, in Keynes's concentration on the propensity to
consume. His emphasis on personal saving behavior to the neglect of
corporate saving behavior reflects Marshall's inability to integrate the
modern corporation into his system of economic analysis. More fundamentally, his stress on current income receipts as the prime determinant of
current consumption expenditure, and particularly his deduction of the form
of the income-consumption relationship from an a priori "fundamental
psychological law," reflects the general weakness of the Cambridge School in
dealing with capital in its relation to economic behavior. Indeed, if one seeks
for a single peg on which to hang a discussion of both the criticism and the
elaboration of this and other aspects of Keynes's theory, one can find it in the
inadequate attention paid in the *General Theory* to problems of capital
theory.

The *General Theory* as Economic Theory

Let me now turn from the *General Theory* as economic literature to the
general theory as economic analysis. The theory presented in the book can be

considered from two points of view. As Keynes presented it, it is a theory of the determination of income and employment, in which the emphasis is thrown on the determinants of effective demand and monetary factors play a subsidiary role. But it can also be considered as a monetary theory, in which the emphasis is thrown on the demand for money as an asset alternative to other assets. The distinguishing feature of the first theory is the concept of the propensity to consume; the distinguishing feature of the second is the speculative demand for money—"liquidity preference proper." Both theories are developed on the assumption—to which Keynes did not always consistently adhere—of a given level of money wages, an assumption incorporated in his device of measuring all aggregates in wage units. It is this assumption which makes Keynes's monetary theory a theory of interest rather than of prices and which raises the central theoretical questions about both his monetary theory and his theory of underemployment equilibrium.

Before I discuss these theories in detail, let me note briefly that Keynes's way of presenting them as static equilibrium theories led in each case to a violent and prolonged controversy which has turned out in retrospect to be sterile. I refer to the controversy over the savings-investment identity, and the loanable funds versus liquidity preference, stocks versus flows, debate. The savings-investment controversy turns on the question of how savings and investment can be identical and yet their equality be a condition of income equilibrium; the answer is simply that the term "savings" (or "investment") is being used in two senses—variously distinguished as *ex post* and *ex ante*, realized and intended, actual and desired—of which the latter is the theoretically relevant one. Most theorists have long since ceased to worry about the necessary identity of savings and investment, since insistence on it clutters up dynamic analysis; but it survives as a bewildering element in various Keynesian theories of income distribution, and, in the form of the proposition that investment creates its own savings, continues to inhibit clear thinking on problems of promoting economic development.

The liquidity preference-loanable funds debate turns on the question of whether the rate of interest is better regarded as equilibrating the flow of funds onto and off the market for securities or as equilibrating the demand for and supply of the stock of cash. The answer, which is now so deeply embedded in mathematical argument that no one can be sure he has got it right, seems to be that the stock-flow distinction is irrelevant, since either theory can be expressed in stock or flow terms; and that it makes no difference whether one works with money or securities, provided, first, that one is concerned only with the determination of the equilibrium level of the rate of interest, and, second, that one realizes that this is a general equilibrium problem which can be reduced only by artifice to a problem of equilibrium in one market. In more formal terms, if one assumes to begin with that the markets for goods and factors are in equilibrium, equality

between the demand for and supply of money implies equality between the
(stock and flow) demand for and supply of loans and vice versa. The two
theories become different, however, when applied to dynamic analysis of
disequilibrium situations, since liquidity preference theory implies that the
rate of interest rises only in response to an excess of the demand for over the
supply of money, whereas loanable funds theory implies that it rises only in
response to an excess of supply of over demand for securities, and when the
goods and factors markets are out of equilibrium an excess demand for
money does not necessarily imply an excess supply of securities. In a dynamic
context, the loanable funds theory definitely makes more economic sense;
and the sustained resistance of Keynesians to admitting it, evident most
notably in the prolonged defense in the English literature of the proposition
than an increase in the propensity to save lowers the interest rate only by
reducing the level of income, is a credit to their ingenuity rather than their
scientific spirit.

The General Theory *as Monetary Theory*

With these preliminaries out of the way, I turn first to Keynes's general
theory considered as a monetary theory. As I have stated, the distinguishing
feature of this theory is the emphasis placed on the demand for money as an
asset alternative to other yield-bearing assets rather than as a medium of
exchange, together with the crucial role assigned to uncertainty of expectations about future interest rates in determining the shape of the demand
curve for money as a function of the rate of interest. Thus Keynes made the
analysis of the demand for money explicitly a branch of capital theory,
whereas the role of money as a form of wealth-holding had been left implicit
in the neoclassical analysis. His theory of the demand for money is, however,
misleadingly presented, very confused, and, as a theory of demand for money
in capital theory terms, seriously incomplete; so that much work has been
required of interpreters and critics by way of clarifying and extending his
central ideas.

As to misleading presentation, I have already made the point that Keynes's
presentation of a general equilibrium system as one of unidirectional
causation creates the false impression, of which Keynes himself was the chief
victim, that holding securities is the only relevant alternative to holding
money, and that the classical alternatives of spending money on consumption
or investment play no part in determining the demand for money and the
rate of interest.

As to confusion, I need only mention the transmogrification of the
precautionary and speculative motives for holding money between the two
chapters in which they are discussed. The precautionary motive starts as the
senior partner, entrusted with the important business of avoiding uncertainty
about future rates of interest, while the speculative motive is the junior

partner who looks after the possibility of profiting from a fall in security prices on an organized market. But when next we meet them, the speculative motive has taken over the whole business of asset management, and the precautionary motive has been reduced to a poor relation eking out his existence in the household of transactions demand. That the speculative motive in Keynes's final formulation of it includes the precautionary is not generally recognized in the post-Keynesian literature, even though the precautionary motive provides the ultimate rationale of the "liquidity trap." James Tobin's important article on "Liquidity Preference as Behavior Towards Risk" does distinguish clearly between the two elements in Keynes's analysis of the demand for money as an asset; but it does not identify them with the two motives that Keynes described.

As to incompleteness, there is first the fact that Keynes dealt only cursorily with transactions demand, which he explained on classical lines of personal convenience and economic structure and took to be a simple proportion of income. Thus demand for money in his theory depends partly on income, in a way not rigorously analyzed, and partly on the influence of current and expected interest rates on the preferred disposition of wealth. Subsequently Baumol and Tobin have shown how transactions demand can be treated as a problem in capital (specifically, inventory) theory, and that the demand so derived varies inversely with the rate of interest and is subject to economies of scale.

Far more serious, however, are the limitations resulting from Keynes's procedure of conducting his analysis on the assumption of a given wage/ price level and lumping all securities together in an aggregate yielding a single rate of interest. Aggregation undoubtedly tends to exaggerate the importance of the speculative, as distinct from the precautionary, demand for money, since it overlooks the likelihood that, with a wide variety of equities and fixed-interest securities of varying maturity available, speculation will take the form of movements between securities of different types rather than between securities and cash. It is Keynes's emphasis on the speculative as against the precautionary motive that more orthodox monetary theorists have tended to find objectionable. The assumption of a given wage/ price level excludes the influence of price expectations on the assets demand for money, and the associated necessity of distinguishing between real and nominal interest and between fixed-interest-bearing securities and equities; Keynes's attempt to circumnavigate these complications by confining the influence of price-level expectations to the marginal efficiency of capital is not convincing.

The theory of liquidity preference has since been extended by Keynesian writers—Joan Robinson, Richard Kahn, and others—to comprise choices between money, bills, bonds, and equities, and more generally between a multiplicity of assets; but the influence of price-level expectations on asset choices has generally been neglected by Keynesian writers, important though that influence has become on investor behavior since the war. For explicit analysis of it one must turn to the modern quantity theory literature, where Milton Friedman's restatement of the quantity theory of money goes far toward providing a synthesis of Keynesian and classical approaches to the demand for money in capital theory terms.

As a theory of the demand for money as an asset, Keynes's liquidity preference theory is incomplete in another significant respect. His concern with the short run in which the stock of physical capital is given, together with his assumption of a given wage level, enabled him to develop the demand for money as a function of current and expected interest rates without explicitly introducing the value of assets. This omission led him into analytical errors of far-reaching significance. In the first place, he did not distinguish between increases in the quantity of money resulting from gold discoveries or budget deficits and those resulting from open market operations, though the former involve a net increase in the quantity of assets held by the public and the latter do not. Secondly, in treating the effect of a reduction in money wages as a reduction in the transactions demand for money—a procedure which incidentally commits the heinous crime of building money illusion into the assets demand for money—he overlooked the effect of the wage reduction in increasing the public's real wealth—the Pigou-Haberler-Patinkin wealth effect. In each case, the significance of the oversight lies less in its implications for the demand for money than in the neglect of the effects of the increase in real wealth on aggregate demand. Keynes's neglect of the wealth-effect of deficit finance undoubtedly contributed to misunderstanding of the postwar consequences of the methods adopted for financing the war; and the wealth-effect of wage reduction has become the foundation of the proof that his underemployment equilibrium depends on rigid wages. The value of wealth and its dependence on the price level have since been integrated with other determinants of behavior in Keynesian theory.

So far I have been discussing Keynes's theory of the demand for money and subsequent developments of it. I have taken his central contribution to be his conception of money as an asset whose usefulness springs from uncertainty about future asset prices and the chief limitation of his analysis to be his concentration on expectations of future changes in interest rates as the determinant of the assets-demand for money. I now turn to the deeper issues raised by Keynes's treatment of the demand for and supply of money as determining the rate of interest rather than the level of prices. As Modigliani showed in his classic *Econmetrica* article, this treatment depends on Keynes's assumption of rigid wages: with perfect wage and price flexibility, liquidity preference and the nominal quantity of money would determine the level of prices and not the rate of interest in Keynes's model, unless a liquidity trap intervenes. But an economy with perfect price flexibility is not the economy with which Keynes was concerned, and it is not an interesting economy to posit for theorizing about the problems with which he wanted to deal. In this judgment I derive support from the fact that the quantity theory has ceased to be a theory of prices and has become the theory that there is a stable demand function for money—a formulation which leaves open the question whether the demand and supply of money determine interest or prices or both.

To leave the matter there, however, is to confine the issue to short-run analysis, whereas it goes much deeper. The fundamental contention of Keynesian monetary theory is that a monetary economy is essentially different from a barter economy—that money is not merely a veil but exercises an influence of its own in the working of the economy. To examine the validity of this contention it is necessary to investigate the role of money in an economy with wage and price flexibility, allowing for the wealth effect of price-level changes. Such investigation is the object of the two major works in monetary theory published since the *General Theory*—Patinkin's *Money, Interest and Prices* and Gurley and Shaw's *Money in a Theory of Finance*. These show (the one largely by inference, the other directly) that in an economy in which a variety of assets exists and money is created by purchase of such assets by a banking system, changes in the supply of and demand for money have a long-run and not merely a short-run influence on the real equilibrium of the economy. The present position can be summarized in the statement that Keynes was right to attack Say's Law, but he attacked it for the wrong reason. Properly understood, the significance of Say's Law is not that it makes the decision to save identical with the decision to invest but that it excludes money altogether from any influence on economic behavior.

The General Theory of Income and Employment

I have been discussing the *General Theory* as a monetary theory; but its main purpose and contribution is the theory of income and employment. Keynes's great achievement was to cut through the conceptual complexity and literary looseness of contemporary monetary theory to an aggregative general equilibrium model of the economy which, once grasped, was simple, readily manipulable, and above all relevant to contemporary problems. The elements in this model, aside from liquidity preference and the quantity of money are the propensity to consume, the investment demand schedule, and the aggregate supply schedule relating employment to output. Keynes's analysis of the last two of these was thoroughly classical in general outline—extraordinarily so in view of the contemporary eruption of monopolistic and imperfect competition theory. The novel and intriguing element in the theory was the propensity to consume, together with its alter ego, that inexhaustibly versatile mechanical toy, the multiplier.

The propensity to consume made the theory of income determination a simple theory in which income was determined by the amount of fixed capital investment, the multiplier playing a role analogous to that of velocity in the quantity theory. The concept of income as the main determinant of expenditure, which Keynes confined to personal consumption behavior, lent itself readily to extension by others to the spending behavior of government, of corporations, of nations in their external transactions, and of an economy disaggregated into output-producing or income-receiving sectors. The statistical estimation of the consumption function offered itself as an important exercise for the emerging discipline of econometrics; and early analysis of time-series and cross-section data seemed abundantly to confirm the hypothesis that consumption is a stable function of income.

Alas for the consumption function, it dismally failed the test of forecasting postwar unemployment. This failure, together with the paradox disclosed by Kuznets' data on the long-run constancy of the savings ratio, prompted a rapid independent development of the theory of the consumption function, and led to substantive modifications of Keynesian income theory. Both developments have been concerned with the same shortcoming of the theory as Keynes presented it, the neglect of the influence of wealth on consumption, a neglect inherent in Keynes's short-period approach and concealed by his deduction of the shape of the propensity to consume from an unexplored "psychological law." The various hypotheses used to reconcile the short-run variability with the long-run constancy of the savings ratio, ranging from "secular upward drift" through the influence of highest previous income or value of assets to the more intellectually exciting life-plan and permanent income theories, are all concerned at one or another level of sophistication with the influence of wealth on consumption. Correspondingly, it has become customary to include the value of wealth in some form among the variables on which the Keynesian behavior propensities depend, both to give explicit recognition to the influence of wealth on consumption in the long run and to incorporate the neglected wealth-effect of wage and price-level changes.

Meanwhile, the propensity to consume and the multiplier have dwindled to relative insignificance both in the purer sort of monetary theory and in popular Keynesian economics. For pure theory, the essential Keynesian concept is the functional dependence of aggregate expenditure on itself in its income-generating capacity. The division of expenditure into consumption and investment is a superfluous complication once one drops the restrictive assumption that consumption depends only on income and investment only on the rate of interest, and permits both to change autonomously; similarly, the multiplier is a tiresome way of comparing general equilibrium positions. At the popular level, the essential Keynesian idea is the dependence of income, employment, and (more recently) the rate of inflation on the level of aggregate spending, together with the understanding that economic policy can attack spending at a variety of points; the notion of consumption as a passive respondent to investment is appropriate, if at all, to a laissez faire society, not to one with conscious economic policies. But the propensity to consume survives as an integral part of modern business cycle and growth theory; it has also become a basic component of the theory of planning economic development.

I turn now from the propensity to consume to the equilibrium of income and employment it helps to determine. As Keynes himself indicated in his chapter "Changes in Money Wages," and as other writers have demonstrated rigorously, underemployment equilibrium in Keynes's system depends on wage rigidity, except in the two possible empirical cases of perfectly interest-elastic liquidity preference and perfectly interest-inelastic consumption and investment demands. Subsequent criticism based on the wealth-effect on demand of a lower price level has circumvented these two exceptions and shown that Keynesian unemployment equilibrium depends on wage rigidity unless the wealth-effect peters out before full employment is reached—an empirical possibility which only a few diehards have been prepared to defend. This demonstration does not controvert Keynes's main contentions about wage reduction as a means of increasing employment in a competitive economy—that the money wage level influences employment through its monetary effect and not by altering real wages, that in practice wage reduction is difficult to achieve and may influence expectations adversely, and that normally monetary expansion can accomplish the same results more easily and justly. But it does mean that "unemployment equilibrium" has to be reinterpreted as a disequilibrium situation in which dynamic adjustment is proceeding very slowly; this is the interpretation of mathematical economists such as Leontief, Patinkin, and Clower, and is, I believe, a fair modern translation of Keynes's short-period equilibrium technique. Empirical research has confirmed that wage adjustment is slow in depressions and has also shown the "real balance effect" to be small.

A more relevant question is whether large-scale unemployment is the typical situation of an advanced capitalist economy, as the theme and prevailing tone of the *General Theory* imply, and as the stagnationists of the late thirties insisted. It is a particularly relevant question because Keynes, unlike many of his followers, was prepared to concede that traditional quantity theory becomes relevant under full employment conditions. A conclusive argument on this question is impossible, given the changes brought about by massive peacetime armament expenditures, social security and farm support programs, aid for the underdeveloped, and the success of the Keynesian revolution in securing recognition of governmental responsibility for full employment. Nevertheless, I believe that Keynes drastically overgeneralized a particularly bad depression which was made worse by errors of economic policy. Whether this is so or not, mass unemployment of the thirties variety has not been a problem of advanced capitalist countries since the war. Stagnationists do still exist in the modern world; but they are concerned either with the underdeveloped countries or with the failure of capitalism to grow as fast as the Russians. In either case they are certainly not underconsumptionists.

If the consumption function is nowhere near as simple as Keynes made it out to be and underemployment equilibrium is a special case of dynamic disequilibrium and anyway not the chronic problem of modern capitalism, what is left of the general theory of income and employment? The contribution of the *General Theory* to modern economics is certainly not Keynes's specific model of income determination, for not only is his consumption function too simple but his theory of investment is incomplete and has had to be extended to make it usable. Rather the contribution lies in the general nature of Keynes's approach to the problem of income and employment. In the first place, he concentrated attention on the expenditure-income and income-expenditure relationships, which are much easier to understand and apply than the quantity theory relationships and which provide, in the multiplier analysis, a key to dynamic processes of change. In the second place, he provided a useful macroeconomic general equilibrium model for the analysis of a monetary economy in which capital accumulation is a specialized activity financed by the issue of marketable securities. In monetary theory, Keynes's crucial distinction between consumption and investment decisions has been dropped and the model refined into the four-market system comprising goods, labor, money, and "bonds"—two flows and two stocks—but the distinction remains essential to cycle and growth theory. Indirectly, also, Keynes stimulated the development of modern dynamic theory. Finally, what is most important for scientific economics but can easily be used to denigrate Keynes's work, he set out his theory in a model in which the important variables and relationships are specified in a form suitable for statistical measurement and testing. The stimulation given by the *General Theory* to the construction and testing of aggregative models may well prove to be Keynes's chief contribution to economics in the longer perspective of historical judgment, since the application of capital rather than income concepts to monetary theory may well produce better and more reliable results, and the present predominance of the income-expenditure approach prove to be a transitional stage in the analysis of economic behavior.

The Policy Implications of the *General Theory*

This brings me to the policy implications of the *General Theory*, which I have hitherto postponed discussing. At this date there is no need to labor the point that the *General Theory* deserves much of the credit for the fact that the maintenance of high and stable employment is now accepted as a governmental responsibility, or that Keynes's theory of effective demand is the origin of the modern theory of economic policy. What calls for comment, rather, is the bias that the majority of Keynesians have drawn from the *General Theory* against allowing money, and consequently monetary policy, an important role in determining the level of activity of the economy. This bias has meant that Keynesian theory has proved a poor guide to the dominant postwar policy problem of inflation and that the Keynesian approach to this problem has tended to degenerate into a confused and often obstructive eclecticism. Now, a bias against money and monetary policy was not characteristic of Keynes's work as a monetary theorist—rather the opposite—and money and the demand for it play an essential role in the *General Theory* itself. It is true that the presentation of the theory plays down the role of money and that despite its title the book contains almost nothing on the thoery of inflation; but Keynes did state clearly that full employment would require a different analysis, and he had after all dealt exclusively with such conditions in the *Treatise*. (The *Treatise* is in fact much more relevant to postwar conditions than the *General Theory*—but that would require another lecture.)

It is an interesting question why a theory in which money is important should have turned into the theory that money is unimportant. Part of the explanation lies in certain features of the *General Theory* I have already mentioned that diverted attention from the influence of money and of price expectations on spending. Part of it lies in the hardening of certain of Keynes's conclusions into rigid dogmas in the hands of his disciples—notably the hardening of his legitimate criticisms of the quantity theory into militant opposition to any form of quantity theory reasoning, and the hardening of his opinion that monetary policy might be ineffective in combating a collapse of the marginal efficiency of capital into the conflicting dogmas (*a*) that monetary restriction is dangerous because it might precipitate such a collapse and (*b*) that monetary restriction is useless because it will have a negligible effect on effective demand. Part of it is that for obvious reasons Keynesians have tended to be politically left of center, a position associated with distrust of central bankers—particularly in England, due to the part the Bank of England played in the restoration of the gold standard and the downfall of the first Labour Government. Much of it is simply that the "vulgar Keynesians" seized on the simplest and most striking version of the Keynesian system—autonomous investment and the multiplier—as the essence of it, ignoring the monetary analysis as an irrelevant complication.

Whatever the explanation, the result has been that in analyzing inflation Keynesians have tended to fall back on one or other of two approaches based on components of the *General Theory* rather than on the complete model. One approach is based on the crude, effective demand model of income determination; combined with the expenditure-income-expenditure sequence, this leads into the demand-pull theory of inflation. The other approach is based on Keynes's habit of treating the wage unit as exogenous; combined with the income-expenditure-income sequence, this leads into the cost-push theory of inflation. The one approach leads toward the prescription of fiscal policy to remedy inflation, the other toward the prescription of some form of wage and price control. Neither prescription is very realistic for postwar capitalist economies: fiscal remedies are difficult to graft onto high-level budgets dominated by defense expenditure and structural social welfare programs; wage and price controls are inconsistent with a free enterprise system, and especially with the principle of free collective bargaining. Both approaches, by ignoring or suppressing the monetary side of Keynesian theory, concentrate on the mechanism rather than the causation of inflation; and both virtually assume away the possibility of controlling inflation by monetary means.

Not all Keynesians have been skeptical about monetary policy, especially after experience of it since 1951. Keynesian theory has in fact had a formative influence on modern ideas on monetary policy. The theory of effective demand suggests the question of what precise effects monetary policy has on spending—a question which it is important to ask owing to the tendency of central banks to judge their policies by their effects on interest rates and credit conditions in the markets with which they are immediately concerned. This question has stimulated the search for the effects of monetary policy on particular sectors of the economy and also furnished the rationale for a broader and more selective approach to the techniques of monetary control. On the other hand, the search for specific impacts of monetary policy tends to promote underestimation of its influence; so does the Keynesian concern with interest rates as determinants of effective demand—which also tends to play into the hands of central bankers—since it is only too easy to fall into the habit of identifying an increase or decrease in interest rates with a deflationary or inflationary policy. Similarly, the theory of liquidity preference, in a more indirect way, has played a part in the evolution of the modern theory of central banking, according to which the function of the central bank is the broad one of controlling the liquidity of the economy rather than the narrow one of controlling the quantity of currency and demand deposits. Again, the recognition of the monetary role of financial intermediaries and other credit-granting institutions which this entails can easily lead back to skepticism about the potentialities of monetary policy. But these are matters far removed from the *General Theory*.

Conclusion

Let me conclude by summarizing briefly the main points I have made in this lecture. The *General Theory* is an uncommonly untidy book, which bears the strong imprint of the Marshallian tradition from which it sprang. Nevertheless, it has shifted the emphasis of monetary theory to the role of money as an asset with special properties in an uncertain world and forced recognition of the fact that a monetary economy is fundamentally different from a barter economy. It provided a simple and comprehensive aggregate model of the economy, which not only facilitated the analysis of aggregative problems but greatly stimulated the development of econometric work with such models. It explained why the competitive capitalist economy does not automatically maintain a satisfactory level of employment and outlined the theory of remedial policy, thereby promoting a revolution in ideas on the responsibilities of government in such a system. On the other hand, the book was weak at a crucial point, in its neglect of the influence of capital on behavior; and its influence has been to distract attention from the role of money in the functioning of the economy. I have not, in this lecture, been able to survey the contributions of Keynes's ideas to the many specialized branches of theory—international economics, public finance, business cycles, economic growth, economic planning, to mention the major ones— where they have proved extremely fruitful. But no one could hope, in a single lecture, to take a census of the progeny of the *General Theory*.

6. Keynes and British Economics

Introduction

The English-speaking world, and especially the world of Cambridge University and King's College, Cambridge, abounds with people who can write with first-hand knowledge of the personality, life, professional work, and amateur interests of John Maynard Keynes, and of the personal, social, and political milieu of his career. Lacking these advantages, and even the English upbringing that would have conditioned me into an understanding and acceptance of British standards for the assessment of his professional achievement, I attempt in this essay to present a rather impressionistic view of that accomplishment, looked at from outside both the United Kingdom and the historical epoch to which Keynes belonged. Much of what I shall have to say is not about Keynes himself so much as about the younger generation of Keynesians, who constitute the older generation of economists to the younger generation to which I belong. And since much of what I shall say on both counts is unflattering, I should emphasize, first, that these are personal views, though derived from considerable thought about the evolution of economics since the First World War; and second, that to trace the subsequent impact of a man's ideas on his subject and his society is not to hold him responsible for the consequences of his thoughts—by the opposite assumption, all the great thinkers who have influenced human history (including most notably Jesus Christ) would be guilty of crimes against mankind.

Keynes's Contribution to Economics—A Reassessment

According to an admittedly drastically oversimplified but widely propagated view of Keynes's professional contribution, the orthodox economic theory in which Keynes was trained held that the "invisible hand" tended to produce automatically a state of full employment in the economy unless prevented by worker insistence on too high a level of money wages. This was contrary to the facts of years of British experience of mass unemployment. Keynes produced an alternative theory that explained the facts, to the effect that the level of production and employment depends on the level of aggregate demand;

An essay prepared in April 1973 for *Essays in Praise of John Maynard Keynes*, ed. Milo Keynes (Cambridge: At the University Press, 1975); reprinted with permission.

aggregate demand is the sum of aggregate consumption—determined largely by aggregate demand itself in its alternative identity of aggregate income according to the "fundamental psychological law" that when income rises consumption also rises but not by as much—and aggregate investment—influenced by business expectations and the rate of interest—with investment determining aggregate demand through its "multiplier effect" on consumption; that the level of aggregate demand is normally not such as to produce full employment; and that money wage reductions can influence employment only indirectly, through their very uncertain effects on investment through the quantity of money in real terms and the equilibrium rate of interest, and through business expectations. Thus unbridled capitalism meant chronic unemployment, and the maintenance of satisfactory employment required policy management of the level of aggregate demand; and while Keynes himself was always confident of the powers of monetary policy to control the level of aggregate demand, both certain aspects of his theory and the apparent failure of "easy money" to achieve economic recovery in the 1930s made it easy for his followers to read into the theory the need for control of aggregate demand by budgetary policy (setting the levels of taxes and government expenditure—"fiscal policy," in American terminology).

In the light of historical hindsight and retrospect, the place of Keynes and of the *General Theory* in the evolution of economics appears very differently; and the above interpretation of it appears strongly circumscribed and biased by the peculiar economic and political situation of the early 1930s against the background of which the *General Theory* was written. To appreciate this point, it is necessary to refer to British economic and monetary history, the state of British academic economics at that time, and the character of Keynes himself. The first reference is relevant to explaining why no Keynesian revolution was really necessary (what was necessary, however, was for economists to apply the economics they had). The second two references are relevant to explaining why a Keynesian revolution nevertheless occurred (and may indeed have been necessary after all, given the inability or refusal of economists to apply the tools of their trade to their society's most pressing social and economic problem).

To recapitulate the history briefly, the mass unemployment in Britain in the 1920s—which, far more than the additional mass unemployment in Britain and the novelty of mass unemployment in other countries created by the Great Depression after 1929, was the focus of Keynes's prolonged professional concern—was the result of two interacting forces, one inevitable but the other the result of a perverse act of policy decision by the British government. The inevitable force was Britain's gradual loss of her early nineteenth-century industrial supremacy, a loss which some economic historians trace back to the 1890s and others to the 1870s (certainly Keynes's great teacher Alfred Marshall was contemporarily aware of Britain's relative decline and anxious about its implications). The perverse decision was the return to the gold standard at the prewar parity for sterling. This made British goods uncompetitive in money terms and necessitated a restrictive monetary policy to retain foreign capital and maintain foreign confidence in the pound, both of which necessitated mass unemployment which in turn aggravated the problems of industrial obsolescence. Somewhat paradoxically, however, the overvaluation of the pound meant a higher standard of living for both the upper class of civil servants and professional people (including academics), on the one hand, and rentiers and owners of established businesses and large estates on the other, and the majority of workers, who managed to obtain full-time employment, than they would probably have enjoyed with an appropriate lower exchange rate. The result was to preserve an increasingly tenuous myth of Britain as a wealthy and powerful country—with obvious implications both for foreign policy and for potential domestic social welfare policy—while widening the gap between the status of the unemployed and the employed and the social and political tensions associated with it. (There is, incidentally, an interesting parallel in economic policy views between that period of overvaluation with mass unemployment and precarious balance-of-payments equilibrium and Britain's chronic post–World War II situation of overvaluation with full employment and a balance of payments deficit; in both cases a way out of the dilemma was sought in "the rationalization of industry" and in lower wages, though in the 1920s the argument was for reduction of money wages and in the 1950s–70s for achievement of essentially the same result through increasing productivity to reconcile rising money wages with lower money prices and more recently through "incomes policy.")

Had the exchange value of the pound been fixed realistically in the 1920s—a prescription fully in accord with orthodox economic theory—there would have been no need for mass unemployment, hence no need for a revolutionary new theory to explain it, and no triggering force for much subsequent British political and economic history. The country would have been worse off than it remembered being before the First World War, due to the inevitable pressures of industrial obsolescence, and the large majority of the assuredly employed or otherwise provided with money income would have been worse off than they actually were, but this would have been more than offset by the gains of those who would have been employed instead of unemployed. With reasonably full employment in the 1920s, moreover, the economic adjustment to industrial obsolescence would probably have been both easier and more effective (involving less concentration on promoting the survival of traditional industries and the preservation of traditional markets for their products—including the Empire) and the political adjustment to Britain's declining importance in the world less crisis-torn and traumatic (for example, Britain might have joined the Common Market at the beginning, or else remained determinedly aloof from it).

The universal mass unemployment that struck the capitalist world after

1929, and enabled a theory developed for the special circumstances of Britain in the 1920s to become accepted as a universally applicable theory of the failure of unmanaged capitalism, can also be attributed to the perversity of monetary management, national and international. What began in 1929 as the depression phase of a normal short trade cycle was converted by the Federal Reserve's failure to prevent a collapse of the American money supply into an unprecedentedly deep and prolonged depression; and the American monetary collapse precipitated the collapse of the international gold exchange standard, including the adoption of a floating pound in 1931 under political crisis conditions that have inhibited rational discussion of exchange rate policy for sterling ever since. Keynes's *General Theory* distracted attention from all this background—which fits without trouble into the orthodox tradition of economic theory, unless one rejects a great deal of work on the trade cycle as not belonging to that theory—by focusing on a closed economy and on mass unemployment as an equilibrium situation instead of a long-lagged adjustment to a severe monetary disturbance. Keynes's followers did extend his theory to an open economy, but regarded exchange rate adjustments—in the light of their 1930s experience of them—as of very doubtful efficacy in affecting employment and the trade balance. In this, they failed to distinguish between a devaluation by one country required to align its domestic price level with world market prices—the British problem of the 1920s—and a devaluation of all currencies against gold as one means (not necessarily the most efficient and least painful) of increasing world liquidity. (The same problem has recurred in recent years in the international monetary system, with respect to inflation, and equally eluded the understanding of many international monetary experts.) In justice to Keynes, it must be recalled that when later confronted directly with the problem of international monetary reform, in the course of preparations for the Bretton Woods negotiations of 1944 that established the International Monetary Fund, he pioneered the intellectual foundations of a system vastly superior to the previous gold exchange standard. (One cannot really blame him for the fact that the IMF system eventually developed internal strains very similar to those that destroyed the gold standard, with the result that it has recently been temporarily dropped in favor of a floating rate system and if reconstituted, as is probable, will incorporate arrangements for much greater exchange rate flexibility.)

Had the policymakers of the 1930s really understood what was occurring in the international monetary system and their own part in it, or the economists of the time understood it (as they could have done by developing available monetary theory) and explained it effectively, the Great Depression of the 1930s would have been nipped in the bud and the *General Theory* either not written or received as one eccentric English economist's rationalization of his local problem. Had Keynes been a different type of personality, he might have produced and published in the 1930s the international monetary reform plan he pioneered in the 1940s, together with an explicit rationale for the plan more firmly based in monetary theory than the IMF Articles of Agreement (and still more, subsequent plans for international monetary reform) have ever been. As it occurred, however, the Great Depression and international monetary collapse set the stage for a view of capitalism and of appropriate government policy to manage it oriented toward the problems of Britain in the 1920s to become the majority view of economists in the Anglo-Saxon countries ever since.

I have argued that the sources of the problem of mass unemployment with which the *General Theory* was concerned lay in severe monetary disturbance created by perverse monetary policies, thoroughly reconcilable with the orthodox neoclassical tradition of monetary theory, and not in any inherent deficiency of capitalism requiring a new causal theory and a new set of policy prescriptions and governmental responsibilities. Clearly what is so obvious to economists now, two generations later, was not at all obvious to economists (or the accepted leaders among them) then. For this there are several reasons, applying either to economics in general or to British economics in particular.

We may begin with the quantity theory of money. In its simplest and broadest form, this theory asserts that in a closed economy the level of money prices will tend to proportion itself to the quantity of money in relation to the volume of transactions to be effected in a given period and the speed with which money turns over in transactions (this last factor can be formulated alternatively and more fruitfully in terms of the ratio the public wishes to hold between its money stock and the money value of its transactions per period). What makes the theory a theory and not a mere tautology is the assumption that the latter two factors are determined by other forces than the quantity of money itself; but this assumption makes the theory true only in a long enough time perspective for the assumption to be approximately valid. The classical and neoclassical economists, living in a world of normally slow economic change, could safely rely on the assumption and the theory, since in the long run the volume of transactions would be governed by the stock of productive resources accumulated from the past because competition would tend to ensure full employment of those stocks and money-holding habits would be stable. Moreover, for various reasons those economists were primarily concerned with the allocative functions of relative prices and wages, and their main interest in monetary theory was to establish that in the long run money was "neutral," merely casting a "veil" over the results of the interaction of real wants and productive possibilities without affecting the "real" equilibrium of prices and quantities toward which the operation of these forces tended; and in the circumstances of their pre–World War I times, this concentration was natural and reasonable.

For the few specialists in monetary theory, however, the quantity theory as expressed in the quantity equation described above was only a starting point. Their interest shifted increasingly toward "the conditions of monetary equilibrium"—that is, the conditions under which money would have to behave or should be made to behave in order to perform merely as a veil and so as not to impede or distort the operation of the underlying "real forces." Work on this problem reached its full flower in the 1920s and early 1930s, with the work, in English, of Robertson, Keynes in the *Treatise on Money*, and Hayek; in Dutch, of J. J. Koopmans; and beginning earlier, in Swedish, of Wicksell and later Myrdal and others. This was a much shorter-perspective problem than that with which the earlier quantity theory was concerned, yet the theory continued to be built on the assumption of full employment as the condition to which the economy would approximate, though the shorter perspective made this assumption questionable, particularly in the case of severe monetary disturbances. In an important sense, the *General Theory* can be considered as a successful (and theoretically useful) challenging of the relevance of the full employment approximation to the problem under analysis. In terms of the framework of present-day monetary-theoretic controversy, Keynes can be interpreted as insisting that both output and prices are variable in the short run relevant to monetary changes, and as dramatizing the need for analysis of the division of response to aggregate demand changes between prices and output by assuming, in opposition to classical and neoclassical theory, that quantities and not prices (except indirectly) respond to short-run changes in aggregate demand. In short, contemporary monetary theory was guilty of sticking to traditional assumptions in the face of the evidence that these were empirically invalid for the problem under examination; and it compounded this stupidity, when questioned, by seeking for reasons why mass unemployment constituted a real equilibrium (witness Robertson's attempt to convince the Macmillan Committee that mass unemployment was attributable to the satiation of human wants). In so doing, it paved the way for a revolution in monetary theory when what was called for was a drastic effort at application.

In similar but less obvious fashion, when international trade and investment are extensive the world as a whole becomes the closed economy of monetary theory, and the relevant related variables are the world stock of money and the world price level. Recognition of this is implicit in Hume's price-specie-flow mechanism, and explicit in important neoclassical studies of such phenomena as the effects of the inflow of precious metals to Europe after the Spanish conquests in Latin America. But monetary theorists faced with the collapse of the 1930s were unable to make this intellectual leap, and instead tended to stop short at the limitations imposed on national stabilization policy by adherence to the gold standard. As mentioned, Keynes's assumption of a closed national economy ruled international monetary phenomena out of the theoretical purview of the *General Theory*, and his followers naturally saw no reason to disturb their logically self-contained view of macroeconomics by introducing consideration of them in more than a peripheral way.

The failure of economists generally to understand the nature and sources of the Great Depression of the 1930s as a matter of international monetary collapse is probably considerably more excusable than the general failure of British economists to relate the mass unemployment of the 1920s to the maintenance of an overvalued exchange rate. For this latter failure there are many explanatory factors, such as the fact that Marshall never managed to write the intended monetary companion volume to his *Principles of Economics*, while Pigou, his successor to the Cambridge Chair, was neither interested nor competent in the field, and the British tradition in monetary economics, which until very recent years was concerned with history and institutions rather than with theory, and with theory only as a part of historical and current policy debates. Something is attributable to the prestige of the Bank of England and its commanding social dominance at the time over politicians, civil servants, and academics, a dominance that it has begun to lose only recently, long since its nominal nationalization. Probably a considerable amount is attributable to the effects of the First World War both in slaughtering a significant proportion of the country's best young brains or making them, as erstwhile conscientious objectors, outcasts for their decision-taking class—alternative fates that Keynes's invaluability enabled him to escape gracefully, despite his early Apostolic beliefs—and in creating something of a national "backs-to-the-wall" attitude which made loyalty to national policy decisions, right or wrong, a virtue and made outspoken and sustained fundamental criticism of policies unpopular and a ticket of assignment to the political wilderness. Such criticism in any case consorted ill with the symbiotic, to some extent parasitic, relationship between the ancient universities and Whitehall and Westminster. (Both elements, national loyalty and symbiosism, have if anything strengthened since the Second World War, and have helped to squelch any fundamental debate over crucial policy decisions such as the failures to float the pound in 1951 and to devalue the pound in 1964 and the decision to enter the Common Market in 1971.) To be blunt, whatever the balance of the reasons, British economics lacked the confident grasp of applied monetary theory and the intellectual courage to insist that the exchange rate was crucial to Britain's problems and that continued overvaluation would make a solution impossible; instead, it joined the government in the hunt for ways around the impasse.

This brings us to the character of Keynes. Keynes was—without any intention of slurring him—an opportunist and an operator, the glowing exception being his expression of moral outrage in *The Economic Consequences of the Peace*—and even that redounded to his personal and professional benefit. He was also—and this helped—a brilliant applied theorist; but the theory was applied when it was useful in supporting a proposal that might win current political acceptance, and dropped along with the proposal when the immediate purpose had been served or had failed. Thus Keynes realized fully, and exposed brilliantly in *The Economic Consequences of Mr. Churchill*, the adverse consequences for Britain of the return to the gold standard. But once that decision had become a part of the order of things, he absorbed it and turned to advocating public works as a way of increasing employment; and in 1931 he came out in favor of protection. These gyrations frequently made him seem inconsistent to his contemporaries; actually the examples cited can be easily reconciled by reference to the modern theory of second-best, but Keynes never spelled out such a theory. The *General Theory* represents the apotheosis of opportunism in this sense, in two ways. Mass unemployment had lasted so long that it appeared to the average man to be the natural state of affairs, which economics was powerless to explain and political processes powerless to alter; a new theory of its causes that promised an easy cure was thus virtually certain to sell, provided its author had impeccable professional credentials. But to be a new theory it had to set up and then knock down an orthodox theory, not merely explain what traditional theory really was and develop its application to the problem at hand—a procedure Keynes had applied frequently in his younger days but which in this case would have required a major effort of theory construction and probably made the product unsaleable to the relevant public anyway. It was far easier to set up the dry aridity of Pigovian reasoning and the labrynthic alien Austrian logic of Hayekian capital theory as the targets, and to sacrifice the subtle and sensitive, intellectually more menacing but emotionally more vulnerable, personality of his former student Robertson to his coterie of young lions in the bitter in-fighting that followed the Keynesian revolution.

To make these points is not to dispute that the *General Theory* is nevertheless one of the few classics in the history of economics. But its importance from the long-range point of view of the development of economics, as distinct from the contemporary and subsequent politics of economic policy in Britain and the United States lies not in its refutation of a classical "orthodoxy" but in its application of capital theory to the theory of demand for money and the stimulus it provided to study of the dynamics of price and quantity adjustments to changes in aggregate demand.

Keynesianism and British Economics

There can be no doubt that, at least in the historical short run, the publication and reception of the *General Theory* gave British economics a prestige in the outside world that it had possessed up to and including the heyday of Marshall but which had been waning ever since, the publication of Joan Robinson's *Economics of Imperfect Competition* constituting the major exception to this generalization. As time has passed, however, it has become increasingly apparent that Keynes's work in a sense marked the end of an era in British predominance in economics, an era which may be termed the Marshallian era and includes both Pigou's contributions of welfare economics and Cambridge work in the 1920s on the problem of reconciling the theory of the individual firm with the assumption of perfect competition. It has also become apparent that other important British work in the interwar period, notably that of Hicks and Allen on general equilibrium systems and of Hicks on demand theory and welfare economics, work of at least comparable importance to Keynes's in monetary economics to the development of modern economics, was overshadowed by Keynes and unjustly denigrated by Keynes's Oxbridge followers—a misjudgment recently underlined by the award of the Nobel Prize in economics to Hicks. Finally, it is a fair generalization not only that leadership in economics has decisively passed from Britain to the United States in the postwar period, but that Britain has contributed very little in the way of new ideas and directions to the process of scientific development of economics. The only exceptions that spring to mind, by this extremely stringent standard, are Harrod's extension of Keynesian economics to the context of economic growth, and, of relatively greater fundamental significance, Meade's monumental though tedious-to-read works on the theory of international economic policy.

For this there is a variety of general reasons, including the vastly superior numbers and resources of the American economists and the economies of specialization and division of labor that size and wealth make possible, the exhaustion of the intellectual curiosity and energy of many of the active contributors of the 1930s in the service of the government during the war, the closing of ranks in loyalty to the national society in a country that felt itself far more beleaguered by uncontrollable internal and external economic forces in the post–World War II peace than it had after the First World War, and the excessive preoccupation with current politics and policy problems generated thereby. But the nature of the Keynesian revolution and of Keynesian economics in its British version have played an important part. Two specific aspects have been especially influential: a view of the nature of scientific work and the character of progress in economics derived from the intellectual success of the *General Theory,* and the identification of Keynesian economics with left-wing politics. Both aspects, it should be emphasized, are the creation of the Keynesians, and quite contrary to the life-work of Keynes the economic scientist and the political stance of Keynes the political economist.

The view of economic science in question consists of positing an orthodoxy which is committed to defense of every aspect of the existing system and denies that any improvement on its performance is possible, and identifying as a contribution the use of clever reasoning to dispute this posited orthodoxy at some point. Thus economics becomes a crooked game, the winning of which by the "good guys" requires intelligence but not sustained hard work. For most of his long professional career, before the *General Theory* (he was in his fifties by the time it was published), Keynes put in the hard intellectual labor of learning monetary theory by study and application; and the book was presented as a challenge to orthodoxy, not merely for the strategic reasons discussed above, but because he honestly believed that he had found a crucial flaw in what his contemporaries regarded as orthodox economics. He was fortunate to be right, at least superficially—and superficiality represented as deeply as a very busy man could go into the foundations of monetary theory as then commonly understood. This made him an easy act to imitate but a very hard act indeed to follow. Unfortunately his followers have tried only too often to imitate the act without putting in the long hours of preliminary practice. Even where they have put in the practice, as is true of the most eminent of his Cambridge followers, the usefulness of their work to scientific progress has been largely vitiated by Procrustean forcing of it into the framework of a straw man of capitalist orthodoxy to be knocked down by the force of superior intellect. Thus Joan Robinson writes the most arid of technical capital theory in the belief that, contrary to all the empirical evidence, capitalism cannot possibly work, because she can to her own satisfaction make a nonsense of the concept of the production function and of distribution by marginal productivity; and Nicholas Kaldor goes her one better by admitting that capitalism does work, but maintaining that it cannot possibly work according to orthodox theories of how it works, proper understanding of it requiring acceptance of revolutionary new but unverified theories of his own devising. Each derives support and satisfaction from the knowledge that there are eminent professional economists in the United States who are prepared to take their arguments seriously, little realizing that if they did not exist it would be necessary for American economics to invent them to meet its own need for an orthodoxy against which to demonstrate its own scientific superiority.

The damage done to professional work by a methodology requiring an orthodoxy to assault unfortunately does not end with its stultifying effect on the work of those who espouse that methodology. The myth of a mindless but majority orthodoxy has to be given some degree of verisimilitude by the existence of a few professionally reputable specimens at whom the finger of scorn may be plausibly pointed. Since no young scholar can afford the professional risk and no senior mature scholar fancies the role, volunteers are not forthcoming, and hapless innocents have to be pressed into service, willy-nilly. The results are personal and professional destruction or at least serious damage for the thinner-skinned scholars such as Robertson, and the suppression of the free spirit of scientific inquiry by the use or threat of the witch-hunt. An economics profession in which people have to think, "before I dare to say what I think, I have to be sure that what I say will not damn me as hopelessly orthodox," is not one likely to discover new and important scientific truths.

This baneful influence of concern about orthodoxy or heterodoxy as the hallmark of "bad" or "good" economics is vastly reinforced by the identification of Keynesian economics in Britain with left-wing or at least Labour Party politics, and the politicization of economics that it has entailed. (Keynes is well known to have had strong Liberal sympathies, but he carefully kept out of party politics to protect his professional reputation, and while he consistently sought for solutions to current problems that might be acceptable politically there is no reason, so far as I know, to suspect him of ever having produced or endorsed a solution because it conformed to the credo of a party he favored.) The evidence of politicization ranges all the way from the scandal attending certain recent appointments to Chairs at Cambridge, through the consensus version of accepted economic principles expressed by economic and financial commentators and journalists and the significant failure of leading economists known to be Labour Party sympathizers to speak out in public against the decisions not to devalue in 1964 and 1966 and to seek entry to the Common Market in 1966, to the report by Samuel Brittan in his recent *Is There An Economic Consensus?* that an unexpectedly large number of academic economists gave the scientifically wrong answer to a question involving comparison of provision of below-cost public housing and direct social security payments to poor people and his suggested explanation that "when they came to as politically charged a subject as homes for the poor, they dug in their heels and were determined to provide no comfort to the opponents of subsidized council building." The adverse effects of political self-censorship on both the progress and propagation of scientific understanding and the professional reliability of economic advice on policy questions are too obvious to require further comment.

Keynesian Economics and British Economic Policy

The success of the Keynesian revolution and its defeat of orthodoxy and the subsequent adoption of Keynesian policies of demand management, is widely credited with responsibility for the fact that the post–World War II period has been characterized by the disappearance for some thirty years of the mass unemployment that characterized the British economy in the interwar period. The critics of Keynesian economics implicitly concur by blaming the chronic inflation that has characterized the same period on the same adoption of Keynesian policies. The validity of the attribution in both cases is extremely doubtful. Other countries have had at least as good luck without following Keynesian policies or even knowing what they are—the "new economics" won acceptance in the United States only as recently as the tax cut of 1964, and Japan's economic policy seems to have been orthodox in the extreme—and one can with fair plausibility attribute Britain's success to prosperity in the rest of the world coupled with the good fortune of a forced devaluation of the pound in 1949. Economic growth is a different story, but even there Britain has done far better than she did for many decades before, stretching back into the nineteenth century; and some would argue that she would have done still better by far had it not been for the crippling load of the mixture of protectionist policies for industry and the regions and of Keynesian policies for employment inherited from her interwar time of torment. (In any case, the promotion of economic growth was no part of Keynes's thinking, or indeed of Keynesian economics until sometime in the later 1950s.) About the most one can say is that Keynes's demonstration that mass unemployment is an avoidable evil has been popularly accepted to the extent that the government could no longer get away with the egregiously deflationary errors of policy it committed in the interwar period; and even this is not necessarily a plus point, since under postwar conditions the temptations have generally been to aim in the inflationary direction, and in a generally inflationary world environment the social costs of inadvertent errors in the deflationary direction have generally been low as compared with those of errors in the inflationary direction.

Leaving those issues aside, it is worthwhile calling attention to the naïveté of the concept of full employment as a policy goal, which has been one of the main legacies of Keynes and Keynesianism to economic policymaking in Britain and elsewhere. That goal, as Elizabeth Johnson points out in a paper in the *Journal of Political Economy* (January-February 1974), is very intimately related to Keynes's essentially aristocratic Victorian view of the economic requirements of a happy society. In that view, social happiness consisted of a job for everyone in his appointed place in life—Keynes was little concerned about providing more equal opportunities for advancement within the ordered hierarchy of employments, since in the typical fashion of successful men he believed that his society was so organized that anyone of merit, if only he exerted himself, could rise to the eminence he had himself attained. Social misery of a severe and completely avoidable kind resulted from the failure of society to keep demand high enough to provide the expected and deserved jobs. (This simple view, incidentally, is consistent with and indeed necessary to another of Keynes's beliefs, one which demarcates him sharply from postwar Keynesianism with its emphasis on the necessity of economic growth to the good society, namely his confidence that it would take no more than a generation or so of capital accumulation at the normal rate to satiate society's demands for goods and services and free man for the cultivation of the finer things of civilized life. There is in fact an obvious disagreement between first-generation and second-generation Keynesians on the issue of the importance of economic growth, reflecting a basic difference between aristocratic and democratic attitudes to the desire of the lower orders for improvement in their material standard of life.)

The identification of social welfare with full employment not only represents an extremely narrow aristocratic and paternalistic attitude to the workers, but leads to serious biases in attitudes on policy issues evident particularly in the pronouncements and writings of some of the leading British Keynesians. For one thing, by neglecting the role of voluntary unemployment in providing flexibility, capacity for adjustment to economic change, and the opportunity for self-betterment by obtaining a better job, as well as in permitting individuals to escape from the boredom of working the same number of hours doing the same thing week after week into the freedom of disposal of their own idle time, it leads to a serious exaggeration of the social loss from unemployment and the social benefit of full employment. If unemployment actually means both total waste of the lost labor time of the unemployed and the psychological and social demoralization of the individuals concerned, then virtually no amount of inflation is too high a price to pay for full employment (and if inflation is bad for the balance of payments, no amount of interference with international transactions to control the balance of payments is too costly either). But, as a logical corollary, if full employment is such a great boon to the workers, they ought to show their gratitude for the full employment conferred on them by Keynesian policies by not making inflationary wage demands in the first place; and if nevertheless they irresponsibly persist in doing so, as some of them do, it is not only socially fair but in their own long-run interests, as they ought to see, to force an incomes policy on them.

For another thing, identification of social welfare with the single simple index of the unemployment percentage, and specifically disregard or denial of the manifold elements of voluntary choice that enter into the determination of the unemployment rate, leads to disregard of the fact that the unemployment percentage that corresponds in principle to what Keynes can be deemed to have had in mind in the concept of full employment is not a social constant determinable by technical calculations based on aggregate labor market statistics but a variable changing in response to other kinds of change. Specifically, there are two major kinds of relevant changes which will tend to raise this unemployment rate. One is the provision of more generous social security benefits. The other is the general progress of affluence and increase in educational levels, which make it easier for individuals to finance voluntary unemployment out of past savings or the current earnings of other members of the family, and more conscious of the possible gains to be obtained by devoting time to the search for a better job. Improved social security is especially important, as an alternative and in many ways more sensible method of preventing the socially evil consequences of unemployment than the Keynesian panacea of maintaining a high pressure of aggregate demand. One of the areas in which the naïveté of the Keynesian concentration on employment is most evident, incidentally, is that of regional variations in unemployment rates. It is extremely difficult to believe, after even the most cursory thought on the matter, that an abnormally high unemployment rate that has persisted in a region for several generations represents a failure of the competitive system to provide job opportunities rather than some sort of social choice in favor of a lower probability of employment at high wages and a higher probability of leisure time in a broad sense, over a greater certainty of employment and less individual free time.

Concluding Observations

All in all, it is difficult to avoid the conclusion that Britain has paid a heavy long-run price for the transient glory of the Keynesian revolution, in terms both of the corruption of standards of scientific work in economics and encouragement to the indulgence of the belief of the political process that economic policy can transcend the laws of economics with the aid of sufficient economic cleverness, in the sense of being able to satisfy all demands for security of economic tenure without inflation or balance-of-payments problems, or less obvious sacrifice of efficiency and economic growth potentialities. A good case could even be made to the effect that Keynes was too expensive a luxury for a country inexorably declining in world economic and political importance and obliged to scramble for dignified survival to be able to afford.

7. The Keynesian Revolution and the Monetarist Counterrevolution

When James Tobin and I agreed on the subject of this lecture last spring, it appeared to be a highly topical subject that would command widespread interest among the membership of this Association. Unfortunately, as so often happens with forward planning for academic purposes, others have also been alert to topicality, and have undermined our forward planning by getting in earlier with their version of the theme. Thus Milton Friedman himself gave a widely publicized lecture on the counterrevolution in monetary theory last September in London, which lecture has recently been published by the Institute of Economic Affairs (*The Counter-Revolution in Monetary Theory* [London, 1970]); Karl Brunner has recently circulated a typically scholarly paper, "The 'Monetarist Revolution' in Monetary Theory" (mimeographed, 1970); and undoubtedly many others have been writing and publishing on the same subject. My treatment of this beginning-to-be-well-worn theme today will, I hope, still retain some novelty, inasmuch as I shall be primarily concerned, not with the scientific issues in dispute in the monetarist counterrevolution against the Keynesian revolution, but with the social and intellectual conditions that make a revolution or counterrevolution possible in our profession. This lecture is therefore an excursion—amateurish, I must confess—into the economics and sociology of intellectual change.

As is well known from the field of economic history, the concept of revolution is difficult to transfer from its origins in politics to other fields of social science. Its essence is unexpected speed of change, and this requires a judgment of speed in the context of a longer perspective of historical change, the choice of which is likely to be debatable in the extreme. Leaving the judgmental issue aside for the moment, one could characterize the history of our subject in terms of a series of "revolutions," very broadly defined, as follows. Economics as we know it began with what might be called the "Smithian revolution" against the established body of doctrines generically described as "mercantilism," a revolution which changed ideas on the nature and sources of the wealth of nations and the policies required to promote

The Richard T. Ely Lecture delivered at the 1970 Meetings of the American Economic Association, reprinted with permission from *The American Economic Review, Papers and Proceedings* 61, no. 2 (May 1971): 1-14.

the growth of what we now call "affluence." The Ricardian revolution turned the attention of economists from concern with national wealth and its growth to the distribution of income among social classes and the interactions of growth and income distribution. The marginalist revolution of the 1870s essentially introduced a new and superior analytical technology for dealing with Ricardo's distribution problem, in the process gradually depriving Ricardian economics of its social content; hence, the results of that revolution have been described as neo-Ricardian or more commonly neo-classical economics.

Contemporary economics is based on this development and on at least four discernible "revolutions" that occurred in the late 1920s and in the 1930s. One was the imperfect-monopolistic competition revolution, which challenged the validity of the assumption of perfect competition on which value theory had come to be built following the marginalist revolution, and particularly the conclusions about the welfare effects of competition to which that theory led. This revolution has more or less fizzled out, though its fossilized remnants continue to plague both students and their instructors in elementary courses. Another was the empirical or econometric revolution, with its insistence initially on the measurement of economic relationships and, subsequently and more ambitiously, on the testing of economic hypotheses—though the "testing of hypotheses" is frequently merely a euphemism for obtaining plausible numbers to provide ceremonial adequacy for a theory chosen and defended on a priori grounds. The third was the general equilibrium revolution, based on the introduction by Hicks and Allen of the continental Walrasian-Paretoan approach into the Anglo-Saxon tradition in replacement of the then-dominant Marshallian partial-equilibrium approach. Finally, and most sweeping in its effect, there was the Keynesian revolution in monetary theory.

By contrast with the abundance of revolutions, counterrevolutions are hard to find in the development of economic thought. About the closest one can come to a counterrevolution in the history of economic thought is to interpret the development of the Austrian theory of value as a counter-revolution against the socialist, and especially the Marxist, tradition of economic theorizing; and that aspect of the work of the Austrian school was a side issue in the marginalist revolution. The monetarist counterrevolution of contemporary times is probably the first significant counterrevolution in the development of our subject. In venturing this judgment, however, I should note that the disrepute into which the theories of imperfect and monopolistic competition have fallen, as theories of contemporary industrial competition, in the period since the Second World War could be described as the result of an intellectual counterrevolution, based on a combination of faith in the preexisting theory of competition and devotion to the empirical revolution; and also that, if one is prepared to disregard the political labels that people choose to attach to themselves, the left-wing student and faculty demand for a politically and socially relevant "radical" economics and protest against emphasis on mathematical and econometric quantification can be classed as counterrevolutionary, inasmuch as it seeks to revert to the premarginalist revolution concern with the economic system as a system of relationships among social classes.

As I have already mentioned, the chief problem in identifying revolutions and counterrevolutions and distinguishing them from slower and more comprehensible and rational processes of change in economic thought is to arrive at a judgment of the relative speed of change and the degree to which the speed is justifiable. From this point of view, some of what I have just now described as revolutions were not really revolutionary—notably the Smithian and marginalist revolutions, the imperfect-monopolistic competition revolution, and the general equilibrium and empirical revolutions. The Smithian and marginalist revolutions spread relatively slowly, through the force of their scientific superiority and intellectual appeal and the process of natural wastage of their opponents. The imperfect-monopolistic competition revolution was the end result of puzzling by many minds over a problem that Marshall had stated but had been unable to solve satisfactorily—the existence of downward-sloping cost curves for individual firms. The general equilibrium revolution was a result of the delayed appreciation by economists of the need for a better command of mathematical techniques, the delay being occasioned by the long association of the subject with philosophy in the English academic tradition and its continuing association with law in the Continental tradition. And the empirical revolution depended on the development of the techniques of statistical inference—most of the historically great economists were quantitatively oriented, or at least paid lip service to the need for quantitative work, but lacked the requisite tools to carry out such work themselves. For real intellectual revolutions, we are left with three major examples: the Ricardian revolution, the reasons for whose propagation were examined some twenty years ago by S. G. Checkland,[1] the Keynesian revolution, and the monetarist counterrevolution. These last two are the subject of my lecture today.

My concern, specifically, is with the reasons for the speed of propagation of the monetarist counterrevolution; but I cannot approach this subject without reference to the reasons for the speed of propagation of the Keynesian revolution, since the two are interrelated. Indeed, I find it useful in posing and treating the problem to adopt the "as if" approach of positive economics, as expounded by the chief protagonist of the monetarist counterrevolution, Milton Friedman, and to ask: suppose I wished to start a counterrevolution against the Keynesian revolution in monetary theory, how would I go about it—and specifically, what could I learn about the technique from the revolution itself? To pose the question in this way is, of course, to fly in the face of currently accepted professional ethics, according to which purely scientific considerations and not political considerations are presumed to motivate scientific work; but I can claim the protection of the "as if" methodology against any implication of a slur on individual character or a denigration of scientific work.

From this point of view, obviously, the first problem is to identify the elements in the situation at the time of the *General Theory* that accounted for its rapid acceptance and propagation among professional economists. Such elements are of two types, one relating to the objective social situation in which the new theory was produced, the other relating to the scientific characteristics of the new theory itself.

As regards the objective social situation, by far the most helpful circumstance for the rapid propagation of a new and revolutionary theory is the existence of an established orthodoxy which is clearly inconsistent with the most salient facts of reality, and yet is sufficiently confident of its intellectual power to attempt to explain those facts, and in its efforts to do so exposes its incompetence in a ludicrous fashion.[2] Orthodoxy is, of course, always vulnerable to radical challenge: the essence of an orthodoxy of any kind is to reduce the subtle and sophisticated thoughts of great men to a set of simple principles and straightforward slogans that more mediocre brains can think they understand well enough to live by—but for that very reason orthodoxy is most vulnerable to challenge when its principles and slogans are demonstrably in conflict with the facts of everyday experience.

So it was in the 1930s, and particularly in the 1930s in Britain, which had already experienced a decade of mass unemployment associated with industrial senescence and an overvalued exchange rate, mass unemployment which the prevailing orthodoxy could neither explain nor cope with. This, it may be noted, was in large part the fault of the economists themselves. There existed already a body of monetary analysis that was quite capable of explaining both Britain's and the industrial world's unemployment problems as a consequence of monetary mismanagement. But, hypnotized by the notion that money is merely a veil cast over real phenomena—the homogeneity postulate of contemporary monetary theory—the economists of the time attempted to explain what were essentially monetary phenomena by real causes. Eminent British economists sought to explain mass unemployment as a consequence of the satiation of real human wants, a satiation that should have produced a general reduction in working hours but unfortunately and inexplicably operated instead differentially to reduce the working hours of a substantial part of the population to absolute zero. Other economists viewed the depression as a punishment justly visited upon enterprises and individuals for past sins of speculation and erroneous microeconomic decision-taking. The concern for microeconomic explanations diverted attention from what the available macroeconomic analysis could have said about the problem; it also led to the recommendation of ad hoc remedies such as public works that lacked any firm grounding in theory as generally understood.

In this situation of general confusion and obvious irrelevance of orthodox economics to real problems, the way was open for a new theory that offered a convincing explanation of the nature of the problem and a set of policy prescriptions based on that explanation. Such a theory, however, would have to possess certain characteristics if it were to win intellectual acceptance and political success. In particular, it would have to come from within yet offer liberation from the established orthodoxy—for one must remember that orthodoxy includes both an established conservative orthodoxy and an established self-termed "radical" orthodoxy, and, since each recognizes and accommodates the other's arguments, there is no real hope of progress being achieved by a switch from one position to the other.

To be more specific, a revolutionary theory had to depend for its success on five main characteristics—here I must admit that I am conducting my analysis in the blinding light of hindsight. First, it had to attack the central proposition of conservative orthodoxy—the assumed or inferred tendency of the economy to full employment—with a new but academically acceptable analysis that reversed the proposition. This Keynes did with the help of Kahn's concept of the multiplier and his own invention of the propensity to consume. Second, the theory had to appear to be new, yet absorb as much as possible of the valid or at least not readily disputable components of existing orthodox theory. In this process, it helps greatly to give old concepts new and confusing names, and to emphasize as crucial analytical steps that have previously been taken as platitudinous; hence, in the *General Theory*, the marginal productivity of capital became the marginal efficiency of capital; the desired ratio of money to income, the k of the Cambridge tradition, became a minor constituent of the new theory of "liquidity preference"; and the ex post identity of savings and investment, which previous theorists including Keynes himself had rightly recognized as unhelpful to dynamic analysis, became the sine qua non of right reasoning.

Third, the new theory had to have the appropriate degree of difficulty to understand. This is a complex problem in the design of new theories. The new theory had to be so difficult to understand that senior academic colleagues would find it neither easy nor worth while to study, so that they would waste their efforts on peripheral theoretical issues, and so offer themselves as easy marks for criticism and dismissal by their younger and hungrier colleagues. At the same time, the new theory had to appear both difficult enough to challenge the intellectual interest of younger colleagues and students, but actually easy enough for them to master adequately with a sufficient investment of intellectual endeavor. These objectives Keynes's *General Theory* managed to achieve: it neatly shelved the old and established scholars, like Pigou and Robertson, enabled the more enterprising middle-

and lower-middle-aged like Hansen, Hicks, and Joan Robinson to jump on and drive the bandwagon, and permitted a whole generation of students (as Samuelson has recorded) to escape from the slow and soul-destroying process of acquiring wisdom by osmosis from their elders and the literature into an intellectual realm in which youthful iconoclasm could quickly earn its just reward (in its own eyes at least) by the demolition of the intellectual pretensions of its academic seniors and predecessors. Economics, delightfully, could be reconstructed from scratch on the basis of a little Keynesian understanding and a lofty contempt for the existing literature—and so it was.

Fourth, the new theory had to offer to the more gifted and less opportunistic scholars a new methodology more appealing than those currently available. In this respect, Keynes was lucky both in having a receptive audience available, and to hit somewhere conveniently between the old and the newly emerging styles of economic theorizing. The prevailing methodological orthodoxy was that of Marshall—a partial-equilibrium approach set within a clear appreciation of the two complex problems of general equilibrium and of historical change, and hence both unsatisfactory at the simple level of partial-equilibrium analysis taken by itself, and extremely difficult to apply skillfully in a broader analytical and social context. The new methodological challenge was coming from the explicitly mathematical general-equilibrium approach of Hicks and Allen, an approach whose empirically and historically almost empty generality was of little general appeal. The *General Theory* found a middle ground in an aggregated general-equilibrium system which was not too difficult or complicated to work with—though it demanded a substantial step forward in mathematical competence—and which offered a high degree of apparent empirical relevance to those who took the trouble to understand it.

Finally, the *General Theory* offered an important empirical relationship for the emerging tribe of econometricians to measure—the consumption function, a far more challenging relationship than the demand for sugar, a relationship for which the development of national income statistics provided the raw material needed for estimation, and which could be estimated with surprising success given the limitation of the available data to approximately a single business cycle.

In my judgment, these factors accounted for the success of the Keynesian revolution: on the one hand, the existence of an important social and economic problem with which the prevailing orthodoxy was unable to cope; on the other hand, a variety of characteristics that appealed to the younger generation of that period—notably the claim of the new theory to superior social relevance and intellectual distinction, its incorporation in a novel and confusing fashion of the valid elements of traditional theory, the opportunity it offered to bypass the system of academic seniority by challenging senior colleagues with a new and self-announcedly superior scientific approach, the presentation of a new methodology that made general-equilibrium theory both manageable and socially relevant, and the advancement of a new empirical relationship challenging for econometricians to estimate.

The very success of the Keynesian revolution, however, ensured that it would in its turn become the established orthodoxy, and as such be as vulnerable as the old to revolutionary attack—which would necessarily have to be a counterrevolutionary attack. Keynes himself, as Leijonhufvud's monumental reinterpretation of his thought[3] has reminded us, had a seasoned and subtle mind, conscious both of the flow of economic history and of the role of theory as an adjunct to policymaking in a given set of historical circumstances. His followers—which means the profession at large—elaborated his history-bound analysis into a timeless and spaceless set of universal principles, sacrificing in the process much of his subtlety, and so establishing Keynesianism as an orthodoxy ripe for counterattack.

There are several factors in this transmogrification worthy of note. The first, and probably most important, has been the conviction of Keynesians that the mass unemployment of the 1930s represents the normal state of capitalist society—more accurately, of capitalist society unaided by Keynesian management—and that unemployment is always the most urgent social problem. This view was elevated into a dogma in the United States under the leadership of Alvin Hansen, whose theory of secular stagnation was the subject of his Presidential Address to this Association.[4] While that theory has been quietly forgotten, or frugally converted into a theory applicable to the underdeveloped countries, vestiges of it linger on in the thinking of American Keynesians. The view that unemployment is the overriding social problem also lingers on among British Keynesians such as Joan Robinson, Roy Harrod, and Thomas Balogh, though I should note that Nicholas Kaldor has for many years taken a much more optimistic view of the resilience of capitalism. The corollary of the Keynesian view of the primacy of the unemployment problem has been a pronounced tendency to play down the adverse economic consequences of inflation, and to assume that, if only the unemployment consequences of anti-inflationary policies were properly understood, society would cheerfully agree to adopt and implement an incomes policy instead.

A second factor in the transformation of Keynesianism into an orthodoxy has been that people who made their academic reputations and earned their present status on the basis of an early and enthusiastic conversion to Keynesianism in the late 1930s and early 1940s have continued to trade on their foresight, to the academic detriment of their juniors, who have never had the same chance to jump onto the front—and not the rear—of an academic bandwagon. This factor has been far more effective in paving the way for a monetarist counterrevolution in the United States, where institutional competition prevents centralized control of professional advancement, than in the United Kingdom, where Oxbridge continues to dominate the academic scene.

A third factor has been that, while the Keynesian revolution in its time offered a tremendous liberation to the energies of young economists in the fields of pure theorizing about concepts, the construction of macroeconomic general-equilibrium models, and the estimation of econometric models of the economy, these activities have run into diminishing returns so rapidly that they have ceased to be appealing to young and ambitious economists.

The result has been that—beginning perhaps sometime in the mid-1950s—Keynesianiam has become itself an established orthodoxy, ripe for attack in exactly the same way as what Keynes chose to call "classical economics" and to attack in the 1930s. It has had the same two vulnerable characteristics: inability to prescribe for what has come to be considered a major social problem—inflation, in contrast to the unemployment of Keynes's time—and a dependence on the authority and prestige of senior scholars which is oppressive to the young. Also, ironically enough in view of Keynes's own long concern with the influence of money on the economy, it has suffered from the same major defect as the orthodoxy Keynes attacked—the attempt to explain essentially monetary phenomena in terms of a mixture of real theory and ad hoc-ery, and specifically to explain inflation in terms of real effective demand and the Phillips curve. The fact that Keynesian economics has stumbled into the same pitfall as the "classical" orthodoxy it succeeded is, perhaps, an indication of the difficulty of monetary theory as contrasted with value theory, as well as the perils of abandoning monetary theory in favor of what appears to be more reasonable common sense.

If, in accordance with the "as if" methodology of positive economics that I adopted earlier in this lecture, one posed the question of how to mount a counterrevolution against Keynesian orthodoxy, and considered the question in the light of the factors that contributed to the success of the Keynesian revolution, one would, I think, be driven inescapably to two sets of conclusions.

The first would be the need to find an important social problem that the established orthodoxy is incapable of dealing with, even though it tries its best and claims to be successful. The second would be the need to develop a counterrevolutionary theory that had the requisite characteristics to be academically and professionally successful in replacing the previous revolutionary theory.

The obvious answer to the first problem—finding an important social problem that orthodox theory cannot solve—is to concentrate on the issue of inflation, the issue that Keynesian theory was least well designed to deal with. The trouble with that answer has been that, under the influence of both experienced inflation and Keynesian theory, the public has for the most part not been much concerned about the economic evils of inflation, and so has not regarded inflation as an important test of the intellectual strength of Keynesian orthodoxy. The history of the monetarist counterrevolution has, in fact, been characterized by a series of mostly vain efforts to convince the profession and the public (a) that inflation is an important question and (b) that monetarism can provide an explanation and a policy whereas Keynesianism cannot. Proposition (b) is eminently plausible; but it can only get a hearing if proposition (a) is accepted first; and, aside from a brief interlude in the late 1950s, the public has become convinced of proposition (a) only very recently. It is no accident that the appearance of monetarism as a strong intellectual movement has had to wait until the aftermath of the escalation of the war in Viet Nam in 1965. It is even less of an accident that its current success has depended on a prior Keynesian claim to, and acceptance of, responsibility for efforts to stop inflation by Keynesian fiscal means, under the auspices of the "New Economics." Monetarism has until the past few years been in the position of investing a great deal of intellectual ability in analyzing problems and producing solutions that no one else has considered worth the effort involved. It has eventually become a public force less by its own efforts than as a consequence of the "New Economics" overreaching itself when it was riding high in the formation of national economic policy. The "New Economics" was favored by the opportunity to sell Keynesian policies to meet a Keynesian problem; it encountered disaster when it tried to sell reverse Keynesian policies to meet a non-Keynesian problem. And the monetarist counterrevolution has been cashing in on that mistake of intellectual strategy.

Nevertheless, on this score of social relevance, the monetarist counterrevolution has had certain factors working in its favor which have enabled it to survive and prosper despite the absence of an overwhelmingly obvious inadequacy of the established Keynesian orthodoxy, for most of the postwar period. One has been that, with the growing professionalization of economics and the expansion of academic support of interest in it, it has become increasingly possible for an issue to be deemed scientifically interesting and worthy of investigation even if the general public displays no visible interest in it. Another has been the rise of the United States to the position of a world power, which has made the exploration of issues of no direct relevance to the economic interests of the United States nevertheless worth pursuing as potentially matters of the national interest in the world economy. Both the hyper-inflations in Europe and elsewhere that followed the two world wars, and the strong inflation that have characterized Latin American economic history, have lent themselves to investigation with the aid of the quantity theory as matters of potential relevance to U.S. economic policy. But, as already mentioned, while these foreign experiences have provided fodder for monetarism, and in the course of time support for the contention that monetarism rests on a far wider base of empirical investigation than Keynesianism, the real counterrevolutionary thrust of monetarism has only developed since inflation became a major problem for the United States itself. Further, it is only since that event—which, given the world importance of the United States, has meant the emergence of inflation as a worldwide problem—that monetarism has been taken seriously by academic and public opinion in other countries.

Practical social relevance apart, the question of success for a new theory, whether revolutionary or counterrevolutionary, depends on its fitting appropriately into the intellectual climate of its time. Here we may apply what has already been said about the reasons for the successful rapid propagation of the Keynesian revolution to the "as if" question of how to proceed to mount a quantity-theory counterrevolution. There were, I trust you will remember, five elements in the success of the Keynesian revolution, and I shall take them in turn.

The first was a central attack, on theoretically persuasive grounds, on the central proposition of the orthodoxy of the time. In the case of the Keynesian revolution, that proposition was the automatic tendency of the economy to full employment. In the case of the counterrevolution, the obvious point of attack, in a world characterized by high employment and inflationary tendencies, was the vulgar Keynesian orthodox position that "money does not matter." As James Tobin has pointed out, there is a world of difference between two alternatives to this proposition, namely, one, "money does too matter," and, two, "money is all that matters." But this difference was easily and conveniently blurred, to the benefit of the counterrevolution, by seizing on the extreme Keynesian position that money does not matter at all as the essence of the prevailing orthodoxy.

The second aspect of Keynesian success was the production of an apparently new theory that nevertheless absorbed all that was valid in the existing theory while so far as possible giving these valid concepts confusing new names. This was the technique followed—again I would emphasize the "as if" character of my interpretation—in Friedman's classic restatement of the quantity theory of money.[5] The restated quantity theory is, as Patinkin has recently pointed out, essentially a generalization of Keynes's theory of liquidity preference on the basis of a more sophisticated analysis of the nature of wealth and the relation of wealth to income. Novelty and the requisite intellectual confusion were provided by the substitution of the concept of "permanent income" for that of wealth, and the dragging across the trail of the red herring of human capital that was emerging from other work being conducted at Chicago at the time. Nevertheless, the restatement of the quantity theory of money did include one important and genuinely novel element, drawn not from Keynes but from his predecessors in monetary theory, which was highly relevant to the problem of inflation and which continues to distinguish quantity theorists from Keynesians; this consisted in its emphasis on the Fisherian distinction between the real and the money rate of interest and on the expected rate of price inflation or deflation as determining the difference between the two.

For the reasons just given, the restatement of the quantity theory provided a new theory meeting the third criterion for success, a degree of difficulty of understanding just sufficient to deter the old and to challenge and reward the young, and hence to reopen the avenues of professional opportunity for the ambitious.

The fourth criterion for success was a new and appealing methodology. Here the counterrevolutionary theory could appeal against the tendency of Keynesian economics to proliferate into larger and yet larger models of the economic system, a tendency which sacrificed theoretical insights to the cause of descriptive realism and which had the incidental but important detractions of demanding large sums of scarce research money available only to senior economists and of turning young economists into intellectual mechanics whose function was to tighten one bolt only on a vast statistical assembly line, the end product of which would contain nothing that could be visibly identified as their own work. In place of this approach, the counter-revolution set up the methodology of positive economics, the essence of which is not to pursue descriptive realism as represented by the largest possible system of general equilibrium equations, but to select the crucial relation-ships that permit one to predict something large from something small, regardless of the intervening chain of causation. This methodology obviously offered liberation to the small-scale intellectual, since it freed his mind from dependence on the large-scale research team and the large and expensive computer program.

The fifth criterion for success was the advancement of a new and important empirical relationship, suitable for determined estimation by the budding econometrician. The relationship was found in the demand function for money, the stability of which was claimed to be the essence of the traditional quantity theory of money. Presentation of the stable demand function for money as the essence of the quantity theory offered a close parallel to the Keynesian consumption function of the 1930s—a statistical relationship simple to understand theoretically and not too hard to estimate statistically, which promised, nonetheless, to contribute importantly to the resolution of central theoretical issues. Moreover, since intelligent and gifted young men and women will persevere until they succeed in finding statistical validation of an allegedly important relationship, and will then interpret their results as evidence in favor of the theory that originally suggested the relationship, their efforts will inevitably be extremely favorable to the theory in question. And so it has proved. A stable demand function for money is by no means inconsistent with the Keynesian macroeconomic general equilibrium model, and indeed is presumed to exist in the construction of the standard IS-LM diagram. But the empirical finding of the existence of such a function has been widely adduced in support of the quantity theory as against the rival Keynesian theory, a procedure justified only by the identification of the Keynesian orthodoxy with the proposition that money does not matter and that velocity is either highly unstable or infinitely interest-elastic.

The quantity-theory counterrevolution could therefore make use of the same factors as facilitated the rapid propagation of Keynesian economics—the attack on a central and widely held theoretical proposition, the development of a new theory that absorbed and rechristened the best of the old, the formulation of that theory in terms that challenged the young and enabled them to leapfrog over the old, the presentation of a new methodology that made more immediate sense than the prevailing methodology, especially in terms of accessibility to the young and to those outside the established centers of academic excellence, and a new and presumptively crucial empirical relationship suitable for relatively small-scale econometric testing.

A counterrevolution, however, has to cope somehow with a problem that a revolution by definition can ignore—though it can trade on it in its propaganda—the problem of establishing some sort of continuity with the orthodoxy of the past. Specifically, the monetarist counterrevolutionaries were burdened with the task of somehow escaping from the valid criticisms of the traditional quantity theory, which the Keynesian revolution had elevated into articles of dogma and self-justification. These criticisms were, first, that the quantity theory had assumed an automatic tendency to full employment, which was manifestly in conflict with the facts of experience; and, second, that velocity was a highly unstable variable, useful, if at all, only for the ex post description of historical events. The restatement of the quantity theory met these criticisms by two countercontentions: that the question of whether the economy responds to monetary impulses by price-level or by output changes is an empirical question falling outside the domain of monetary theory properly defined, because the quantity theory is a theory of the demand for money and not a theory of aggregate response to monetary change; and that the essence of the quantity theory as a theory of the demand for money is not presumptive constancy of velocity but the stable functional dependence of velocity on a few major variables. The former countercontention freed the quantity theory from the charge that it was too silly to be worth considering, and opened the way for fruitful scientific controversy and development in monetary theory—though, as I shall explain later, the abnegation of responsibility for explaining the division of the effects of monetary change between price and quantity movements has subsequently proved a serious short-coming of the counterrevolution, now that the counterrevolution has come to be taken seriously. The latter countercontention, involving emphasis on the existence of a stable demand function for money, permitted the absorption of the best of Keynesian ideas into the quantity theory cause, without any recognized need for acknowledgment of their source. The problem in the case of both countercontentions was to establish a plausible linkage with pre-Keynesian orthodoxy.

The solution to this problem was found along two lines. The first was the invention of a University of Chicago oral tradition that was alleged to have preserved understanding of the fundamental truth among a small band of the initiated through the dark years of the Keynesian despotism. The second was a careful combing of the obiter dicta of the great neoclassical quantity theorists for any bits of evidence that showed recognition (or could be interpreted to show recognition) of the fact that the decision to hold money involves a choice between holding money and holding wealth in other forms, and is conditioned by the rates of return available on other assets.

Don Patinkin has very recently—over-belatedly, from the standpoint of the history of economic thought—exploded these efforts to provide bridges between the pre-Keynesian orthodoxy and the monetarist counterrevolution.[6] He demonstrates conclusively that in their theorizing the neoclassical theorists did assume a tendency to automatic full employment, and that in their analyses of practical policy problems they regarded the inherent instability of velocity as a major disturbing element and made no use whatever of the functional relationship between velocity and other aggregate variables implied by their own obiter dicta. And he shows specifically that the Chicago quantity theorists—Simons and Mints—were no different from their quantity theory colleagues elsewhere in these respects. There was no lonely light constantly burning in a secret shrine on the Midway, encouraging the faithful to assemble in waiting for the day when the truth could safely be revealed to the masses; that candle was made, and not merely lit, only when its light had a chance of penetrating far and wide and attracting new converts to the old-time religion.

Nevertheless, one should not be too fastidious in condemnation of the techniques of scholarly chicanery used to promote a revolution or a counterrevolution in economic theory. The Keynesian revolution derived a large part of its intellectual appeal from the deliberate caricaturing and denigration of honest and humble scholars, whose only real crime was that they happened to exist and stand in the way of the success of the revolution. The counterrevolution had to endow these scholars, or at least their intellectual successors, with a wisdom vastly superior to what their opponents had credited them with. Obiter dicta and an oral tradition are at least semilegitimate scholarly means to this polemical end. Moreover, as time has passed and the counterrevolution has acquired increasing academic respectability, it has become increasingly possible to admit, and even to brag, that the useful ideas have been drawn from the revolution and not from the preexisting orthodoxy. Indeed, this is a necessary element in a successful counterrevolution, an element for which a previously successful revolution inevitably provides the foundations—because it ultimately becomes possible to draw an intellectually acceptable distinction between the sophisticated ideas of the revolutionary leader and the unsophisticated ideas of the revolutionary followers and executors, and to absorb the former into the counterrevolutionary ideology while discarding the latter as beneath intellectual contempt. The service of drawing this distinction in intellectually acceptable terms has been performed for the monetarist counterrevolution with great scholarly distinction by Axel Leijonhufvud's book on Keynesian economics and the economics of Keynes.

I have in this lecture been concerned primarily with the intellectual and social factors that make it possible to launch a successful revolution or counterrevolution in economic theory. However, I would judge that the key determinant of success or failure lies, not in the academic sphere, but in the realm of policy. New ideas win a public and a professional hearing, not on their scientific merits, but on whether or not they promise a solution to important problems that the established orthodoxy has proved itself incapable of solving. Keynes, and many other economists in Britain and elsewhere, spent much time in the 1920s and 1930s advocating public works as a cure for unemployment—a cure that, because it conflicted with prevailing orthodoxy, was unacceptable. The *General Theory* was successful, precisely because, by providing an alternative theory to the prevailing orthodoxy, it rationalized a sensible policy that had hitherto been resisted on purely dogmatic grounds. Similarly, the monetarist counterrevolution has ultimately been successful because it has encountered a policy problem—inflation—for which the prevailing Keynesian orthodoxy has been able to prescribe only policies of proven or presumptive incompetence, in the form of incomes or guidelines policy, but for which the monetarist counterrevolution has both a theory and a policy solution.

No particular point would be served in a lecture of this kind by recounting the stages of accomplishment in the monetarist counterrevolution.[7] The advance from strength to strength is summarizable in a few key phrases: the restatement of the quantity theory, a statistical illusion in the judging of Keynesian models, velocity versus the multiplier in U.S. monetary history, monetarism versus fiscalism, and "the new new economics." The question of interest is whether the monetarist counterrevolution will sweep the board and become the orthodoxy of the future, itself ripe for attack by a new revolution, or whether it will gradually peter out.

Personally, I expect it to peter out, for two reasons. The first, and most important, is that I believe the Keynesians are right in their view that inflation is a far less serious social problem than mass unemployment. Either we will vanquish inflation at relatively little cost, or we will get used to it. The odds at present are that we will accept it as a necessary price of solving other pressing domestic issues—this seems to be the current view of the present administration—and in that case monetarism will again be reduced to attempting to convince the public of the importance of the problem it is equipped to solve before it can start arguing about the scientific superiority of its proposed solution to the problem. The second reason is that monetarism is seriously inadequate as an approach to monetary theory, judged by prevailing standards of academic economics, and in the course of repairing its intellectual fences and achieving full scientific respectability it will have to compromise irretrievably with its Keynesian opposition.

The most serious defects of the monetarist counterrevolution from the academic point of view are, on the one hand, the abnegation of the restated quantity theory of money from the responsibility of providing a theory of the determination of prices and of output, and, on the other hand, its continuing reliance on the methodology of positive economics. Abnegation of responsibility for analyzing the supply response of the economy to monetary impulses, and particularly the disclaiming of the need for an analysis of whether monetary changes affected prices or quantities, was, as I have explained earlier, necessary to the restoration of the quantity theory to a position of academic respectability. But this need was transitory: once the quantity theory regained academic respectability, it was obliged to resume responsibility for the short-run forecasting of aggregate movements of prices and quantities.[8] This it has begun to do, most importantly through the research work of the Federal Reserve Bank of St. Louis, and with appreciable success; but it has been lured into playing in a new ballpark, and playing according to a different set of rules than it initially established for itself.

In similar fashion, the methodology of positive economics was an ideal methodology for justifying work that produced apparently surprising results without feeling obliged to explain just why they occurred, and in so doing mystifying and exciting the interests of noncommitted economists and wavering Keynesians. But the general equilibrium and empirical revolutions of the recent past have taught economists to ask for explicit specification of the full general equilibrium system with which the theorist or empiricist is working, and to distrust results that appear like rabbits out of a conjurer's hat—and an old-fashioned top hat at that. The demand for clarification of the mechanism by which results can be explained is contrary to the methodology of positive economics, with its reliance on the "as if" approach. But it will have to be answered satisfactorily if the monetarist counterrevolution is to win general acceptance among the profession; and the attempt to answer it will necessarily involve the counterrevolutionaries in the opposing methodology of general-equilibrium systems and multi-equation econometric models. The quantity theorists have already begun to extend their efforts into simultaneous-equation formulations and estimations of economic relationships. In so doing, they have been making important methodological compromises with the Keynesian opposition—or, to put it another way, reaching out for a synthesis between the revolution and the counterrevolution.

In summary, it seems to me that the monetarist counterrevolution has served a useful scientific purpose, in challenging and disposing of a great deal of the intellectual nonsense that accumulates after a successful ideological revolution. But its own success is likely to be transitory, precisely because it has relied on the same mechanisms of intellectual conquest as the revolution itself, but has been forced by the nature of the case to choose a less important political issue—inflation—to stand on than the unemployment that provided the Keynesian revolution with its political talking point, and has also espoused a methodology that has put it in conflict with long-run trends in the development of the subject. If we are lucky, we shall be forced as a result of the counterrevolution to be both more conscious of monetary influences on the economy and more careful in our assessment of their importance. If we are unlucky (those of us who are not good at jumping on bandwagons), we shall have to go through a post-counterrevolution revolution as the price of further progress on the monetary side of our science.

8. Cambridge
in the 1950s

I first arrived at Cambridge in 1945. The Canadian Army had excited a series of riots by its troops in Aldershot, due to its inability to claim the shipping to send them home immediately as expected, and then decided to cool them off by sending the longest-service of them home on ships that suddenly and not inexplicably became available, and as many as possible of the remainder who possessed adequate educational qualifications back to school on the spot. So I arrived in Cambridge in October 1945, in my corporal's uniform, which I wore for most of the rest of the year. When I finally tried to enter the college dining hall in resplendent new mufti, the head porter stopped me and said, "Sir, you must wear a gown—otherwise the gentlemen will think you're a freshman"—and kindly lent me one for that evening. Fortunately I was not the only Canadian soldier there—there were nine other Canadian soldiers—or I might have felt either lonely or snubbed. There were also 150 American GIs there, and they bore, as usual, the brunt of discrimination against North Americans. (Nowadays, with no British-style uniforms and not much recognizable Canadian accent to distinguish them from Americans, Canadians often find themselves bitterly resentful at bearing the discrimination which the British love to inflict on ordinary Americans.)

Cambridge was quite a change from the academic background I came from, the University of Toronto, which functioned in those days with fairly small classes, and instruction mostly by informal lectures and seminars. Cambridge ran on a different system—and still does—whereby the lectures are few in number from any one individual staff member, and very formal. Most of the weight of the instruction is carried by a weekly hour you spend, alone or in small numbers, with someone known there as your "supervisor" (and in Oxford as your "tutor"), for whom you write an essay every week for discussion in your "supervision" or "tutorial." Moreover, examinations were set on the field and not on the lecture series, and would probably be dominated by what the external examiner happened to think were important current problems. This gave us an extra degree of freedom from attending

A revised version of a talk given at Converse Hall, Amherst College, on Monday evening, 19 February 1973; reprinted with permission from *Encounter*, January 1974. I am grateful to Dorothy Ives, of the Amherst Economics Department, for the preparation of an excellent transcript of the spoken talk. The invitation came from Professor Arnold Collery, and the program included a paper by Elizabeth Johnson entitled "Keynes: Man of Contradictions."

lectures that was difficult for the more regimented North American to get used to. I played it safe, Canadian-style, and attended most of the lectures. My colleagues did not suffer visibly, given their ambitions and work capacity, from doing without most of the supervisions as well as most of the lectures.

On the personal side, I was allotted a room (actually a bedroom-study, livingroom, and kitchenette for making tea and soup) in Jesus College. I had not been forethoughted enough to stipulate King's College, which shows something about my lack of understanding of economics at the time, since King's was where A. C. Pigou was and Gerald Shove was and J. M. Keynes still had rooms: in short, where the action was. Jesus College did not even have a supervisor. I was paired with a lively little American whose interest in economics was shown by his classic remark "Cambridge is a great place: Yuh get yur own who'house" (referring to the fact that he could entertain girls in his room); but I soon arranged to halve my supervision hour with him and to be supervised alone.

It was a pretty miserable winter. There was no coal, and they managed also to contrive a shortage of bread. In England, then, with a lack of central heating, coal and bread were substitutes. You could heat yourself either internally with bread and marmalade or externally with coal. One ate starch five times a day and relished proximity to a roaring fire. I can remember doing my studying in my army overcoat and gloves and trying to leaf through the pages of the *General Theory* while I shivered away in my little set of rooms.

I was assigned for a supervisor Maurice Dobb, the well-known Communist intellectual, and this was probably the saving virtue of being at Jesus College, because everybody else was involved in the fight over liquidity preference versus loanable funds. Dobb, having no intellectual commitment to either side, was capable of being dispassionate when it came to discussing those issues. So I did not wind up brainwashed one way or the other on that fundamental issue, as it was put to us, of whether liquidity preference or loanable funds was the only possible approach to monetary theory.

Well, I went to lectures, not being able to shake off the habit of a North American education and the belief that lecturers somehow were there to teach us something—a great mistake, I now realize. And the first lectures I heard were by D. H. Robertson. I sat down on a sort of bench, and I looked down at the desk where I was going to put my paper to take my notes, and staring at me in the face was a deeply carved inscription, *"Pigou mumbles."* And then Robertson came in and talked. They were brilliant lectures, but you had to know at least enough economics for a Ph.D. before you could understand them. In his youth he had been quite an eminent amateur actor, and his delivery was beautiful. It was not until you got to know him better that you realized that every single word had been written out. He allowed no questions. Toward the end of the year he would announce that anyone who wished to write out a question was welcome to do so, and he would take them home and write out his answers and read them to us the next time.

He and many other Cambridge people at that time remarked that the lecturing load was very light. We used to refer to it, when I became a member of the faculty, as "the forty-hour year." Our standard lecturing commitment was forty hours, and when spread over the whole winter it was indeed no burden—something like two lectures a week for two terms out of three. But Robertson was in the habit, as many other Cambridge people were, of writing those lectures out fresh every year. They would take the whole month of September and spend it writing and rewriting. The lectures did not turn out all that differently, as I found out by going to some of Robertson's lectures after I returned to Cambridge. But it seemed to give them pleasure to do this and a feeling of assurance.

I asked Maurice Dobb about this after I became a lecturer, and he said that he wrote his out every time, every year. But in his case he did not have any elocutionary talent. He used to read these things in a flat monotone, and I went to those lectures out of a sense of duty, which was certainly required. They were supposed to be about the economics of socialism, which was a fairly hot topic in 1945-46; and he would start off with a large crowd of forty or fifty students. Toward the end there would be nobody left except myself and a very small band of Communist party members who felt obliged to reciprocate the services that he had done for the party, by listening to the lectures. They were mostly about the 1930s arguments about socialism, which started with von Mises's assertion that socialism simply "could not work" because you could not "coordinate all those decisions." And quite a number of socialists had set out to challenge this by showing that "Yes, indeed, you could coordinate decisions—by making a socialist economy work like a capitalist economy with prices serving as signals to decentralized managers." This was a rather abstruse debate involving at least three people who had published on the subject, and it took the whole term to work through it all. One never really discovered what would happen in a communist society except that it would indubitably be "far better"—a matter on which, if you lasted the course, you would have at least a few doubts.

There was another lecturer who, while not involved in such fantastically fundamental issues, produced more or less the same impression. This was a man called J. W. F. Rowe, who was by way of being an expert on commodity markets. He would take a whole hour to explain to us the difference between retailers and wholesalers. This left one plenty of time for writing letters home; I cleared off most of my relatives during those hours.

The only exciting lecturer was Joan Robinson; and this, again, was a bit of a surprise. We had had female lecturers at Toronto who appeared nicely dressed and perfumed and wearing skirts and other kinds of recognizable sex symbols. But we all assembled for Joan Robinson's lecture—and in strode a mousy-looking woman, wearing a sort of blouse-and-vest combination on top and a pair of slacks down below, and sandals. She proceeded to put an elbow on the lectern, peered out at us, and started out in a rather flat monotone. "Well, it's very difficult these days to lecture on economic theory because now we have both socialist countries and capitalist countries." Everyone thought, "Gosh, what a wonderful new idea!" I found out from one of my students some ten years later that he heard her start her lecture course exactly the same way, and he came to me and said, "Gosh, what a wonderful new idea!" At any rate, you got used to the image that she was not recognizable as a female of the species and did not behave like one, and that was one of the main lessons one had to learn. Once she came to Chicago to talk to my students there; they looked at her and decided, "Well, we'll certainly show this old grandmother where she gets off." After they picked their heads up off the floor, having been ticked off with a few well-chosen blunt squelches, they took a much more respectful attitude.

Even at that time the fight between the liquidity preference and loanable funds groups was going on. Robertson had a little coterie of people who believed in loanable funds. Unfortunately for him, they were not really sharp theorists. They were mostly involved in peripheral subjects like industrial organization (on which the British have always been extremely weak), labor economics, and other similar subjects, so about all they could do was declare their faith and maneuver behind the scenes in the academic politics of the place, trying to get more of their kind elected to positions and keep out the opposite crowd. The Keynesians were the sharp theorists, and they made their points by caricaturing an orthodoxy that no one equally sharp (apart from Robertson) was there to defend.

Things went on like that. We were, I am afraid, not paying too much attention. It was too easy to drink beer and argue politics. As is well known, English public licensing hours are rather barbarous; but they do have the one great advantage that the pubs open at 10:30 in the morning, which makes it possible to cut a lot of lectures and feel no pain. They stay open until afternoon (when one is supposed to go out and play healthy field sports), and reopen an hour or so before dinner. Of course, you have to stop drinking at ten o'clock at night, unless you can afford your own private stock; but that did not make too much difference because in those days you had to be in by midnight or you got either gated or sent down (unless you knew how to climb over the walls). There were well-charted routes by which one could get into and out of colleges, including the female colleges, after midnight. Actually, the rule in the women's colleges was that, after 7 P.M., all men are beasts. Up until 7 P.M. they were angels, and the girls simply had to learn to live with the routine and practice love in the afternoon.

It was during that year that I saw Maynard Keynes for the one and only time. They had in Cambridge a "Political Economy Club" (it had been founded by Keynes) which had a set of rules based on the society of the "Cambridge Apostles." The Apostles included many of the people who later figured in "the Bloomsbury group" and a great many famous people in various walks of life. One of the rules was that somebody would read a paper, and before the paper was read those present would draw numbers from a hat. The numbers would run from 1 to 6, and this would determine the order in which you spoke. If there were more people present than six there were blanks in the hat, and if you drew one at the Political Economy Club you could heave a sigh of relief and devote yourself to getting close enough to Robertson's coal fire to keep warm. Robertson was pretty much of a miser, and the coal fire was always lit but it never generated too much warmth. So that if you arrived a little late for the meeting you found yourself frozen, and you had to follow the lecture carefully as you shifted from foot to foot, or else you spent so much of your effort combatting the cold that you could not follow what was going on. It made a great difference whether you had a number or not. If you had a number *and* came late, you were really in trouble.

I was eventually invited to join this club. The membership included only those students who were *2-1's* or *firsts*, that is *top B* or *A* students, and I was invited to come along to my first meeting: Keynes was the guest. They passed the hat and I drew number one, which was a pretty daunting experience. I spent the time that Keynes was talking trying desperately to think of something that might be wrong with his argument; and failing that, something that might be right, but could somehow be still more right, if you follow what I mean. My colleagues were kind and they offered to take my number and give me a blank, since it was rather unfair to put me up against Keynes the first night. But I refused manfully to accept this lifeline that was being offered to me. The paper he gave is the one that was published post-humously on whether or not there would be a long-run dollar shortage. He argued fairly convincingly (at least as far as he was concerned and we were concerned) that there would not be. His argument depended very heavily on an appeal to the long-run classical mechanism, basically the influence of balance-of-payments surpluses on money, wages, and so forth.[1]

Keynes was a brilliant phenomenon; he was a sparkling man and a great experience for me. The speaker had the good fortune of sitting right beside Robertson's hearth fire, so he had no trouble keeping warm. Keynes sat there in an armchair with his legs slumped out in front of him—and he had very long legs; he was in some ways, physically, a slightly miniaturized John Kenneth Galbraith. He had some notes on the table beside him, but he never seemed to look at them. He gave us a very elegant talk, beautifully constructed, every sentence a piece of good English prose and every paragraph cadenced—just a wonderful performance. But it was in the discussion afterwards that I learned so much from him. I got up and struggled through a rather lame argument. It was to the effect that, given the availability of lots of farm labor in the United States, it would take some time before the pressure of demand for American industrial products would force up the general level of wages, just because the labor could be drawn off the farms. I was not really convinced of this myself, particularly after having listened to Keynes. But he was very kind, and he picked up the point and made something of it. And I noticed that this was what he did. One of the secrets of his charm was that when it was a student, he would go out of his way to make something flattering out of what the young man had said. If the student had made an absolute ass of himself, Keynes would still find something in it which he would transform into a good point. It might well be the very opposite of what the student had said; but the student was so relieved to find that he was not being cut to pieces that he was really impressed by the brilliance of what he was told he *had* said. On the other hand, when a faculty member got up—faculty members had the right to get up at any time, having interspersed themselves among the students, and at that time Joan Robinson stood up and attempted to argue with him—he simply cut their heads off. No matter how ingenious what they said was, he would make nonsense of it. And that, again, flattered the students, because they had been told that they were really incisive and then somebody they knew was really clever was being reduced to rubble before their very eyes. That was a doubly flattering thing. I think that this has something to do with the various well-known reactions to Keynes as a personality. When he was out of the public eye, he could be extremely kind and charming, and could make somebody feel glad to be alive. On the other hand, when the chips were really down, he could be quite ruthless in the way he dealt with people.

I happened to meet Robertson a day or two after this, and I expressed my tremendous appreciation both for the invitation and for the paper itself. He said to me, "Ah, but you missed something that used to be there—the impishness of his mind." And that, of course, reflected Robertson's very long concern and intimacy, first as a student and then as a junior colleague, with Keynes. He missed the flash of brilliance, or penetrating remarks of an unexpected kind. The paper was impressive, but it did not have the cut and thrust and mental agility that Keynes had formerly displayed. And, of course, it was only about two or three weeks afterwards that Keynes died.

That was my first year at Cambridge, and then I went back to Toronto and then to Harvard. But in between I worked my way across the ocean on a cattle boat and returned to visit some Cambridge friends. I. G. Patel, I think it was, told me I should go to see Robertson. So I went to see him, expecting it to be a pretty lame encounter, a sort of visit of respect; and so it was, more or less. We did not have too much in common, but at the very end he stunned me by asking whether I would like an appointment in Cambridge. I recovered enough to say, "Yes, yes, yes, yes, yes," and later, after I got to Harvard, I received a letter from him, written in his own hand. He never used a stenographer except for typing papers, conducting all of his correspondence himself; and this had been true even when he was the secretary (or chairman) of the faculty. Everything was done by hand, and it was infernally difficult to read.

I later discovered this was the done thing, and mail delivery happened to be very good. I became involved several times in controversies with Joan Robinson. She would send me a handwritten note in the morning, and I would scribble my answer by noonday; and then I would get a note back in the evening saying, "Where you made your mistake is as follows . . ." I could keep that up for two days; but I soon wearied of the game. Why was I the only one who made hopeless mistakes in pure theory?

At Harvard, I was educated in Keynesian economics by Alvin Hansen and Seymour Harris. I cut a lot of ice around Harvard, since Cambridge was where they all would have liked to have gone. That eased my path as a graduate student considerably, and I duly recrossed the Atlantic and went back to Cambridge.

By that time two other members of the cast had appeared on the scene, Richard Kahn and Nicholas Kaldor. That set up a situation for the next ten years or so, which became a situation of considerable strain. Without, I hope, going too far in personal terms, I think one has to understand what lay behind the bitterness of the controversies in terms of the personalities involved. When you become a member of the Cambridge faculty, you are there for life; there's nowhere else to go. And each of you is attached to a particular college, and you teach that college's students. You give your lectures (but that is a rather minor part of the responsibilities). Is there anything more likely to generate personal bitterness (and a penchant for overstepping the bounds of civilized discourse) than the knowledge that you and that other person are stuck there for the next thirty years? You cannot really do them any harm: they are not going to apply for a job anywhere else, so your opinion on their incompetence will never be solicited. And the same applies to you. You can be as incompetent as you want to be; you still have most of the weapons in your hands, in the sense that you can tell your students what you like and carry on the war that way.

The physical environment and the nature of the academic appointment had quite a bit to do with the bitter personal animosity of Cambridge controversy. There is something of the flavor of it in C. P. Snow's novels, which refer to a college that is really a composite of Cambridge colleges and their gossip. That kind of situation makes for considerable acrimony and for dissatisfaction in the long run among the students, because they are being told one thing by one teacher and another thing by another. Then the examinations are not set by the individual teacher, which would make life easy: you could be a Keynesian in one examination and a "Loanable Funds

Man" in another. But you have somehow to straddle the issues in a paper which will possibly be marked by one of each, which means that the ability of one to influence the other is going to have a substantial influence on the outcome. There will also be an external examiner whose name you may not even know (since they make every effort to keep the external examiners secret until the last possible moment). He may well set you a question innocently, into which you can drag liquidity preference or loanable funds. All those traps lie in wait. In addition, most students at Cambridge were not planning to become professional economists; so spending a couple of years trying to master the ins-and-outs of liquidity preference versus loanable funds before going back to India as a government planner was not exactly a wise investment of their time. Nevertheless, that was the prevailing ethos.

Robertson had been a supervisee (or a "pupil" as they used to describe it) of Keynes, and there was a great personal attachment between them. It lasted through the 1920s, but broke up with the publication of Keynes's *Treatise* (1930). The *Treatise* introduced a great many new concepts and a few equations that turned out to have nothing very much in them. On one of the final-year examinations (these are compulsory examinations, incidentally; there is no getting around it), Robertson set the question, "In the *Treatise* Mr. Keynes says—. . . . Does this mean that the quantity theory, besides being a tautology, is not true?" And this kind of thing would go on in the exams in my days as student and don.

Robertson had been very deeply attached to Keynes; they broke over the *Treatise* basically, but it became worse as the *General Theory* began to emerge. And Keynes had a group of young people around him—Richard Kahn and Joan Robinson, in particular, though there were a number of others who were involved who didn't stay at Cambridge but went elsewhere. He deliberately egged them on to attack Robertson—not that they needed much urging.

Now to understand the implications of that one has to know a bit about the characters of the persons involved. Robertson was a very shy, gentle person. I suppose he might be best described as "an English gentleman." He had served in the First World War and been awarded the Military Cross, though nobody ever spoke about this, and I never found out for what act of valor he received it. It certainly was not anything he ever talked about. He was a bachelor and lived all the time in his college; and his attitude toward economics was pretty much of a gentleman's attitude and an Establishment attitude. He had been trained as a classicist and that, I suspect, was where his heart really lay. His attitude toward economics was that it was something one did lightly. And, of course, some people at least who have read his little book *Money* (1922) will remember the quotations from *Alice in Wonderland* with which he started each chapter. This truly reflected his character: whimsical, somewhat withdrawn, and very shy, and it expressed itself in what

I have already mentioned—his writing out every word of his lectures and entertaining no questions, the lectures being a theatrical performance, scripted by himself. The most you would get out of him at the Political Economy Club was a sentence ot two of a not very informative nature. And Keynes had egged his young people on against him.

Their attraction to economics, particularly in the case of Joan Robinson, was basically a radical political attitude. This led to them being described by Joseph Schumpeter as "Marxo-Keynesians." In that respect one has to accord an important influence to Michael Kalecki, who had arrived in Cambridge and become one of the group in the middle 1930s, and who had actually produced much of the *General Theory* in his own writings in Polish (which were eventually translated), though with a very strongly Marxist flavor. Where Keynes had an "aggregate propensity to comsume," which is the key pin of his apparatus, Kalecki had the division of society into workers and capitalists. On the Marxist assumption that the capitalists save and invest most of their income and workers consume most of theirs, you can regard the capitalists abstractly as having a unitary marginal propensity to save, and the workers a zero one. In fact, some of the empirical work of that period was devoted to this problem. Much to people's surprise they found that workers *also* save, and that the difference in marginal propensities was not all that great (though it was certainly statistically significant).

Keynesian economics originally (at least on a majority interpretation of it) started out really as a way of saving capitalism from the stupidity of its managers, and this, I think, remains the majority tradition of monetary economics outside England. The general proposition—that policymaking does have to pay attention to macroeconomic management (but once that is properly looked after, microeconomics comes into its own)—became, in the Cambridge concept, very much tied up with questions which go a long way back in the history of economics, particularly the question of the justification, if any, for the payment of interest. On that question the classical economists often showed their complete failure to distinguish science from emotion. That certainly survived in this tradition at Cambridge. It is one thing to say that people who own property "do not deserve to own it," that inheritance of property is "a bad thing socially," and so forth. It is another thing to say that property, therefore, must be *unproductive*—because we want to believe that the people who own it have no real social function.

This, of course, has been one of the major problems in Soviet Russian economic planning. The Russians are exceedingly good at developing human capital. One of the major sources of their rapid growth has been the attention they have paid to developing the characteristics of the individual as a worker, or as administrator, or whatever else, fostering human talent as far as possible by intensive emphasis on education. Where their chief difficulties come are from attempting to argue that interest has no justification and no meaning, that capital is not scarce, that you should treat it as if it cost you nothing (and naturally if it *is* scarce you get into trouble). The same sort of problem arises in Russia with respect to the rent of land, which again (according to the Marxist and pre-Marxist tradition of various writers such as Ricardo) implies there is something wrong somewhere since no work is being done to generate the rent of land. Much of the development of economic theory, of course, concerns the separation of the economic *logic* of prices being attached to things that are scarce from the question of *morality*. Well, that confusion of logic still runs right through the Cambridge Keynesian school (and I will say a little more about that later).

My point of departure is this characteristic of Robertson: a man who was very aloof about relationships with other people and was not cut out for the rough life of politicking behind the scenes or for public debate. This was fully realized by the other chief protagonist in the argument, Joan Robinson. She—I would not say necessarily consciously—certainly used the attitudes of the opposite sex toward her as an excuse for behavior which often would not have been acceptable from a male economist, I mean in terms of distorting arguments and abusing the privileges of academic discourse. It was her favorite ploy with the students to say, "Well, I don't mind—I'll galdly have a public debate with Robertson on any issue at any time." Well, take—on the one hand—Joan Robinson, whose forte in life has been standing up in front of audiences and announcing her political conclusions (with much economic nonsense) without feeling any compunction about it; and—on the other hand—Robertson, who had to write out every lecture in order to give himself the confidence to deliver it. This was certainly no contest. It was a giant challenging a baby to a boxing match. And this went on continually.

The background to all this was the harrying of Robertson through the 1930s both in print and personally; the latter was much more serious. He had been prevented from receiving what he (and many others) considered was the final reward of a serious academic career, namely the professorship at Cambridge; for that reason he had gone to the London School of Economics as a professor. Fortunately for him, the war broke out—and the London School of Economics moved to Cambridge. When he left Cambridge, it was for temporary war work with the Government. At the end of the war, when it was clear that Keynes was never going to come back to academic life, these people got together and persuaded Robertson to take the chair on the basis of promises by them that they would "stop the persecution," would "live and let live," and so forth. But those promises were very quickly forgotten. The bitter controversy and intellectual guerrilla warfare resumed full sway.

I remember taking Anthony Scott, a friend of mine from Harvard (who is now a professor at the University of British Columbia) to one of Joan Robinson's lectures. She was holding forth about liquidity preference and loanable funds. One of her main remarks was first of all to call attention to some analysis of Maurice Dobb's (about the Benefits of Planning) in terms of an analogy. A man is walking along a road across the field from his dog, and the dog tries to catch up with him. It starts off and each moment it is aiming for the man; but as it goes along the man is also going along, so it traces out a sort of curve: the "pursuit curve." Yet, if it had the brains, it would realize that if it did its canine calculations properly, it could go in a straight line to the point where the man had now arrived and save itself a lot of legwork. Joan Robinson called attention to this analogy, and then she said, "and loanable funds is the fly buzzing around the nose of the dog." This may be good polemical tactics, but not exactly very instructive to somebody who wants to know what the real economic issues are. A great deal of this sort of thing went into her lectures, and much of the controversy was concerned with debating issues which had been raised in the 1930s. Here I want to fill in some background history which, I think, would help clarify the basic questions.

The quantity theory as we think of it now, thanks to the atavism perpetrated by my colleague in Chicago, Milton Friedman, is usually conceived of as $MV=PT$, or $M=kOP$, or whatever. The Cambridge formulation which we used to have a lot of fun with as students was $M=kOP$. We always referred to it as "M equals cop," where M is the nominal quantity of money, k is a functional relationship representing the ratio of money people want to hold to their money income, O is output, and P is the price level. If we go back to Knut Wicksell we notice that for Wicksell this was merely the starting point: interpreting what this equation meant and how it operated. But very quickly Wicksell, in his own work (and in the development of the theory, based on his work) got quite a way off from the equation of exchange, which was just a starting point, to a discussion of the conditions under which money will be neutral—that is, under which monetary developments will not interfere with the achievement of the real barter equilibrium of the economy. Now Wicksell stated the conditions for that in terms of three principles which he thought were equivalent: namely, that savings should equal investment; or that the money rate of interest and the real rate of interest should be equal; or that prices should be stable.

A young Swedish economist, Johan Akerman, pointed out that in a growing economy these conditions are not the same—that, in a growing economy, keeping savings and investment equal (at least as these are commonly defined) would not necessarily mean stability of the price level, and in particular as output increases with a given quantity of money the price level will tend to fall. As this becomes expected, then the money rate of interest will lie below the real rate—because people who hold money will be getting the automatic benefit of an increase of the purchasing power of money.

That set the framework for the development of the general quantity theory tradition, particularly with the Austrian economists who came to be represented in England by Friedrich Hayek of the London School of Economics. It also characterizes Keynes's work up to and including the *Treatise*. The basic mechanism which determines whether the economy is going through a "boom" or a "recession" is whether Savings are *less than* or *greater than* Investment. But savings there are defined as voluntary savings out of a full employment level of income, and investment is defined as the investment that businessmen want to make. So that if you have an excess of investment over voluntary saving you will get a rise in incomes and increases in saving which will accrue to businessmen as windfall profits. Now in ex post accounting terms you would count these as part of "savings," as in the *General Theory*. But in the *Treatise* these are windfal profits and not part of savings as defined by Keynes. Similarly the other way around. If full-employment Savings tends to exceed full-employment Investment, then you get a fall in the price level with windfall losses for entrepreneurs. Again, the mechanism is inequality of Savings and Investment (in the special sense defined).

Robertson's major contribution to the development of monetary theory was concerned with this question of the conditions for monetary equilibrium, in which he introduced two kinds of factors. There was the balance of real savings and investment, but then there was also the balance between the desire to accumulate cash balances and the willingness of the monetary authority to create them. So you had a market for loanable funds in which (in the short run) equilibrium would require that the sum of savings and new money creation would be equal to investment plus hoarding, the desire to accumulate cash balances.

It is a feature of Robertson's writings in this field—and one which comes as somewhat of a surprise to someone who has read Keynes's frequent diatribes against central bankers—that he was very much in touch with policymaking. He was, in fact, the only economist in the country who could invite himself to lunch at the Bank of England. While the Bank of England was not quite as august or eminent as it used to be, still, there were many others who had to wait to be asked. In my own case it was only two years ago that they asked me, and then it was not the Governor, it was just one of the Court. (The lunch, incidentally, was rather austere, though the wines were good.) Robertson kept writing into his monetary theory an assumption which to our minds would seem very strange (particularly given the twenty years or so of criticism of the U. S. Federal Reserve System that there has been), namely that "the monetary authority is pretty smart." Robertson always assumed that the monetary authority was "smart" enough to know whether a disturbance in the market is due to a change in the real factors, Savings and Investment, or due to a change in "the hoarding factor," namely the desire of people to hold idle balances. So from place to place you find him remarking that a normally astute central bank will recognize this difference; and if people want more money because there is a scramble for liquidity, the central bank will provide it. That, of course, is good, standard, central banking theory. It even goes back to Walter Bagehot. But it makes a big difference to the model whether you assume that the authorities are "smart" and intelligent or not. The consensus among American monetary economists is, on the whole, that they are *not*, and that their efforts to be "smart" cause more trouble than they are worth. Not just Milton Friedman, but a number of others (including the Joint Economic Committee of the U.S. Congress) have come out in favor of limiting the power of the central bank to introduce arbitrary disturbances in the market by subjecting it to some sort of rule (or band limits) on what it can do to the money supply.

Robertson's contribution, then, was to set the problem up *this* way with loanable funds and to take account of hoarding. But it was very easy to make fun of the concept of hoarding. When I was a student at Harvard, for example, it was not Robertson but Hayek that people were having great difficulty with—because he had the concept of "forced saving." This is a concept, which after forty more years of monetary theorizing, we can understand pretty well. All it amounts to is that, if you inflate the money supply of an economy, this will drive up prices; and the rise in prices will cause people to try to restore their real balances; and, to do that, they have to spend less on goods and services. So, you are extracting goods and services from them through the inflationary process. This is known in the modern literature as "the inflation tax."

But it is very easy to poke fun at the idea of hoarding and forced saving—who has the money? who has the savings?—and all that kind of thing. This was what Cambridge in the early 1950s was spending most of its time on. Richard Kahn was giving his lectures on monetary theory; in fact, there were several series of lectures going on this particular kind of issue. That, frankly, is why I chose to specialize in money and banking institutions—and to leave monetary theory alone—while I was teaching there.

It was primarily Kahn who carried on the Keynesian tradition of liquidity preference theory. It is important for the understanding of Keynes to realize that he started his life as a lecturer—talking about the stock market and the financial markets generally—and that he kept on with those lectures through much of his career. Kahn took over from him both in lecturing on that subject and in managing the College's finances (where this analysis is really of great practical importance). Kahn was a rather peculiar lecturer. He would always spend something like twenty minutes of an hour summarizing what he said *last* time and then, by the time he got through that, of course he could not finish what he was going to do *this* time, so that had to go into the *next* lecture's summary. And so you went on from week to week, being told either what he said last week or what he was going to say next time, with a very thin sliver in between of what he was actually saying this time.

But Kahn's main function in Cambridge economics was not the contribution of his own subtle analysis of liquidity preference. It was (on the one hand) to direct the strategy and tactics of left-wing academic political maneuvers in the Faculty, and (on the other hand) to marshal all the intellects in support of Joan Robinson's version of Keynesianism. For this purpose, he played the affable host to the self-styled "secret seminar," which met in his King's College rooms virtually every Tuesday evening in the Michaelmas and Easter terms and increasingly became a forum for the advance testing of the technical analysis of Joan Robinson's *The Accumulation of Capital*.[2]

Anyway, Kahn was lecturing on liquidity preference theory, and Joan Robinson was lecturing on aggregate demand theory. She, of course, lacked the rewarding subtlety of Kahn's mind. Kahn was juggling, long before anyone else, with the question of extending liquidity preference theory to allow for more than two assets—treasury bills and equities as well as Keynes's money and bonds—and grappling with complicated issues of portfolio management theory.

Robertson, meanwhile, was giving essentially what was by then very old-fashioned stuff. He began with $M=kOP$, went on to loanable funds, and wound up with "the four crucial fractions" (which Paul Samuelson sneeringly dismissed in his *Quarterly Journal of Economics* obituary of Robertson).

Actually, the four crucial fractions, which I do not want to go into here, had a lot more sense to them than Samuelson allowed. Let me explain very briefly what the problem is. One has a banking system in a growing economy; and one has a certain rate of growth of the demand for money. The supply of money has to be provided by the banking system. The banking system has a desired relationship between the amount of commercial lending it wants to do and the amount of reserves it holds. The business community has desired ratios between financing by bank credit, financing by security issues, and financing by ploughed-back profits. Robertson's problem, which originated in the circumstances of the 1930s when bank lending dropped very sharply and banks came to be loaded up with government securities was this: Is there anything in the natural course of evolution of a society that will make all these ratios work out correctly? Or will there be troubles because the money people demand does not match the money that they want to see supplied, as reflected in their borrowing from banks?

That formulation, again, was easy for a more mathematically trained generation to ridicule. Professor Samuelson, I think, behaved rather badly in using an obituary of Robertson to make fun of it and of other efforts by a subtle but hopelessly literary mind to tackle serious problems. If Samuelson had drawn the analogy with Don Patinkin's *Money, Interest and Prices*, which was by then available, he might have been more perceptive. And if we had studied Robertson more carefully ourselves, we undoubtedly would have understood Patinkin much better. Anyway, Robertson was lecturing away on pre-Keynesian quantity-theory lines, $M=kOP$ and loanable funds and the four crucial fractions; and Joan Robinson was slashing away at Robertson, using a very simple version of liquidity preference theory; and Kahn was making liquidity preference theory a general—and difficult—exercise in the theory of portfolio management.

As I have said, the early part of that period was devoted to making fun of Robertson, who more and more did his writing in the form of interpretative essays, full of allusions and quotations. Richard Kahn once said that he wanted to stage a debate between Dennis Robertson and Thomas Balogh. The contest would impose only one condition: neither of them was to be allowed to quote or cite anyone else—they had to make a straightforward argument. That might have been a good competition, except that neither would have made it past the starting point without being disqualified. The Keynesians all amused themselves by asking what "hoarding" meant, and travestying Robertson's "period analysis" to show that, in the short run, the loanable-funds approach led to the conclusion that the rate of interest might go either up or down. This is a result easily achievable. One repeals Walras's Law (the law that all money must be either spent or held), or one incorporates a concealed change in liquidity preference along with a change in the real factors (saving and investment). Joan Robinson's famous 1951 *Econometrica* article on the rate of interest had played this game. But eventually they got tired of that, which was not very enlightening for the rest of us anyway. Then along came Roy Harrod with his dynamic growth equation; and Joan Robinson latched on to that and proceeded to create a new confusion which Cambridge has insisted on ever since in the realm of capital theory. It is the mistaken belief that to prove capitalism to be logically impossible is sufficient to dispose of its existence.

To understand that controversy, one has to understand something about the politics of academic debate in England; more particularly, to appreciate the sharp division between the London School and Cambridge over Hayek versus Keynes in the 1930s, which eventually led the younger people to start publishing *The Review of Economic Studies*, so that those interested in serious technical economics (rather than academic polemics) could publish their ideas.

Joan Robinson's work in this connection is essentially a criticism of the aggregate production function. (This relates total output produced by the economy to the total labor and capital it employs, via the technology which permits productive factors to be converted into products.) It was developed by J. R. Hicks and R. G. D. Allen at the London School of Economics at the turn of the 1930s, and so implicitly carries on the Cambridge 1930s myth of a "revolutionary Cambridge" battling a dinosauric London orthodoxy. But by the 1950s F. A. Hayek had departed from London for Chicago, and there was no one left in London either capable of or interested in debating pure "capital theory" with Cambridge. Had it not been for Cambridge (U.S.A.)—I mean MIT not Harvard—responding eagerly to Joan Robinson's challenge to "orthodox" production function theory in order to display its mathematical-economics muscle—Cambridge (England) would have been revealed—even to its own captive student audience—as a voice crying nonsense in an imaginary wilderness. It would long since have been a dead duck professionally.[3]

A major break-through in economics in the 1930s, as it appeared at the time, was the imperfect competition revolution. In the post–World War II period this was reconstituted in the proposition that prices do not reflect any rational profit-maximizing process, but instead are determined by the mark-up that entrepreneurs choose for their own unexplained reasons to add on to their prime costs. As a consequence, running through the works of Joan Robinson (and quite a few American Keynesians of the same 1930s vintage like Sidney Weintraub and others) you find the notion that we really have no theory of income distribution and price determination that has any rational basis. One, therefore, has to construct one out of whatever pseudo-sociological materials lie to hand. This position, among other things, provides the scientific vacuum from which recommendations for Incomes Policy as a cure for inflation are derived.

The two major Cambridge protagonists in the attack on the aggregate production function were Joan Robinson and Nicholas Kaldor. While they agreed on the utter imbecility of neoclassical production and distribution theory, they differed radically on what should be put in its place. Joan Robinson has put vast efforts of both analysis and personal assertiveness into developing the theory of capital to the point where she has proved conclusively to her own satisfaction that Capitalism Cannot Possibly Work.

Nicholas Kaldor once commented that if you really believe in capitalism, it is worthwhile doing all the work required to explain how it functions. If you do not believe in capitalism, it is not worthwhile exploring how it is supposed to work in order to show why it doesn't. But to do all that work in order to show that it cannot work is a waste of time.

Well, Cambridge is a very isolated place, and the message still has not reached there that, by and large, the world has enjoyed full employment and fairly successful capitalism for over a quarter of the post-War century and that, that being so, the fact the Britain had mass unemployment for twenty years and the rest of the world for about eight years in the inter-War period is not really a very great violation of the long run of historical experience. Joan Robinson's effort (and that of many of her disciples) had been to prove that capitalism cannot work and to do this on purely intellectual grounds. This is not a scientific game at all; it is not even an interesting divertissement; but with enough prestige inherited from superior minds, and with enough vociferousness, you can make a lot of the profession think it must be important. One of the major elements in the radical case is the ancient idea that the rate of interest really has nothing to determine it. It is modernized into the contention that what determines the rate of profit is whatever it is that makes entrepreneurs decide on various kinds of mark-ups (or else some extension of the concept of "liquidity preference").

Nicholas Kaldor, on the other hand, being a man who rolls with the times fairly fast, decided early on that capitalism actually was working. So for him the problem was, given that it works, it cannot possibly work because the theory of it is right. It must work for some quite unsuspected reason which only people as intelligent as himself can see. He developed a great deal of new theory to that effect, opposing Joan Robinson on theoretical fundamentals but joining her in rejecting the production function. In particular he developed a new "Keynesian" theory of income distribution to oppose to marginal productivity theory, and something called the "technical progress function" to reconcile production theory with his new distribution theory, thereby scoring twice over orthodox theory while not violating the crude facts of empirical observation. So that, you will see, is having it both ways. I was wrong the first time in saying it did not work. Now I must be doubly right, because I can show you that it cannot possibly work for the reasons that people always said it works; but that it nevertheless works, after all, according to a new theory I have developed to replace the theory I claim cannot possibly work. The consistency of the results—that is, with the obvious facts the others started with—irrefutably demonstrates the brilliance of my own contribution.

I want to return briefly to the "production function" as the subject of the Cambridge debate. One of the leading figures at London was J. R. Hicks, who won the Nobel Prize in 1972. He was instrumental in developing "general equilibrium theory" in the United Kingdom. As a preliminary, in his *Theory of Wages* he applied the aggregate production function to the determination of the distribution of income. I want to say two things about that.

1. If you use a simple aggregate model, which produces only one "product," of course demand has nothing to do with distribution of income—it is purely technologically determined by the production function. The total amounts of labor and capital suffice to determine how much each contributes to total output, and hence receives under competitive market conditions. So naturally, anyone who does not like the distribution of income (and is not smart enough to realize that there is a difference between the economic functions of factors of production and the social function of the distribution of their ownership) has a natural incentive to attack the production concept as a way of laying an intellectual foundation—though a completely unnecessary one—for his beliefs about the just distribution of property and income.

2. If you go beyond the one-sector model to a two-sector model, demand

does come in again. The distribution of income is not determined by technology and factor supplies alone, as the one-sector model necessitates. In a two-sector model there are two goods—which may for present purposes be identified with Consumer Goods and Capital Equipment—and two industries producing them, these industries using labor and capital in different proportions. A shift of production toward the labor-intensive industry increases the demand for labor, raises its price, and lowers the value of the services of capital (and vice versa). Hence, to determine the prices of factor services to production and the distribution of income, we need to bring in the demands of the two groups of factor owners for the two goods, weighted by the distribution of income corresponding to the allocation of production between the two industries.

The Cambridge mind however never stretched to the two-sector model, until they began working on the line of proving that capitalism could not work. They then developed the production side of the two-sector model, but they never fed back the implications of that for demand through the distribution of income between labor and capital and the preference systems of these two factors of production for the consumption of goods. Instead they relied on the Keynesian assertion that investment is subject to no budgetary constraint. Investors can undertake any amount of investment they want; saving is a fixed proportion of income (the proportion differing between labor and capital owners). Then you arrive at a model which is "overdetermined" in the sense that you have investors determining how much investment there is and, therefore, how much has to be saved. This, in turn, implies a distribution of income which sees to it that amount does get saved. On the other hand, you have a production side of the economy which implies typically a different rate of return on capital and wage rate than is consistent with the assertion that investment is not subject to a budget constraint.

My own view is that the Keynesian assertion is the one that has to go—because it is inconsistent with the observable facts. It implies that investment has nothing to do with the rate of interest, that entrepreneurs can always find all the money they want for investment, and that everything depends on their high animal spirits.

It was about that time—the 1950s—that I began to appreciate the difference between scientific and ideological motivations for theoretical work. I began to realize more and more that Cambridge people in my judgment were perverting economics in order to defend intellectual and emotional positions taken in the 1930s. In particular, for them Keynesian economics was not a theoretical advance to be built on for scientific progress and improved social policy. It was only a tool for furthering left-wing politics at the level of intellectual debate.

So I decided to leave Cambridge and go somewhere else where I might learn something useful—namely to Manchester.

I eventually left Manchester to go to Chicago, in spite of the fact that my days in Manchester were probably the happiest in my life, professionally speaking. Over the years I became fed up with the intellectual poverty of English economics, which provided increasingly inadequate spiritual compensation for the material poverty that English academic life in the provinces imposed.

But that is another story.

Part 3   **Economics
                              and the
                              Universities**

9. National Styles in Economic Research: The United States, the United Kingdom, and Various European Countries

Any attempt to discuss national styles in economic research, and the institutional arrangements that influence them, has to start with recognition of the fact that in the post–World War II period, and especially in the sub-period beginning somewhere in the early or middle 1950s and running up until two or three years ago, economics has been undergoing what may be called a "research revolution." On the intellectual or purely scientific plane, the 1930s witnessed the production of a variety of important new ideas. The most apparently revolutionary idea was Keynes's *General Theory of Employment, Interest and Money*—though from a policy point of view the theory of monopolistic competition has also had a significant impact. But with specific reference to research, the most important ideas, from a longer-run point of view, were the introduction of mathematically based general equilibrium theory derived from the Continental theoretical tradition, the acceptance of mathematics as a more powerful analytical tool than literary logic and commentary, and the transmogrification of economic statistics into econometrics—the use of statistical methods to measure and test relationships specified by theory.

These ideas were barely launched before the interruption of scientific economic activity by the Second World War, which diverted a large proportion of English-language economists—and an even larger proportion of those who otherwise would have become graduate students—into work in the government economic service or into the armed forces. After the war, many of the prewar generation of economists returned to academic life, but typically with a commitment to positions they had adopted in the 1930s and without the drive to resume the hard intellectual exercise that characterized them earlier. On the other hand, thanks in large part to generous veterans' benefits supplied by governments, the number of graduate students expanded greatly; and those students were quick to absorb the most readily learnable aspects of the discipline and the aspects most likely to give them both respect from their teachers and demonstrable superiority over them, namely the new techniques of mathematical analysis and econometrics, as contrasted with the social wisdom and philosophizing that characterized the older style of "political economy." Hence economics shifted from an orientation toward

Reprinted with permission from *Daedalus* 102, no. 2 (Spring 1973): 65–74.

"political economy" to an orientation toward "economic science"; and the essence of science is research, the application (with more or less ingenuity) of known or knowable techniques to the solution of suitable problems (which may or may not be of general social interest, but usually are not because problems of general social interest are usually very untidy).

The relevant point about the "research revolution," in the context of the present discussion, is that its focal point and indeed its revolutionary frontier were located in the United States. For this there were many reasons. One was the intellectual tiredness, the sense of themselves as anachronisms, and the inferiority complexes of both Continental Europe and the United Kingdom after six years of an all-out war which was finally won by the resources of the United States and Russia, together with their lack of resources and intellectual capacity to mount the kind of graduate training program required to equip students for the research revolution—and the repugnance of such programs to the historical tradition of the lonely scholar working on his own and deriving his satisfaction as much from the work itself as from sharing its results with others. Another reason was the historical dependence of ex-colonial countries like Canada and Australia on the mother country to provide ideas, teachers, and graduate instruction for their own students; they were incapable of picking up the ball of the research revolution themselves but their teachers and students saw clearly that the United States was the place to get graduate training and began to go there rather than to the United Kingdom or Continental Europe. (The European students, especially those from the United Kingdom and northern Europe, got the same message; those from France and Italy were inhibited from studying in the United States by the difficulty of fitting themselves back into their own university systems—with the result that France and Italy are of virtually zero significance on the contemporary economic scene.)

The most important reason, however, lay in the characteristics of the United States itself. First, in contrast to Europe, and to a lesser extent Canada and similar countries, where a professor is a member of the national elite and is accordingly judged by his behavior in relation to what the elite think he should be doing and saying, so that he has to be in some sense a "rounded" member of society, in the United States—except for brief periods of political esteem for what the academic can do to solve society's problems—the academic world is a fairly self-contained world, within which entry and promotion are fairly strictly governed by academic standards. Hence students attempt to acquire, and aspiring universities try to provide, instruction in techniques of analysis and research that will give them an edge over their rivals and the promise of future publication performance. Second, in contrast to the European tradition of doing graduate work on one's own under an eminent professor or supervisor, the United States has a long tradition of explicit and organized programs of graduate instruction, a tradition in which the program adapts itself sooner or later to the incorporation and transmission of new development in the field. Third, and related, the United States has the resources to support such programs by the offer of handsome fellowships to students of high quality, and competition for good students among university graduate departments extends this support to foreign as well as domestic students. Fourth, the interest of American society in knowledge has always been pragmatic rather than philosophical, so that an orientation toward techniques and research comes more naturally to the American than to the European scholar. Finally, the U.S. concern for the promotion of science and scientific research that followed in the wake of Russia's success in launching the Sputnik in 1957 extended to embrace economics as a science, thereby creating an inflated demand for "economic scientists," that is, those who at the junior level would demonstrate satisfactory training in mathematics and econometrics and at a senior level could prove research performance by published output of ceremonially adequate scientific papers.

The results of this outburst of technique-and-research-oriented training and activity in the United States have been that the profession of academic economics in most countries, including the United States, is divided rather uncomfortably into three groups: those who have been to a top-notch graduate school in the United States, or a school there or elsewhere good enough for them to have acquired the research techniques and orientation, and who have stuck with them in a research-and-publication-oriented career, wherever they may be teaching; those who have attended a good graduate school to acquire the qualifications necessary for respectable academic employment, but thereafter have receded into non-research interests and activities, regarding a bare minimum of research as a necessary cost of academic reputability; and those who have never gone through the mill of a top-notch graduate school, though they may have attended one as a short-term student or a senior visitor.

The first group constitutes the elite of the profession—those who communicate with each other by exchanging papers before publication and by attending international conferences, rather than by reading each other's work with a long lag in journals and still longer lag in books. Their style is an international style, though primarily American in origin and outlook, and frequently they have to maintain it in the face of hostility and resentment from their departmental colleagues and of inadequate institutional support. One reflection of this problem is the strong desire on the part of such people to establish research institutes with financial support from outside the university, in order to free themselves from the restrictions imposed on their research ambitions by the departments and universities within which they work. Another is their anxiety to take as much leave of absence as possible from their main employer university to spend visiting, or teaching if necessary, in one of the livelier American (or even British) graduate centers. Still another is their eagerness to obtain short- or long-term visitors from the international world who share their style of scholarship, through the offer of visiting lectureships and professorships and the holding of conferences, the published proceedings of which will serve as validation of their belief that they belong in the large cosmopolitan world of economic scholarship and research.

It is the other two groups that constitute the repository of differences in national styles. And these differences reflect differences in three major factors: national culture; university tenure and promotion systems; and outside funding for research. With respect to national culture, it would perhaps be more accurate to subdivide that factor into differences in national culture, and differences in the way in which the economist, either as such or as an academic generally, is involved in that culture. One could discuss the factors separately, using different nations as illustrations, but it is more convenient to compare nations in terms of the influence of the factors. (The reader is warned that what follows consists of condensed personal impressions, which may well be considered offensive or inaccurate by other people.)

In the United States, the economics profession has shared the general freedom of the public to disagree with its government—except in wartime, when all the population is expected to close ranks in defense of its peacetime freedom. In this respect it has had the advantage that its relation to government has been that of a hired independent expert; and since the profession is large, there are always competent economists available who will work for a government of any political complexion, and who will neither suffer opprobrium from their fellow economists nor enjoy undue professional advancement for so doing (in this respect, economists are probably a tougher intellectual lot than, say, atomic physicists). In other words, the national culture values economists primarily as experts, not as potential or actual rulers.

Perhaps as a result of this respect and freedom, the most impressive characteristic of the economics profession in the United States is its consistently high quality across the country. Wherever one goes to visit a university, one finds people who have been very competently trained, who maintain a keen interest in the subject and its development, and who have a serious research interest of some kind. In part this may be an optical illusion: the rapid expansion of American universities in the past decade has meant that most departments consist predominantly of young faculty members ("young" means under forty), and the few seniors, unless they are really competent, have been squeezed out of real participation in the department and can be kept decently hidden from sight. Discounting that fact—which in any case applies to other countries as well—the explanation for this excellence consists of a number of factors. One is the rather isolated role of the academic in the American society, already mentioned, which tends to concentrate his attention on his subject. Another is the pragmatic nature of American society, which in this connection means that a university teacher has to take his stand, not on the greatness of his personal thoughts about and reactions to life, but on how good he is in his subject and how well he can teach it. A third is the ability of American universities to insist on the Ph.D. as a qualification for academic tenure, which means that most people teach in a university of lower quality than the one from which they received their Ph.D., are conscious of that fact, and are anxious to prove to themselves and others that individually they are better than one would expect from their institutional affiliation. A fourth is the stringency of American standards for promotion and tenure, which typically require a man to continue to demonstrate competence by research and publication well into his forties. Allied with this is a fifth, the mobility of American academic life, which means that a man who demonstrates research competence may at any time receive an offer of better pay and higher rank from a university of higher (or equal or not much worse) quality than his present one, which will enable him to bargain for a better deal from his own university. In other words, the academic in America is being continuously evaluated, by his own or other universities, until a very late stage of his academic life; and this provides strong incentives for him to keep up with his subject and to engage actively in research. An important point here is that in contrast to the British and other university systems, pay and title are based largely (though not always) on performance and not on age. A sixth factor is the multiplicity and diversity of the American governmental structure, and the geographical dispersion of the country. This means that if an individual is looking for the opportunity to do sponsored research of an academically respectable kind, and is prepared to turn his mind to other people's definitions of research problems, he can usually find research support from some branch of the federal or his state government, or from some local industry or national industry with a local branch, or from some foundation.

This implies, of course, that research in the United States tends to be "outer-directed" rather than "inner-directed." This is probably not too serious a defect, given a plethora of competently trained people who are obliged to do research of some sort but lack the originality to devise their own problems, and the scarcity of original ideas anyway. However, the general tendency is for research to be directed to small problems rather than large ones. To correct this tendency, and to steer research toward problems of more general and immediate national interest, the United States has developed the technique of granting government and foundation money for research. This system, however, has its own defects. It encourages people to venture beyond their intellectual depths in order to get research money (also to organize big research teams that are not necessary to the purpose in hand

and are hard to administer) and to produce research results that are technically competent but of little value in relation to solving the original problem. Also, the foundations, because their administrative structure calls for regular turnovers of staff each new wave of which seeks to monumentalize itself by initiating something new and imaginative, exercise a disturbing influence on research by encouraging economists to embark on research endeavors that have no long-run future, incidentally leaving universities stranded with staff whose research interests are at variance with the university's central teaching responsibility.

Mention should also be made of those foundations that conduct research themselves, either in-house or on a contract basis. The most well known and influential of them, the National Bureau of Economic Research, which began as a powerful center for the quantitative study of business fluctuations, gradually became ossified and antiquated in its concepts and methods and is struggling to reestablish itself under new management. For a long time, however, it exercised a strong influence on the direction and character of American economic research. In particular, it has supported the work of Milton Friedman, leader of the "monetarist counterrevolution" (against the "Keynesian revolution"). More uniquely characteristic of the American scene, however, are a number of foundations devoted to the study of policy problems—the outstanding one being the Brookings Institution, which has played a very active entrepreneurial role in the funding of research in recent years. The studies supported by these foundations provide an ongoing independent research-and-theory based evaluation of policy problems and alternatives, something that governments do not have time for, and that in other countries nongovernmental agencies and academics lack the resources and the incentives to undertake.

For several reasons, the situation in the United Kingdom is very different. For one thing, the United Kingdom, with which I am most familiar, has been bitterly scarred by its historical experience. The period before World War I gave its economists the impression of an incredibly affluent society, in which context all sorts of free thought were possible and only the just distribution of the affluent income constituted a real economic problem. But two world wars, and the associated capital losses and recognition of superior American affluence, have closed in the intellectual perspectives of British economists. The problem is no longer to determine what is true about the economic side of society, but how to use economics to defend the British economy against the onslaught of adversity and how to work the miracle of restoring Britain to its former position of economic dominance (or at least respectability) in the world. Thus economics is converted from a scientific subject into a species of political necromancy.

Furthermore, as the affluence of the British (or European) economist declined, so did his political independence. There was a time when an economist was also a propertied gentleman; if asked for advice, he would give it—frequently he published it before being asked—but he was an independent citizen who did not identify himself with the country's rulers though he thought of himself as an equal. That situation has changed, again mostly as a result of two world wars and the emergence of the United States and Russia (and more recently China) as dominant world powers. The result has been that the national society has closed in on the economist, and he has lost his role as an independent citizen distinguished by his scholarly knowledge. Instead, he has tended to become an intelligent parrot, concerned either with maintaining that his country is still as great as it used to be—or could be if only it followed his advice—or with asserting that if it would only follow some policy adopted by the dominant countries, it could restore its greatness.

This politicization of the economist is not unrelated to the academic situation in the United Kingdom, where a B.A. plus some research time at a "good" university (rather than the Ph.D.) is all that is required for an academic post, so that there is no formal graduate training in research methods and little real emphasis on research other than as a minimal requirement for promotion and tenure. In addition, salary scales are more or less constant across the country, and salaries increase with age regardless of performance, apart from the points of major review: for tenure, for the lecturer efficiency bar, and for the possibility of elevation in rank to Senior Lecturer, Reader, and Professor. Service to a department and university rivals, and sometimes takes priority over, research performance as a criterion for promotion. Moreover, there is a tradition set by the Oxford tutorial and Cambridge supervision systems for undergraduates, that a teacher proves his academic quality by his ability to find fault with the published work of others, a tradition which inhibits the average academic from sticking his neck out by publication of research on any but the most innocuous and dull subjects, while at the same time giving free rein to charlatans who do not care what is said about them so long as their name is spelled correctly and they get a reputation for originality. The Oxbridge tradition, which involves training economists primarily for the civil service or politics, and only secondarily for academic careers, has also perpetuated a polarization of the profession into left wing and right wing which originated in the deep political tensions that rocked the country in the interwar period. This has been a pariculary serious impediment to scientific research and progress because both Oxford and Cambridge have been held by the left wing since the war, and through their eminence over other universities in British cultural and academic life, they set the public image of economics as a political subject and maintain it by the practice of applying political criteria to the assessment of scientific ability and achievement. One result has been to steer aspiring young economists out of mainstream economics into mathematical economic theory and theoretical econometrics, fields in which British economics has continued to maintain a reputation for international quality.

The general tendency in Britain toward desultory and dull work on unimportant problems is reinforced by the nature of research support, and more generally by the social position of the academic economist in relation to government. The imperial history of the country, and the two world wars through which it has passed, have created an ethos in which it is accepted on both sides that the academic is generally inferior both socially and intellectually to the civil servant—an acceptance reflected in the relative pay scales of the two. His function is to do humdrum research of mundane usefulness to government, applying whatever part of existing knowledge he has encountered and is capable of apprehending. The function even of the better academics is either to provide sophisticated rationalizations for government policy decisions or to provide new and challenging ideas on policy that government (or its opposition) might be able to use sometime. This function involves no research at all, only cleverness in making forensic use of other people's research for political purposes. In accordance with this socio-political structure, research money is available in austere amounts for applied research projects deemed socially useful; in much more generous amounts for applied research projects demonstrably useful to governments such as the construction of large-scale forecasting models of the British economy, represented by those of the National Institute for Economic and Social Research (which is essentially an indirect branch of government and produces virtually no basic economic research worthy of the name), and of the London Business School (the large University of Southampton model is designed for relationship-testing rather than forecasting); and in still more generous amounts for academic economists prepared to take leave from their universities and accept much higher-paid temporary employment in government in order to write policy-oriented papers that rarely if ever get published, except when necessary to refute academic criticisms of government policy decisions. It is no wonder that Britain has completely lost the reputation it established in the 1930s as the world center for the serious scientific study of economics, and that its only hope of regaining its repute lies in the small group of its economists who belong to the American-based world community of highly qualified and research-oriented scholars.

In Canada the colonial tradition still prevails: "Them as can, do; them as can't do, teach." The Canadian academic has an uneasy place in his national culture: his society believes that he is overpaid for the mere possession of knowledge and the imparting of it to the young. He has two alternatives. The majority choose to acquire still more learning without using it to raise any new questions about Canadian society, though they may legitimately use it to refute the wilder public answers to old questions, provided they do so decorously and without having any real impact on public opinion. A minority choose to abandon all academic standards and to use academic status as a platform from which to encourage the wildest of public emotions, especially in support of a form of nationalism which would guarantee its academic exponents academic promotion without academic delivery.

These tendencies are encouraged by the slackness of the university system itself. Most of the better young Canadian economists, by now, have been educated at American graduate schools; but of these, a large number regard acquiring a Ph.D. as an initiation rite into adulthood of an extremely painful kind that does not have to be repeated, while those who have acquired the scientific research orientation find that it has little payoff once they return to Canada. For Canadian universities have slack tenure and promotion practices, in which age and service to the university count for more than research performance, and there is little competition among universities for staff of superior qualifications. Research does, however, get done, as a result of the fairly generous funds available, but the research is not necessarily of a kind scientifically useful from a long run point of view. There are two main sources of funding. One is government, which finances research either directly for a summer vacation or for one or two years' leave or indirectly through successive Royal Commissions. This kind of research involves the application of existing techniques to applied policy problems and does little to advance basic knowledge in the science as a whole; concern has in fact been expressed in Canada about this aspect of the dominance of government funding of economic research. The other source is the Canada Council, which has ample funds without strings tying them to applied research, but which tends to grant applications which are essentially for comfortable sabbatical leaves rather than for serious research of general interest. Since many Canadian economists at the present time are immigrants from other countries, or else have been involved in granting foreign aid, much of the money goes in reality on travel grants. (This, of course, is not the fault of the Canada Council, but rather the fault of the Canadian university system for not requiring its academics to deliver a sustained research performance, but instead allowing them to regard a year of idling at someone else's expense as a just reward for involvement in undergraduate teaching and university administration.)

In Europe, the north (Scandinavia, the Netherlands, and Germany), where competence levels are high and research is well understood, must be differentiated from the south (particularly France and Italy), where research is misidentified with literary facility and a capacity for grandiloquent rhetoric. France, for example, lives on dreams of grandeur and on rhetoric instead of scientific analysis from its economists. Big prizes go to those so-called economists who can snatch ideas from the English literature and translate them into French concepts and the French language; and due to the unreality of French culture in relation to the rest of the world, prizes are often won by snatching unscientific pseudophilosophical ideas from the Anglo-Saxon world and translating them into even more pseudoscientific French. In this respect, the most esteemed French economists are the most fraudulent economic scientists. Any hope that France has of restoring the scientific repute it had before it expelled Walras to an exiled existence in Switzerland lies in the undervalued economists who staff its technical schools, and in the young English-language-oriented economists who have risen to positions of power as a result of the university expansion precipitated by the events of May 1968.

All of the European countries, however, have some common convictions (vestiges of which also remain in the United Kingdom, especially in the provincial universities): that research is a necessary requirement for obtaining a professorship, but not a requirement for retaining a professorship once acquired; that the research in question has to be approved by the reigning professor, and support his long past accomplishments and current prejudices; and that a professor, by virtue of his past research, must be an expert over the whole field of economics, an expectation which leads him to believe that he is competent to be such—a belief supported, in turn, by the deference accorded him by his obligatorily deferential students and by his fellow members of the elite. Academic research is not well funded; instead, it is subsidized heavily by the students who have to do it to make their own names and earn their professorships; and the subsidization extends to their professors, whose own research, such as it is, is largely extorted from the dependence of their students on their goodwill. It is thus not surprising that one encounters three types of Continental academic economists: the young man (probably not all that young by American standards, say late twenties or early thirties) who is extraordinarily competent and well-read because he is still striving to receive his professorship; the formerly promising young man who has turned into an incompetent blusterer, rhetorician, and public figure in his society; and a very few dedicated economists who have continued and built upon their youthful interest in scientific economics and research, often by moving out of the university environment into a research institute. (Of course, a European research institute is frequently merely a retirement home and annuity source for academics who are no longer able to compete in the main stream of their subject, and find solace in pursuing portentous pseudoresearch into nonresearchable amorphous topics.)

Despite a certain amount of criticism of my position, I maintain that economics has, in fact, become an English-language discipline. I would cite the career histories of any number of young European economists to prove that they got their professional start, and their comparative advantage over their contemporaries, by means of a shorter or longer visit to the United States, where they came into contact with real scientific economics. I personally wish that this were not so, that Europe could generate graduate training of a kind that could rival the United States not only in technique but in insight into economic problems. The technique is easy—any intelligent young man can learn mathematics and statistics—the real problem is to learn to observe and try to understand the economic system, not as it functions in one's own country, where one's vision of its functioning may be highly distorted by governmental policies that, as a citizen, one does not question, but as it functions in general. For that, one has to go to the United States, the only country where governmental policies are still not regarded as sacrosanct and where a man is not only free but encouraged to think of government policies as arbitrary interferences rather than as unquestioned national necessities.

Of the three factors mentioned earlier as influencing national styles in economic research—national culture and the economist's relation to it, university tenure and promotion systems, and outside funding for research— this paper has stressed the first two, though it has also paid attention to the third. In concluding, it is relevant to remark that concern with research is an extremely modern phenomenon in the history of the academic community. For the vast preponderance of that history up to modern times, what was valued was knowledge or "scholarship"—the possession of knowledge—not the capacity or determination to discover new knowledge. Different national styles, at least with respect to economic research, may be associated with each nation's position on the path of transition from valuation of a man for what he knows, whether or not that knowledge is useful and communicable, to valuation of a man for the new knowledge he can produce and communicate, whether or not he is a reputable scholar or a civilized member of the elite. From a social point of view, and in general terms, it is by no means clear that the latter standard of judgment is a better one than the former. Nor is it clear that the emphasis in recent years on high-technology scientific research in economics is independent of the fact that, as a result of the various intellectual revolutions of the 1930s and the interruption of the war years, economics was left with a vast amount of unfinished business, the execution of which, incidentally, was greatly accelerated by the introduction of computer technology. It may well turn out, in the near future, that the possibilities of acquiring useful new knowledge by further research along scientifically respectable computer-and-mathematics-oriented lines will play out, and that the world will discover that what it needs, after all, are political economists and not economic scientists.

10. Scholars as Public Adversaries: The Case of Economics

Introduction: An Economist's View of the Problem

The terms of reference for the study to which this essay is a contribution state:

> Unlike other social sciences, economics has achieved—or so it seems to the outsider—a working etiquette which allows people to disagree vigorously without engaging in recrimination about "unscientific" or "unprofessional" behavior. Moreover, the educated public seems well accustomed to the expectation that economists will disagree, and yet the status of economics as probably the hardest of the hard social sciences is unchallenged. How has this happened? What lessons, if any, can be drawn that might illuminate the situation in other social sciences?

These questions were further amplified as follows:

> Politically significant debate among scholars takes place often in explicitly political contexts. Scholars take sides before Congress, in public commissions, as advisers to the bureaucracy, before the press, with regard to issues such as the ABM controversy, wage-price guidelines, or poverty programmes. What issues affecting the authority and integrity of scholarship do such activities raise? It's hasty to assume that taking sides on a public issue is incompatible with objective scholarship and an honest examination of the alternatives. Nevertheless, partisanship may affect the selection of topics for research, the designing of the investigation, and the formulation of general conclusions based upon it. And this partisanship is all-the-more partisan, perhaps, when it is hidden, or disguised as "neutrality." The effects of involvement in controversial public issues with regard to the authority of scholarship therefore merit attention.

These two paragraphs defining the scope of this essay, read in reverse order and critically interpreted as an economist would criticize them, constitute in themselves a good starting point for the explanation sought. The reason is that they typify—or perhaps more fairly to the editor, accord academic respectability and potential validity to—an unsophisticated and

Reprinted with permission from Charles Frankel, ed., *Social Science Controversies and Public Policy Decisions*, a study prepared for the American Academy of Arts and Sciences, to be published by the Russell Sage Foundation.

primitive methodology that economics, at least in the United States, has long since outgrown. The second paragraph presents, in barely qualified form, the general hypothesis that participation in public policy discussions must be corruptive of scientific work and of the maintenance of scientific standards; the first expresses puzzlement that economics, which is more deeply involved in public discussion and formation than many other social sciences—with the exception of political science in the specific contexts of foreign policy formation and the winning of elections—seems to be an exception to this rule, and asks for an explanation. An economist would observe that the hypothesis is badly formulated to begin with, and that the fact that the strongest available expirical test falsifies it is strong evidence that the opposite hypothesis possesses more validity. The opposite hypothesis is that the stronger a social science is, the more its members can afford to participate in adversary debate over public policy issues without jeopardizing scientific integrity and freedom. There are several reasons for this: first, the scientific basis of the discipline helps to develop roles in relation to public policy formation that are scientific and politically neutral; second, because of the scientific base, scholars are well aware of what they and others are doing when they step outside academia into public policy discussion and advice, and can establish fairly clear lines of demarcation between scientific work and conclusions and political partisanship; and third, both the scientific base of the subject and the members of the scientific community operate to inhibit or police transgressions. These points will be illustrated in the following discussion.

The hypothesis of the second paragraph of definitions is badly formulated both in terms of fundamental conceptions and in detailed argument. Implicit in it is the academic concept of the pure scholar searching for truth. But the raw material of the social scientist is not nature but society; he has to draw his problems from events in society, of which many consist of public policy decisions and their consequences, and his task as a scientist is to develop general principles reliably governing the workings of society and elaborate on their applications to particular cases; and he has some obligations as a citizen or merely as a human being to feed some of his findings back into the social process. It is thus difficult either to define what purity in social science would be, or how public policy participation could corrupt it, in the terms traditionally conceived of for the natural sciences. Any such definition would have to run in terms of either violation of accepted scientific standards for the sake of partisanship, or diversion of effort to scientifically peripheral studies and excessive emphasis on application as contrasted with "pure" research—the latter alternative being difficult to define for reasons already given. Equally important, one must distinguish between the individual scholar and the scholarly community, and recognize the implications of the transition that has occurred from the few isolated scholars of past history to the large number of members in each social science discipline today.

To turn to the details of the second definitional paragraph, the various contexts of participation in politically significant debate listed in the first sentence carry widely different political overtones. Testifying before Congressional committees is commonly a matter of analyzing the nature of a problem and the alternative policies that might be adopted; and while their own values may lead individuals to different policy recommendations, the procedure is not so much adversary as competitive in the presentation of economic analysis, since ultimately it is Congress and not the winner of the case that makes policy. As to public commissions, economists connected with them are usually research staff engaged in scientific studies of relevant problems; economist members of commissions are usually appointed to represent their profession, and try to do so honestly, whereas if they are appointed on account of their political views these must have been at least as well known to the profession as to the government that appointed them, and will be appropriately discounted in professional assessments of the resulting report. Advice to the bureaucracy is usually engaged on the basis of professional expertise with respect to such matters as the effects of taxation, monetary policy, and foreign economic policy. Appearance before the communications media is typically a matter of explanation of economic policies and issues, though the willingness to explain often comes from political partisanship (though as citizen rather than as scientist). Not on the list, but probably the most potentially dangerous corrupting influence on economic science, is actual participation in the policy-decision process, since such participation confuses the sense of scientific integrity and objectivity in the need to achieve politically acceptable compromises, and turns the object of activity from scholarly understanding and inquiry to achieving effective influence on policymaking. (Very few indeed of economists who have served on the Council of Economic Advisers have returned quietly and happily to the calm of academic life.)

It is true enough that partisanship may affect the selection of topics for research, the designing of the investigation, and the formulation of general conclusions based upon it. However, it should be noted that, equally, partisanship may follow from the completion of a study embarked on for scientific reasons; and also that participation or partisanship in politically significant debate may suggest new problems that need to be tackled by scientific methods. Here the existence of the scientific community is relevant in several ways; on the one hand, it judges the value of research topics, the quality of the design and performance, and the scientific validity of the conclusions drawn; on the other hand, both the scientific demand for demonstration of originality of topic selection and competence in execution and inference of conclusions, and the scientific objective of basing general principles on as wide a body of tested evidence as possible, give value to the scientific study of problems even if their motivation or origination is partisanship.

After all this argumentation, which in a sense is an explanation of why economics is not seriously troubled by the problem of partisanship as envisaged in the overall study, it is necessary to state that the "outside view" of economics referred to in the Chairman's first paragraph is significantly rosier than the inside one, for two reasons. First, the view is based on economics as understood and practiced in the United States; economics elsewhere is very different, and especially in the United Kingdom, which used to be the leader of the subject. The reasons include such factors as the much larger scale and more advanced professionalization of American economics, the politicization of British economics in the 1930s which has continued in Oxbridge ever since (in the U. S. a similar politicization went less deep and was halted by the McCarthy era), and the difference between a congressional and a parliamentary system of government. (In the latter, the majority government makes economic policy, and the minority opposition has to criticize it, so that economists' participation in policy formation has inevitably to be partisan or considered such if conducted from the outside, and can be conducted from the inside only by joining the bureaucracy, exception being made for the odd consultant and royal commission.)[1] Second, recriminations about "unscientific" or "unprofessional" conduct are significantly present in the United States, though they typically relate to the adequacy or validity of the evidence alleged to support policy conclusions and are fought out in the professional journals and meetings. There are also cases of an eminent economist bending his economics to support his political party in public speeches or debates; but control over this is exercised through the gossip grapevine, which spreads news of such lapses from scientific integrity. No economist can get away for very long by disguising partisanship as "neutrality." In fact, as will be explained below, economics long ago outgrew the phase of believing that an individual could achieve neutrality, and has come to rely on mutual policing by the members of the profession or on the revelatory effects of competition of biases for attention.

The Evolution of Economics Into A Social Science

How has economics developed to the point where it maintains its own confidence and its public reputation as a science while being able to engage extensively in public policy debate and public policy formation? Part of the explanation lies in its subject matter, which is in a sense more "objective" and amenable to logical and empirical analysis than those of the other social sciences, and to its scope and method, which have from the start been concerned with whole societies as such rather than with the analysis of groups or individuals in society, and with the study of complex contemporary societies (illuminated, of course, by historical knowledge) rather than with the small and apparently simple and static primitive societies that intrigued the scholars and thinkers of social sciences generally. A different angle of approach to the same point is to say that in a world evolving from feudalism into the national state, economic issues were more important—and were realized earlier to be important enough to deserve analysis, because they were immediately vital to the survival of the nation-state—than were the issues that concern the other social sciences, which assume the continued existence of the nation-state (or of primitive societies) and are matters of internal social organization rather than of external survival.[2] (This indeed may be a fundamental factor in the explanation of the problem set: economics is too important to the state for governments and the public not to expect experts to disagree over important and difficult problems.)

The remarks in the preceding paragraph are essentially static observations on the social sciences, whereas the question is posed in terms of evolution. To answer the dynamic question properly would require a tremendous knowledge of both economics, in the sense of mainstream economics as the core of economic science, and of the evolving social context in which economics itself evolved. The following sketchy treatment of the subject is confined to English-language economics, which fortunately has been dominant in the historical evolution of the subject—though with important importation of and incorporation of general equilibrium theory, capital theory, and monetary theory from various European traditions after the First World War—the lead being taken by the British classical and neoclassical traditions and in the 1930s the "Keynesian revolution" up until somewhere in the late 1930s, and then shifting decisively to the United States as a result of the involvement of British economists in the economic management of the British war effort and subsequent involvement in British politics and economic policy, on the one hand, and of the vastly greater numbers of well-trained American economists on the other.

While both British and American economists had from time to time before the Great Depression of 1929 onwards been involved in public policy formation, it was almost exclusively as expert witnesses before or professionally representative members of public commissions. (It is necessary to emphasize, though, that the subject was from the start concerned with public policy issues. Adam Smith, founder of the subject, enunciated the doctrines of laissez faire; Malthus produced his population theory as an answer to the utopian socialism of William Godwin; Ricardo enunciated the principle of freedom of trade; and later Marshall, Sidgwick, and especially Pigou turned utilitarianism into a case for policies to reduce the inequality of income distribution.) It was not until after the Great Crash that governments began to seek the help of economists in solving immediate issues of public policy—as distinct from long-run issues of economic organization—and economists became extensively involved in the kind of political participation with which this study is concerned.

By that time, and indeed since the emergence into dominance of the neoclassical (marginal utility and marginal productivity) school in the last third of the nineteenth century, economics had a hard and consistent scientific core of both real and monetary theory.[3] It thus should have been ready to cope with the new public policy demands being made on it. Unfortunately, the monetary theory, while a logically beautiful and sophisticated structure, rested on the assumption that the economy reacted quickly enough to monetary changes to maintain full employment of labor, so that such disturbances would produce price changes and not fluctuations in employment. And, faced with the fact of mass unemployment caused essentially by monetary deflation (which prevailed in England from the First World War on and throughout the capitalist world from 1929 until the Second World War), instead of questioning their assumptions about price flexibility and admitting that real quantities rather than their prices might do the adjustment to monetary disturbance, they sought for explanations in terms of real factors such as excessively high real wages or a glutting of wants. These explanations appeared as silly and stupid to the public as they in fact were in terms of scientific method (if the facts do not fit the predictions of the relevant theory, reexamine the assumptions of that theory rather than retreat into an alternative theory).

The correct answer, scientifically, was provided by Keynes: wages and prices are "sticky" and quantities bear most of the brunt of short-run adjustment. But Keynes's answer, aside from being cluttered with new terminology and concepts and specifically British controversies that produced much bitter but on the whole fruitless scientific debate, disregarded the background of monetary deflation that had produced the problem of mass unemployment, and instead made mass unemployment the characteristic condition of a capitalist society. This proposition was quickly seized on by economists of socialist persuasion. In addition, Keynes pointed to certain conditions under which expansionary monetary policy would be incapable of producing full employment, and government expenditure involving budget deficits might be necessary to this end. These propositions were quickly translated by his followers, especially the Americans led by Alvin Hansen of Harvard, into the proposition that monetary policy was powerless and that fiscal policy (specifically deficit financing) was necessary to the management of a capitalist economy, the reverse of the traditional view that government, like private citizens, should balance its budget and that the central bank and not the Treasury should be responsible for stabilizing the economy.[4]

Both messages made the scientific division between Keynesian and "orthodox" economists a political division between radicals and conservatives, and this division has survived into present times, though it has gradually ceased to exercise the strong influence on both academic appointments and or politicians' choices of economic advisers and evaluation of economic advice that it once had.[5] Three reasons for the fairly rapid erosion of the sharpness of the adversary conflict of the 1930s and early postwar period can be adduced.

First, Keynesian economics proved essential to wartime economic management, though the reason was less the theory itself than the fact that it emphasized "real" aggregate variables and relationships, rather than "monetary," and so indicated that the crucial wartime problem was the allocation of labor among armed forces and productive sectors (an approach that Keynes himself had espoused during the British conscription debate in the First World War and successfully got implemented as government economic adviser in the Second World War) and that the monetary and financial side of wartime management should be secondary to the real side and coordinated with it. This emphasis was right, and gave Keynesian economists a lasting edge over the more orthodox financial approach in terms of levying additional taxes and raising war loans, even though the postwar consequences of Keynesian war finance proved strongly inflationary.

Second, and most important, the problem of capitalist countries since the war has been of a chronic tendency toward inflationary excess demand for labor; hence the debate has become one of a little more versus a little less unemployment in the management of the economy, a practical problem in the management of a capitalist system as contrasted with the 1930s debate on whether capitalism could produce satisfactory results without radically new methods of management. Since this is a question which politicians have to decide, and advice on which does not threaten the system from which they derive their political power, and moreover a question on which there are legitimate reasons for differences of opinion which have to be evaluated, economists pronouncing or testifying on the issues can disagree in public without jeopardizing their status as scientific experts. (Indeed, the fact that they can give both logical expression to and quantitative information on considerations that the politician or civil servant senses only vaguely may be important, probably enhances the public esteem of economics as a scientific subject.)

Third, the Keynesians commanded the most prestigious economics departments (Oxford and Cambridge in Britain, Harvard in the United States); and, what is perhaps more important, those that attracted the best graduate students. Through successive generations of undergraduates, particularly in the United Kingdom, Keynesian economics become part of the intellectual culture of the elite and eventually of common culture. Through successive generations of graduate students who become academic teachers and economic civil servants, it gradually conquered academic economics and became the orthodoxy on the macroeconomic side of economics. There was, however, and remains, a noteworthy difference between the United Kingdom and the United States in the way in which Keynesian economics came to dominate, relevant to the problem of this study. In the United Kingdom it remained politicized and identified with the left wing in politics; and it became dominant through the left-wing Keynesian conquest of Oxford and Cambridge and the automatic control over the minds of prospective civil servants, politicians and academics and of academic appointments in other universities that Oxbridge commands. The orthodox tradition was less reasoned with than stamped out or retired without replacement, the process resting on the fact that, in contrast to the United States, graduate work involving formal instruction and leading to a formal graduate degree has not been a requirement of either academic or civil service employment until very recently (less than a decade ago). Hence economic advice is regarded in Britain as political advice, sought from economists of proven loyalty to the party or, if offered uninvited, treated as propaganda for the government or the opposition party, and discounted as such, with the effect that in Britain economics is publicly regarded not as a science but as a set of ground rules and techniques for a rather arcane type of political debate, and the economist enjoys far less public respect (if any) than does his American counterpart. (In fact, the public respect he gets is proportioned to his academic rank and the public status of his university, and not to his professional accomplishment.)[6] In the United States, on the other hand, with its large size and democratic tradition, its large number of good universities, and its already long-established tradition of formal graduate instruction leading to a Ph.D., drawing students from all over the country, as the prerequisite for academic appointment or for appointment to good prospects in the civil service, it was impossible for Keynesian economics to conquer the profession and the country by conquering one or two major universities. Even if it had been, the standards of professionalism already achieved by American economics, together with the pragmatism characteristic of pioneer societies, would have prevented the parading of political partisanship as neutral scientific recommendation. In the United States, Keynesianism had to compete for attention with the more orthodox approaches (sometimes, as in the case of "institutionalism," more radical approaches) on the scientific grounds of being able to produce better answers to scientific problems. And, in a competitive process, one attempts to take over and use as many of one's competitors' good ideas as one can, while still advertising that one is producing a far better product than he. Hence, in the United States, Keynesianism became dominant in economic science on the basis of its scientifically valid and useful new ideas, as sifted by the competition among and judgment of the economic scientific community, rather than on the basis of its political overtones or of an all-or-nothing choice between Keynesianism and professional success, and orthodoxy and professional failure.

In an important sense, "we [economists] are all Keynesians now," scientifically; but this permits, on the one hand, plenty of room for scientific debate over specific theoretical and empirical issues and, on the other hand, economists' identification of themselves alternatively as Keynesians or monetarists as a statement of personal political orientation which reflects no basic disagreements on the nature and methods of economic theory and enquiry and which therefore, when exposed to the public in the context of public policy debate and policy formation, does not detract from the public esteem of economics, because it displays the esteem that eminent economists have for each other—the only possible basis for reasoned debate among them—far more than it advertises disagreements among them on political stances or the diagnosis of particular cases calling for the application of economic analysis. The public, after all, is accustomed to the idea that medical doctors may disagree on the diagnosis of and prescription for a particular patient, without losing its general respect for the medical profession; and it also believes that that profession is genuinely concerned about the patient's health, and that the patient's doctor is not motivated by the desire to kill him in order to inherit his wealth.

The foregoing account relates to the central issue that has divided economists into bitter scientific controversy in this century—the causes of mass unemployment and the policies required to deal with it. But once, either as a result of good economic fortune or of the acceptance and application of Keynesian analysis,[7] the economy returns to and maintains a normal state of full employment, the "real" economics of resource allocation subject to overall limitation of available quantities of resources—the crowning achievement of the evolution of economics from Smith's *Wealth of Nations* to Marshall's *Principles of Economics* and Pigou's *Economics of Welfare*, which may be regarded as the flowering of neoclassical economics—comes into its own again.[8] This is for two reasons: first, apart from the conditions of a great depression such as followed the Great Crash of 1929, in which idle resources could be reemployed at no social cost, and the capacity of man to satisfy his wants thereby improved, the natural condition of man is a shortage of resources and the necessity of making choices among alternative uses of them—and this is what the science of economics is fundamentally concerned about, both as a positive (descriptive) and normative (prescriptive) analysis of the results and implications of these choices; second, by far the majority of the policy issues that concern the public and the politicians pertain to questions of resource allocation and the effects of resource allocation on the incomes of individuals and social groups (e.g., farm price supports, tariff policy, government regulation of industry, minimum wage laws), except in transitory periods of either mass depression or abnormal inflation, both of which disrupt private and social calculations of optimal allocations, and also lead to the mistaken effort to use microeconomic resource allocation policies to compensate and correct for errors of macroeconomic policy. (For example, during the stagnation and abnormal unemployment period of the early 1960s, the idea that unemployment was due to automation or to inadequate education of workers became very popular; in the late 1960s and earlier 1970s, the idea that inflation was due to the greediness of monopolies and trade unions became equally popular. In both cases the result was the adoption of policies that distorted resource allocation without correcting the fundamental error in macroeconomic policy.)

In the context of microeconomic resource allocation policies (assuming that macroeconomic policy is being managed reasonably satisfactorily), the problem in establishing an economic science as distinct from a political propaganda is to separate the value judgments of individual economists from the scientific logic and the empirical facts established by the methodology of the subject, and to develop a methodology for establishing those facts. From this point of view, three episodes in the history of the development of economics are important.

First, as already mentioned, the neoclassical economists of the late nineteenth and early twentieth centuries, basing themselves on utilitarianism and the hedonistic calculus, believed firmly that a more equal distribution of income would contribute to an increased social welfare in the same sense and on the same grounds of scientific principle as would an all-around increase in individual incomes. Thus the desirability of income redistribution from rich to poor became one of the presumed scientific findings of economics—and remains so both in the minds of many economists and in popular economic mythology. Lionel Robbins, in his *Nature and Significance of Economic Science*, published at the beginning of the 1930s, exploded this belief by pointing out that it required interpersonal judgments of the welfare of individuals—specifically that an extra dollar for a rich man adds less to total welfare than an extra dollar for a poor man—which the economist as scientist is not entitled to make. A number of younger now eminent economists attempted to get around this point by proposing "compensation tests" of economic changes—that is, a change is an improvement if the gainers could compensate the losers—but this was a logically unacceptable dodge unless the compensation were actually made, which it normally is not or cannot be. The resulting "new welfare economics" arrived at the position that potentially welfare could be improved but actually it might not be, by a change that increased total output. This implied that the economist could usually say nothing about the effects of changes on economic welfare, and therefore nothing about economic policy. But nature abhors a vacuum, or a position of abstention from the social process of those engaged in under-standing it. The end result has been that economists are conscious that their own values are not necessarily those of society, and that they need informa-tion on society's values in order to make policy recommendations.

An alternative view of this matter, propounded by Gunnar Myrdal and still influential among his followers in Sweden, Oxford, and elsewhere, is that a social scientist should state his personal values at the beginning of his work on a problem, and leave it to the readers to evaluate his conclusions in the light of knowledge of his values. The difficulty with this solution is that any real social scientist who was aware of his own biases would attempt to prevent them from interfering with the objectivity of his work. Consequently the serious problem concerns the biases the individual has that he is not himself aware of, and no amount of introspection can make him aware of. (Myrdal's own work exemplifies the failure of the methodology he propounds.)

Myrdal's position on the problem of individual values in the social sciences parallels a larger debate over social science methodology initiated by Mannheim's *Sociology of Knowledge* and answered by Popper's *Open Society and Its Enemies*. Essentially, Popper's argument as it relates to the present study is that the problem of values is to be overcome, not by investigating values themselves, and attempting to develop a "value-free" social science, but by applying the tests of scientific experimentation and proof. In short, it is the community of scholars policing and accepting or rejecting each other's work, according to scientific standards of verification, not the individual scholar researching his own soul, that produces a social science that is genuinely scientific and not propagandistic. Of course, to Popper's Marxist opponents, this reply has the limitation that social restrictions on entry to the social sciences may produce a community of scholars that is thoroughly scientific in its approach to the questions it asks, but blind to certain kinds of questions, especially those raising fundamental issues about the nature and justification of the existing economic organization of society. One can indeed argue both that the McCarthy era in America strengthened economics in the United States as a hard social science, by squelching the freedom of scholars to ask questions of this kind and forcing them to concentrate their attention on the more innocuous question of how the capitalist system works (or by confining the rewards of the academic career to those interested in the latter type of question), and laid the profession open to legitimate student protest when American capitalism lost its self-confidence as a result of the war in Viet Nam. On the other hand, it was the Marxists who initiated the debate by claiming to found their analysis of capitalist self-contradiction on a scientific economic base, and Popper was thoroughly justified in challenging their assertion that no economic science other than Marxism could exist in a capitalist society, combined with their failure to satisfy the standards of science itself.

Popper's book, though largely unread now, constituted the second relevant episode in the recent development of economic science. The third was the methodology of positive economics propounded by Milton Friedman in his *Essays on Positive Economics* (University of Chicago Press, 1953)—though its roots lie in a book by Keynes's father, John Neville Keynes, *On the Scope and Method of Political Economy*, published before the turn of the century. The background of Friedman's contribution was the climate of economic debate that grew out of two revolutions in economic thought that occurred in the 1930s—the Keynesian revolution already referred to, and a somewhat prior "revolution," known variously as the imperfect or monopolistic competition revolution (the two terms incorporate the key adjectives in the titles of two books published almost simultaneously by the Cambridge economist Joan Robinson and the Harvard economist E. H. Chamberlin.) The Keynesian revolution, as already explained, attacked the assumption of neoclassical economics that capitalism tends to produce full employment. The imperfect/monopolistic competition revolution attacked the assumption of neoclassical value theory that competition tended to produce the lowest-cost production of goods for consumers, and payments to the owners of factors of production equal to their contributions to the social product, on the grounds that in the real world of observation firms had some degree of monopoly power. As a consequence, it became standard practice among self-proclaimedly radical economists to attack their more orthodox opponents on the basis of the "unrealism" of their assumptions about the nature of the real world. Friedman's positive methodology asserted that the question to be asked of a theory is not whether its assumptions are realistic or otherwise, but whether it possesses predictive power. This position too has some philosophical difficulties, since the assumptions of one theory may be the predictions of another, and the methods for testing predictions are themselves controversial, but it did a great deal to shift the emphasis of economics from the interpretation of the economic system to the ability to say something about how it works.

The importance of these background episodes, however, can only be appreciated in relation to the vast increase in the numbers of competent professional economists that has occurred since the 1930s. The United States, in particular, now has perhaps fifty economics departments of an average quality comparable to the average quality of the four or five best departments in the whole world in the pre–World War Two period (though not, it should be remarked, ten times the number of really original minds, because one of the laws of intellectual society is that originality is measured by comparison with the average, and the higher the average the fewer comparatively are those rated as genuinely original.) The consequence of this expansion is that, in contrast to the preceding period when academic scholars in economics could set themselves up as across-the-board personal adversaries expounding conflicting holistic views of the subject, the modern economist's adversary is a faceless host of his professional colleagues; and to be effective he must accept most of what they accept and choose carefully a limited piece of the territory on which to challenge them collectively.[9] For this very reason economists can afford to engage in public debate over policy issues without sacrificing either their own reputations among their colleagues or the reputation of their science among the public at large.

The Lessons to Be Drawn

On the stipulation that lessons have to be drawn, the main lesson for the other social sciences to be drawn from the experience of economics would seem very strongly to be that participation in the public policy formation process will be less corruptive of the scientific work and of the public reputation of a social science, the more of a science it is and the larger the scientific community it comprises. The problem of the other social sciences from the viewpoint of the economist—to the extent that there is one—is that individuals become qualified as "scientists" competent to hold academic posts by virtue of an ill-specified academic process, and thereafter feel free to abuse their academic positions in advocacy of their personal and social prejudices, without being subject to the discipline of the judgment of a professionally trained and scientifically competent academic community agreed on the nature of scientific procedures as applied to their discipline and armed with an extensive body of well-tested and validated empirical knowledge. With no real science at his command, but with the pretense of having one, the academic pseudo-scientist can command undue attention for his own propaganda at the expense of exposing his alleged science to public contempt for the pseudo-science it is, and also of demeaning the efforts of his more scientifically minded and responsible colleagues to improve its scientific status by honest hard work. The key to individual policy participation without scientific community degradation is to have a profession that has a common scientific core; and this means a consistent body of theory validated by empirical knowledge and testing and policed by professionals, in place of a congeries of conflicting untested hypotheses carrying conviction proportional to the persuasive power of their proponents.[10]

11. The University and Social Welfare

The natural response of the economist, faced with political pressures to reduce the costs of higher education and worried about the implications of more severe budgetary constraints for his own and his department's welfare and freedom of action, is to look at the question of efficiency, with the idea that increased efficiency could reconcile the political pressures and the academic resistances to them to the general satisfaction. There are obvious inefficiencies in the university education system.

In a sense, it is only too easy to apply to the university the economist's usual tools of analysis, and especially the ideas of the price-system as a universal solvent of efficiency problems, and of the university as a potential profit-maximizing competitive firm. It is not so easy to do it with adequate appreciation either of the complexity of the objectives a university is supposed to serve in the contemporary community, or of the conflicting interests of the outside social groups which in one way or another influence both the financial support and the government of universities, or of the conflicting interests of the groups inside the university for whose activities it caters.

The purpose of this paper is to attempt to provide a map of this territory, as a preliminary to a study of the issues.

The Functions of a University

The university has many different functions in society. The most general is as a symbol and repository of "civilization," that is, a demonstration that the society is civilized both in the sense of actively belonging to Western culture, and in the sense of being both able and willing to afford the support of scholarship out of the surplus of its resources over subsistence. In addition, the university is thought of as contributing in some vague sense to the advancement of civilization, by either setting standards of taste for the rest of the population or enabling the rest of the population to increase its productivity, income, and command over consumption goods, or both. In this sense, a university is a public good, broadly like good weather or pleasant

Reprinted with permission from *Minerva* 11, no. 1 (January 1973): 30–52.

geography (which, however, cost no resources to produce), or like a forest reserve, an efficient police force, judiciary, or an army (which do).

This general function is to be distinguished from the performance of tangible social and economic functions, for which it is possible at least in principle to specify benefits which can be related to costs. This is important in any discussion of efficiency in universities, because it justifies on both sides the support of universities by both private and public subscriptions of resources, regardless of considerations of efficiency, as long as universities behave as they are traditionally expected to do and as most other universities do. In this respect, the support of universities is like adherence to a religion or church—the benefit is incalculable and problematical, but it is wise to insure against unknown risks.

Second, a university is a home for research. The products of research are a public good in the strict economic sense that once produced they can be used by anyone without precluding use by others. This poses the standard economic problem of how to finance research. It has to be financed somehow, but if it is financed by allowing those who do it a monopoly over the use of the results, the amount of it will be too small in quantity and its composition biased toward the applied research with the maximum privately appropriated results, and the social use of it will be inefficient to the extent that a charge for private benefit is made for something which costs society nothing for another person to use. The university, which generates research as a by-product of its scholarly activities and has a nonfinancial (prestige and promotion) reward system which entails the research product being made freely available to any potential user, solves the problem by the optimal method—public support of research allied with cost-free availability of the results—at the expense of leaving open the two questions of efficiency in deciding the allocation of research effort by leaving it to be decided by individual scholars motivated by scholarly standards of what is worth doing.

A third important function of the university is information storage. In the earlier history of universities, books were expensive and scarce, and still scarcer were the persons who had the time to read them and the wit to understand them. Knowledge was stored both in collections of expensive books and in learned men who had read all or most of the relevant ones. Nowadays, books are relatively cheap and plentiful and many persons have both the capacity to read them and the normal intelligence required to understand them. But this simply creates the same problem in another form: housing a large enough collection of books in a way readily accessible to those who want or might want to use them requires both large capital and advanced technology, and knowledge either of the books relevant to a particular problem or of how to locate them quickly remains a scarce and expensive talent. (There is, further, the fact that much modern scholarship requires not published books but data and the facilities for using them for computation.)

The fourth, and most clearly and popularly recognized function of the university at present, is the teaching of young adults. This includes two types of teaching: professional training, preparing a person for a career which he or she has already decided to embark on, and general education, preparing a person for a future position in the upper ranks of society. Economically, general university education can be thought of as consisting in some mixture of current consumption (i.e., an enjoyable way of passing a few years before assuming adult responsibilities in the economy), the formation of consumption capital (i.e., development of more sophisticated standards of taste and a capacity for more discriminating choice among later alternatives of consumption), and the formation of production capital ("human capital," i.e., the capacity to contribute more productive service to the economy, and hence to earn more future income, than would be possible in the absence of the university education).

In the case of professional education—medicine, law, engineering, and most of the natural and physical sciences—the human capital element predominates, though the elements of current consumption and of the formation of consumption-capital are also present, being derived from the fact that the professional training is provided within the broader, humanistically oriented framework of the university. In the case of general education—the arts and humanities and social sciences—there is considerable room for disagreement as to which element predominates or should predominate; and such disagreement motivates much of the contemporary tensions between university spokesmen anxious to preserve their traditional independence and government spokesmen anxious to ensure that the taxpayer who pays the bill receives something tangible for his money. From an economic point of view, there are three possible hypotheses regarding the main economic function of general university education, each pointing in a different direction of public policy toward universities and university policies themselves.

The Economic Functions of University Education: Three Hypotheses

The first is the hypothesis of "maturation." This asserts that the main purpose of the university is to provide students with the opportunity to grow to adulthood in surroundings which will broaden their minds and heighten their sensibilities. (Suitable choice of marriage partners among a wide range of prospective candidates is one aspect of this process, and from a long-range genetic point of view might well be the main contribution which a modern university, or at least the vast majority with no special claim to excellence of academic teaching and research, might make to the improvement of mankind's economic and social existence. Universities, by facilitating marriages among the intelligent, breed higher intelligence, though an unfortunate by-product seems to be a higher incidence of physical and mental handicaps among the resulting offspring.) On the hypothesis of maturation, what the university offers is a cultural ambience, direct contact with first-rate intellects, and the opportunity for tutored reading of books written by other first-rate minds. It does not matter much what is taught, provided the teacher knows the literature, logic, or technical apparatus of his subject and is prepared to spend enough of his time in personal contact with his students.

Research is his method of proving his competence, and of acquiring and maintaining up-to-date knowledge of his field, but it should nevertheless be secondary to and motivated by his pedagogical responsibilities. Both pure research motivated by idle curiosity, and, even more clearly, applied research undertaken for commercial gain, detract from his responsibilities as a teacher and should not be encouraged; and if allowed, should be financed otherwise than from the university's budget for teaching. (Curiosity-impelled research might also be condoned as eccentric self-indulgence, provided it is conducted in the teacher's leisure time.) This hypothesis, it should be noted, is both most directly in line with the medieval conception of a university as a place where scholars studied and argued with each other and allowed students to come and listen if they were interested and could afford it, and most favorable to the academic "ideal," since the only test of efficiency it suggests is scholarly excellence (as contrasted with the economist's and the government's test of the cost of producing persons of specified educational characteristics). But in a university system in which parents or their children do not pay directly for the opportunity to mature in a university environment, but instead all parents pay taxes for some gifted children to be allowed that opportunity, the questions of scale, efficiency, and tangible social benefit are bound to be raised about what is clearly a luxury good for the students provided as a by-product of a luxurious (and parasitic) way of living for the staff.

The second hypothesis is the "filtering" hypothesis, analyzed recently in rigorous theoretical terms by Professor Kenneth J. Arrow but familiar through the Mandarin Chinese system of civil service selection by competitive examination in classical Chinese scholarship; this underlies much of the philosophy of the British university system as it is now organized. In broad outline, this hypothesis asserts that society has "good jobs" and "bad jobs" to offer, and that it has somehow to select from the general population those who deserve the "good jobs." Higher education adds nothing to a man's or woman's original capacity to fill a "good job"; it is simply a screening device or obstacle course which contenders for the "good jobs" must pass through in order to qualify. Since the same number will eventually wind up in "good jobs" anyway, the unsuccessful candidates will have wasted their time, and the cost of the screening process, in terms both of staff and student time and of real resources, can be easily increased, at least up to the point where even a candidate certain of success does not find it economically attractive to compete, without (by assumption) any effect in increasing the gross output of the economy; this clearly raises problems of efficiency. The problem, broadly speaking, is to achieve a combination of probability of failure and rigor of the filtering tests which will minimize the total cost, including the waste of time and resources and the disappointment of the unsuccessful, while maintaining the apparent reasonableness of the filter itself as an exacting obstacle course. This suggests, incidentally, a rationale for both the recent efforts of university students everywhere to "water down" the rigor of course contents, examinations, and course prerequisites, and the British government's current pressure on British universities to turn out B.A.'s more quickly and cheaply. In both cases, the implicit presumption is that university admission constitutes the major part of the filtering process, and that the degree itself, including the final grade achieved, is primarily an official certification of what was known about the candidate at the time of admission.

The third hypothesis is the "human capital" hypothesis. According to this, attendance at a university adds value to a person's potential productive contribution to the economic system, and is to be regarded as an investment in one particular form of society's stock of productive assets or capital. This view best fits the professional training activity of universities, but it runs into serious difficulty both in specifying what an arts education actually teaches which improves productivity, and in assessing the role of research in improving the teaching performance of university teachers. It also has difficulty with the necessity of distinguishing between the possibility that a student performs well in examinations because he was a good student to begin with and would have learned the relevant material without any help from the teaching staff, and the possibility that he performs well because he has been taught things which he otherwise would not have learned. This distinction corresponds to the economist's distinction between the value of the sales of a firm—which might consist mostly of the cost of raw materials and other purchased inputs used, the extreme example being that of a dealer who sells the products of others for a small commission—and the value added by the firm to its purchased inputs (the dealer's commission for bringing producer and consumer together). Universities have a marked preference for selecting the best available students, as judged by admission qualifications, rather than the most teachable poorly qualified students, so that the staff of an "excellent" university might merit no credit, while a "mediocre" or "backwoods" university might be doing an excellent job of teaching, even though it never produces a first-class graduate qualified to go to a first-class graduate school or destined for a high business or political career. Be that as it may, the human capital approach, at least in its simplest and most naïve (though still scientifically respectable) form, raises the question of university efficiency in a direct and economically sensible form. If the function of a university is to turn out graduates understanding a particular field of specialization up to a particular level of competence, or graded according to defined levels of competence, what is the most efficient way of doing it? How long should it take? Is the traditional structure of the academic year, geared to a past of agricultural pursuits and slow transport between home and university, superior to the industrial practice of year-round work with one short vacation, though the work is frequently characterized by seasonal spurts and respites? What courses are really necessary as prerequisites to others in a training program? What is the optimal combination of reading, lectures, classes, and tutorials? Should lectures be "live," or recorded on tape, or video-taped for minimum cost of adequate instruction? At what point does enrollment in relation to cost of staff and other overheads, combined with quality of output, make a course or a whole department uneconomic and its discontinuation desirable? How many graduates of given specifications will the market absorb at remunerative prices for their services?

Obstacles to Efficiency

Once we can define the type and quantity of product desired, we can proceed to apply all the economist's techniques of cost-benefit analysis and efficiency evaluation, together with his understanding of how markets can be made to ensure social efficiency by giving the appropriate incentives to private choice, to improving the efficiency of university education. But there are three major snags. First, many politically important groups, including many parents and students as well as many members of university staff and administration, do not accept the view that the primary function of the university is to produce graduates of clearly defined attributes suitable for convenient insertion as well-rounded pegs into the round-hole job opportunities offered by business and government. Second—and a good reason for the contrary view—it is not clear either that the essence of a university education can be broken down into the attainment of specified levels of comprehension of either courses or subjects measured at the immediate point of completion of an examination or series of examinations, or that the attainment of specific bodies of knowledge as measured by conventional university standards results in a corresponding income-earning capacity in the future. Rumination and reflection on the one hand, motivation or ambition on the other, may be more important. Third—especially in Britain—the price system which is applied to the allocation of effort by both teachers and students contains many elements of arbitrary subsidy or tax. For example, why should a teacher spend much time in private conversation with students when his salary is conditional only on delivering a standard number of formal teaching hours, his promotion depends on his research publications, and after a certain point his salary is quite independent of his own efforts. And why should a student study hard when his grant or fellowship is conditional only on meeting a minimum standard of examination performance. Superior teaching is difficult for colleagues to evaluate while published papers are generally evaluated according to the status of the journal or the number of pages rather than content; student "swatting" is socially disapproved of among students as dangerously competitive, while the ability to pass examinations without apparent effort is generally admired, without reference to the difference between potential and actual performance. For such reasons as these, it is virtually impossible to determine whether the introduction of more competitive pricing somewhere in the system will actually generate more rather than less efficiency.

The final function of a unversity, and one which imposes an extremely difficult obstacle to a consideration of means of increasing university efficiency, is to redistribute income from the community in general toward its youthful, intelligent and studiously inclined citizens, on the presumption that these are on the average poor and deserving, or else poor but potentially useful to society. This attitude goes back to the Middle Ages, when the church, the state, and the landed nobility needed continual recruitment of literate, numerate, and generally scholarly and rational employees for their service, and had a monopoly of the posts available to propertyless students. In those circumstances, it was a good investment for the rich either to pay privately for the education of particularly gifted and poor children, or even—especially for the monarch—to endow the education of gifted and poor children in general—disregarding the moral virtue which the Christian religion attributed to such acts of charity. In modern times, however, given the availability of familial resources, personal earnings, and capital markets as means of financing higher education and nearly perfect competition, or at least, the absence of monopoly, it is highly questionable whether the subsidizing of higher education for the children of poor families who prove academically capable of attaining university admission is socially desirable, since such students are virtually guaranteed access to the high-income groups of society. It is far more questionable whether, if the objective is the relief of undeserved poverty, the subsidy to higher education should be given without a means test, on the basis of educational qualification, through a general publicly financed subsidy to education which reduces tuition fees to a point well below the level of costs. In fact, a large body of research indicates that this particular income subsidy involves a transfer from the poor (and some of the very rich) to the middle class. Nevertheless, there prevails a strong belief that universities ought to price the education they offer so as to subsidize the poor student. (Thus, private American universities think that they must not raise fees without earmarking some of the resulting revenue for increased scholarships, and the Independent University in Britain has been obliged, at considerable risk to its financial position, to provide generously for scholarships, though its original intention was to have the students take out loans to pay their fees.) The result of this belief in the accepted principles for the setting of tuition fees is appreciable artificiality in both student choices and staff behavior, which makes the achievement of efficiency in university education extremely difficult. Why should teachers be concerned about efficiency in teaching students who do not pay the costs anyway, and why should students be concerned about the efficiency of their teachers when others than themselves pay the costs of inefficiency?

External Interest Groups

The traditional Anglo-American conception of the university is that it is a self-governing community of scholars, in large part self-financed or some-times subsidized by the willingness of its scholars to live humbly for the sake of pursuing truth; and drawing upon outside funds, in the form of student fees or endowments, which were voluntarily subscribed by students interested in learning or donors motivated by charitable and religious feelings of obligation which carried no reciprocal rights of control and management. What disputes there were lay either between students and teachers, or between the university and the church—the latter giving rise to the concept of academic freedom. The university persisted in this pattern more or less into modern times, though increasingly, especially in the United States, parental beliefs that a university should teach their children practically useful subjects began to be influential. In the more recent period, the medieval practice of providing subsidized university education for a few of the intellectually talented poor, either on charitable grounds or to provide recruits for the clerical services, was gradually fused with the contemporary notions that universities and especially university-educated persons are good for society, over and above the tangible benefits to the university staff and students themselves; and that university education should be heavily subsidized by the state, both for this reason and to provide equality of opportunity for children to whatever station born.

The haziness of this conception of the university's functions, which is an uneasy compromise between the university's traditional view of itself as superior to, because apart from, the world of material concerns and the belief of the rest of society that the university provides social benefits in the form of a mixture of externalities, human capital formation, and egalitarian income redistribution, makes it very difficult to apply the economist's concepts of the market, the producing firm, and cost-benefit and cost-efficiency analysis to the university.

The modern university depends typically on government for the major part of its operating expenses on the teaching side, and on government, founda-tions, private endowment, and business firms for support of its research. Hence the university is dependent on the goodwill of these social institutions for its financial support. Parents and their student offspring contribute relatively little to the university's financial resources in any direct manner, and have to depend on political pressure directed either at government, in the case of parents, or at both government and the university itself in the case of students. In addition, since much of a university's activities involves professional training, which usually has to be of an acceptable form and quality to meet the standards of organized professional associations, these associations can achieve considerable influence on this side of the university's activities.

Because these major outside interest groups have very different ideas about the proper functions or ends of university activity, it is usually impossible to define a consistent social welfare function defining what is to be maximized subject to the relevant cost constraints in these circumstances.[1]

Consider, first, the government. It has, or at least must pretend to have, a concern for the support of the university as an institution and symbol of civilization, and also for its operation as a presumptive instrument of income redistribution. Since the 1950s, it has also come to be concerned with the university as a contributor to civilization in the limited form of contributing to the country's or province's economic growth. But its concern has embraced the two possibilities of specific contribution through the formation of human capital by teaching, and general contribution through the formation of intellectual capital by research. In recent years, governments generally have become disillusioned with the potentialities of research, especially "pure" or "basic" research, for economic growth, and have been anxious to cut their expenditure on basic research and to pass the costs of pure research to foundations and of applied research to the private sector and mission-oriented departments of government. Furthermore, the government is concerned on a very large scale with the recruitment of civil servants and of quasi-civil servants such as teachers, social workers, nurses, physicians, and so on. This turns its concern with universities toward professional training, the professionalization of nonprofessional arts or humanities courses, and an emphasis on teaching rather than research. Finally, because it has to raise taxes to finance its contributions to universities, and taxable capacity is limited in the aggregate, and the proportion of it which can be used either for income redistribution or the maintenance of intangible cultural symbols is restricted still further by taxpayers' opinions, the government is under strong pressure to insist on economy in expenditure on universities. This implies a number of widely observed phenomena—preference for expenditure on university buildings over expenditure on staff salaries, emphasis on the primacy of teaching over research, preference for spectacular rather than fundamental research, and a tendency to side with students (and indirectly their parents) rather than with university staff and administrators in cases of student unrest. The university can always be blamed for not delivering as much output as the politicians and public expect for their money.

Consider, second, foundations and private donors. These are motivated by a general belief in the university as both an element of civilization and an instrument of charity. They are also motivated, often quite legitimately, by concerns with social or scientific problems to which they believe universities do not pay sufficient attention. Unfortunately, they are also strongly influenced by current fads of opinion on these matters which then become integrated into the university's structure and impose on it certain financial and organizational problems. The propensity to monument-building, to name an institute or building for the private donor, and—in some ways more dangerous to the university—the desire of the foundation official to make his mark by starting some kind of new research in an established university, all contribute to bringing about these burdens for which the university, after its first enthusiasm, must ultimately pay.

Third, the professional associations often exert important influence over university professional training courses and standards by virtue of their control over the qualification of new members. In some cases, this may be beneficial to the teaching program by setting professionally necessary standards; in other cases, it may simply be a means of restricting entry to the profession in question by insisting on excessively intensive and prolonged, and inefficient, instruction. The raising of standards generally—which must be sharply distinguished from the raising of standards in a particular institution, in order to improve its competitive power against others—is generally defended as being in the interests of the public; attention is thereby diverted from the fact that it increases the monopoly profits of those already qualified. (Insisting that everyone must drive a Cadillac or a Rolls-Royce or nothing would improve the average quality of cars available to consumers, and simultaneously increase the profits of the companies producing Cadillacs or Rolls-Royces; but only those who already can afford such cars would benefit from the resulting increase in road safety.)

Fourth, the main concern of business firms is in the university as a source of recruitment of trained professional experts and potential executives. In this connection, the three alternative hypotheses of maturation, filtering, and human capital formation are relevant. The first two give the business firm no real interest in the efficiency of the university, only in its quality as judged by the standards of the university itself; it may even give the firm an interest in the preservation of university inefficiency. The secondary concern of the business firm is with the university as a source of research talent and research facilities which can be purchased cheaply—here the business firm (like government departments) has a direct interest in university teaching inefficiency, in the sense of maintenance of a stock of underemployed teachers whose promotion depends on research performance they may lack the originality to initiate, and a stock of underemployed buildings and equipment for which the university is not prepared to charge an adequate rent. It also has an obvious interest in letting the university—or government, or foundations—pay for the discovery and incorporation in its students and staff of the basic research on which applied research is based. This is an important and now an economically well-understood problem of both national science policy and university finance. If pushed, both industry and mission-oriented government departments will pay the current and overhead costs of applied research, but who is to pay the costs of the underlying investment in basic research?

Finally we come to households, the fundamental consumers of the process of university education. Here it is necessary to recognize, in contrast to the standard theory of consumption, that the household is not an individual with a single consistent utility function but an aggregation of individuals whose choices might well be inconsistent, intransitive, etc. Moreover, the household somehow, smoothly or painfully, goes through a transition from an extremely paternalistic utility function which covers young parents and their babies, to another such—the grown-up children and their children—via a process of simultaneous ageing and maturation of its members. In contemporary society it is precisely at the point of prospective or actual participation of students in the process of university education that the children make the transition from child to adult status, and move from the role of being paternalized to being paternalist. Hence their expectations of the function of the university differ—often very sharply—from those of their parents. Since the parents tend to dominate the decisions while the neoadult students have to live with the results, one major result in recent years has been student protest over their experience at universities, and parental conviction that the university administration and staff, not their beloved children, are responsible for the trouble.

Many parents, of course, are interested in human capital formation in their children, either through professional training or through general education. Many have other often very different conceptions about what the university will provide, whether they themselves have been to a university or not. Both groups will usually overestimate, in the light of obsolete belief regarding what happens in universities, the intellectual, cultural, or social attractions and advantages of attendance at a contemporary university. Still others will regard the university merely as a place to leave their children while they mature into adulthood and they will value above all peace and quiet during the process and will blame the university if such does not prevail. And still others, with pretty much the same results, regard the university merely as a filter. Only the first group of parents is likely to be at all concerned with the efficiency of the university as the economist conceives it.

Prospective and actual students, on the other hand, will have significantly different views. Some will accept the maturation function, and be especially interested in spending the time enjoyably. All students, however, have a certain interest in the current consumption possibilities offered free or at subsidized prices through the university's amenities, though these may be a waste of resources from the university's own and the social point of view. Other students, in place of maturation, will regard the process of becoming social and economic adults as a process of transformation.[2] The difference will correspond broadly to that between students from socially and economically well-established families and those from marginal families; also between those who have regarded their schoolteachers as bores to be listened to for the minimum possible time and those who have been inspired. The students who look for inspiration and stimulation might conceivably get more of it from "poor" than from "good" teachers. For the students who seek maturation, as for those who wish to increase their value as human capital, tests of efficiency in terms of least-cost achievement of a given level of educational attainment make eminent sense. For those who seek the end of transformation, it is extremely difficult to define either the "product" or the methods by which it can be produced.

The student who is concerned with his formation as human capital might in fact be concerned either with his formation as consumption capital, that is, being a person superior in knowledge, taste, and habit, so that whatever postuniversity life might be in store will be a more enjoyable and rewarding life to live, and his formation as production capital, that is, a higher-income earner, so that whatever his tastes are or may become he can indulge them more fully. This distinction corresponds very broadly to the traditional one between the arts and the sciences, but that distinction has become extremely blurred by the fact that in modern democratic, equalitarian, but competitive society one has to demonstrate one's competence in adulthood as both a superior producer and a superior consumer. The two criteria clearly indicate somewhat—but not necessarily very—different tests of efficiency in university education. The course content and emphasis, rather than comprehension of the material, becomes the differentiating factor between the two conceptions.

Finally, and especially evidently in the student disturbances of recent years, many students accept the filtering hypothesis. For them, the problem of optimization is a complex one of weighing probable employment prospects against the pleasantness of their time at a university, which in turn involves a balancing of the consumption of university amenities (including opportunity for pseudoadult political activities) and efforts devoted to surmounting the obstacle course of examinations. Clearly, one very attractive short-run choice is to use the political activity to demolish the obstacle course, relying on the assumption that admission to a university constitutes most of the effective screening involved in the filter process to safeguard employment prospects. From the point of view of efficiency in the longer run, it might be optimal to concentrate on improving the predictive efficiency of university admissions standards, and minimizing the costs of staff and plant arising from having students actually in the university once they have been admitted.[3]

Internal Interest Groups

The university is under the pressure of a variety of external interest groups, varying in their conceptions of the functions of a university and their ability to enforce these conceptions via both political influence and direct or indirect control of university finance and hence university policy. It is also under pressure from a variety of internal interest groups which also vary in their conceptions of what the university "product" should be and their ability to enforce these conceptions—although in this case ability to enforce is an outcome of the interaction of bureaucratic organization, political skill, and exploitation of the opportunities for choice and substitution which the university affords to its staff and its students. The last includes the opportunity for staff members to substitute among the courses they are equipped to teach—for example, elementary or advanced teaching, seminars or lectures, etc.—and between teaching and research supported from either internal or external sources. It also includes the ability of students to put competitive pressure on their teachers either downwards or upwards by choice among alternative sections of the same course or among optional subjects in the same degree program.

There are in general six major internal interest groups in universities; some universities have more, others less. The balance of power among them varies.

Students

In addition to what I have said above about the preferences of students and their parents, I should like to mention two major points. First, the students in residence have a strong interest in having the university provide subsidized housing and recreational facilities, and this interest coincides in large part with parental concerns, even though such provision may serve no educational purpose and constitutes a serious drain on university resources. The private market—which includes student cooperatives and enterprising student unions, as well as private clubs—could provide such facilities on a commercial basis if the demand warranted it, thereby sparing university funds for properly educational purposes. In this connection, one should note a recent trend respecting student housing: traditionally, both parents and the university authorities have favored the provision of subsidized student housing on the dormitory model as a means of transferring parental moral responsibility for their offspring to the university authorities and enabling the university to supervise and control its students' lives. Students have generally accepted the moral authority for the sake of the housing subsidy;

but recently they have increasingly rebelled against acceptance of moral supervision and have sought the greater freedom of the private housing market—largely because they have become affluent enough not to be completely dependent on the subsidy—with the result that dormitories and halls of residence have been beset by protests against quality of food provided, moral restrictions imposed on student liberty, and so forth. Another consequence is that the universities have found their dormitories standing unfilled because of the students' ability to give effect to their distaste for the authority of their elders by paying more for lower-quality but less regimented and collectivized housing than the university provides. (It should also be remarked that university provision of student housing on a high and subsidized standard affords a tangible talking point for demonstrating university quality to parents and politicians, who know little or nothing about what university education is about but who can appreciate a well-designed bedroom, bathroom, or pseudo-hotel when they see one.)

Second, students other than those strictly interested in their own formation as human capital saleable at the best possible price in the postgraduate market, have a strong interest in the watering down of the quality of the courses offered, and particularly in the lowering of failure rates and the proliferation of "soft options." Once they have surmounted the hurdles of university entry, they naturally prefer to minimize the remaining number of hurdles before graduation, unless they believe themselves capable of hurdling any examination obstacle. For a long time this motivation has expressed itself in the quest for "soft options" and more generally for universities with slack standards for the B.A.; much more recently it has expressed itself in demands for "relevance" of courses—that is, easy comprehensibility to the adolescent student mind—the removal of stipulations of prerequisites for attendance at certain courses, and the abolition of grading systems. In short, the student recognizes that in winning admission to the university he has already acquired a monopoly privilege in society, and one of the ways he can take advantage of it is to adulterate the product of his monopoly position. In this endeavor, he has the joint support of parents and university administrators who are bent on both currying parental and alumni favor and winning political approval. The latter have a strong bias toward believing in the efficiency of their admission procedure (which selects their educational clientele) and measuring its efficiency by the proportion of its intake of students who complete the entire degree course.[4]

Teaching Staff

The second internal interest group is the teaching staff, or faculty, as it is called in the United States. According to the concept of the university which came increasingly to prevail in the course of the late nineteenth and early twentieth centuries, its primary function and interest is research, in a very broad sense, and its teaching is an incidental by-product. In the contemporary university, however, its prime function as far as society is concerned is teaching; but tests of the quality of its teaching are poorly defined, and the teacher is shielded from too searching an inquiry into this aspect of his behavior by the absence of explicit training and criteria in this matter and by the tradition of respecting collegial privacy, so that teaching capacity is judged very largely by published research output. Hence, as a teacher, the university staff member can regard his teaching as a means of disseminating his own ideas to inferior minds, or he can use it to exploit his students so as to improve his research output. Then there is the question of the alternative tests of accomplishment of teaching itself: is a teacher's output and contribution greater in proportion to the value he adds to the raw material with which he starts—for example, is raising a student from failure to pass level more or less valuable than raising a student from a top second- to a low first-class rating—or by the total value of the students he teaches? In other words, is teaching performance to be measured by the capacity to improve low-quality students or by the capacity to attract and instruct high-quality students? Given the emphasis of university promotion systems on research output and their lesser emphasis on teaching as an activity involving the improvement rather than merely the passing-through of the raw material, the teaching staff tends to prefer the selection of high-quality students who will do them credit in terms of final grades rather than the selection of low-quality but improvable students. This is one of the major sources of conflict between the university as traditionally conceived and the current political and social emphasis on the function of the university as a leveler of social opportunity and democratizer of society; it is in the interest of the staff to meet the demand for equality, not by making the teaching effort required—which has no reward for the ambitious in the traditional university system—but by watering down the course offerings and hiring inferior colleagues to do the teaching of them. This is indeed the practice of many who claim that in so doing, they are promoting equality. Because of the prevalent use of research performance as a criterion of teaching ability, the faculty insists on research time and research facilities as a nonsalary attraction of an academic job, and the university does in fact offer such requisites—one financial reason being that salaries are subject to income tax whereas research facilities are not. The university has another incentive to act in this way since its quality as a teaching institution is likely to be known only to a small group of parents and a small group of scholars elsewhere who welcome its graduates as participants in their own graduate teaching and research operations, whereas its published research output is clearly visible for all to see. To justify this emphasis on research it is frequently asserted that research is useful because it improves the teaching of the person doing the research and in the long run raises the average quality of teaching—a debatable proposition because the two are both substitutes and complements to an unascertainable degree. This emphasis on research also heightens the propensity of university staff to prefer institutionalized and mechanized research of a rather mundane kind, with quickly published results, over personal research by library reading and private thought with a slow result or none in impressively publishable papers or books. A third is staff preference for senior undergraduate and graduate teaching which might lead to research ideas or testing of research results, rather than for elementary teaching, which probably has no consequences for research.

A third aspect of the faculty's interest in the university is as a consumption good for themselves. This includes good public facilities for themselves—common rooms, lounges, refectories, and bars, supply of current newspapers and magazines, inexpensive tea, coffee, and pastry—and good facilities in the form of individual offices, secretaries, and paper reproduction facilities, and imposing buildings in which to house them. Here there is to some extent a conflict between the desire of the academic staff for munificence and the desire of the political sphere and the university administration to house them as decently kept servants but still as obvious servants.[5] It is questionable, from the educational point of view, whether low salaries and attractive offices or high salaries and miserable offices—unless the individual chooses to spend his own money on office furniture and decoration—is the better enticement to good academics. Pure economic theory says the salary should be the important thing; but the nonliability of university-provided offices and facilities to income tax, together with the incentives provided by the "public good" aspect of the university to both university administrators and faculty to make the offices of the professors impressive to the nonuniversity community, works the other way. In any case, the teaching staff, which usually does not recognize the balancing of the alternatives of salary and nonsalary perquisites, has an incentive to maximize the consumption-good dimensions of university life, whether this is educationally optimal or not. (For example, teachers could maintain their own studies at home and frequent neighboring private clubs and commercial bars, rather than expect the university to provide office space and subsidize amenities. Also, the faculty could attend commercial performances of music and drama at commercial prices, instead of attending campus performances of musical and dramatic work which are subsidized by university funds.)

A fourth aspect of faculty interest is the opportunity to invest in the formation of their own human capital at the university's expense—that is, to improve future earning power, whether in this university or another one (the two going together in a competitive market for human talent) by being a staff member for a period of time. This has two aspects: the opportunity to earn a salary by a nominal obligation to teach, while actually doing research designed to establish a professional name and a market for the individual's talents; and the opportunity to consort with both senior and junior colleagues who will both suggest research problems of significance and instruct them in the techniques necessary to solve their own research problems. This aspect of a university improves its performance as a producer of research output, through the operation of economies of scale and agglomeration; but it may well also serve to reduce its performance as an institution which is under obligation to teach efficiently its undergraduate, and possibly also its graduate, students.

Finally, university teaching staff are interested in their own promotion, as a question both of status and of income. Promotion to higher academic and income status may conflict with teaching performance and with quality of research output, for two reasons. First, promotion is decided by senior persons who are likely to undervalue teaching as compared with research, and to judge research by their own preconceptions and pride. Second, the research output which leads to promotion is likely to be judged by quantity rather than quality—though there is a contrary tendency to regard a man who publishes a lot in a short time as insufficiently scholarly, and a man who publishes little but that little of extremely abstruse character as a very worthy scholar whose small quantity of output is justified by its high quality—and by topicality of subject and results in relation to current research concerns rather than by fundamental scientific significance. The rate of discount applied to current scholarly work promising future returns in knowledge is higher than the socially optimal, and the valuation of the social product of research reflects the immediate market valuation of a novel product rather than its long-run worth.

Internal Administration

The administration serves, among other things, as a buffer between staff and students on the one hand, and the external interest groups on the other. The buffer function is responsible both for the most widespread structure of university government in the English-speaking world, which involves the sharing of administrative and particularly decision-making functions among the formal administrative apparatus, a senate composed of senior academics, and a board of trustees or governors representing the public but selected from those sympathetic to the university, and for the standard practice of recruiting at least senior administrative staff from the ranks of successful (or, at least, reputable) academics. These are justified as ensuring the "independence" of the university from outside pressures. It may be noted that governments, as the main source of university funds, have become increasingly restive with this system of university government and are eager to replace it in many specific instances by a more direct and subservient relationship between university management and its own civil service.

The administration has a variety of interests which often do conflict with those of other interest groups in the university. First, it has a strong interest in the university being and remaining popular with the local community and the larger society, which above all requires maintaining peace and quiet on the campus, and minimizing the extent to which the university acquires a reputation for unacceptable ideas and activities. This objective often conflicts with the principle of academic freedom. The objective of internal and external peace is a prerequisite to a second, institutional growth, which is a characteristic objective of bureaucracies, since it both demonstrates their successful management and social importance and increases their power and appropriate remuneration. Growth, especially if rapid, is not necessarily conducive to efficient teaching, research, and staff selection or to the happiness of students and staff. Moreover, growth in response to the demands of outside interests, whether for an increase in the aggregate scale of the university or for the undertaking of new kinds of teaching and research activities, is not necessarily conducive to the maintenance of a happy academic staff. A school of undertaking, passively, and a school of journalism, frequently actively, are sources of embarrassment to the traditional academic community, while in recent years defense research and military training on campus have been bones of bitter contention among both staff and students.

A third administrative objective is efficient internal management of the university, although in most universities the principle of academic freedom means that the criteria of efficiency are primarily budgetary and are applied mainly to the allocation of incremental funds rather than to the spending of established fund allocations. In this respect, university efficiency is like governmental efficiency, and consists on the one hand in carefully checking to ensure that allocations of funds are spent for the purposes intended in the allocation, whether that purpose is still useful or not, and on the other hand in carefully scrutinizing requests for additional funds, though once the fresh funds have been allocated, the pattern of allocation tends to continue automatically. A university administration can and often does deny a poor department funds for expansion; but it is almost never prepared to close it down. And if there is a budgetary shortage as a result of inflation or a reduction in revenue, it is translated into an equiproportionate cut in sub-budgets throughout the university (with modifications for special cases), rather than a thoroughgoing review of the university's activities and elimination of those of marginal value. In short, a bureaucracy's criteria of efficiency entail painstakingly honest accounting, rationality in the allocation of incremental funds, and political justice in the continuation of fair shares in the established allocation of funds, in contrast to the economic criteria of efficiency, according to which existing and incremental allocations should be considered together and existing allocations continually reviewed. University administrations in many universities moreover tend to be excessively receptive to offers of fresh outside funds, regardless of the consistency of the objectives of their donors with the general purposes of the university, and as a result frequently find themselves obliged to find funds for the maintenance of the graveyards of outside donors' ideas.

The sacrosanctity of existing budgetary allocations is in part explained by a fourth objective of university administrations, internal popularity with students, teaching staff, and library and other auxiliary staff. This objective is complementary to the first objective of external popularity, since it helps to ensure peace and quiet within the university. Its price, however, is toleration of wide margins of inefficiency in all sorts of directions, and compromises also with the principle of academic freedom. Academic freedom is the right of scholars to proclaim the conclusions of their scholarly studies without political penalty. It is not the right of either staff or students to use their privileged position in the university to impose their political and personal views on the rest of society. Nonetheless, in recent years many university administrations have tamely succumbed to the politicization of the university—that is, its transformation into an agency for the expression and execution of "radical" ideas on the nature of higher education and its role in society. (It must be conceded that one reason why university administrations have been willing to do this has been that in the past they were willing to bend the rules of academic independence to discriminate against radicals.)

A fifth motivation of university administrations is personal consumption at public expense, expressed both in private salaries and perquisites and in the "public good" aspects of university architecture and landscaping. There is little reason to believe—aside from the consideration of impressing visitors from the outside world—that university efficiency requires that the university president, vice-chancellor, rector, or director needs an office and number of secretaries three times the size of that of a professor, and a larger multiple of what an aspiring junior staff member commands; or that the administration inhabit an ornate building surrounded by expensively cultivated grass, shrubbery, and flowering plants; or that air conditioning and central heating contribute more to the efficiency of the administration than they would to the efficiency of the teaching and research functions of the academic staff. On the contrary, it is reasonably clear that the luxury consumption which university administrations afford themselves at university expense creates a social gulf between the administration on the one hand and students and staff on the other, and so works against the achievement of the previous objective of internal popularity.

The extreme of gratification of the desire for personal consumption by university administrations is found in the final objective in the list, the objective of monument-building. Like politicians, university administrators find a great deal of satisfaction in changing the physical appearance of the landscape by erecting new and impressive buildings for the sponsorship of which they claim credit, regardless of whether the buildings serve any useful social purpose. The pyramid-building propensity works against efficiency in two major ways. First, it prompts a quest for large external donations to found new schools or institutes for research which might fit badly into the general structure of the university as an academic community. Second, it biases administrative choices in the allocation of fresh funds toward expenditure on buildings and equipment and against expenditure on staff salaries and staff secretarial assistance, even though quality of staff might be far more important than quality of buildings and other plants in determining the quality of education and research.

Library

The fourth important interest group within the university is the library, which can be thought of mainly as library staff members but also as comprising the support of some administrators and some members of the teaching staff. In relation to the teaching and research activities of the university, the library serves two main purposes—as an accessible repository of books which students have to read or should read, and as a repository of books staff members might want to use for their own research. However, a university library acquires a life of its own, partly because it serves as a sort of monument to the social importance and prestige of the university, partly because its books serve the interests of scholars outside as well as inside the university (both local nonuniversity intellectuals and scholars from other universities), and largely because its staff is specialized in the business of acquiring and storing books, administering their usage, and preserving them from damage and theft.

As a result, the interests of the library are not necessarily wholly harmonious with the interests of the university as a teaching and research institution. The professional librarian naturally has an interest in building the best and most impressive library he can, according to librarians' standards. This involves, among other things, biases toward maximizing the number of titles he can display rather than optimizing the numbers of the same title he possesses in relation to reader demand; toward acquiring collections of books and papers as complete as possible, regardless of the interest of teaching staff and students in having such collections available or the cost-benefit ratio for the university involved, in order to enhance the local or world reputation of the library as such; and toward the acquisition of rare books, which no one in the university might wish to read or even see on display, and access to which (in the case of pornographic books or very expensive collectors' items) might even be denied to students and the junior teaching staff. To house these books requires an expensive building or buildings, involving special architectural features, such as reinforced flooring and rooms with closely controlled temperature and humidity for the storage of rare old books and manuscripts—buildings the contribution of which to the functions of the university, as distinct from the prestige of the library, might not be justified by the expense. The preservation of the library's stock of books in number and condition or physical quality also requires extensive policing of borrowing and reading rights, and an explicit attempt to restrict physical usage of at least the rare books.

Finally, librarians are naturally interested in achieving technical efficiency in information storage—that is, efficiency in both storage and data retrieval. While this concern with efficiency is in general beneficial to the rest of the university in its capacity as user of the library, it is marred by the library's tendency to concern itself with systems of storage and data retrieval which accord equal treatment to the rarely used and the frequently used books. A rational system—which some libraries approximate—would distinguish between books and journals in current heavy demand, which could be made quickly accessible both by good cataloging and ordering procedures and by the maintenance of adequate stocks of copies in the shelves, and rare and rarely used works, the availability of which interests only a handful of scholars who should be expected to be patient in obtaining access to them.

Service staff

The fifth interest group in a university comprises the service staff; that is, the research assistants, teaching assistants, teachers of service courses in languages or elementary mathematics, etc., and technicians of all sorts. These people usually have little power within the university, though they may occasionally be able to acquire significant power by forming coalitions with one of the other interest groups (i.e., either students or teaching and research staff).

As mere employees of the university rather than central parts of it, they have the normal interest of employees in income and job security. But they also have desires to acquire the status of university teachers and research officers, including especially the privilege of tenure after a certain period of service, and a voice in university government. The purpose of tenure, insofar as it still has a reasonable purpose, is to protect the academic freedom of the scholar against outside and inside political pressure, not to guarantee him a stable income for life regardless of his performance, within very broad limits. Similarly, the purpose of maintaining a role for the teaching and research staff of the university in university government is to enable them to give voice to academic values, which they are presumed to be capable of distinguishing from personal interest, not to entitle them to run the university to suit themselves, at the expense of the public. The interests of the service staff in acquiring tenure and governing power run contrary to the requirements of university efficiency, precisely because these persons provide services ancillary to the main functions of the university and their conceptions of its functions are correspondingly limited, in particular with respect to under-standing why and on what terms the polity of the larger society is prepared to subscribe money for the support of universities. A trades union attitude toward the relation between the university and the state is conducive neither to the welfare of the members of the university nor to efficiency in the university; but it is attractive to some regular university staff members in the contemporary situation, in which the university system has been vastly expanded at the behest of the state and the state is rapidly tending to treat university teachers like the employees which secondary and primary school teachers have long since become. The interests of the service staff reinforce the tendency to the defensive adoption of the trades union attitude toward the university.

Research institutes

Research institutes, having no formal teaching function and being divorced from the general university interest in ideas and scholarship by their very specifically defined "mission" or area of research, are not usually involved in the university as a community of scholars and students. The university simply defines their geographical location and their prestige. Virtually their sole interest in it—apart from its library and computer facilities, which are directly useful and relevant—lies in the maintenance and enhancement of their public and scholarly prestige through association with it. Otherwise, their orientation is toward the outside world of other scholars and of research markets. Their concern with the university's prestige is a general and long-run interest; but it does not preclude the staff of research institutes either from undertaking types of research which undermine a university's reputation for dispassionate scholarship, or from attempting to influence university policy in favor of their own institutional interests at the expense of the teaching and research obligations of the university as a whole toward its staff, students, and society in general. In short, the research institutes, like the library and the service staff, constitute only a partial sample of the university's activities, and their interests in the university are not necessarily conducive to the efficiency of the university operation as a whole.

Concluding Remarks

In the technical terms of economics the university is a multi-product firm, important constituents of its line of products being "public goods" of one or another ill-defined kind. Both the consumers and producers of these goods have widely divergent preference functions, so much so that it is virtually impossible to define a social welfare function containing university outputs as variables which would be sufficiently well-behaved to be amenable to maximization subject to a cost constraint. It is, of course, always possible to impose a limited social welfare function, for example, student comprehension of course content at examination time, and to maximize that function subject to a budgetary constraint in terms of expenditure on alternative methods of teaching. But to do so begs the fundamental question, which is: is this what the university is all about?

To say this is not, of course, is to deny the usefulness of analysis of teaching effectiveness, or the efficiency of any other aspect of university "production." The university purportedly produces *something*, and it is useful to know how well it produces the things it claims to produce, even though it can always reject the results on the grounds that the particular product in question is a mere by-product of the process of producing some more important product, the quantity of which cannot be measured. The university system is right now under strong pressure to justify itself by its contribution to society, and any contribution that can be measured and tested for its efficiency is well worth investigating. It is important, however, to appreciate that the results of such investigations do not answer the more fundamental questions.

12. Some Political and Ideological Influences on Contemporary Economics

Introduction

The development of any discipline concerned with man as a social animal is inevitably influenced by the evolution and characteristics of the contemporary milieu. Scholarship itself is a luxury good, in economic terminology, social support of and interest in which is, broadly speaking, an increasing function both of the level of average income and of the concentration of income distribution. Scholars themselves are part of their society and influenced by their role in it, and this has become an increasingly important influence as the evolution and secularization of postindustrial revolution society has transformed universities from isolated centers for the training of young men for the priesthood and the gentry and the storage in celibacy of the scholarly eccentric oriented however vaguely toward eternity, into institutions involved in the training of an evergrowing industrial as well as clerical and governmental elite. The universities are qualified for this responsibility by themselves being the respected lodging of the intellectual elite, enjoying an increasing monopoly of cultural eminence as a consequence of social implementation of the principle of specialization and division of labor. Thus history tends to be rewritten from generation to generation to reflect the prevailing mood (usually majority sometimes minority) of the times, albeit rewritten according to rising professional standards in the use of historical evidence, while English literature, being a happy hunting ground for those interested in quaint manners and morals or in recognizably truthful human experience, has recently been reexamined for the intellectual benefit of the Women's Liberation movement. Economics, as a combination of social science and moral philosophy concerned with man's means of meeting his most fundamental requirement, physical survival, both personal and social, has been particularly subject to feedback processes operating between scholarship and society. This essay attempts, in a rather impressionistic way, to state and discuss the more important of these influences of society—broadly conceived—on economics. Some are more obvious than others, but nevertheless in my judgment important, especially for what they suggest

Revised and abridged version of section III of a paper entitled "The Current and Prospective State of Economics in Canada," presented to a conference held on the occasion of the formal opening of the Social Science Centre, University of Western Ontario, in March 1973.

about the future. I divide the discussion into three major categories: economics and government (government being viewed as society's major agency of influence and used as shorthand for the broader manifestations of public opinion); academic politics in economics; and ideological influences on economic controversy.

Government and Economics

Government has played an important supporting role in the expansion and professionalization of economics in the post-World War II period, in several major respects. First, the Second World War, during which Keynesian economics triumphed over conventional "financial" approaches to wartime economic management and government became deeply involved in economic planning and administration, including the widespread use of controls over wages, prices, and allocations of materials and foreign exchange (at least in the English-speaking countries) vastly increased the respect for and use of economists in the government service. Perhaps it would be fairer to say that what triumphed was the application to the aggregate level of total available resources, in the name of and under the leadership in Britain of Keynes himself, of the much longer-standing concern of economics with the budget constraint on the allocation of scarce resources and its understanding that money is merely a veil—sometimes deceptive and mischievous—over the interaction of unlimited wants with limited resources, since Keynesian methods of wartime monetary and financial management planted and watered the seeds of postwar inflation. Moreover, the increased governmental demand for trained economists proved permanent, because, in contrast to the First World War which followed a long period of sustained prosperity and social self-content and hence appeared as a temporary interruption followed by a return to business—including government business—as usual, the Second World War was preceded by an unusually deep and prolonged depression which shifted public opinion strongly toward supporting a continuing vastly enlarged role of government in the society and in the economy. Note in passing that, owing to the operation of Parkinson's Law, war or any other reason for the temporary expansion of government tends to leave a permanent residue of expanded government; but the expansion that followed the Second World War reflected not merely the inherent laws of bureaucracy but a major change in social attitudes. This change had two aspects: assignment to the government of responsibility for achieving the major macroeconomic objectives of full employment, price stability, and economic growth (and on some lists, greater equality of income distribution as well); and assignment to the government of operational responsibility for or planning and regulatory control over large sectors of the economy, on both the producing and consuming sides of economic activity (as examples, natural resource development on one side, health care and social insurance on the other). Both assignments, it may also be remarked, have tended to have a long-run disintegrative effect on countries with federal constitutions (Canada and the United States) in the form of efforts to shift economic powers toward provincial and state governments, and, in countries with unitary constitutions, in the development of regional nationalism and the demand for devolution of powers. The primary reasons have been the differential regional impact of macroeconomic management policies, and the desire to escape from or compensate for errors of central decision-taking by an appeal to lower and more politically sensitive levels of government, on the one hand; and the fact that as society waxes in affluence its social concerns become more localized and hence more the province of local than of central governments, on the other (the major examples being education, the cities, and "the environment").

The role of government as the major employer of trained economists, especially those with one or more graduate degrees, exercises a variety of influences on the teaching and professional practice of academic economics. On the one hand, progress and the maintenance of professional scholarly standards in an academic subject depends in a familiar way on economies of specialization and division of labor, which in turn depend on department scale; this includes the externalities that accrue, on the lines of the "vintage" approach to capital theory, from the regular (but not too proportionally large) recruitment of newly trained people to existing departments. The existence of a steady and substantial government demand for the product has both permitted the enjoyment of these economies, and provided a larger pool of talent from which to select the academic economists of the future, by affording a safe alternative route to those who fail to make the academic grade to success. On the other hand, the presence of a large-scale government demand for the product cannot help but bias the tone or ethos of the subject toward conservatism, through the subtle interaction of student concepts and faculty response to them concerning the useful as contrasted with the "airy-fairy" aspects of the subject. Radicalism tends to get hived off into peripheral optional subjects, or safely shackled into the discipline of elementary bread-and-butter teaching—if it does not quit academic life entirely out of sheer boredom with prosaic minds applying technical steam hammers to the cracking of intellectual nuts. (Of course, conservatism eventually becomes the psychological bent of almost anyone who devotes his life to the study of how a system works, though it may be conservatism in preserving traditional definitions of "radicalism.") The presence of an assured market for economists in government service, in contrast to the position confronting students in other social sciences, especially sociology, accounts incidentally in my judgment for the universally contrasting behavior of students and faculties in economics and the other social sciences during the "student troubles" of the late 1960s.

One particular aspect of the importance of government as a large-scale employer of economics graduates, relevant especially to the present and prospective state of the subject, evident to the author especially in Canada and the United Kingdom, is worth noting at this point for later discussion. In both countries, and presumably other British countries like Australia, government has come to respect the superior technical qualifications and seriousness of purpose of the M.A.-holder or all-but-thesis-qualified Ph.D. candidate over the B.A.-holder, and is accordingly more or less happy to support graduate work to the M.A. level. But it is not convinced of the training-value of the writing of the dissertation itself, and even regards the Ph.D.-holder as constituting an awkward item to digest into the civil service apparatus. This creates a conflict between the academic interest in lower-level graduate work, as preparation for the Ph.D. and a research-oriented subsequent career, and the social interest in lower-level graduate work as reflected in the marketplace, which conflict has serious implications for the planning of institutional development of economics in a period of increasing financial stringency for universities.

One reflection of this conflict is that the "A.B.D." ("all-but-dissertation") standard of professional qualification tends to become the de facto standard both of graduate student aspiration and of academic appointment. This has created perennial problems for those Canadian departments that have been trying seriously to elevate themselves to first-rank international status by insisting on high standards of research performance by staff and graduate students, only to have many of both drain off to other Canadian universities content with A.B.D. qualifications for staff appointment and tenure. In Britain the picture is even more extreme, possession of a Ph.D. by those who make their careers in that country (in university or elsewhere) frequently denoting insufficient competence, personal charm, or quickness of wit, to achieve academic appointment without one (though often the Ph.D. is necessary to enable the student from a backward country to break into the charmed concentric circles of British academic life). The problem is less obvious, though still there, in the United States, where financial support for completion of the Ph.D. has been relatively lavish; but it is likely to become more evident as a result of recent cuts in government funding and the financial squeeze on the Universities.

In addition, the dominance of a fairly steadily growing governmental demand means that the total demand for A.B.D.'s and Ph.D.'s is geared by a species of accelerator mechanism to the rate of change of the demand for academic economists, and hence to the rate of change of (predominantly undergraduate) enrollment, thereby incorporating strong elements of the "corn-hog" cycle into the process of expansion of graduate work and complicating the planning problems of both departments and university administrations.

A second way in which government has influenced the evolution of professional academic economics has been through the large-scale use it has made of economists to conduct research into a wide variety of policy problems. Here a sharp distinction must be made between the United Kingdom practice and the North American. The U.K. practice typically employs economists to research "in-house" on policy problems regarded as too sensitive for the results to be made public (except occasionally for defensive purposes) and hence distracts good economists from regular academic research without yielding subsequent benefits to the advancement of the subject in the form of published research results. The North American practice, on the contrary, typically involves treatment of the economist as a hired professional expert with the right or even guarantee of subsequent publication. This practice has in my judgment had a very beneficial effect on the whole on the development of the North American and particularly Canadian profession, by providing immediate incentives for research, a specific topic and a deadline for delivery, and sustained supervision by and contact with other professional researchers—none of which are provided at all adequately to graduate students and especially junior staff in either Canadian or most American graduate departments. On the other hand, the dominance in Canada of government as a source of research money for economists, and the influence of this dominance on the standards applied in the award of Canada Council and private research grants, tends to divert professional attention away from basic theoretical and/or "curiosity-oriented" research, thus making the Canadian profession less independent and less interesting to economists in other countries than it could be.

This weakness of Canadian economics is most evident in two respects: one is the tendency of Canadian theorists to become competent combat troops in intellectual wars whose strategy is planned in other countries, the danger of which I shall illustrate later; the other is the temptation to Canadian academics with either insufficient professional competence by present standards or a taste for easy popularity among the masses to take the easy route of imitating and regurgitating the unscholarly and rabble-rousing pseudointellectual outpourings of their opposite numbers in foreign countries, predominantly in the United States but also in the failed and bitterly jealous quondam rival empires of the United Kingdom and France. It would be extremely difficult to discern, from the shallow and frequently near-psychotic writings of some Canadians employed in otherwise reputable economic departments, on such subjects as American investment in Canada and the destruction or pollution of the environment, that serious Canadian economics scholars have achieved world-wide professional recognition for their contributions to the economics of resource utilization and of the multinational corporation.

Australian economics, perhaps because of its ties to the amateur British academic system and remoteness from the professional American system, has displayed significantly more originality in basic economic theory at least in the post-World War II decade, though there are signs that this may be changing as an increasing proportion of young Australians have turned to the United States for their graduate training.

A third, and important, way in which government has exercised a controlling influence over the development of economics to its present professional status has been through providing financial support, direct or indirect, for graduate students in this and other subjects. Direct support means cash maintenance of students, indirect support refers to the provision of part-time or full-time positions in the teaching of undergraduates, research assistance, and so forth. These tend to expand or contract together. There have been two major waves of such support. The first, immediately after the Second World War, was associated with the public belief in the English-speaking countries that those who had served in their countries' armed forces were entitled to special opportunities to reinsert themselves into civilian life, a large part of which consisted of educational opportunities. This contributed greatly to the emergent dominance of the British (now American) tradition in economics, as contrasted with the various Continental European traditions, which till fairly recently remained fettered by the medieval traditions and social formalism of the University. It also introduced into the university—at least in economics—a new type of personality, broader in social origins and experience, and pragmatic and professional rather than scholastic in its approach, one result being greatly to reduce the gulf created by the traditional university between the academic scholar and the man of affairs. (The longer-run effects of this transformation, reinforced by the next wave of government support, have since become a focal point of student radical criticism: radical students, being an unselfconscious social elite, tend naturally to be appalled by the consequences of social democratization.)

The first wave of governmental support for scholarship in general and academic economics as part of it derived from an interpretation of democracy's obligations to its warrior-citizens, not from any perceived or actually realized need for a vast expansion of the proportion of the population qualified by higher degrees. It was succeeded by nearly a decade of lean years characterized by low real salaries and slow promotion for academics during which many drifted or were dislodged out of academic life into other pursuits, especially the civil service, where they constituted a hidden reservoir of senior talent available for employment in the next wave of expansion. Those who remained in academic life, whether through superior talent and devotion or through lack of alternatives as cosy as low-level academic tenure, eventually cashed in heavily on expansion. The second wave of expansion, unlike the first, derived from a popular conviction that higher education for its young citizens was socially, and especially economically, beneficial to a nation, sufficiently so to warrant massive public subsidization of expansion of university education. This conviction, like the concurrent and reciprocally reinforcing rise of faith in the national benefits of scientific research, was superimposed on the general tendency of increasing affluence to create both increasing economic incentives for and increasing economic capacity to bear the costs of expanding higher education. And it owed much more than was appreciated at the time or has been generally appreciated since to the American acceptance of the achieved rate of economic growth as the key test of competence of alternative systems of economic organization in their cold war rivalry with Russia, and the blow to American confidence in the supremacy of American science dealt by Russia's success in launching the Sputnik in 1957.

The many problems that have been associated with the forced rapid expansion of universities in recent years are matters of too recent observation and experience to be worth detailed summary here. The most fundamental facts are, first, that university expansion has, at least temporarily, reached or exceeded a market limit set in an interdependent way by job opportunities for university graduates and students seeking university enrollment; this reaching of the limit impinges, or is in process of impinging, most heavily on graduate work, which as already mentioned is closely connected through an acceleration mechanism with the rate of expansion of undergraduate enrollments. The problem threatens to be a serious one indeed for economics departments in Canada, Britain, and Australia, which have been set on a path of expansion of graduate work in an excessive number of relatively small departments which could only be realized and justified by a very large-scale expansion of the total number of qualified students seeking higher university degrees. Second, the consequences of approaching this "natural limit" have been exacerbated by a revulsion of public and governmental opinion against the universities, based partly on disgust with the antics of students, and even more of university staff and administrators, during the period of student troubles, and based still more firmly on alarm at the mounting financial burden of supporting what again has come to be widely regarded as an over-privileged elite class of drones.

Academic Politics in Economics

The professionalization and expansion of economics in the post–World War II period and the broadening of the social origins and outlook of economists beyond the traditional origins and outlook of the previous generation have involved various kinds of strains, which I describe as "political" in a very loose sense, within economics departments. Some manifestations of these phenomena are university-wide, and as such fall outside the scope of this paper. These include the frequent absence of real understanding of the university tradition of privileged but responsible intellectual independence for the teachers, which has underlain the willingness of significant groups of staff to condone and concur in the politicization of the university into a pressure group promoting minority political opinion on national political issues—including the application of coercive pressures for conformity to fellow scholars—and to view the university quite wrongly as a self-sufficient community that should respond "democratically" to the wishes of its "constituency" of students, irrespective of the facts that both staff and students are supported at public expense on the assumption that their activities serve a useful social purpose and that students are a transient population with no responsibility for keeping the academic house in order for their successors. At a more mundane but in important respects potentially equally corruptive level, these factors among others have been responsible for the diffusion from the applied natural sciences to the social sciences of the assumption by university staff that university employment provides a respectable address and a safe bread-and-butter income on the basis of which one is entitled to establish a commercial consulting, research, and literary enterprise. This has been one of the more legitimate focuses of student criticism (by no means exclusively "radical") of present-day universities, though it is admittedly difficult to draw a clear line in an increasingly oral culture between outside activities that compete with and those that are complementary to good teaching and scientific research. (Other legitimate points of criticism concern course contents, which are often monuments to the eccentricities of past scholars or the intellectual eminence of other universities, and teaching methods, which frequently combine the technological primitiveness of Socratic method with virtually complete absence of Socratic wisdom.)

As regards economics itself, professionalization and expansion have introduced broadly political conflict in several dimensions. The fundamental source of these conflicts is that there is a profound difference in personal and scholarly life styles between the older and the newer generation of economists. At the risk of caricature, the older generation of scholar qualified himself for academic appointment by displaying mastery of his subject through his B.A. written examinations, a form of test that leaves a great deal to be desired through its provision of a wide range of questions lending itself to strategic planning of study, its encouragement to brightly packaged regurgitation of material digested from lectures, and its absence of adequate testing of capacity either for genuine originality or for the sustained hard work that is almost invariably a prerequisite for genuinely original scholarly contribution. B.A. performance might or might not be seasoned with postgraduate study, usually not leading to a degree. Upon appointment the scholar usually picked out for himself a long-range field or topic of study, confident in the knowledge that competition would be minimal and that he would have mostly his own intellectual standards to satisfy. His teaching commitment was mostly to expose the undergraduate to the experience of seeing an older, more versatile and experienced mind at work. His scholarly commitment was almost invariably to one university in which he counted on spending his lifetime; his judges accordingly were his colleagues in that university, who not being expert in his field judged him by personal impressions of his conversation and reading of his occasional literary productions; and the nature of his career allowed considerable time for assuming the responsibilities of amateur and unpaid university administration, a field into which the more ambitious university man could profitably graduate himself to professional status. His social life was in a relatively small community but socially somewhat detached from it.

By contrast, again at the risk of caricature, the younger-generation economist is qualified by formal graduate instruction culminating in the Ph.D., which almost invariably is undertaken at a university different from both his B.A. university and the university that eventually employs him. His intellectual environment is his professional discipline or his specialization within it, rather than his department and university. He tends to regard administration as a distraction from his main work and as a necessary chore to be minimized, rather than as a vital part of his life and responsibilities as he matures and a possible stepping-stone to superior status in his community. And he is actively involved in the world of affairs, and not timidly so, because he is a confident expert capable of delivering wanted performances and not merely a luxury of social aloofness that a busy society affords itself. The price of his different kind and degree of freedom is continuing active participation in the scholarly and research-completion process, rather than early demonstration of brilliance and continuing promise of a single great performance.

There are, of course, both virtues and vices on both sides of the coin—as well as considerable misunderstanding when the two styles of scholarship become confused in the mind of the outside world, and even more so when they become confused in the mind and behavior of the scholar himself. But I believe that the two contrasting styles of scholarship have to be viewed in the context of an evolving society waxing in affluence as a consequence of the conscious application of knowledge to the improvement of the human condition. In the perspective of history, the older style of scholarship represents the determination of a few dedicated men to preserving and painfully increasing man's scarce stock of fundamental truth against the destructive pressures of cultural barbarism, and is an anachronism, or nearly so, in an age of large-scale, collective pursuit of new and usable truth by the organized and cooperative activities of a host of scholars supported by a public keenly interested in the answers.

Be that as it may—and one must bear in mind that one is not legislating compulsory conformity of all scholars to one monolithic concept of scholarship—the conflict between the older and new styles of scholarship shows up at a variety of points in the process of academic self-government. A number of the resulting lines of political division are fairly self-evident: brightness and promise versus sustained performance as the standard for first appointment, and more importantly as the criterion for tenure and promotion, where still another criterion enters, administrative and/or teaching service to the department and the university; the debate over "publish or perish" as a rule for academic advancement within an institution; and a variety of questions concerning departmental management, including the attention to be paid to teaching and the extent to which department members should be allowed freedom to teach what they are interested in as they want to teach it, and allocated timetable space and examination course-credits accordingly. This range of conflicts is especially acute at the level of graduate work, where the older style of scholarship tends to regard such work as an apprenticeship to be served by youth in the casual company of the old, and to be catered for by the offering of courses, and preferably of seminars, in the subjects that interest senior staff members, to standards set individually by themselves, while the newer style of scholarship favors more structured courses focusing on the core of the discipline as agreed by the generality of the profession at large, with more or less uniform standards determined collectively by the department (or its senior members). This division, in turn, has far-reaching implications for standards and criteria of hiring and promotion of staff, notably for whether a department (and its university) should aim in its staff selection policies at a balanced range of high competence or at a few stellar appointments supported by a majority of mediocrities.

I myself (as already hinted) am strongly of the view that the older style of scholarship is outmoded; in particular, that contemporary universities are preparing their students for the transition from the small local environments from which they predominantly come, to competition in a broader provincial, national, or international arena and that, accordingly, they should aim at providing the best possible portable training rather than one dominated by the ultimate idiosyncrasies of the small group of scholars on whom they have conferred initial appointments and a virtual guarantee of tenure. This implies thinking in terms of departments of economics rather than of individual stellar economic personalities. Similarly, "publish or perish," properly administered, seems to me a necessary corrective to the propensity of the individual scholar to hoard his knowledge against the possibility of its productive use by others and to use it to build a monopoly position with and for his own immediate students. The traditional structure and practices of universities encourage the formation of antisocial monopolies of knowledge in all sorts of ways, and these tendencies have been reinforced by the combination of public finance of universities and consequent rationing of access to university admission by faculty judgments of academic qualifications. "Publish or perish" counteracts the influence of monopoly by forcing its products to be made available to scholars—and much more important, to students—everywhere; and it is no real restraint on the academic actively involved in the world of scholarship, for whom publication of results is necessary to the completion of research and not merely an infinitely deferable frill on self-satisfaction or exposure of personal vanity to collegial criticism.

Nevertheless, it must be recognized that the rise of the new style of scholarship in economics represents to a significant extent the influence of two probably transitory forces. The first is the longer-run effects of the various revolutions in economics of the 1930s, which afforded the new generation a chance to overleap the old by the exploitation of new theories and techniques that they could master more easily and at a relatively early age. The second is the recent rapid expansion of economics departments, in response to the general public desire for expanded opportunities for university education. This "undergraduate-propelled expansion," as Professor A. D. Scott labeled it in his 1967 Presidential Address to the Canadian Political Science Association, has meant a sharp increase in the proportion of freshly trained Ph.D.'s and A.B.D.'s in the average economics department, with consequent emphasis on advanced technique, more rational organization of instruction, and involvement in graduate training in the style of the major centers from which the new recruits have largely come. A slowing down in the rate of technical progress in the advance of economics itself, combined with a deceleration of the growth of demand for economists in academic institutions, may well mean a trend back toward the older style of scholarship—as a matter of accumulating wisdom through aging and experience—and the older style of treatment of graduate students—as a minor adjunct to the main job of producing good undergraduates.

Ideological Influences on Economic Controversy

The most striking characteristic of the development of economics since the Second World War has been the professionalization of academic economics, a professionalization built, on the one hand, on the various "revolutions" of the 1930s and, on the other hand, on the great expansion of both the demand for and the supply of economists in academic and related careers. With professionalization, and in particular as a result of the intense preoccupation with the status of value judgments in economics that followed Robbins's challenge to Pigovian utilitarian welfare economics and the subsequent concern with the empirical and quantitative study of economic phenomena and issues, has come a marked decline in the attention given to and emotional heat generated by ideological issues, by contrast particularly with the 1930s, among the mass of qualified professional economists. However, economics as a subject for discussion by educated laymen has always involved ideological issues, centering on moral aspects of the role of capital and of the pricing process for labor in the economic system, and professionalization of the subject has been accompanied to a significant extent by "internalization" of some of these issues within the profession itself.

In discussing this aspect of contemporary economics, it is necessary to distinguish between the level of discourse at what might be called the marginal or rank-and-file professional level (which includes the pronouncements of or debates among some quite high-ranking economists, addressed to the rank-and-file and the outside literate intelligentsia) and controversy at the theoretical core of the subject, the latter being by far the more interesting.

At the rank-and-file level, the possession of superior economic insight has traditionally and typically been confused with the expression of plausible doubts about how far capitalism approximates some usually unspecified ideal of human perfection, by those who for one reason or another find comfort and personal identity in the expression of such doubts.[1] (I would be the first to admit, and even to assert, that the scientific approach and scientific progress depend on the expression of doubt and the demand for confirmation of alleged truth; what I refer to here, however, is making a career out of the expression of doubt as if its expression provided its own empirical confirmation.) Some of the revolutions of the 1930s provided, and continue to provide, new and more sophisticated techniques for the pursuit of this apparently respectably scientific but in fact fundamentally antiscientific type of academic and intellectual activity. Thus the new welfare economics offered limitless possibilities of positive or negative externalities as a reason why the competitive market system could never possibly be efficient, and the impossibility of arriving scientifically at value judgments about the desirable distribution of income as a clinching reason why competition could never possibly arrive at interpersonal justice, while by scaring away the angel-philosophers of the older utilitarianism it created a vacuum into which any self-appointed spokesman for society's moral feelings about income distribution could happily rush. Similarly, the imperfect competition revolution provided new and more sophisticated analytical support for the long-standing ideas that profits originate merely in illegitimate monopoly privilege and serve no social function, and that the mass of the public does not know what is good for it, the alleged evidence for the former being product differentiation and for the latter being commercial advertising—though both phenomena are far more evident, and far more evidently socially costly, in the political rather than in the commercial realm. (Far more people have been consistently far more expensively taken in by promises of something for nothing, or of satisfaction beyond all price through the purchase of a cheap and commonplace product, offered by politicians, than promises of the same sort made by the manufacturers of soap—soap at least makes you cleaner and less obnoxious to your fellow human beings, whatever it may or may not do for your psyche.) Finally, the Keynesian revolution, and more specifically its policy residue in the form of the assumption that the capitalist system ought to be capable of delivering at all times a politically determined minimum percentage of unemployment within an equally politically determined tolerable maximum rate of inflation, usually equated with zero, was widely interpreted as setting the seal of scientific legitimacy on a standard of performance impossible for any economic system to fulfill. (It also santified two much longer-standing tenets of radical belief: that the self-seeking activities of monopolies of labor have a social legitimacy denied with loathing to monopolies based on capital or industrial knowledge, and that society possesses vast reservoirs of resources that only the stupidity or self-seeking of the capitalists prevents from being used for noble social purposes.)

Superficialities of this kind are remarkable only for their capacity to seduce self-respecting and otherwise reasonable and educated people, and perhaps as demonstrating that P. T. Barnum's dictum that "there's a sucker born every minute" is a masterpiece of understatement. Fairness requires one to acknowledge, however, that there are plenty of dogmatists on the other side of the argument who refuse to meditate on such matters as the influence of inheritance and the inefficiencies of the educational and legal systems on the actual distribution of opportunities for self-betterment among individuals equally placed to superficial observation.

Far more interesting, from both a scientific-professional and a social point of view, is the fierce controversy that has been raging at a high level— between the arcane pure theorists of Cambridge, England, and Cambridge, U.S.A., no less, to distinguish two identically named institutional locations by their respective intellectual provinces—over the nature of capital and the role of capital and the production function in the theory of distribution. This controversy centers on the rediscovery by Joan Robinson of Cambridge, England, that capital, being a man-made embodiment of original resources in machinery and structures, cannot in strict logic be treated as an easily quantifiable input into a production function, and that the distribution of income therefore cannot (at the same level) be regarded as determined by the quantity of capital relative to labor. This general point has since become embodied in the specific proposition that the rate of return on capital is not a unique monotonically decreasing function of the quantity of capital, a point originally treated as an exceptional case—"the Ruth Cohen case"—in Robinson's *The Accumulation of Capital*, but since come to be dignified as "the reverse switching problem."[2]

Had the reverse switching problem been discovered by someone other than the high priestess at Keynes's shrine in Cambridge, it would in all probability have wound up as a short journal article, or even been left in its original form as a possible but empirically uninteresting exceptional case pointed out by a bright junior colleague, to be duly noted but otherwise ignored by conscientious scholars thereafter—like the "Giffen good" case in which the negative income effect outweighs the positive substitution effect of a price decrease and leads to an upward-sloping demand curve over a range, or the possibility of unstable equilibrium and multiple equilibrium which mathematical economists have sought to bury in the assumption that all goods in general equilibrium systems are "gross substitutes." Instead, in the hands of Joan Robinson and her followers, it has become the final convincing demonstration that capitalism cannot possibly work, "orthodox" or traditional mainstream economics is a bunch of nonsense, and socialism as both an alternative economic system and an emotional protest against capitalism is the only viable alternative.

This sweeping claim reflects the rudimentary and confused state of economics in the 1930s from which the basic ideas involved spring, and is in an important sense a counterrevolution against the validated revolutions that have occurred in economics since that time rather than the radical revolution in economic thought it claims to be. First, the choice of the aggregate production function and the older, more literary theories of distribution that preceded it and remained its penumbra reflects the very early stages of the introduction of mathematical methods into economics, in the form of Douglas's joint invention and empirical application of the Cobb-Douglas production function and Hicks's use of the aggregate production function and the elasticity of substitution to tackle classical Ricardian problems of distribution theory in his *Theory of Wages*.[3] (Joan Robinson was herself involved in the long intellectual straining to understand the elasticity of substitution that filled the pages of *The Review of Economic Studies* in its early years.) A single aggregate production function necessarily makes the distribution of income depend technologically on relative factor quantities and the technology shaping the production function, to the exclusion of both the demand factors that Marshall taught economists to emphasize at the microeconomic level and the questions of morality, monopoly power, etcetera, that concern the critic of capitalism. But such an aggregate production function is a transitional stage to a general equilibrium analysis of a many-sector model, from which analysis it becomes evident both that it may not be possible to construct a "surrogate" aggregate production function and that nothing important depends on whether one can do so or not—a point with which theorists of capital in the classical tradition were quite familiar.

Leaving aside the possibility of multiple equilibrium, which in no other economic context would be held to be fatal either to economic analysis or to capitalism, the distribution of income is perfectly determinate on marginal productivity principles within a general equilibrium model incorporating demand factors. The assertion that the contrary is true is this generation's Cambridge (England) myth. Joan Robinson supports it sometimes by relying on the imperfect competition theory view that profit is determined by monopoly power and sometimes by reference to the short-run, Great Depression-oriented Keynesian view that savings and investment do not tend to equality at full employment. Her colleague Piero Straffa[4] supports it by constructing a brilliant precursor of the modern linear programming theory of production in which relative prices depend only on the real wage rate or the interest rate, and refusing to attempt to explain the interest rate except by a vague reference to liquidity preference. Their colleague Nicholas Kaldor[5] goes them one better by accepting the premise that capitalism works but maintaining that the reason cannot be anything so simple as that provided by the classical theoretical tradition. Instead, in his view, it requires two new theories: a Keynesian theory of income distribution to replace marginal productivity theory, and a Kaldorian theory of technical progress to make the rate of capital accumulation which entrepreneurs want consistent with the rate of population growth.

In the second place, the underlying methodology of the Joan Robinson exercise reflects the fallacious methodology popularized by the imperfect competition revolution, itself the outcome of much work in the 1920s on the question of what Marshall and his contemporaries meant by the assumption of "perfect competition," and subsequently by the welfare economics revolution. This methodology rested on the belief that one can dispose of a theory by finding an unsuspected error in its logic or a lack of "realism" in its assumptions. (Note that this same belief motivates Marx's attack on the "classical school" of English economics.) That belief is false: the contemporarily accepted methodology of positive economics maintains that one can falsify a theory only by falsifying its predictions.[6] By that test, no amount of logic-chopping designed to show that capitalism is impossible in pure theory can dispose of the fact that capitalism actually exists and actually works—and has worked fairly well as a system for most of its history, the major exception occurring in the Great Depression of 1929 and after when the recuperative powers of the system were insufficient to overcome the crises imposed by gross national and international monetary mismanagement.

Third, in line with the Kaleckian version of the Keynesian theory,[7] the renewed interest in capital and growth stimulated, but by no means entirely aroused, by Joan Robinson's work has thrown modern theory—in spite of, or perhaps because of, the extreme sophistication of its treatment of the production side of the economy—back into the crude Marxist model (cruder, it may be noted, than its predecessor Ricardian model, which allowed for rents earned by sheer scarcity) of an economic system employing only two factors of production (homogeneous labor and capital) identified with two social classes ("workers" and "capitalists") distinguished by different average propensities to save.

In view of the theoretically, methodologically, and sociologically reactionary nature of the model involved and the deliberate sacrifice of much intellectually hard-won understanding of the economic system that its use entails, the interesting scientific question is why this particular controversy has excited so much theoretical attention and absorbed the time and effort of so many able theorists, especially the younger students of the subject. One obvious reason is the success of the mathematical/general equilibrium revolution, which requires no knowledge of the history of economic thought, even of mathematical economics itself, and imposes no obligation to establish social relevance, beyond a plausible assertion, documented if possible, that some reputable economist has uttered a mathematical error which science requires should be cleared up. Unfortunately with sufficient determination the clearing up process can always be shown to have created further messes requiring further clearing up, and so on ad infinitum.

A more interesting explanatory factor, with broader implications, concerns the politics of institutional leadership and institutional rivalry for leadership. In very sketchy outline, the preeminence of Cambridge, England, in economics achieved at the end of the 1930s, largely due to Keynes's *General Theory*, both enabled Keynes's successors to exploit Cambridge's prestige for the propagation of their own political beliefs (which were vastly different from Keynes's own), and attracted to Cambridge a continuing stream of able students. The able student's optimal career strategy, assuming the normal degree of risk aversion, is to go to the best place available and try to distinguish himself by doing better what the teachers established there are already doing, or doing what they think should be done. By so doing, students both advance their own careers and serve the institution by becoming devoted proselytizers for the true faith among the heathen from whose ranks they sprang. At the same time, the preeminence of Cambridge, England, accepted by Harvard University as a result of the conquest of that institution by the Keynesian revolution, offered the newly established department of the Massachusetts Institute of Technology an opportunity to spring to prominence over Harvard in the United States profession by challenging Cambridge, England, on its chosen ground of pure theory. Thus Cambridge, England, became a punching bag for M.I.T.; and, if one may be permitted to personalize a punching bag, it continued to consider itself a champion because it could never be dislodged from its initial position and occasionally scored when the real champion missed a punch through overconfidence. Students taught by a punching bag are very unlikely to question their teacher's assessment of who is winning the fight, let alone learn what the fight is about or how to rate a fighter properly.

Furthermore, to abandon the boxing metaphor abruptly and turn to broader international political considerations, the post-World War II period has been characterized until relatively very recently by the international political and economic dominance of the United States, and in economics itself by the somewhat vulgarly ebullient dominance of the American scientific approach. In the meantime, the United Kingdom has been dwindling in importance in the world economy, and losing or throwing away the international prestige gained by a graceful abandonment of the erstwhile British empire, to the point where economic integration with Europe has become the last available desperate gamble on reversing the downward trend. This process of apparently inexorable decline has occurred in spite of the self-assumed superiority of British over foreign economics, derived to a not inconsiderable extent from the strong socialist and nationalist leanings inherited from the intellectual and political turmoil of the 1920s and 1930s; in fact, this inheritance has meant in practice that at every point of crucial economic policy decision British economics has reacted either with political dogma or with political opportunism. Under the circumstances, it is understandable that a developing and increasingly despairing national inferiority complex should have expressed itself in an attempt at the intellectual level to dispose of United States hegemony by ostensibly purely scientific debate about the intellectual foundations of the American economic system, and—as so often happens in such matters—that the intellectual weakness of the challenge should have been disguised by stridency of assertion of propositions and by an unrelenting quest among the counterarguments of the challenged for firmer and more plausible grounds for dispute. It is equally understandable, though no less pitiable, that intellectuals professing economics in other countries with less objectively justified but emotionally equally strong leanings toward anti-Americanism should have seized on the challenge initiated by Cambridge, England, as an apparently purely scientific rallying point for their anti-Americanism—and specifically that Joan Robinson should have become the folk heroine of the American radical minority, much of the Italian economics profession, and certain economics departments in east central Canada and the remoter parts of Australia.

The Future Prospects of Economics

Several predictions about the future prospects of economics, some obviously more reliable than others, can be made on the basis of the themes developed in the foregoing sections.

First, it is fairly certain that the halcyon days of rapid and well-financed expansion of economics training in universities, especially at the graduate level, are over—probably for a decade at least—in the English-speaking countries. That golden age rested on a sublime faith in the importance of economists and of economics to the growth and well-being of society, on the one hand, and on "undergraduate-propelled growth" on the other. The public and its politicians have lost their faith in the social benefits of science of all descriptions and in the value of spending lavishly to support it; and they have become increasingly restive over both the financial costs of university education and the elitist implications of transferring so much income and privilege to the most educationally gifted portion of the population. Economists, however, in contrast to natural scientists, are fairly well cushioned against such adverse changes in public sentiment. There is a broad and resilient market for their services, embracing government, industry, and administration of various kinds, both national and international, as well as academic employment in universities; and they do not disdain teaching their subject in high schools (or even kindergartens) if the price is right. Moreover, almost nothing can happen in a sufficiently affluent society that will not create new opportunities for the application of economics to replace those it incidentally destroys. Economists have in rapid succession turned from problems of promoting economic growth and maximizing the "bang for the buck" in defense expenditure to studying poverty and the remedies for it, and are currently massively engaged on studies of the economics of medical care, education and its finance, urban problems, and the pollution of the environment. The only serious losers are likely to be the high-powered mathematical economists, who probably quite unjustifiably established themselves in the immediate postwar period as the supreme-prestige "pure scientists" of economics; and even they have been hedging their bets by producing elegant mathematical analyses of ("modeling," in the current fashionable jargon) problems in pollution, income distribution, and health care. Economics is likely to continue to thrive, though maintaining a lower scientific profile than recently and concentrating on bread-and-butter analysis and research oriented to the social problems society is willing to spend money on studying.

Secondly, the academic end of the profession is likely to experience a marked change of tone as departments stabilize in numbers and size (or even decrease in size), promotion becomes harder and slower, and seniority comes to count for more relative to youthful promise. This will have some beneficial effects in disciplining the impatient young, over-anxious to set the world on fire, though it may extinguish some potentially illuminating fires in the process. The most serious adverse effect is likely to result from the fact that the earlier rapid expansion led many departments to award promotion and tenure to available personnel of second-rate talent or worse, in the expectation that they would eventually be outnumbered by more able new appointments in the course of a further expansion that now will not materialize. Efficiency would indicate replacing the older second-rate by the younger first-rate; but university traditions of tenure will force most of the young aspirants to look to alternative careers, and force university students to put up with worse instruction than is necessary at a time when they will need the best they can get.

Finally, the emerging less dynamic academic environment is likely to have conflicting effects on the strength of the ideological element in economic debates, effects that will be reinforced by the passage of time and political evolution. Specifically, the great Cambridge-versus-Cambridge debate over capital theory should wane as, on the one hand, leadership passes from the relics of interwar British socialism on the one side and the vanguard of American scientific imperialism on the other to a more pragmatic generation of primarily mathematically oriented theoretical specialists, for whom the British-American rivalry for domination of the subject is already a historical anachronism in an increasingly cosmopolitan profession; and, on the other hand, as mathematical virtuosity (either literary or more formally symbolic) declines as a ready-because-rare key to professional preeminence. On the other hand, the university unrest of the late 1960s, and the more general public questioning of the meaning and quality of life in a materialistic industrial society (the unease is not confined to avowedly "capitalist" countries) characterized by an inhuman and intolerable scarcity of major ideological and nationalist conflicts, are likely to mean some tendency for the average economist in future to trade rather less on his professional competence and rather more on his versatility in verbalizing and rationalizing commonly felt doubts about the beneficence of the "invisible hand."

A final point, not directly but implicitly related to the main themes of this essay, is that leadership in economic science is likely to be increasingly diffused among nationalities and languages, and decreasingly a monopolistic preserve of the speaker and writer of English, native or learned. In particular, the Continental European countries are likely to move back toward the parity of contribution that they displayed in the nineteenth century, before two world wars distracted them from scientific pursuits and anti-Semitism recruited some of their best brains to the English-speaking world. Their younger generation has all the incentives to absorb the techniques of American economics as a means of overleaping its seniors that Keynesian economics and the other 1930s revolutions offered to the younger generation of that time. In the longer run Asia may also emerge as a potent source of scientific advance in economics, though the social conditions necessary to produce the detachment and specific curiosity of the social scientist are not yet evidently sufficiently strong to generate new concepts of the economic system and its social implications. (To espouse Marxism is simply to accept a secularized western religious protest against social and economic modernization of traditional society.)

Part 4 Economics and
Contemporary Problems:
Inflation and Inequality

13. The Problem of Inflation

Inflation is most conveniently (and neutrally) defined as a sustained rising trend in the general price level, or—what is virtually the same thing—a rate of expansion of money income greater than the rate of growth of real output. Other definitions abound, but they typically attempt to insert into the definition of the observed phenomenon either some elements of a theory of causation (for example, "inflation results from excess demand") or an implicit policy recommendation (for example, "inflation results from excess money creation," or "inflation occurs when money wages rise faster than labor productivity"). Some are essentially meaningless, like the famous *Economist* catch-phrase of the immediate post-World War II period, "too much money chasing too few goods"; still others involve the economic fallacy of assigning "real" or "microeconomic" causes to a "monetary" or "macroeconomic" phenomenon, notably the popular views that inflation is caused by the monopoly power of trade unions on the one hand or large oligopolistic companies on the other—the point being that efficient exploitation of monopoly power involves fixing the most profitable price for the labor or product in question relative to the wages of other labor or prices of other products, the money wage or price required for this purpose being geared to the general levels of wages and prices.

The definition employed here concentrates on the objective phenomenon to be explained by analysis and dealt with by policy. It does, however, entail two difficulties. The first, which constitutes a trap for the unwary, is that not all price increases are "inflationary" in the sense of contributing to the inflationary process: increases in interest rates or sales taxes increase business costs or consumer prices at the time of introduction, though their purpose is to counteract inflationary pressures. The second is that the rate of price increase deemed to constitute an inflationary problem is not a scientific question but a political question determined by public opinion; and public opinion vacillates on the issue.

The problem of inflation has been a chronic problem of the "Western" or "mixed free enterprise" economies throughout the post-World War II period. This fact has been contrary to the almost universal late-wartime

A revised version of the first of the 1971 de Vries Lectures, reprinted with permission from *Inflation and the Monetarist Controversy* (Amsterdam: North-Holland Publishing Co., 1972).

expectation, grounded in Keynesian theory and especially in the American Keynesian tradition established by Alvin Hansen, that the end of the war would be followed by a disastrous depression of 1930s dimensions unless drastic Keynesian expansionary policies were adopted. That expectation, it is evident in the blinding light of hindsight, overlooked the historical fact that, for reasons easily explainable in terms of traditional monetary theory, major wars have inevitably been followed by severe inflations, for a varying but non-negligible period. It is also evident that the measures adopted for Keynesian reasons to cushion the expected deflation, especially large-scale deficit financing of war efforts at low interest rates supported by money creation and enforced in real terms by price and wage controls and physical rationing, made the immediate postwar wave of inflation more severe than it needed to have been. That particular wave of inflation was aggravated, for the European economies, by the sequential coupling of the currency devaluations of 1949—which appear, again in the light of hindsight, to have been excessive and to have contributed to the serious problem of international monetary disequilibrium that has plagued the capitalist world since the late 1950s—with the inflationary impact on primary product prices of the war in Korea. It is important for the maintenance of historical perspective to note that the inflation that has been concerning public opinion and policy makers in most countries in the past few years is attributable at least in important part to the same combination of factors—on the one hand, a major war measured in economic terms, financed by deficits and money creation rather than by taxes, and on the other hand currency devaluation or reluctance to appreciate undervalued currencies.

The fact that the chronic problem of the postwar Western world has been inflation rather than mass unemployment is associated with the fact that on the average the countries comprising that world have maintained rates of economic activity and employment unprecedentedly high by interwar standards. Some would, and still do, attribute this eminently desirable accomplishment, and the economic growth that has gone with it, to the intellectual success of the Keynesian revolution in teaching governments the techniques of demand management, and the practical success of governments in applying those techniques. This explanation is highly implausible. On the one hand, the Keynesian revolution in economic theory and policymaking has had relatively little impact outside the two countries of its origin and major intellectual development—the United Kingdom and the United States—and it was less than a decade ago that the advent of the "new economics," personified by Walter Heller's chairmanship of the Council of Economic Advisers, was hailed in the latter country, while even in the United States the governmental machinery is ill-adapted to the execution of Keynesian-style economics policies, to the extent that the timing of fiscal policy changes has generally been pro-cyclical rather than anti-cyclical. On the other hand, there are good reasons, rooted both in the "real" analysis of the economic historians[1] and in monetary theory, as to why capitalist economies should be expected in normal circumstances both to maintain a high level of employment and to enjoy some non-negligible rate of economic growth. Put very briefly, "real" analysis calls attention to the opportunities for the profitable investment of savings that the world of reality constantly throws up, while monetary analysis assumes as a matter of empirical fact that the economic system tends toward a rational full-employment allocation of resources so long as the management of money is well-behaved, and can only be thrown off course by severe monetary mismanagement.

This latter assumption is, of course, in a sense the crux of the issue prevailing between Keynesians and monetarists: the Keynesian position is that the real economy is highly unstable and that monetary management has both little relevance to it and little control over it; the monetarist position, on the contrary, is that the real economy is inherently fairly stable but can be destabilized by monetary developments, which therefore need to be controlled as far as possible by intelligent monetary policy. The monetarist position—in this very general sense, which leaves open all the important scientific questions about how monetary impulses affect the economy and how money should be managed—seems to me the only alternative consistent with the facts (as distinct from the myths) of historical experience. And though I do not wish at this particular point to go into the empirical evidence in detail, I should remark that I have arrived at this judgment, not by dogmatic conviction, but out of growing dissatisfaction with the explanatory power of the theories and the empirical results of the policies of Keynesian economics in which I was instructed during my youth at the two major centers of the revolution.

I should also remark, in passing, that I find not merely implausible but completely incredible two other variants of a Keynesian explanation of the success of the Western capitalist world in maintaining high employment since the Second World War, both of which rest on the Keynesian assumption that capitalism cannot prosper without a large and sustained exogenous—and preferably both irrational and immoral—demand for goods and services. One, which has appealed greatly in recent years to so-called intellectuals trained in the emotional and religious self-indulgences of vulgar Marxism, is the idea that the survival of capitalism depends on the wastage of vast amounts of resources in unjust imperialistic adventures in military aggression. This explanation deliberately disregards, or, more likely, is simply naïvely ignorant of, the economic implications of the considerable swings in levels of military expenditure that have occurred over the postwar period, in terms of their theory of capitalism. The other, which has recently been put into circulation by my former colleague Nicholas Kaldor in three prestigious articles in the *Times*,[2] is the pseudomonetary hypothesis that capitalism has been kept going in the postwar period by the willingness of the United States to inject an exogenous expansionary item of demand into the world economy by running a persistent and growing balance-of-payments deficit. Neither Kaldor's assertion that the United States has suffered sustained heavy unemployment as a result of this benevolent irrationality of its macroeconomic policy, nor his assumption that a net demand injection of the order of $3 billion on average—a small fraction of a tenth of one percent of total world output—has sufficed to make capitalism a success in the postwar period, can make any empirical sense to economists schooled in the scientific view that an idea is to be tested by its empirical relevance rather than by its intellectual brilliance.

Keynesian theory, then, offers no satisfactory explanation of why the quarter century since the Second World War has been characterized by reasonably full employment in the capitalist countries, and therefore of why its chronic problem has been inflation rather than Keynesian mass unemployment. At most, Keynesian theory can offer an explanation—which, incidentally, is not Keynesian but merely a Keynesian description of phenomena well understood by pre-Keynesian monetary theorists—of why high employment tends to generate price inflation. And even this description is marred, as I shall argue later, by the tendency of Keynesian theorists, following their master, to reason in terms of a closed economy and to ignore the linkings between price developments in the various countries of the world economic system created by the system of fixed exchange rates on the one hand and the maintenance of relatively liberal international trade and payments arrangements on the other. As a consequence, the problem of inflation has tended to appear in the literature as a series or collection of individual national problems, essentially sociological in origin, rather than as an international monetary problem.

In sum, neither the adoption of Keynesian stabilization policies by governments, nor the application of the simple Keynesian view that if capitalism is successful this must be attributable to some "uncapitalistic" exogenous demand factor, seems capable of explaining the sustained stability and prosperity of the world economy since the Second World War. The broad facts fit much better with the traditional assumptions that the system possesses a great deal of inherent stability and that—though this anticipates subsequent argument—monetary factors play a determining role in the long-run development of prices and interest rates. The intellectual and popular success of the Keynesian revolution in economic theory has, however, nevertheless brought about a fundamental change in the atmosphere or climate of public opinion in the postwar period as compared with the prewar, a change vital for economic policymaking and specifically for the problem of inflation. This change consists simply in the general acceptance of the proposition that government has both the power and the responsibility to maintain a politically satisfactory level of employment. Moreover, by a not entirely logical connection of ideas based on the identification of new investment as the source of productivity increase, government has also come to be charged with the responsibility for maintaining a satisfactory rate of economic growth, while one natural consequence of the extension of governments' economic responsibilities has been that the maintenance of a satisfactory balance of payments has become a policy objective or at least a constraint on the pursuit of other policy objectives that must be satisfied. Thus, the standard list of policy objectives reeled off whenever appropriate by government and central bank spokesmen, official commissions, and independent policy commentators has come, even in the Netherlands, to consist of four items: high employment, economic growth, price stability, and a reasonable balance of payments. (Tastes vary internationally regarding the inclusion of a fifth objective, described in Canada as "an equitable distribution of income.")

The acceptance of "full" or "high" employment as an objective of government policy has been a fundamental change, with widespread implications of varying degrees of subtlety. One obvious implication, which was in fact recognized by a number of earlier Keynesian writers on economic policy, though against the background of the 1930s experience of mass unemployment they either played down the point and hoped for the best or were dismissed as inhuman and immoral dogmatists and preachers of doom, is that a serious government effort to maintain continuous full employment implies loss of policy control of the wage and prices levels, since the monetary authority will have to validate any wage and price increases determined by competitive pressures or—the more usual bogey—administrative price-fixing by oligopolistic firms and collective wage-bargaining involving oligopolistic unions.

This basic point, which has been elegantly formulated in particular by M. W. Reder[3] and J. R. Hicks,[4] has persisted throughout subsequent discussions of the inflation problem in two specific forms. One has been the pragmatic recognition that the commitment both inclines the political policymaking process to take calculated risks on the inflationary consequences of demand-expansive policies, and obliges it to accept inflation once it has occurred rather than attempt to fight wages and prices back down toward their starting point. The other is a strong propensity, even among professional economists who should know better, to blame inflationary developments on the immoral self-seeking activities of monopolistic industries and unions. The elementary economic theory of value teaches that monopolies, either firms or unions, will seek to set a relative price for their product that maximizes profits in real terms, while monetary theory suggests that the money price so determined will be adjusted by rational maximizers in conformity with general changes in the price level, so as to maintain the maximizing real price relativity. (One has, however, to recognize a potentially important qualification here: If established businesses and union managements are slow to make adjustments to the fact of inflation, they may be challenged by more junior people in their organizations with the result that the organization comes to regard a higher relative real price for the product as the optimal profit-maximizing strategy; and, particularly in the case of "union militancy," this may lead to efforts by rival organizations to restore traditional real price relativities through inflationary adjustments of money prices.) With this view of inflation as being due to the selfishness of monopolistic organizations, ungrateful for the politically conferred benefits of full employment, naturally goes the propensity to prescribe an incomes policy of some kind as a panacea for inflation. And with that prescription comes the typical and insoluble dilemma of incomes policy: that its aim is to substitute for a politically imposed constraint on the use of monetary policy against inflation, but that its implementation becomes embogged in the effort to correct real distortions in the operation of the competitive system, or even more hopelessly in the effort to distort the workings of competition in order to secure a more ethically satisfactory distribution of income.

A more subtle implication and one that is not recognized by the traditional Benthamite-Fabian approach to the nature and functions of government characteristic of economic policy theory and the theory of welfare economics, though it has increasingly been made the subject of the recently evolving economic theory of government, and is recognized rather uneasily and uncomfortably by economists concerned with economic policy formation, is associated with the fact that, whatever the rhetoric of the public good involved, the prime problem of politicians is not to serve the public good but to get elected to office and remain in power. The knowledge both that the public holds them accountable for its experiences of unemployment and of inflation, and that they do have their hands on levers that influence these experiences, naturally suggests the use of these levers to maintain and strengthen political support among the electorate rather than to serve a larger-range concept of the public good if the public finds what is good for it hard to live with. Specifically, politicians elected on the basis of promises of anti-inflationary policies who attempt to carry them out are under strong social-psychological pressures to abandon them in the face of their growing unpopularity and the approach of the next elections; and politicians facing an election they fear they may lose are under similarly strong pressures to inflate the economy to gain votes, in the expectation that if they win they will have time to clear up the mess they have created sufficiently soon for the public to forget their deceitfulness before the next elections, and that if they lose, their opponents will come into office with a cripplingly embarrassing mess to clean up, any failures or unpleasantness involved in the effort constituting ammunition for the next election. This process has been evident in the United Kingdom and the United States in recent years; it is so well known in Europe as to have been christened "the political cycle" (i.e., business or trade cycle).

A third, and still more subtle, implication, is one that is virtually universally disregarded in economic theorizing and model-building. It is associated with the fact that the effective economic decision-taking sector of the public is fairly fully aware of the political nature of and constraints on economic policy decisions, and uses this knowledge in its own decision-taking. Contrary to the standard assumptions of economic theory, the economic public does not simply respond mechanically, according to econometrically determined behavior relationships, to signals reaching it through the blind and impersonal operations of price and quantity determination in competitive markets. Instead, the relevant economic public engages in two kinds of political transactions with its governmental policymakers, both of a game-theoretic rather than atomistic-competition type. First, one of its major concerns is to guess how determined the government is about implementing its announced economic policies, and particularly how soon the government will be forced by the pressures of political unpopularity to reverse its policies before they have become clearly effective in securing their objectives. This has been a favorite subject of discussion in informed economic circles in both the United Kingdom and the United States in the past two years—with the British government being able to hold out longer than the American because it had a longer run up to the next election, but with both sacrificing their policies to political pressures well before success was more than an optimistic possibility. Second, the relevant economic public, aware of the sensitivity of government to political pressures, has an incentive to generate such pressures in its own favor so far as it can, through both private representations and public pronouncements, the latter often of a contrafactual or contra-analytical nature.

The consequence of these implications of the commitment to full employment as a policy objective is that academic analyses of the causes of inflation and of the relative merits of economic policies for dealing with it are to an important extent unreal. They are about knowledge and its limits, rather than about the uses to which society chooses to put its existing limited knowledge. Further, presumably scientific debates about economic policy are frequently poisoned—sometimes quite deliberately and intentionally—by the engagement of the economists concerned in the political process itself. The proclamation of politically unpalatable truth becomes an invitation to pseudoscientific character assassination, while the invention of so-called boldly unorthodox theories that seek to repeal the laws of economics because they stand in the way of the politicians' desire to maximize their political utility function without reference to the economic budget constraint becomes an avenue of professional advancement. Still, this is a fact of life with which scientifically minded economists have to learn to live, in the hope that sometimes, or in the long run, truth will somehow prevail.

The fact that inflation has been a chronic problem of the Western capitalist world for a quarter of a century implies that the processes of political decision-making have been in fact prepared to tolerate it as an element in a politically optimal system of economic management. There has been, in other words, a "revealed preference" for inflation. In view of the ostensible and often highly vocal political resistance to inflation and insistence on governmental responsibility for stopping or at least minimizing inflation, this is a rather paradoxical situation. Economic theory suggests two alternative possible lines of explanation.

The first rests on a presumed irrationality of governmental decision-taking. There are three conceivable variants of this explanation.

The first, which I would regard as definitely untenable, is that government is simply ignorant of the causal factors in inflation and unaware of the inflationary consequences of its own policy choices.[5] This hypothesis is completely implausible, given both the sophistication of contemporary economic understanding and the fact that even politicians are capable of learning from their own and others' experience; and dismissal of it out of hand is not inconsistent with the observation that, for their own purposes, politicians frequently deny or attempt to deny that a particular policy action will have the inflationary consequences that such a policy action has always had in the past.

The second variant is that, in technical terms, the political preference function violates the standard axioms of consistency and transitivity, so that political preferences as revealed in actual decisional behavior are inconsistent. This explanation is plausible as an observation based on governmental behavior over relatively short periods of years, and can be supported by reference on the one hand to the responsiveness of politicians to political pressures emanating from the electorate, together with the fact that the public tends to complain most vociferously about whatever is currently annoying it most about its economic situation, and on the other to the internal decentralization of government policymaking, according to which two institutions with different traditions are assigned separately primary responsibility for what may be termed the "real" and the "monetary" aspects of policy, the Treasury being primarily responsible for employment and growth and the central bank for price stability and the balance of payments, with the results both that their policies may conflict and that now one and now the other achieves command in overall policymaking. The problem at hand, however, is not one of random inconsistency or alternation in the pursuit of policy objectives, but of a long-run systematic bias in the policymaking process toward an inflationary outcome.

This brings us to the third variant of this line of explanation, which is that the political decision-taking process is rational in its own terms, but systematically biased toward underestimating the social value of price stability and the social costs of inflation. This explanation also can claim considerable plausibility on various grounds. One, already mentioned, is the necessary preoccupation of politicians elected for short terms of office with short-run achievements to the neglect of the longer-run consequences of their policies. If government were conducted in the same way as the management of the large industrial, commercial, and financial corporations, it would probably do much more, and much more intensive, long-range planning.[6] Another comes from the economic theory of democracy,[7] which stresses the cost-benefit aspects of acquiring the information required for intelligent voting behavior as explaining the dominance of producer over consumer interests in political decision-taking. In the context of the explanation of persistent inflation, the argument would be that the losses from inflation come on the side of consumption, and that two important classes of potential losers lack political organization as producer groups to defend their interests as consumers. These are, on the one hand, the retired and other socially dependent groups who are out of the active labor force and do not currently produce the incomes on which they live, and on the other hand the numerically important group of the currently occupied who produce, not goods and services for the private market, but services for the governmental, educational, health-care, and other institutions of society and are subject both to the problems of confronting a monopoly purchaser and to ethico-sociological constraints on their capacity to pursue unashamedly their economic self-interests. This explanation, also, lacks plausibility in the longer run, for two economic reasons. First, a reason now familiar from the "permanent-income" and "life-cycle savings" theories of consumption and the more general theory of human capital, rational active producers should appreciate that they will eventually themselves retire, and in the meantime may fall victim to life's various accidents, and so in their political behavior have regard for the economic position of the ailing and the retired—as in fact the political process does, through periodic revision of the monetary values of social security and retirement benefits. Second, one would expect that in the longer run the supply of employees to what may be loosely called the public sector would respond to the real income prospects there as compared with those in the private sector—including possible victimization by inflation; and in fact public sector salaries are also adjusted periodically to the fact of inflation.

The "irrationality of government" explanations of inflation, therefore, plausible as they may appear, do not hold up very convincingly as explanations of a long-sustained period of what may be termed "creeping" or "strolling" or "briskly walking" rather than "galloping" inflation. The alternative line of explanation assumes that, on a long-run average, government is both rational and informed about the alternatives confronting it, and broadly representative of the preferences of the public as a whole; and it attributes the revealed preference for inflation to the hypothesis that inflation of the kind under discussion has relatively little social cost and hence is not too irksome to tolerate as the price of achieving other economic objectives.

In contemplating this hypothesis, an economist has to be (or at least ought to be, since so few are) acutely aware of social and intellectual pressures to prejudge the issue in terms of emotional, political and social commitments. The pressures come from both sides. On the one hand, the origins of Keynesian economics in interwar and still largely Victorian England predispose Keynesian economists—particularly those sequestered in the medieval environments of Oxford and Cambridge—to the belief that economic nirvana consists in everyone being fully employed in his allotted station in life, which implies that no price in terms of other economic disturbances is too high to pay for full employment. This is an attitude only too happily shared by the organized labor movement and by those who identify socialism with espousal of the conservative self-interests of "the workers." But economic rationality requires recognition that society has other interests with which those of full employment for workers may conflict, including some of the interests of the workers themselves, and that the social and economic costs of unemployment are a function of the other social policies that society chooses to adopt. "Love on the Dole" meant misery and degradation in the 1930s in the north of England; in the 1960s it came to mean the liberty and economic irresponsibility of hippiedom in California.

On the other hand, the voices that speak against inflation and in favor of price stability as a policy objective are not to be trusted either. Concern about preservation of the purchasing power of money is characteristically the special responsibility of the financial community, headed by the central bank as that community's special representative in the governmental machinery. As such, it expresses the self-interest of a vested interest group with no more claim to respect for its economic understanding than any other interest group. Much of the respect that its claims nevertheless command derives from the historically irrelevant circumstances of medieval history, when debasement of the currency by the monarch was a desperate last-resort method of taxing honest merchants and other commoners by deliberate fraud. There was, therefore, a need for a moral pressure group to keep the monarch honest (and frequently conveniently penurious) in defense of the hard-earned wealth of honest citizens. That logic does not apply to the modern world of democratically selected governments, in which (except in the case of major wars, where outright confiscation of wealth and income is the only alternative to inflationary taxation) the main consequences of inflation are redistributions from one group of citizens to another—insofar as inflation can constitute a method of redistributory taxation, which theory suggests is doubtful in the longer run.

In recent times, however, partly as a result of the subordination of central bank policies to the fiscal needs of treasuries, a major source of political complaint about inflation has come to be the consumer. Here the alert economist should observe and contemplate the economic implications of the contemporary institution of marriage, and particularly of the customary division of economic responsibilities between the husband as the earner of income and the wife as the household-utility-maximizing major spender of it—an application of Adam Smith's principle of specialization and division of labor that only the advertising men and their economists have tried to accommodate to. This division of responsibility in the earning and spending of income, and particularly the time-lag in the adjustment of the husband's nominal budgetary allocations to his wife to the fact of inflation, besides making inflation a powerful enemy of the Women's Liberation movement and guarantor of male supremacy, makes inflation a serious political issue for women, and to some extent for the more hen-pecked of their husbands, even though when the family balance-sheet is consolidated, inflation may have a zero or positive effect on total family welfare. As politicians are well aware, men vote for jobs and women vote for lower prices.

If one can dodge these political opinion-traps, the scientific question for consideration is, what are the main elements in the economic costs of inflation. As already suggested, much of the argument about the evils of inflation concerns effects of inflation which may or may not be considered to be social costs, but which actually do not involve economic costs in the sense of waste of resources and sacrifice of potential consumption or investment— that is, redistributions of income from creditors to debtors, or from old age pensioners, social security recipients, and public sector employees to private sector employees and entrepreneurs, or from wives to husbands. With respect to the social costs—which, incidentally, are sometimes, at least as regards the first two, regarded as socially desirable rather than undesirable—economic theory suggests, first, that if they are considered serious they could be compensated by appropriate institutional changes, rather than requiring the battling of inflation by economic policy, and, secondly, that the institutional mechanisms of a society based on freedom of choice and competition will, if the system of contract is reasonably flexible and inflation not too erratic, act to bring about the elimination of major inflationary injustices. If one is to find genuine economic costs of inflation, therefore, one must look for costs that cannot or will not be eliminated by the processes of competitive contract adjustment.

One obvious problem arising from inflation, which has much exercised economists and economic policy in the contemporary era, has been its adverse balance-of-payments implications. This problem, however, has to be properly understood as a problem itself created by government policy, and moreover as one that has come to cut in the opposite direction to that formerly assumed, as the Western world has become an inflationary environment. The standard argument against inflation based on external economic considerations is that inflation will render a country's export and import-competing goods internationally uncompetitive, and so face it with a balance-of-payments problem. But that problem is created not by inflation per se but by the government's tolerating domestic inflation while trying to adhere to a fixed exchange value of its currency, which policy dishonestly pretends that the purchasing power of the currency is stable when in reality it is being eroded by the governmentally tolerated inflation. And the economic losses associated with inflation are those imposed by government itself in its efforts to avoid admitting the inconsistency between its inflationary domestic policies and its fixed exchange rate, either by deflating its domestic economy severely occasionally in order to try to restore its international price competitiveness, or by imposing distorting restrictions on the international trade and payments of its citizens, thereby sacrificing the advantages of international specialization and division of labor, rather than by following the theoretically proper policy of devaluing its currency or allowing it to depreciate in order to reconcile internal inflation with external economic viability within a liberal trade and payments system. Moreover, for many countries in the contemporary inflationary world, external balance with a fixed exchange rate requires more or less deliberate inflation, to avoid the necessity of transferring real resources to more inflationary countries at the expense of the living standards and growth prospects of the domestic public. In the context of world inflation, domestic arguments against inflation, when not firmly allied with insistence on upwards exchange rate flexibility, are pleas for trying to hold back an inflation ultimately inevitable so long as the exchange rate remains fixed while other countries are inflating, by means of low-yield or negative-yield loans of real domestic resources to foreigners.

Turning to domestically oriented arguments against inflation, recent theorizing has turned up only two significant such arguments. The first— which rests on the assumption that inflation comes to be fairly rapidly anticipated, and so translated into the determination of money prices, wages, and interest rates, which therefore preserve their real equilibrium values and relativities—stresses the costs and welfare losses arising from the inability of the public to recontract the holding terms on the one asset whose supply is monopolized by the government, namely money, along with money-substitute assets such as government debt and various kinds of savings media, the terms on which are controlled at least partially by the government. This cost, it can be shown by relatively simple empirical calculations, is likely to be trivial for mild inflations occurring in a financially advanced economy. The second economic argument against inflation, on the other hand, stresses the costs of acquiring information and taking decisions in the face of uncertainty about what the rate of inflation in fact will be. It should be noted that this aspect of the cost of inflation is not a cost of inflation as such, but a cost of variations in the trend of the general level of prices; and that consequently the costs of stopping inflation on this account may be greater than the costs of letting it continue at its current rate. Further, given the previously mentioned political constraints on the capacity of government to adopt and to adhere to for long a sharp change of direction in economic policy, combined with the ability of the more important economic decision-takers to forecast trends and changes in government policy with some degree of reliability, the costs involved may be relatively small in advanced countries, though they may well be high indeed in less-developed countries with unstable governments.

These brief remarks reflect what I hope is a consensus of common-sense economics on the question of the costs of inflation of the kind experienced during the past twenty-five years. It may be useful, however, in concluding this lecture, to survey briefly what more formal monetary theory has had to say about the welfare aspects of inflation. As already mentioned, formal monetary theory up into the 1930s, when the Keynesian revolution struck, was dominated by the Wicksellian concepts of monetary equilibrium and of "neutral" money. The essential concern of that tradition was with the conditions under which money would remain merely a "veil," in the neoclassical phrase, over the workings of the underlying barter economy, conditions which Wicksell summarized in the principles of equality of the real and money rates of interest, equality of (ex ante) savings and investment, and stability of the price level. Later theorists in this tradition realized that, in a growing or changing economy, price level stability rather than deflation might be inconsistent with monetary neutrality, and (a postwar finding) that ex ante equality of savings and investment was an inadequate criterion for real equilibrium because neither was an operational magnitude; such equilibrium required equality of both with ex post investment and saving. The concern with preventing monetary developments from distorting real equilibrium rested on the assumption that, left to themselves, the real economic forces would tend to produce a welfare-optimizing equilibrium, an assumption that the Keynesian revolution effectively blasted, so that the concept of monetary equilibrium has now to be interpreted as a non-normative, purely positive, technique of analysis, as I understand it is in contemporary Dutch monetary theory. Moreover, recognition of the fact of economic growth destroyed the necessary equality of the real and money rates of interest—the relevant theory, which introduces expectations of the rate of price change as a wedge between the two, was provided by Irving Fisher but seems never to have made its way into European theorizing, whose efforts to cope with the problems of the interrelations among real growth, price trends, and interest rates remained groping. Thus my great teacher

D. H. Robertson used to assert that the money price level should fall in proportion to the rate of increase of productivity, a proposition very similar to some modern results to be discussed later; but his argument rested on the desirability of enabling those retired from the active population to continue to share in the growth of productivity; through the resulting increase over time of the purchasing power of their annuities; and that argument was invalid, because it neglected the influence of the expected trend of prices on the money interest rates at which the retired would have accumulated their savings.

For what it was worth, however—and some of it was extremely subtle— monetary theory up into the 1930s suggested that the proper monetary policy would aim at a deflationary trend of prices related somehow to productivity growth. The contemporary popular emphasis on price stability as an objective of economic policy is a political simplification with no comparable theoretical justification. During the same period, however, some "monetary heretics," including Keynes in the 1920s, had been developing an alternative view, namely that price inflation was good for prosperity and growth because it redistributed income from rentiers to entrepreneurs and so raised profits and stimulated investment. A further and related argument in the same vein, though one usually kept veiled in decent moral obscurity, is that inflation stimulates growth by redistributing income from workers to capitalists, with similar effects on investment. This view has its representatives among contemporary Keynesian growth theorists. But it involves the same basic theoretical flaw as its more orthodox contemporary, namely that it neglects the influence of price expectations on the determination of monetary rates of interest and of money wage rates. If inflation—or deflation, for that matter—comes to be anticipated with fair certainty on all sides, it should have no influence in redistributing income among the owners of factors of production, assuming that these owners behave rationally. (This does not deny that unexpected inflations or deflations do redistribute wealth between the holders and the issuers of fixed-interest securities.)

As already mentioned, the concern of monetary theorists up to the mid-1930s with monetary equilibrium, monetary neutrality, and the desirable trend of the price level was swept into limbo by the Keynesian revolution, at least in English-language economics. Contemporary monetary theorists, however, have been returning to these problems in a somewhat different and more explicitly growth-oriented context, namely the role of money in models of economic growth and the somewhat misleadingly named problem of "the optimum quantity of money."[8] The essence of the problem as theoretically constructed is that money is assumed to cost nothing to produce and also to bear no explicit yield, but instead to bear an implicit negative or positive yield determined by the rate of inflation or deflation maintained by government monetary policy. The problem, then, is to choose the optimal rate of monetary growth and corresponding price trend, to maximize the community's welfare along an exogenously determined growth path (the rate of growth in the long run being determined exogenously by the rates of growth of population and of labor-augmenting technical progress).

The answer is complicated if the economy is assumed to save irrationally according to a fixed savings ratio or desired wealth-to-income ratio, because then its consumption may fall short (on either side) of the technically maximum possible consumption per head, and if it falls short through insufficiency of capital per head (the more reasonable case) increasing capital stock and therefore consumption per head by manipulating the cost of money-holding and therefore the amount of saving that goes into material capital involves an intertemporal choice problem insoluble in terms of the model. If, on the other hand, saving can be assumed to be motivated by rational utility maximization, welfare maximization requires satiating the demand for real balances, which in turn requires deflating the economy's price level at a rate equal to the rate of return on material capital. In short, with much theoretical pyrotechnical display, contemporary pure monetary theory arrives at the same broad conclusion as the interwar style of monetary equilibrium theory, according to which optimality requires a deflationary trend of prices.

This conclusion, however, assumes that money is inherently non-interest-bearing, so that price deflation is required to endow it with the real yield necessary to satiate the demand for it (which demand by assumption is socially costless to satisfy). If, instead, it is assumed that in practice money is predominantly produced by a competitive banking system paying competitive interest rates on deposits—a situation which could be created by government policy where it does not now exist—the conclusion falls to the ground, because any rate of inflation maintained by the monetary authority would be reflected in money rates of interest on bank deposits as well as on other monetary assets and hence cause no distortions from the optimum quantity of money. The theoretical analysis would then have to turn to other considerations not currently allowed for, most obviously the relative economic costs of operating an economy with rising or falling prices as compared with stable prices. Such an analysis would probably lead to the common-sense conclusion that price stability is optimal in this respect and that inflation imposes additional welfare-reducing information and trans-actions costs. But the resulting loss from mild and not too erratic inflation on this account would probably be of a negligible order of magnitude, certainly not large enough to justify a strong policy of resistance to inflation.

14. Some Microeconomic Observations on Income and Wealth Inequalities

The subject of inequalities of income and wealth is one of perennial concern in the history of modern society, erupting into acute concern from time to time. Such eruptions show a high degree of correlation with two frequently but not necessarily or always related phases of economic and political development. One is serious and/or prolonged depressions, which frustrate prevalent expectations of prosperity, security, and rising standards of living, and generate private and public concern about the distribution of existing income in place of normally overriding private and public concern about the growth of income and the exploitation of opportunities for increasing income through application and planning for the future. The other is loss of national self-confidence, with respect to both the purposiveness of the political process and the quality of life provided by the economic system which the political process is presumed to direct to the service of nobler aims than the satisfaction of "mere" material wants. In the modern world, with its rapid international communications system focused on the world's greatest nation, the United States, concern in that country with inequality tends to spread to other countries that lack the same objective domestic reasons for discontent. Thus, for example, recent concern about poverty and inequality in Canada and the United Kingdom can be traced back fairly reliably to U. S. domestic concern arising in the early 1960s from the evident and well-publicized failure of blacks and of poor people generally to participate in the national affluence, and later from the demoralizing effects, especially among educated and draftable young males, of the expensive fiasco of the war in Viet Nam.

The underlying foundations for sporadic acute concern with inequality in modern society would seem to consist of two elements. One is a naïve and basically infantile anthropomorphism, according to which, because men are physically identical (or at least men in reasonably homogeneous ethnic or other social groupings are so), inequalities in the socially determined capacity to satisfy biological and social wants are considered unjust, in disregard or denial of the social role of such inequalities in motivating and rewarding contributions to the organization of the society for survival and progress in

Prepared for *Income Inequalities*, ed. Sidney Weintraub, a special issue of the *Annals* of the American Academy of Political and Social Science, 1973; reprinted with permission.

the face of erosive internal and external pressures. The other is the historical Western inheritance of the Judeo-Christian tradition of the equality of man before God, originally primarily an affirmation of the right to survival and self-fulfillment of a discriminated-against minority group, and now shorn of its countervailing affirmation of the religious legitimacy of duly constituted authority and status differentiation by the materialistic secularization of culture following the advent of the industrial revolution and the associated rise of popular democratic government.

Both of these foundations for concern about inequality are emotional rather than rational in essence; and their emotional character lends itself both to the interpretation of current social organization in terms of archaic myths and to the projection of the personal self-doubts and strains engendered by life in modern society. In particular, there are strong tendencies to interpret modern society in terms of feudal or early industrial structure based on the family inheritance of landed or accumulated property in the nonhuman means of production, an interpretation especially ana-chronistic for societies based on immigrant opportunity to escape the limitations on economic and social mobility imposed by a "class" society, of which the American is the explicit prototype but not the only one, other societies increasingly incorporating elements of social reward for economic achievement. Also, there are strong tendencies to identify equality with the opportunity for all to enjoy the advantages of affluent cultivation of self formerly reserved to the few who had monopolized the economic surplus above subsistence through capture, accumulation, and ownership and careful administration of scarce nonhuman factors of production—without worrying about how a surplus of sufficient size can be created and maintained if no one is entitled to the profits from minding the store. These misperceptions of the problem lead both to an exaggerated and naïve concept of the importance and urgency of inequality, reflected in the use of such superficial and irrelevant statistics as "the top x percent of the population receives ax percent of the income," where x is a small fraction and a a sufficiently large integer to convey the impression of obscenity; and to the recommendation of superficial and analytically weakly-based or unsupported policies for remedying inequality by taking large sums from those who have currently high incomes and giving them to those who have not.

This is not to deny that there are serious problems of inequality in an ethical sense, about which something should be done, but to assert that the problem ought to be viewed and analyzed in terms of a sophisticated understanding of the mechanisms of economic organization of modern society for the purpose of serving man's wants, rather than in terms of an absolute ethical principle that all men ought to be economically and socially equal.

The essential point in this assertion is that observed inequality in income distribution is to a large extent a by-product of the success of the modern economic system in providing opportunities for free choice and self-fulfillment of man, considered in the short run as a being with diverse tastes, preferences, and attitudes, and in the long run as a mortal being with a limited life span characterized by patterned change in physical, mental, and social characteristics, whose hopes of transcendental immortality are dependent on the procreation of his species—and to do so in consistency with the survival and progress of human society and the absence of dependence on the institutions of legal or de facto slavery that characterized earlier systems of society. The problem of inequality is therefore in a broad sense that of determining the areas in and the extent to which modern society falls short of this ideal generalization, and of devising appropriate remedies for these shortcomings, insofar as this is possible given the complex nature of both man and his society and the danger of solving superficial problems at the expense of creating new and more intractable basic problems.

In traditional debates on the subject of inequality, the conservative defense of "things as they are" is usually rested on the proposition that inequality is necessary to provide "incentives" for hard work, discipline, inventiveness, accumulation, and so forth. This position is not defensible, however, not merely because it is easy to pick holes in its blanket endorsement of all inequalities—the only exception customarily allowed being the legitimacy of the claims of the "deserving" poor (those who are poor through no fault of character or circumstance of their own) on the conscience of the rich—but more fundamentally because it entails an antidemocratic instrumental concept of the relation of the citizen to the state. The point being made here is the quite different one that the exercise of the alternatives of choice provided to the citizen necessarily give rise to observed inequalities of income as conventionally measured, and that efforts to prevent this outcome or to cancel it out by post facto income redistribution run the serious risk both of depriving the citizen of the benefits of freedom of choice and self-fulfillment and of eventually requiring a reversion to a more authoritative or totalitarian structure of the society and the state.[1] This point rests firmly on various recent developments in the microeconomic analysis of the functioning of labor markets, most notably the life cycle theory of the consumption function, the concept of human capital, the analysis of the implications for career choices of varying attitudes toward risk and toward future versus present consumption, and the detailed theory of leisure as a consumption good.

To put the point very briefly and generally, as is necessary in a short essay of this kind, let us ignore for the moment differences among individuals in opportunities and capacities for economic performance, and concentrate on the implications of significant differences in tastes and preferences.[2] We would expect to observe the following phenomena, as well as others not listed, all of which would lead to observed differences in labor income on a cross-section basis, and some to observed differences in wealth and property income as well.

First, the individual life span is characterized economically by non-synchronous patterned variations with age in both material consumption needs and potential productive contribution. On the consumption side, the typical pattern involves limited but gradually expanding needs during a first period of upbringing and education, a multiplication of needs in the phase of family formation and child-bearing and child-raising, a phasing-out of these needs as children in their turn mature and leave home, and a subsequent diminution of needs with aging and the approach of death, possibly with a final upsurge of needs for medical attention and physical care. On the production side, the individual begins life incapable of productive contribution and dependent on parental provision, foregoes exploiting productive potential immediately as it develops for the sake of investment in education increasing future productive potential, acquires increasing potential through job experience up to some peak point after which capacity gradually depreciates, and retires from active participation in production long before death. These nonsynchronous consumption and production patterns over the life span would imply cross-section inequality of income and wealth both because incentives to earn money rather than enjoy leisure vary with age and family responsibilities (in youth, claims on family resources) and because it is rational to convert human capital (earning power) into material capital and vice versa in order to finance family formation (and possibly education of self and/or children) by borrowing, and retirement by investment in income-yielding property. Such cross-section–statistically-created evidence of inequality where in essence there is none should obviously not be interpreted as indicating a significant social problem.

Second, individual choices reflecting differences in preferences will produce observed inequalities of labor income and property income or wealth among individuals at the same phase of the life cycle. People obviously can legitimately differ in their preferences as between living an austere and hardworking early productive life for the sake of a comfortable old age as an independent worker or affluent retired person, and living it up in youth while hoping that their future will take care of itself. They can also legitimately differ in their preferences for family formation and child upbringing as compared with more personal leisure or material consumption in the potential child-raising and subsequent phases of the life cycle, in their preferences as between a fixed commitment to regular but limited hours of work and the freedom to work in concentrated spurts punctuated by periods of voluntary idleness, and in their preferences as between high material consumption and scant leisure, and low material consumption and ample leisure—where leisure should be interpreted broadly to include such phenomena as the long paid holidays available to schoolteachers and civil servants, and the opportunity to serve one's fellow men through political, charitable, and civic-minded activity, as well as the opportunity to entertain oneself by exercising one's own mental and physical talents.[3] Finally, given the uncertainties of career choice in an uncertain world, people may legitimately differ in their attitudes toward risk, those who dislike risk settling for careers offering greater security at the expense of a lower prospective average income for such people as a group, and those who enjoy risk opting for careers with a prospect of an exceptionally high income at the expense of a possibility of a substantially lower individual income and also of a lower average income for such people as a group than would be obtainable in safer occupations. A society composed of a majority of risk-averters would be characterized statistically by the presence of a relatively small number of extremely high incomes and of incomes not far below the average; by contrast, a society composed of a majority of risk-lovers would be characterized statistically by a relatively high number of very low incomes and of incomes not much above the average. The former society would presumably view its income-distribution problem as one of inordinate income inequality, the latter as one of unwarranted large-scale poverty, though in both cases the statistical facts are the outcome of voluntary choice and to make a social problem of them would require introducing the additional (though not unreasonable) assumption that the choices which the facts reflect are biased by ignorance of opportunities and risks or lack of resources to exploit opportunities on the part of a significant number of society's members, and/or that inequalities in the achievements of parents are unfairly passed on to their children as inequalities of knowledge and resources for exploiting opportunities.

The conclusion to be drawn from this brief analysis is that the proper focus of ethically motivated social concern about inequality should be inequalities of opportunities and the knowledge and resources required to exploit them properly, rather than the statistical facts of measured inequality, which reflect both inequality of original opportunities and rational voluntary choices among available opportunities intended to maximize individual self-fulfillment. Analyses and remedies that focus on the resultant income distribution and the correction of it by redistributive progressive income and inheritance taxes and social security systems will if implemented have the unintended (or, perhaps worse, even intended) effect of disproportionately burdening with taxation those who have preferences for non-procreation or for high-quality low-number families as against high-quantity low-quality high–public-expense families, preferences for future over present consumption, preferences for high-skilled over low-skilled careers, preferences for material consumption over consumption of leisure, and preferences for risky high payoff careers over secure low payoff careers. At least some of the preferences that would in effect be subsidized are definitely antisocial. Apart from the public or taxpayers' expense imposed by private indulgence in fecundity, losses accrue to society from choices by those with creative talents in favor of leisure rather than work, or against further development of their talents through rigorous training, while the absence of social devices for pooling many career risks implies that private risk-taking tends to be on too low a scale for social optimality anyway. Moreover, advocacy of redistributionary taxation and expenditure policies almost invariably assumes that habits of hard work and honesty will survive intact through fiscal mauling, whereas tax avoidance and evasion respond readily to profit incentives for them (especially if the taxes are thought to be unjust), and in the long run social institutions and customs adapt to produce the kind of people favored by the fiscal system. [4]

The suggestion to focus equalitarian policies on providing information about and resources for exploiting available opportunities carries with it a number of obvious implications for the types of policies that might effectively be pursued: for example, better schooling for the children of the poor, better public health care for children generally, loan finance to cover maintenance costs and fees for education for the older children of impecunious parents, earlier and more directive career counseling, and public assistance to or provision of more information about alternative jobs available, coupled with grant or loan assistance to geographical and occupational mobility. Even policies of that kind, however, raise questions about how they might work out in practice. A variety of evidence tends to show that, as a rough approximation, existing government tax and expenditure policies redistribute income from very rich and very poor toward the middle class. There is also massive evidence from the results of the short-lived "War on Poverty" launched by President Johnson in 1964 that crash programs and bright ideas directed at the surface of the problem mostly waste resources, since low and uncertain incomes are not merely low and uncertain incomes but a way of life, a culture that will take a long-sustained and expensive effort to transform. A large part of this problem is related to the role of the family in relation to its junior members (offspring) in the long period of social conditioning that precedes the signaling of full adulthood by entry into the labor force and to all appearances dominates over the social conditioning provided by the formal education system.

In an important sense, modern society has created this problem for itself, as a by-product of its success in achieving affluence and in consequence in the narrowing down of the extended kinship system to the nuclear family and of the socially ordered community to casual social relationships with business acquaintances or a few economically-similarly-situated neighbors. The result of this, along with the extreme specialization of parental participation in the economic system, is to limit severely both the knowledge of the economic world at the growing child's disposal, particularly in the least affluent families confined to the ghetto life, and the resources available from the family for investment in the exploitation of economic opportunities. In addition, the pace of economic change and increasing affluence is such as frequently to make what knowledge parents have of the outside world out of date and misleading—as well as to make youth less willing to take parental advice than in former days when both boys and girls could expect to live, when they grew up, more or less as their parents had done, and could benefit from their parents' instruction and example.

The role of the family in child-rearing raises two major difficulties for policies seeking to increase equality. One, which is relatively minor, is that either a motivation for or the by-product of achievement of material success is the capacity to accumulate material property and pass it on to one's children, thereby relieving them of the necessity of working for a living. Much contemporary inheritance taxation, and still more crushing inheritance tax proposals that have been advanced, aim at eliminating this effect of economic success as far as possible. The results seem to have been nugatory by and large, to judge from the relative stability of statistics on inequality of ownership of property, partly because to be effective in decreasing inequality inheritance taxes should be graduated according to the amounts received by individual beneficiaries and by their individual personal means as well, rather than by the size of the estate; but largely because such taxes can be avoided in countless ways by foresighted and perfectly legal action. On the other hand, there is plenty of qualitative evidence to the effect that large individual accumulations of wealth tend to get dispersed in a generation or two, frequently into worthy charitable purposes, so that excessive concern with the unearned economic advantages enjoyed by the first generation of descendants of the rich may well be too myopic a basis for equalitarian economic reform. (Of course, it is our own generation of children of the rich that irk us most acutely, and it is only as we age and see their children turn out no better than ours, and sometimes far worse, that we realize too late that our childhood resentments were unjustified.)

The far more serious problem of inequality associated with inheritance is concerned, not with the passing on of material property from generation to generation, but with the passing on of less tangible but probably far more important productive assets. In the modern economy, as J. K. Galbraith has made it his major lifework to emphasize, it is not property as such but the ability to manage property and to combine it productively with other inputs under shrewd management that counts. And success in this context depends broadly on three characteristics of the individual that may be classified in one way or another as inherited: native ability inherited genetically; education, which though nominally provided equally for all through the formal education system is dependent for its absorption and effective use on "inheritance" in the sense of a family background of parental interest and encouragement and willingness to spend real resources and parental time in complementing and augmenting the formal educational experience; and an elusive quality incorporating determination and the ability to accept responsibility and to work hard for no immediate return in discharging it, again a matter of family background and parental example (which unfortunately does not appear to get communicated equally to children of the same parents.)

The late Frank H. Knight was fond of pointing out, in criticism of the equalitarians of his day, that there is no more ethical justification for inequality of capacity to exploit opportunities deriving from genetical inheritance and family background than there is for inequalities deriving from unequal inheritance of property. This point seems incontrovertible, though it suits the book of critics of society whose superior position in it derives from intellectual brilliance and literary facility to identify inequality with inequality deriving from property income. In fact, such inequality is probably less of a fundamental social problem than the other forms of inherited inequality just mentioned, since personal concentrations of material property are probably more easily dissipated by foolishness and force of circumstance than are personal concentrations of familial genetical and behavioral characteristics.

Knight was firmly convinced that it would be impossible effectively to eliminate or reduce significantly inequalities associated with nontangible familial inheritance. Utopian philosophers throughout history have struggled with the problem, but their thoughts concentrated on the organization of relatively small communities living an austere life based on a relatively simple and unchanging economic technology, and the societies they idealized were highly regimented and joyless constructions certain eventually to run out of great ideas whose contemplation would liberate the human spirit—as has in fact been amply demonstrated by the unhappy experience and eventual collapse of the majority of utopian communities. Nowadays, with the vast scientific resources of modern genetics available, as well as the material resources and administrative knowledge necessary to the raising of children under far more comfortable regimentation, psychological as well as physical, than is currently provided even by the best orphanages, one could conceivably do far better to ensure equality of juvenile training and opportunity. But what bold but socially respectable philosopher, let alone what political party, would have the courage seriously to suggest the complete supersession of the family by the scientific orphanage, now or in the foreseeable future?

15. Inequality of Income Distribution and the Poverty Problem

Introduction

There are two possible sources of concern about the personal distribution of income which do not amount to the same thing: concern about inequality in the personal distribution of income, which may exist even if no one is actually poor by generally accepted social standards, and concern about the prevalence of poverty, which may exist even if incomes are not very unequally distributed among individuals. These concerns reflect different philosophies of the "good society" and indicate different types of social policies to move toward such a society, though the differences are often obscured by concentration of both philosophies on the low-income groups in society.

In the United States, beginning around 1963, there was a rise of concern about poverty in the population, leading to the announcement of a "war on poverty" and to the Economic Opportunity Act of 1964. The emergence of this concern had certain striking economic similarities with the previous occasion of American concern about poverty under President Roosevelt in the 1930s. Roosevelt found one-third of the nation in poverty that should be remedied by social action; President Johnson found one-fifth. In each case, the finding of poverty of a nationally shameful kind followed a period of prolonged recession (much less serious in the case of President Johnson than in the case of President Roosevelt) during which real incomes may be assumed to have fallen well below the expected trend. This suggests that there is a causal relation between the downswing of a relatively severe depression and the upsurge of concern about poverty, the upsurge of concern being motivated less by Christian feeling on the part of the majority middle class for the poor who are always with us than by the uneasy feeling on their part that they are, through no fault of their own, poorer than they expected or deserve to be. (There is a well-documented relationship historically between the downswing of the business cycle and the upswing of religious revival movements, the psychology of which is equally simple to explain.) Be that as it may, the mid-1960s concern about poverty as a national problem has led to considerable analysis of it with the aid of the techniques of the economic theory of income distribution.

Originally chapter 18 in Harry G. Johnson, *The Theory of Income Distribution* (London: Gray-Mills Publishers, Ltd., 1973).

To begin with, it is necessary to arrive at a definition of poverty. To the economist, such a definition is in principle simple: poverty consists in having insufficient spendable resources to maintain a standard of living deemed by some standard to be adequate for civilized survival. And it carries with it the simple policy recommendation, at variance with the recommendation of most social philosophers and poverty experts, "don't come yourself, just send money." (The non-economists view poverty as a sociological phenomenon requiring the administrations of social workers rather than the mere dispensing of cash.) But such a definition, while satisfactory in principle, necessarily raises problems. First, there is the question of what is an adequate standard of living, falling below which indicates poverty. The definitions are set by social workers and show a strong tendency to rise over historical time more or less proportionally to the average income of society. In the United States, over the past hundred years or so, the generally accepted poverty standard as revised from time to time by social workers has been approximately half the average income per head. In the United Kingdom, researchers repeating Rowntree's famous work on poverty in the city of York for the immediate post–World War II period found that by Rowntree's prewar standards there were virtually no poor left in the city; so they hastily revised his standard so as to create an adequate showing of poverty in the period they studied. Apart from the definition of poverty, there is the question of measuring it; this involves on the one hand the definition of the spending unit whose poverty or otherwise is to be assessed, the general tendency being that the larger the family unit is defined to be the smaller is poverty as measured (because the typical nuclear family passes through a stage of youthful struggle to make ends meet into a stage of middle-aged affluence and then into a stage of penurious retirement, whereas if all generations of the family—parents, young or middle-aged married couples, and children—are lumped together in one reckoning the average will pass the test of non-poverty). On the other hand it involves the measurement of spending power: both young people and retired parents living independently tend to receive subventions respectively from their parents and from their children, and young people can borrow against their future income prospects whereas old people can live on their accumulated savings, neither source of spending power appearing in the usual statistical measurements of "income." The question of actual family size to be supported from a given income is also important, as is the question of dwelling location: the Council of Economic Advisors made a big mistake in 1964 in defining the poverty line at $3,000 per year per family, a definition which led it to overlook both the influence of family size on the prevalence of poverty (and especially to overlook the prevalence of poverty among unmarried female black heads of households) and the influence of high urban rents in causing poverty among people who, had they lived in the country, would have been accounted well off by comparison with their neighbors.

These questions apart, the fact that the definition of poverty is not a matter of objective specification of minimum cost of physical survival but of subjective specification of what money it takes to lead a life considered socially decent means that the definition of the poverty line keeps rising over time as average income per head rises, so that one cannot rely on the general progress of society to remedy poverty. Instead, the reduction or elimination of poverty requires a reduction in the inequality of distribution of income, raising the incomes of the lowest-income groups relative to those of the highest-income groups. This in turn means that poverty so defined can only be reduced or eliminated if general economic progress raises the share of productive assets owned by the initially lower-income groups at the expense of the share of the initially higher-income groups. There is nothing in the theory of economic growth to suggest that growth will be biased in this direction, though it does perhaps signify something that, whereas Roosevelt found a third of the American nation in poverty, Johnson found only a fifth—but a cynic might interpret these figures merely as showing that Roosevelt wanted to dramatize the problem to the electorate whereas Johnson wanted to prove that it was not too large to be manageable. Consequently, poverty will not cure itself through economic progress; there are only two broad ways to cure it: redistribution of income from the rich to the poor through the fiscal mechanism, and redistribution of property (the source of income) from the rich to the poor, either directly or, more acceptably, through public investment in increasing the human capital of the poor, for example, by public education, retraining programs, and so forth.

Growth Models and Poverty

Assuming that the poverty standard involves a fixed minimum of command over goods and services, the question arises as to how economic growth will affect the proportion of the population in poverty. Consider first the aggregative models of economic growth that economists use. On the one hand, there is the Malthusian-Ricardian model. According to this model, population breeds to the level of subsistence, and there is no hope for growth to relieve poverty unless the poor can be persuaded to raise their minimum subsistence level to something above the poverty line. Malthus and his followers preached abstinence from marriage to begin with and from sex to follow. (It is an interesting reflection that the first birth control movement, in the early nineteenth century, was a movement to relieve the poverty of the working class; the second one, in the late nineteenth century and early twentieth, was a movement to relieve middle-class women from the dreary obligations of childbearing and consequent second-rate-citizenship; it is interesting too, that the contemporary movement is again one designed to raise the subsistence level of the working class, both in the underdeveloped countries and in the ghettos of the United States.)

On the other hand, there are the contemporary growth models. According to these models, which assume an exogenously given growth rate of the labor force, wages per worker tend to rise toward a level set by the accumulation of capital relative to labor and the equilibrium ratio of capital to labor on the equilibrium growth path, and to rise on a trend path per worker to the extent that there is Harrod-neutral technical progress. In terms of these models, poverty, if defined by a fixed level of consumption per head, should be eliminated eventually; but if poverty is defined in relation to average income per head, it will become a permanent feature of the economy, though the proportion of the poor may be larger or smaller depending on the characteristics of the growth model.

Turning to microeconomic approaches to the theory of economic growth, T. W. Schultz has stressed the question of the incentives that the economy offers to people to investment in the augmentation of their human capital and the acquisition of educational and other skills. A general characteristic of economic development in the twentieth century has been that human skills and education have accumulated without appreciably driving down the rates of return on human capital investment—in other words, technological progress has created a relatively expanding market for human capital, and permitted people to elevate themselves out of poverty by investing in such capital. This is a "stylized fact"—there is no more fundamental explanation of it, though students may like to speculate on one, and some observers have raised the question whether the tendency will continue, or whether in future the education of more and more students to increasingly higher educational levels will simply result in a reduction in the rate of return on educational investment and a rise in the educational and gentility level of the poor.

A further point emphasized by Schultz, and worth mentioning, is that measured poverty is to some extent a consequence of voluntary choice, and that choices which make people better off in terms of utility may make them worse off in terms of measured income. A particular case in point is the "undoubling" of families: if people are poor enough, unmarried sons and daughters have to live at home and make do with their share of the family accommodation and living space; similarly, widowed parents can only be supported by provision of a room in their married children's homes. As incomes rise, children prefer to set up independent establishments even before they are married, and retired parents prefer an independent room or apartment of their own to more luxurious but freedom-restricted accommodation with their married offspring. When peoples' incomes are measured on a per household basis, even allowing for the number of people supported by the family income, the multi-generational family unit appears to be affluent whereas the single-generation unit frequently appears to be poor by statistical standards. A further point in this connection is that the greater freedom of divorce in contemporary times, and the greater opportunities for women to earn an adequate income to support themselves and their children, albeit with financial stringency, have led to an increase in the relative number of households with female heads which by statistical standards fall below the poverty line. In a significant sense, statistical poverty may be the price of freedom, privacy, and independence, and hence its measured existence may represent an improvement and not a deterioration of the condition of mankind. Of course, this conclusion does not amount to a contention that poverty does not exist, only to a warning that measured poverty may not be a measure of the constraints of the economic system on human liberty.

A Classification of the Sources of Poverty

Poverty can be simply defined as inadequacy of income receipts to support a standard of life considered socially to be decent. This brings into the question the relation between the income earned by the family unit and the size of the family supported. The family can in this connection be conceived of as a utility factory selling productive services in the factor markets in order to earn income to spend on satisfying its wants for ultility-yielding goods and services. This in turn suggests a broad classification of the sources of poverty into two sorts, corresponding to the size of the family relative to its income-earning opportunities on the one hand and the value of the services of its income-yielding assets in the market place on the other.

The first type of poverty is associated with an excessive number of people dependent on the earning capacity of the family unit for their sustenance and support. This type of poverty is due on the one hand to the system of free enterprise in the supply of labor, which makes the family's spending power a function of the productive services it can supply and not of its need for economic support, and on the other hand to various cultural restrictions on rational family planning and weaknesses in the legal system governing the economic claims of mothers on the fathers of their children. If there were a fully rational and adequately informed free enterprise system in the formation of families, supported by adequately enforced rules of contract between spouses, the size of the family would be an economic choice variable governed by preferences and the budget constraint. Large families living on relatively low incomes per head would be the result of rational choice between material and "familial" welfare and no cause for social concern; and the result of decisions by spouses to separate would not, as it so frequently does now, consist in the imposition of poverty on the children, through the unwillingness or inability of the father to support his offspring and the inability of the mother to earn enough by her own labor to do so. (In this connection, economic irrationality in childbearing interacts with the effects of discrimination against women in the labor market to enforce poverty on the children of unmarried, separated, divorced and widowed mothers—a type of poverty particularly prevalent among the black popu-lation of the United States, where the slavery tradition still makes the mother rather than the father the head of the household, but also prevalent in other countries.) An alternative social arrangement, which is partially but not wholly reflected in the social security and other arrangements of various countries, would be for society to regard the raising of children not as a family responsibility but as an activity in the social interest, providing population for the future, and to assume social responsibility for the economic costs through the provision of children's allowances, free edu-cation, and so forth. (The United States is exceptional among advanced countries in not having some sort of system of family allowances payable by right to the mother.)

The second type of poverty—inadequate income to support the individual or a normal-sized family—is attributable to several reasons. One is inadequate employment opportunities for workers of sufficient skill to support themselves and their families above the poverty line if they were normally employed. Inadequate employment nowadays has to be the result of deliberate choice by the macroeconomic policymakers, and while this choice may be necessitated by domestic or international difficulties (and the need to enforce unemployment for macroeconomic disciplinary reasons cannot simply be denied on the grounds that unemployment is distasteful), it is arguably unfair that a subset of citizens should have to suffer poverty to discipline the others, and reasonable to argue that unemployment benefits should be generous enough to shield those made unemployed by national economic policy from being forced to descend into poverty. There are two further considerations pointing in this direction, both the result of research in the United States into the consequences of unemployment. First, crimes against property (robbery, etc.) tend to increase as unemployment rises; second, a transitory period of unemployment tends to lead to a permanent increase in poverty, for two reasons: elderly people get thrown out of work and cannot find their way back into the labor market at their customary wages; and youths entering the labor market cannot put their foot on the first rung of the ladder of promotion to a non-poverty lifetime income stream via on-the-job training.

A second cause of poverty of this kind is inadequacy of the factors of production the individual or family can supply to command a non-poverty level of income. In a broad sense, this can be regarded as due to the immobility of the family's factors of production, either between occupations or between regions, the assumption being that the normal individual could earn a non-poverty income if either he were located in a prosperous instead of a declining region of the country or his native skills had been trained to the needs of expanding rather than contracting industries. One of the problems here is that indigent parents tend to produce and raise children who retrace their own poverty-stricken footsteps: if the children grow up in a poor environment, they tend to face opportunities and make choices that keep them condemned to poverty. This is a major reason why "regional development policies," which have existed under one or another name for over a century, have tended to fail consistently to remedy regional poverty; by attempting to resuscitate industries declining in response to economic pressures they both doom themselves to failure and guarantee the preservation of a next generation of poor people who will have a legitimate claim for public help.

There are exceptions, however, to the implied antipoverty policy of solving the problem by retraining or assisted migration. First, some individuals are physically or mentally incapable of rendering sufficient labor service to the productive system to be capable of supporting themselves, so that relief of their poverty would be more cheaply accomplished by direct cash payments. One suspects, however, that some of the prevalent unwillingness to employ physically or mentally handicapped people is due to discrimination against them on the part of the able-bodied and/or normal-minded, an indulgence in the avoidance of negative personal consumption externalities (who likes to be reminded of the risks of human existence by the daily sight of a one-armed, one-eyed, dwarfed, or otherwise disfigured elevator operator when for a somewhat higher wage one can obtain the services of a fully-able-bodied man or woman whose presence in the elevator daily reminds one that one's superior income is due to one's superior ability and not merely to one's physical health?). Second, the payoff from public investment in assisting labor mobility depends on the remaining length of productive life of the assisted, in conjunction with the cost of the investment, and the payoff may be too small—as probably in the case of the retraining of unemployed clerks in their late fifties—to justify such investment as contrasted with the award of a cash income stream. Even so, it may be socially profitable to make economically unprofitable investments of this kind, for the sake of providing a normal family life (father regularly employed in a respectable job, mother keeping house within a reliable budget constraint) for the children.

A third source of inadequate earnings from the individual's or the family's stock of productive assets is, in a broad sense, discrimination against the hiring of those assets. Modern society has more or less reduced discrimination on grounds of religion to negligibility; but it continues to discriminate for various (and usually philosophically very confused) reasons against the colored, the aged, the uneducated, and the female. Color discrimination, it should be noted, is not peculiar to predominantly white societies; it also exists in countries like India and Pakistan where variations in climatic conditions produce people of differing shades of brownness, and among American blacks, as well as in countries like Brazil which pride themselves on their lack of color discrimination, but are still capable of discriminating between more and less acceptable shades of brown. Discrimination against the aged reflects a variety of forces: intergenerational rivalry; the tailoring of jobs to the assumption that the typical worker is young, muscular, adroit, and clear-sighted, even though the job may technically require none of these characteristics; and the fact, noted long ago by Jeremy Bentham in his *Book of Fallacies*, that in a changing society in which most people survive into adulthood it is youth and not age that has the widest and most flexible grasp of human experience. (This proposition obviously requires qualification; as a person matures he acquires more knowledge of the society he lives in but loses flexibility in adaptation to change, so that he is at his best somewhere between adolescence and middle age. However, Bentham was calling attention to the important point that in a literate society one can acquire knowledge of the past by reading about it rather than having lived through it, and the former is often more informative than the latter.) Discrimination against women reflects an archaic view of the function of the family in contemporary society. In primitive nomadic or settled agricultural societies, women's inferior strength and probably superior manual dexterity— themselves probably the result in part of cultural definitions of the desirable characteristics of female mates, since no culture that I am aware of has extolled size and muscularity as a criterion of desirable womanhood, matrilineal societies apart—provided a natural basis for a division of labor between men and women that was mutually satisfactory on the whole if not always mutually tolerable. In advanced industrial society, where reasonably good health and trained intelligence rather than muscular strength constitute the foundation of productive contribution, the traditional assignment of women to household management and child rearing is an anachronism, and discrimination against women in employment based on the view that this is either their preferred social role or the role to which society should assign them prevents them from realizing their full economic potential and condemns many of them—especially those who have essayed marriage and emerged at the other end as heads of households of children whom they must support largely by their own economic efforts—to unnecessary poverty. Discrimination against the uneducated reflects the desire of the educated to enjoy the consumption externalities of communication with others of the educated, and their instructed faith in the socially discriminatory value of educational qualifications. It is an interesting question whether a society which does not discriminate on grounds of race, color, creed, religion, sex, or age, but does discriminate by educational attainment, will be a better society than one that regards educational differences as secondary to the others.

In any case, if society is concerned about the problem of poverty, one line of solution is to eliminate the various kinds of discrimination that help to create and preserve it; or else to recognize that the discrimination is based on a social philosophy which penalizes unjustly those who are discriminated against, and to award adequate compensation for this discrimination. Thus, in the case of the elderly, society should either redesign its work specification and hiring rules to give equal opportunity to the older in competition with the younger citizens, or if it wishes to push the elderly out of the labor market provide an adequately non-poverty system of pensions. In the case of the colored, if they are accepted as citizens, they should have the same opportunities to earn income as other citizens (if the sight of their presence offends the while fellow citizens, it should be possible to assign them to less visible jobs without jeopardizing their incomes—as Becker points out, color prejudice may lead either to segregation of jobs among white and colored, each earning the same wage, or to discrimination involving the colored earning less than the white for the same job). Note that the easy way out for the whites—to deny the blacks the opportunity to immigrate and become citizens—has not been available to the United States because of its history of slavery but has been resorted to by other ex-imperial countries. This makes the United States easy game for criticism by the intellectuals of other countries whose governments have thoughtfully prevented them from having to think seriously about the manifold problems of racial integration; English intellectuals, whose contacts with colored people have mostly consisted of meeting the prospective rulers of colored colonies as fellow students at Oxford and Cambridge, have a particularly easy task in telling the United States how to handle its racial problems. In the case of women, society has to face a difficult and unacknowledged choice: either women are really equal to men as citizens, discrimination has to be abolished, and the family has to be redesigned to eliminate the differential burden it imposes on women as compared with men; or society has to recognize explicitly that the woman's role in managing the household and rearing children is as exacting as that of the man's in earning the income to maintain the household, and deserves the support both of contractual arrangements specifying the financial obligations of the husband toward the partnership involved in marriage, and of public subvention of the costs of rearing the children that result. In the case of the uneducated, society should recognize that lack of education is a lack of human capital, brought about by the unwillingness of society itself to invest resources in individuals unpromising in their ability to accumulate such capital, and that such individuals should in equity be compensated by the transferral to them of material capital. (Eighteenth-century plays and nineteenth-century novels abound in individuals who have to be admitted to civilized society because they have a substantial property income, even though they lack the graces conveyed by education; contemporary society might well be better off if it had to allow for a lower degree of correlation between education and income than now prevails.)

Apart from these forms of social discrimination, contemporary society contains important forms of discrimination on other grounds, nominally economic, which help to create a poverty problem. One such is trade unionism, which by establishing a differential wage for union members over nonunion members helps to keep the nonunion members poor. Another is minimum wage laws, which benefit those fortunate enough to obtain employment in minimum-wage-law industries at the expense of those not so fortunate. A third is the practice of recruiting civil servants on the basis of educational attainment, which discriminates against those who lack the capacity for such attainment but may nevertheless have the capacity for arriving at intelligent public policy decisions. (Related to this is the practice of business firms of using educational attainment as a "filter" for the selection of potential executive material; this particular filter may be both unnecessarily expensive socially, and inefficient in selecting effective business executives.) Finally, the legislation of "equal pay for equal work" for the public sector only, when the private sector is characterized by discrimination against the employment of women, may contribute to poverty among women by creaming off the most talented and leaving the rest to serve as examples of the proposition that women are less efficient than men. Insistence on equal pay in one sector only, when discrimination in conjunction with relative supplies makes pay for women generally lower elsewhere, will result either in women taking over employment in that sector completely, or in the women who obtain employment in that sector being in fact considerably better qualified than the men employed in it.

Poverty Programs: Promising and Unpromising

Assuming the existence of a social concern about poverty, there are a number of points at which the economist has questions to ask or suggestions to make and advice to offer.

First, there is the question obvious to the economist of what the effect of transfers of income to the poor will be on their incentives to work and to improve their economic position by their own efforts. In posing this question in modern times, however, economists frequently make the mistake of thinking themselves back into classical times, when life really was a hard struggle for survival and the blunting of incentives to work was a really serious matter, because it entailed a drain on the meager resources of the responsible hardworking citizens for the benefit of the social drones, or else a tax on the god-given rightful income of the propertied classes for the benefit of those who should be grateful for the opportunity to find gainful employment in their service. In contemporary affluent times, there is both less obvious necessity for hard work on the part of everyone—as reflected in the increasing cultivation of leisure-time activities for the middle and lower-middle class—and less moral certainty about the rights of those who earn high incomes by virtue of possession of material or human capital to spend the income from it according to their own desires. In other words, the insistence on efficiency of the economic system at the cost of poverty for some is no longer a tenable starting point; and the classical concern about efficiency has to be modified into a weighing of costs and benefits of poverty relief against one another. This is not to say that efficiency and incentives are unimportant, only that one has to recognize that it is not only the poor that may be inefficient, and that a certain amount of inefficiency may be and probably should be tolerable if the overall outcome of such toleration is socially desirable. But there are still potentially important problems where the economist's concern with efficiency is relevant, notably the possibility that generosity in providing for the poor may result in a proliferation of their numbers as a result of both voluntary choice of poverty status rather than work, and natural increase through procreation.

Second, there is the question, assuming in general that poverty can be identified with insufficiency of income received or receivable through the market mechanism, of how best to arrange for the poor to receive sufficient incomes. (Note that to social and charity workers, poverty is often identified not with its market results in terms of income but with the social and personal characteristics of the poor, and its relief with a reformation of those characteristics; this corresponds to a long-standing social differentiation between the "deserving" and the "undeserving" poor, the former being regarded as poor through no fault of their own and entitled to the provision of work and opportunities, the latter being feckless and entitled only to what charitable gifts the conscience of the rich was prepared to offer.)

One way of attempting to transfer incomes toward the poor, which is obvious and appealing to the non-economist, is to allow or legislate tinkering with the market mechanism in order to provide prices more favorable to the poor. Previous analysis suggests that programs of this kind are not likely to be promising. As economic theory shows, neither trade unionism nor minimum wage legislation is likely to benefit the working class as a whole; on the contrary, both are likely to ensure adequate incomes for a favored group at the expense of a large degree of poverty for the disfavored group. This is particularly true of minimum wage laws, especially if as in the United States the minimum wage is set regardless of the age and position in the labor force of the workers covered. Similarly, a policy of farm price supports or output controls is likely to do little to raise the incomes of farm workers (as distinct from farm owners) and has the undesirable side effect of raising the cost of food to the urban poor, a side effect which it is difficult to counteract effectively and efficiently by food stamp plans and other methods of subsidizing the food consumption of the poor. To the economist, the most efficacious way of transferring incomes is to transfer incomes by direct fiscal means.

Benefits in Cash Versus Benefits in Kind

A standard controversy concerning measures to relieve poverty, which puts the economist in general conflict with the non-economist humanitarian, is over the issue of payment of subsidies to the poor in cash versus payments in kind—economists favoring the former and humanitarians and professional poverty workers the latter. Standard economic theory leads to the conclusion that cash is always better than kind (because it permits individual utility maximization and preserves consumers' sovereignty) unless *either* benefits in kind amount to less than the poor recipients would have freely bought if they had received cash instead, *or* the recipients are free to sell benefits in kind in the market and the transactions costs entailed are negligible—in which cases it makes no difference to the ultimate consumption pattern of the poor whether benefits are paid in cash or in kind. To this argument, the economist usually adds the observation that costs of administration and policing of benefits in kind absorb a large proportion of the budgetary allocations nominally destined to the relief of poverty—much of this in the form of salaries for middle-class people appropriately qualified by higher education. He is also inclined to feel that the bureaucratic control involved entails discriminatory interference with the civil liberties of the poor—discriminatory because the rich are allowed to waste their money and their lives as they like, and only if they want psychiatric treatment and financial discipline do they need to hire experts in these subjects to help them to live better; they are not obliged to accept a "tied sale" of such help as the price of receiving their incomes.

It is such considerations that in the mid-1960s led economists such as Milton Friedman and James Tobin, otherwise strongly divided on almost every conceivable fundamental scientific issue, to concur both in recommending the "negative income tax" (i.e., income subventions from the Treasury to people whose cash incomes put them below some socially accepted "poverty line") and in exploring the difficult technical question of reconciling this scheme with the existing income tax system. (The technical problem here is that most existing poverty relief systems impose a 100 percent or near 100 percent marginal income tax rate on the poor, in the sense that their benefit payments, whether in cash or in kind, are reduced more or less to the extent that their earned income rises, up to the point at which they cease to be classified as poor, receive no benefits, and become ordinary taxpayers. This feature obviously discourages the poor from attempting to earn income in the market place. On the other hand, it would obviously be inequitable—and expensive to government as well—for persons who once succeeded in getting themselves classified as poor to go on receiving their benefits as of right regardless of what they earned on top of their benefits, paying the same taxes on their earned incomes as the non-poor who earned all their cash receipts for themselves and paid the normal taxes on them. The technical problem is to devise a schedule of tax rates for the poor that will not have the disincentive effects of a 100 percent marginal tax rate on the earnings of the still-poor, while restoring equality of tax treatment between the two groups at some non-poverty level of income.)

Nevertheless, there are various legitimate or at least plausible arguments for giving benefits in kind. One, which goes back at least as far as John Stuart Mill's arguments for public education as against private education, is that the poor, like children, do not know what is good for them and need, in both the social and their own true private interests, to have imposed on them the superior judgment of more intelligent and better-educated and more successful people. (The counterarguments are that the preferences of such people are not necessarily superior to those of the poor; that under the guise of improving the poor they are really seeking to create a society more deferential to people like themselves; and that the poor will not learn to be self-reliantly independent if they are denied the opportunity to learn by making their own mistakes in the spending of money.) A second argument is that the competitive market, at least as it confronts the poor, is less efficient than centralized administration in providing the goods necessary to the relief of poverty. (The counterarguments are that if a centralized administration and not the collectivity of the poor determines the spending of the funds allocated to the relief of poverty, the private market system will naturally cater to the tastes of the administration rather than attempt to determine and educate the tastes of the poor.) A third argument is that centralized administration and distribution of benefits in kind can offset market imperfections that would otherwise prevent or impede the poor from making choices in accord with true social costs and benefits. One example concerns food stamp plans, which can be interpreted as devices for relieving the poor of the necessity of making consumption choices in the face of artificially high food prices created by farm price support policies. Another, more complex, example is the imperfection of the market in human capital that makes it extremely difficult for the intelligent poor children to invest in their own human capital via education. (The counterargument, a rather idealistic one, is that government should abandon economic policies such as farm price supports that involve regressive taxation of the consumer, and correct the imperfections of the markets in human capital, rather than preserve these policies and then seek to mitigate their impact on the poor.)

These arguments for benefits in kind stress questions of economic efficiency in the relief of poverty, considered as a program of transferring resources in general to the poor. But it is quite conceivable that those who wish to relieve poverty do not conceive of it (as the economist does) as consisting of a general shortage of income or spendable resources, but instead are concerned about certain aspects of the condition of poverty that impinge on their consciousness as a species of negative consumption externality, and seek to eliminate such externalities by making transfers of specific benefits in kind. Thus James Buchanan has argued that the popularity of benefits in kind rather than in cash is attributable to the fact that the affluent do not like the thought of (say) starving people, especially children, of bright children whose parents cannot or will not give them a decent education, of shabbily-clothed people infesting the streets, and of crowded, littered, and dangerous neighborhoods. Hence the public preference for benefits in kind in the form of cheap or free food, clothing, slum clearance and public housing, and subsidized education. The fact that the poor frequently resent and even refuse to take advantage of such benefits in kind implies that they are less willing to sell positive externalities than the affluent are eager to purchase them.

It should be noted in conclusion that benefits in kind may have the contrary effect to that intended, of improving the lot of the poor, because such benefits may carry side-costs with them. For example, efforts to relieve poverty in the long run by forcing the children of the poor to stay in school and acquire an education by the imposition of a minimum school-leaving age may impose considerable extra costs of child maintenance on the poor family during the extra years at school, without providing the child (if he or she is incapable of learning beyond a certain point) with additional education-based income-earning capacity, and even have the effect of inculcating irresponsible habits and antagonistic attitudes toward authority that reduce the child's employment prospects in the labor market. As another example, in the 1930s in England there was a widely told tale to the effect that it was useless to provide the poor with modern apartment-block housing containing all modern conveniences, because they simply used their bathtubs for storing their coal; the facts seem to have been that the architect put the coal storage bins at the ground level, on the assumption either that the poor would have the time and the strength to carry coal upstairs in small lots as needed for fuel, or that they would have servants to do the job for them.

Income Transfers Versus Investment in Poverty Relief

As mentioned already, public concern about the relief of poverty tends, in contrast to the economist's identification of poverty with inadequacy of money income or spending power, to see poverty as a problem of changing poor people's habits and relation to the economic system, and hence to favor investments—in education for poor children, in retraining of adults, and in the provision of capital to buy better equipment for poor farmers or self-employed workers—over the cash income transfers that appeal to the economist. This orientation is a mixture of prejudice and prescience. The prejudice involves the attitudes already referred to, which discriminate between the deserving and the undeserving poor and assume that, with some public help, the deserving can be given a place in the productive system that will enable them to be self-supporting at a non-poverty level. To the economist, two questions arise concerning this attitude. First, do the poor typically represent some sort of social disequilibrium situation, in which people who could participate effectively in the economic system at a non-poverty level of income are somehow disbarred from the opportunity to do so but could be restored to participation by a relatively small amount of social expenditure? Or do they represent an equilibrium situation, the result either of their own choices to disregard opportunities for higher incomes— choices based either on myopia or on a strong preference for leisure and aversion to industrial discipline, or on their own limited talents and capacity for acquiring the education necessary for success in the industrial system? Economic analysis suggests that the equilibrium explanation is more reasonable than the disequilibrium explanation—see T. W. Schultz's book on *Transforming Traditional Agriculture*—and that, consequently, the rate of return on investments designed to overcome the presumed disequilibrium is likely to be low and not, as implied, incredibly high. A corollary is that it might be economically and socially more efficient to allocate to the poor a block of stock in General Motors, or even a chunk of government debt (rigged as the rate of return on that is to give the owners less than a fair rate of return on their capital), rather than give them their benefits in the form of a specific investment in their human or material capital. Second, and related, is investment in the creation of human capital in the poor a better investment than a cash income subsidy? If the object is to give people adequate spending power to maintain a decent standard of living, rather than to transform them into a different type of person, a cash income subsidy may be far more economical than an investment in the formation of human capital, especially if the investment is chosen by the governmental bureaucracy in the light of the social circumstances of the poor person concerned. To put the point another way, it is not clear that a poor person is benefitted more, in terms of relieving his poverty, by an educational investment than by the gift of an equivalent allocation of government bonds.

The prescience of this point of view enters the picture when one considers (*a*) the externality aspect of poverty—if poverty is offensive, not because the poor have low standards of living, but because they behave in an offensive way affronting the middle-class belief in responsibility and hard work— giving the poor more money to spend as they like simply adds insult to injury, and the money should be used instead to bribe them into conformity with middle-class standards of good citizenship; (*b*) the intergenerational aspect of poverty—some (but not all) of the children of poor parents constitute a poverty problem for the next generation, either because they have acquired poverty-prone attitudes toward life from their parents or because their parents' choices for them have left them insufficiently equipped with productive capacities to achieve a non-poverty level of participation in economic society. In such cases, social investments in the transformation of the parents into worthy citizens may not pay off, in terms of the returns in parent income, but may be well worthwhile when the side effects on the attitudes and educational attainments of the children (and of subsequent genrations as well) are taken into account. An important implication for United States policy, in contrast to the policy expressed in the Economic Opportunity Act, is that instead of trying to relieve rural southern poverty by subsidizing loans to farmers to buy capital equipment, the government should retire farmers on pensions paid ex gratia to "victims of economic progress," on condition that they move to California, or Florida, or if they can stand the climatic misery to one of the big northern cities, where their children will have the educational opportunity to fit themselves into industrial society at a non-poverty level of income. A rational economic attitude toward the poverty problem would probably accord consumers' sovereignty to the preferences of parents, pay income subsidies to those deemed poor and let them spend the subsidies on current consumption or investment as they saw fit, but intervene in one way or another to rescue the children from the psychological conditioning and the inappropriate choices that irresponsible parents impose on them. (Some social philosophers, including most of the utopian socialist philosophers, have so despaired of the family as an efficient agent for child-rearing that they have proposed that all children be reared communally.)

Part 5

Economics and
Contemporary Problems:
World Inflation, Money,
Trade, Growth,
and Investment

16. World Inflation: A Monetarist View

According to a long-standing and historically well-documented theory of monetary phenomena—the quantity theory of money, currently frequently described as the "monetarist view"—inflation is associated with and ultimately causally dependent on a rate of increase of the money supply significantly in excess of the rate of growth of real output—the difference between the two rates being the rate of inflation. The theory, it should be noted, does not assert that inflation is attributable to monetary ignorance or mismanagement; monetary expansion and the consequential inflation is a method of taxing the holders of money to which governments may well be driven by political circumstances, in full knowledge of what they are doing. The theory rests on the proposition that there is a stable relation between real income and the amount of real purchasing power the public wants to hold in monetary form; that this money-to-income relationship is inversely related to the expected rate of inflation, the erosion of the purchasing power of money through inflation constituting an important element of the cost of holding money; and that in the long run people will come to expect the rate of inflation induced by the authorities through their policy with respect to monetary expansion.

The assumption that the public forms expectations about inflation, adjusts them in the light of experience, and acts on these expectations in its behavior, is a crucial difference between the quantity-theory approach to inflation and the currently dominant Keynesian approach. It has some important implications for the assessment of the social costs of inflation. One is that, if inflation proceeds for long enough at a steady rate (and the evidence of recent history is that long is not very long) interest rates on securities fixed in money terms will adjust to include an allowance for the expected rate of inflation. This implies, contrary to popular belief, that it does not necessarily redistribute income from lenders to borrowers on fixed-interest securities (from "rentiers" to "entrepreneurs") or impair the efficiency of the capital markets. The main redistribution is from the holders to the issuers of non–interest-bearing money and of money-like assets with conventionally fixed yields; and this causes a social loss through the efforts of holders of money and money-like assets to avoid the inflation tax imposed on

Reprinted with permission from *The Journal of World Trade Law* 6 (January/February 1972).

them by economizing on the use of money. In parallel fashion, one would expect the political process that fixes the money receipts of so many public sector employees, pensioners, and other social security beneficiaries in the modern world to recontract these payments in the light of realized or anticipated inflation, so that in the long run there would be no significant redistribution of income among social groups resulting from inflation on this account.

A second and related implication is that the major social and economic problems associated with inflation stem from changes in the actual (and consequently the expected) rate of inflation *in either direction*. Such charges falsify the expectations on which past decisions have been based, leading to both economic waste and arbitrary redistributions of income and wealth among sections of the population. Such distortions are exacerbated, when inflation accelerates, by governmental efforts to suppress its manifestations by imposing restraints on increases in the wages and prices over which the government happens to have direct or indirect control or influence. Apart from the arbitrary redistributions already mentioned, a change in the rate of inflation imposes considerable social strains in the process of adjustment of wage and price determination processes to the new circumstances and expectations.

The quantity theory approach to inflation and other monetary problems fell into disrepute and virtual oblivion for two decades following the intellectual revolution in the 1930s generated by Keynes's *General Theory of Employment, Interest and Money*—a book which was really about the economic stagnation of Britain in the 1920s but which was received as a fundamental advance in understanding of the capitalist system. The *General Theory* was concerned with the economics of depression but its basic theoretical model—or at least the standard analytical model drawn from it by the leading Keynesian theorists—lent itself readily to theorizing about inflation on lines alternative to the quantity theory. In fact, most contemporary thought about inflation (apart from the monetarist view) can be related to two basic elements of the Keynesian model: the assumption that in the short run relevant to policy the money wage rate can be taken as given, and the conclusion based on this assumption that the levels of output and employment will be determined by aggregate demand for output (private consumption and investment and government demand). The latter conclusion suggests the obvious proposition that inflation will occur when aggregate demand exceeds the economy's aggregate productive capacity at current levels of wages and prices—a situation usually referred to as "demand-pull" inflation—and the equally obvious policy recommendation that the government should remedy inflation by using fiscal and monetary policy to deflate aggregate demand to the measure of the country's productive resources.

The assumption of short-run fixity of wages, transformed to a dynamic context of increasing productivity, suggests that if inflation is occurring despite the absence of evidently excessive aggregate demand, the reason is that wages, and therefore production costs, are, quite irrationally, rising more rapidly than productivity—a situation commonly described as "cost-push" inflation; and that the proper remedy is to introduce an income policy or wage-price freeze to replace the presumed irrationality of wage-fixing behavior. The simple but superficial logic of this policy is that, since real income in the aggregate can rise only at the rate of productivity increase, everyone should be willing to cooperate in an agreement to settle for an increase in money income that will give him his fair share in increased aggregate real income consistently with stability of the overall price level. The superficiality lies in the assumption that, in a large and diversified economy in which myriads of economic decisions are taken in the light of information on demand and supply pressures in particular commodity and labor markets and integrated by the use of money as the common unit of account, entrepreneurs and workers can be persuaded both to accept a centralized determination of where individual wage and price decisions ought to come out in real terms, in place of their own judgments of relevant sectoral demand and supply conditions, and to accept substitution for the familiar monetary unit of account of a "real" unit of account to which monetary calculations have to be adjusted. It may be obvious to the economists inside and outside government that on the average real incomes can rise by, say, only 3 percent a year; but this statistical fact should not and will not persuade employers and workers in individual industries and firms that a 3 percent increase in money wages will give the worker the increase in real income he is entitled to and the employer the labor supply he wants. Both will try to find a way around the centrally imposed constraint on their freedom of negotiation; and there are many ways of doing so without breaking the letter of the law.

These two strands of Keynesian theory on the subject of inflation have been integrated, since 1958, in the concept of the "Phillips curve," named after its inventor, Professor A. W. Phillips, then of the London School of Economics. The Phillips curve is essentially an inverse statistical relationship between the rate of increase of money wage rates and an index of the balance between demand and supply in the labor market, usually but not necessarily identified with the percentage rate of unemployment. By subtracting the rate of increase of productivity from the rate of increase of money wages (a procedure which involves a rather simple theory of prices and production) one obtains an inverse relationship between the rate of unemployment and the rate of inflation. Analytically, the rate of inflation corresponding to the unemployment rate associated with some conventionally determined concept of full employment can be taken as an index of the cost-pushfulness of the economy, and the relation of the actual unemployment rate to the full employment rate of unemployment as an index of the presence or non-presence and the magnitude of the demand-pull factor. For purposes of policy analysis, the Phillips curve represents the menu of choices open to the policymakers—the so-called trade-off relationship between inflation and unemployment—under given circumstances, but also a constraint that might be made less binding by improvements in the efficiency of the labor market (which would tend to equalize demand pressure disparities between individual sectors of that market) or altered or eliminated by an incomes policy.

The statistical data until a year or two ago appeared to lend fairly substantial support to the reality of the Phillips curve for a number of countries, and therefore to the analytical and policy theories based on it—though the same kind of evidence cast considerable doubt on the efficacy of incomes policy, which apparently had little statistical effect in shifting the Phillips curve in a direction favorable to the policy-makers. The theoretical foundations of the Phillips curve were, however, frontally challenged by the neo-quantity theory, or monetarist school, led by Professor Milton Friedman of the University of Chicago, who argued that the wage-determination process will be influenced on both sides by the rate of inflation expected, so that a Phillips curve can be drawn only for a given state of inflationary expectations, and will break down if the authorities attempt to use it to secure a different combination of inflation and unemployment rates than the expected inflation rate and the corresponding unemployment rate shown on the curve. More generally, Friedman argued that in the long run there is a "natural" unemployment rate, which balances real demand and supply factors in the labor market, and which cannot be altered by fiscal and monetary demand management policies. The trade-off is not between the average rate of unemployment and the average rate of inflation, but between less or more unemployment now and more or less inflation later. In the long run, the authorities cannot choose the rate of unemployment they want; all they can choose is the rate of inflation that will accompany the "natural" rate of unemployment.

This attack on the fundamental assumptions of the Phillips curve naturally led to attempts to test the Friedman argument by introducing the expected rate of inflation (hypothesized to be based on past actual rates of inflation) into the statistical estimation of the curve. The results showed that the rate of money-wage increase did depend on the expected rate of inflation, but not to the extent required to invalidate the existence of a trade-off relationship. The estimated long-run Phillips curve was considerably steeper than the short-run curve—making inflation a substantially less attractive policy for reducing unemployment—but was not vertical, implying no long-run leverage for inflation with respect to the rate of unemployment. (Contrary to what I originally thought, the incomplete feedback of prices to wages does not imply a changing share of labor in income, because another equation ties wages-minus-productivity-increases to price increases; what reconciles constant shares with apparent incomplete adjustment of wages to prices is the extra influence of the rate of unemployment on wage pushfulness.) Further, the fact that the Phillips curve relationship for both Britain and the United States has recently broken down, in the sense that the rate of wage increase in the past year or so has been unprecedentedly high at unprecedentedly high rates of unemployment for the postwar period, precisely in a period of exceptionally strong (and well-publicized) inflation, suggests that the expectational factors to which Friedman has called attention are more important than even the more sophisticated recent Phillips curve analysis has allowed for.

The alternative theories of inflation reviewed in the preceding paragraphs have one fundamental element in common: the assumption that inflationary developments in a national economy can be explained by factors endogenous to that economy, whether those factors are conceived to be excessive monetary expansion, permission of excessive aggregate demand, or the willful wrong-headedness of the wage determination process. This assumption may be completely arbitrary; just because a political nation exists, with its own national economic institutions and a government charged with responsibility for striking an acceptable balance between unemployment and inflation through the exercise of the policy instruments it controls, is not sufficient cause to ensure that economic developments are endogenously and not exogenously determined and that the government actually has the power to control those developments by use of the instruments it commands.

In fact, the major nations at least of the Western world are linked together in a world economy by the maintenance of a system of fixed exchange rates, just as the regions of a single country are linked together in a single monetary domain by the use of a common currency. Within a nation, the different regions generally experience more or less the same rate of inflation, as a consequence of the common currency in conjunction with the freedom of movement of goods, capital, and labor among them—and it should be noted that this occurs in spite of substantial differences in unemployment percentages among the regions. The assumption that nations linked by the equivalent of a common currency into an integrated world economy still have significant independence with respect to both the causation and remedification of inflation depends heavily on the assumption that the barriers to freedom of international movement of goods, labor, and capital—including money itself—are both high enough and variable enough by national economic policies to provide the requisite insulation for national economies against the impact of general influences emanating from the world economy. In the short run, the existence of barriers provides some insulation; in the longer run, variability of barriers is necessary, since the limits of the insulation provided by given barriers will be exhausted.

One such insulator could be the freedom to change the exchange rate against foreign currencies provided constitutionally by the International Monetary Fund system. But this freedom is severely restricted by the conventions of that system as they have developed over the postwar period. Moreover, as will be discussed in more detail later, the freedom of maneuver that a country obtains through the ability to change its exchange rate according to the IMF rules—that is, from one parity to another, in contrast to letting its exchange rate float on the market—is dependent on the degree of openness of its economy, which determines how rapidly a change in its exchange rate is neutralized by offsetting movements of domestic wages and prices.

Given adherence to a fixed exchange rate as the normal rule, reliance has to be placed on the influence of market imperfections, tariffs, and barriers to international capital movements in fragmenting the international economy and so insulating and providing significant policy autonomy for the constituent national economies. But since the Second World War freedom of competition in international trade has been greatly increased both by successive negotiations of tariff reductions under the General Agreement on Tariffs and Trade, culminating in the successful conclusion of the Kennedy Round in 1967, and by the formation of the European Common Market and the European Free Trade Association; and, as the experience of Britain's introduction of tariff surcharges in 1964 demonstrated, the accepted rules of international trade made it extremely difficult to increase barriers to international trade to counter a balance-of-payments deficit (i.e., to insulate the economy from international competitive pressures). National economies are, to a good first approximation, now linked together in a single world market for manufactures and primary commodities (though not for agricultural products, where national protective policies have a free rein, with chaotic results for international agricultural trade).

Further, since the restoration of currency convertibility at the end of 1958, the national capital markets of the major countries have become increasingly linked in a single international capital market. This has occurred not so much through liberalization of access to national capital markets—there have been marked tendencies in the opposite direction in some countries, notably the United States—as through the development of new institutions in the form of the Euro-currency and Euro-bond markets, which constitute an international money and capital market alternative to and imposing competitive pressures on the national capital markets. The rules of the international economic policy game permit national governments to intervene in international capital movements by methods and to an extent that would not be condoned if applied to industrial trade; but it is doubtful how effective these interventions are in insulating national capital markets from international tendencies. Again, to a good first approximation, national capital markets can be regarded as linked together in a single international capital market.

On the two approximate assumptions of an integrated world market for industrial products and primary materials and an integrated world capital market, it makes sense to consider inflation as a world phenomenon and problem, rather than as a collection of individual national phenomena and problems. This view has several important implications. One is that discussions of the reasons for inflation, and particularly of accelerated inflation, in certain countries that concentrate on the detailed development of wages and prices—and especially "wage explosion"—as causal factors are largely beside the point: they assign causality to the mechanisms by which more fundamental causes operate to diffuse the world inflationary process. A second is that national policies such as deflation or an incomes policy will not be effective in stopping inflation in one country if inflation is rampant elsewhere in the world economy. Deflation will create unemployment without stopping inflation; while an incomes policy, to the extent that it is successful, will simply distort resource allocation and produce unwanted balance-of-payments surpluses. The only effective method by which a country can avoid sharing in a world inflation is to combine anti-inflationary domestic policies with a floating (upward) exchange rate, as Canada has been doing since the beginning of June 1970. A third is that if inflation is considered a serious problem, it must be tackled at the world level by coordinated national, or by international, economic policies.

As has been well documented in a recent report by the secretary-general of the Organisation for Economic Cooperation and Development (*Inflation: The Current Problem*, December 1970), the rate of inflation in the member countries (which includes all the major noncommunist industrial nations) has been significantly higher since 1965 than it was before and has been accelerating recently. In accordance with the well-known institutional bias of the OECD toward regarding each country as a special case, the report tends to explain this by special factors operating in each country, and particularly the development of inflation in the United States, which bulks large in the aggregate; but it does recognize (though it does not explore) the possibility of common causation. To cope with the problem, it reiterates at length its long-recommended policy solution, the adoption of incomes policies by the various national governments.

It is possible, on the basis of the evidence of the OECD report, to interpret the increase in the average rate of inflation since 1965 on Keynesian lines, in terms of a world Phillips curve, since on the average countries appear to have been maintaining a higher rate of productive-capacity utilization than in the preceding period. Such an explanation would call into question the OECD's recommendation of universal incomes policies, and suggest that to moderate world inflation countries would have to agree to increase their average rates of unemployment permanently—which would appear a formidable problem for international negotiation.

This Keynesian explanation leaves unanswered, however, the question of why countries committed to fixed exchange rates should have felt free to allow higher levels of activity and employment at the risk of more inflation and—more important—balance-of-payments difficulties. The answer lies in the position of the dollar as an international reserve currency, and the freedom this has given the United States to run balance-of-payments deficits and hence to allow domestic inflation. In brief, the United States has had no external reason for trying to avoid inflation, because any consequential deficit would be financed by accumulations of dollars in the rest of the world; and because a U.S. deficit implies a surplus for the rest of the world, the rest of the world as a whole has had no external reason for trying to avoid inflation either. In fact, their policymakers have been faced with the awkward dilemma that the more they try to resist inflation for domestic reasons, the more dollars they accumulate in financing the U.S. deficits— and without being very successful in resisting inflation.

This brings us to the "monetarist" view of the reasons for the acceleration of inflation since 1965: that it has been the ultimate consequence of an increase in the rate of world monetary expansion, an increase attributable primarily to the excessively expansionary monetary policy pursued by the United States in recent years, and diffused to the rest of the world through the U.S. payments deficit.

The monetarist interpretation has been strongly disputed, on a variety of grounds that recall older debates about the international application of the quantity theory of money, and which boil down to the difficulty of finding statistical evidence of changes in monetary and trade flows large enough to appear capable of accounting for the international transmission of inflation. Objections of this kind, however, appear to depend on a rather naïve interpretation of the relevant theory. In the first place, if, as suggested above as a useful first approximation, the world market for manufactures and primary materials is assumed to be integrated, prices and wages in individual countries will tend to adjust directly to world market levels for prices and comparative-efficiency levels for wages, without the need for either excess demand generated through a current account surplus (on a Keynesian theory of inflation) or prior movements of international reserves and domestic money supplies to bring about these adjustments (on a quantity theory view of inflation). In the short run, depending on the domestic monetary policy followed, this adjustment may involve an increase in unemployment; in the longer run, on the second approximation of an integrated capital market, the extra money supply required to support higher domestic wages and prices can be obtained through the capital account of the balance of payments (international borrowing) as well as through the current account (an excess of production over expenditure being used to buy money in the commodity markets). But—and this is the second important point—the extra money required does not have to be obtained through a balance-of-payments surplus. It may instead be created by domestic credit expansion; and it will be so created if the authorities do not wish to accumulate large additional foreign exchange reserves. In short, adjustment of domestic prices and wages to world inflation does not require a prior export surplus or monetary inflow; and the monetary flows that actually occur will be determined by domestic credit policy, rather than being an independent causal factor.

The "monetarist" view of world inflation has two important implications for policy. The first is that the new Special Drawing Rights at the International Monetary Fund, created in response to an assumed prospective shortage of international liquidity, may in fact provide fuel for further world inflation rather than facilitate the reduction of barriers to world trade and payments as intended. The second is that if the rest of the world seriously desires to moderate or halt inflation, it must either float its exchange rates against the dollar, on the Canadian model—which might seriously disrupt the whole fabric of world trade and payments—or persuade the United States to alter its monetary policy to a less expansionary one consistent with price stability in the United States and therefore in the world economy. This latter alternative poses a serious problem for international diplomacy, since many American experts are convinced that monetary expansion (and inflation) are essential to the maintenance of high employment. The monetarist position on the other hand suggests that this is not so, though monetarism in the United States has recently gone into decline owing to the fact that monetary restraint has involved a high cost in unemployment in return for a low benefit in terms of slowing inflation. The most recent, and as yet highly controversial, monetarist theorizing on the subject, by Professor R. A. Mundell of the University of Chicago, argues that monetary policy governs only the rate of inflation, and that fiscal policy governs the level of unemployment. On this theory, a swing of U.S. policy from fiscal tightness and monetary ease to the converse would serve both U.S. and world interests.

17. Political Economy Aspects of International Monetary Reform

Introduction

In the background of the international monetary crisis of 1971—the so-called dollar crisis—were the three long-recognized problems of a gold exchange standard based on the use of a national currency as a reserve-currency substitute for gold. These were the problem of liquidity, associated with the gradual deterioration of the liabilities-assets ratio of the reserve currency and the resulting danger of loss of confidence in the continuing convertibility of the reserve currency into gold; the more general problem of confidence in particular currencies associated with shifts of funds among them and between them and reserve assets—the so-called composition problem; and the problem of adjustment of exchange rates.

In a reserve currency system, the adjustment problem operates asymmetrically: the non-reserve currency countries can adjust against the rest of the world by changing their par values in terms of gold, but the reserve currency country cannot do this unilaterally, for a variety of reasons including both the effects on private commercial contracts entered into on the basis of the status of its currency as the lynch-pin of the system, and the difficulties posed both for itself and the other countries by general uncertainty on both sides as to how the non-reserve currency countries will react. Adjustment of the value of the reserve currency against the others in general requires either coordinated action by the rest to change their individual rates on the reserve currency, or concerted action by the reserve and non-reserve currencies together to change the pattern of exchange rates, including the reserve-currency price of gold. The former is difficult to achieve, given the extent of exchange rate and domestic policy autonomy afforded by the reserve currency system to non-reserve currency countries. The latter is even more difficult to achieve, owing to national jealousies of the reserve currency country and of each other among the non-reserve currency countries, and requires the use of some sort of force majeure on the part of the reserve currency country. It was indeed the failure of the major non-reserve currency countries to take some sort of action, coordinated well or badly, to appreciate

Reprinted with permission from *Journal of International Economics* 2, no. 4 (September 1972): 401–23; © North-Holland Publishing Company.

their currencies against the dollar that provoked the United States administration into taking the crisis action of 15 August 1971 and forcing a realignment of currency values, including a token increase in the dollar price of gold (token in two senses: the percentage increase was small, and the U.S. shows little sign of willingness in the near future to resume official gold transactions at that price.)

A rationalist might have expected that the crisis would have led to recognition of the need for coordinated adjustment, in either of the two forms mentioned above, together with plans to reform the international monetary system so as to make exchange rate adjustment less painful by adoption of some combination of the various proposals that have long been advanced by academic experts to this end—the wider band, the crawling peg, and temporary flotation of currencies obviously undervalued in order to facilitate the difficult exercise of establishing a viable new exchange rate. On the latter score, the Smithsonian agreement of 18 December 1971 provided only for the wider band, which under the circumstances was an obvious insurance policy against some margin of error in agreeing on the new pattern of exchange rates—and in principle is a means of passing more of the burden of stabilizing exchange rate speculation in defense of the par value from official central bank speculators to private market speculators, while enabling the central banks to penalize destabilizing private speculators more severely for the error of their ways. It provides no long-run improvement in the adjustment mechanism in the face of sustained divergences of price trends among the major countries of the system. As to coordination of adjustment, the Common Market countries have produced the "snake within the tunnel" scheme, under which variations in their exchange rates on each other will be confined within narrower limits than the now permitted range of variation, the level of European rates on the dollar on average floating up and down against the dollar within the full permitted range. But to achieve this will require more coordination of European demand management policies than now exists, and more sacrifice of domestic policy autonomy than the European governments have so far proved willing to concede to the concept of a United Europe. Apart from this reinforcement of the political appeal of the idea of a common European currency, the crisis has had the effect of rupturing the halting trend of the late 1950s and the 1960s toward closer international economic cooperation in international monetary adjustment, and focusing the attention of official and academic experts back on the problems of liquidity and confidence.

Specifically, there has been a retreat from the concept of cooperation and coordination into the concept of establishing a new international monetary system that will remove the tensions manifest in the 1971 crisis between reserve-currency country and non-reserve-currency country by establishing a system in which national currencies will figure symmetrically, on the basis of consolidating the present variety of reserve assets into a single, non-national currency, into which all currencies would be convertible, and convertibility into which would subject all countries regardless of international economic importance and the role of their currency and their capital markets in the private international economic system to balance-of-payments discipline over their domestic economic policies along essentially traditional gold-standard lines. This retreat from the concept of cooperation in adjustment into the concept of an automatic self-disciplinary system involves a rather strange and potentially dangerous meeting of minds between European monetary officials and academic experts anxious to deprive the United States of the power its reserve-currency status has given it to pursue both domestic policy objectives, and particularly employment at the expense of inflation, and international policy objectives, notably the war in Viet Nam, in disregard of the balance-of-payments consequences; and American officials and monetary experts some of whom share the European objective of disciplining the United States for its own good but most of whom have the opposite objective of freeing United States domestic economic policy from the conflicts between domestic and international economic policy responsibilities that the reserve-currency status and the unwillingness of the other countries to adjust in relation to the dollar have created for it, and that have gradually forced it into adopting a string of policy measures contrary to the self-announced principles of a free enterprise system, such as aid and defense expenditure-tying, controls on capital exports, and wage-price policies.

The problem that arose in Aesop's well-known fable was the technical difficulty for the mice, having decided that the ideal solution for their cat problem was to bell the cat, of determining precisely how to do it. The present problem of the international monetary system, as currently conceived, is far more difficult: assume that the cat can only be belled by its own consent, but it is willing to be belled because it is tired of standing on guard over its master's household and would like to move freely among the mice in order to enjoy the mice's privilege of raiding the kitchen without worrying about the effects on the household's fortunes. The cat knows, and the smarter mice also know, that the cat can accept the bell but can scratch it off at any time it wishes to and revert to being a lethal cat. The technical problem then is to work out conditions of belling the cat such that the cat will stay happy with the arrangement and not scratch off the bell.

This, in allegory, is the problem with which Richard Cooper's companion paper[1] is concerned—how to turn the U.S. cat into a pseudo-European mouse, on terms that both cat and mice can live with. The problem is that if you turn the cat into a pseudo-mouse, he may revert at any moment to being a cat again and eat you up. Cooper's survey of the problem is most able, thoughtful, and useful; and there would be no point in my surveying the same issues and debating on points of detail, since I agree with him on the general principle that reducing the U.S. dollar to equality with other currencies would require far more radical change in the existing international monetary system than has generally been realized.

But there is another, and more general, problem suggested by that particular fable of Aesop's: supposing either that the mice are clever enough to figure out how to bell the cat successfully and lastingly, or that they achieve it with the cat's consent, what are the long-run implications for the viability of the household in which they jointly live? Can the mice, including the pseudo-mouse cat, devise rules of fair mouse behavior and discipline among mice that will enable all to live comfortably and consistently with the available food supply in the household, or will anarchy emerge with results dangerous to collective survival? To drop the analogy, can a more or less automatically operating modernized replica of the theoretical classical gold standard be devised, that can govern international monetary affairs and adjustments without the continuing necessity for the exercise of responsible, and occasionally self-sacrificing, leadership by one or a few of the world's largest countries? This is a problem in political economy, not in technical economic analysis, though as Cooper's paper shows one cannot discuss the technical issues intelligently without reference to the political economy of vast inequalities among nations.

In posing this problem, I am of course assuming, as a fact of international political life, that the governments, central banks, and financial communities of the various nations have a strong preference for fixed exchange rates and aversion to adjustment of exchange rates, and especially to a system of genuinely floating exchange rates. (The industrial and commercial sectors come down on sometimes one side and sometimes the other of the fixed versus floating rate issue, depending on the general tenor of government's success or otherwise in domestic economic stabilization policy, but their views are usually presumed and expressed for them by the defenders of fixed exchange rates.) There are economic reasons for this preference, associated more with the abstract functions of money as a unit of account and standard for deferred payments than with its concrete functions as medium of exchange and store of value.[2] The well-known difficulties to which this preference gives rise can be stated in terms of the observation that revealed preferences as implied by the domestic economic policies actually pursued do not correspond with the stated preferences obtained by indirect questionnaire; together with the related observation that governments are reluctant to admit the inconsistency overtly by changing their exchange rates. These circumstances make international politics an essential ingredient in the functioning of the international monetary system, and necessitate the exercise of international political cooperation, and of international political leadership by the largest countries.

It is for this reason that the disruption of the degree of international monetary cooperation among the United States and the major European countries, slowly and painfully built up through the 1960s, by the sequence of European reluctance to revalue against the dollar, the use of a demonstration of American power to force the indicated currency realignment, and the consequential European and Japanese resentment against U.S. power as expressed in the asymmetrical role of the dollar in the international monetary system, could be extremely dangerous for the future of the international monetary system. The resulting proliferation of plans for putting the dollar on the same footing as the other national currencies—especially with the conflicting motives on the two sides noted earlier—is headed in the opposite direction to the increasingly close international political cooperation needed to make the system work.

Unfortunately, economic theory offers no easy prescription for methods of inducing individual entities to cooperate for the common good; indeed, its standard prescription, dating from the time of Adam Smith—let competition prevail and if it will not prevail enforce it—is not only irrelevant but downright misleading in the international monetary context, since it assumes atomistic competition is possible whereas the international economy more nearly resembles a situation of oligopolistic competition. It is misleading, because it encourages the notion that institutional devices can be found to reduce large national oligopolies to the status and performance of atomistic firms under perfect competition—a notion embodied both in the original structure of the International Monetary Fund until it was modified to recognize the special status of the dollar as the intervention currency and the power position of the "Group of Ten" in the international monetary system (the latter through the General Arrangements to Borrow), and in present efforts to establish an institutional system under which the position of the dollar would be symmetrical with that of other currencies. It is further misleading because it ignores the crucial difference between legislation and institutionalization: in the national economy, laws can be passed and enforced by sovereign authority stipulating the maintenance of competitive conditions under impartial legal penalties for noncompliance; in the international system, institutions must rest on general consent to their fairness, and there is no central sovereign authority to penalize transgressors— punishment must be administered by consent of the damaged parties, if they can agree on and enforce it. In these circumstances, disinterested advice to all parties to behave less selfishly and more responsibly is highly likely to fall on deaf ears; about the most the economist can do is to keep reminding governments and the public of the consequences for the system as a whole of irresponsible behavior on the part of individual members of it. Unfortunately, governments and publics are more concerned about the motes in their neighbors' eyes than about the beams in their own; and government economic advisers are usually paid either to devise or to defend self-interested national policies, rather than to be their own government's conscience.

In this paper, I can offer no better hope for improvement of the international monetary system than that, on the one hand, academic and official economists will realize that institutional tinkering or even drastic institutional change offers no alternative to acceptance of increased international responsibility in the game of international power politics, and that governments and their publics will gradually accept and practice the obligation of international responsibility. The paper itself attempts to present some aspects of the political economy of the international monetary system, in the hope that they will be either illuminating and informative, or at least provocative with respect to the contemplation of the future of the system and of the prospects for beneficial reform.

Two Traditions of International Monetary Analysis

To begin with, it is worth remembering that there have always been two traditions in the analysis of international monetary phenomena and problems, a political-economic one and an economic-scientific one—though these two traditions are often mingled in the work of a single writer, and indeed the development of a scientific approach to economics has forced the politically oriented to acquire at least a smattering of scientific language and logic, while exposure of the theorists to practical policy problems has obliged them to acquire at least some dim awareness of the political process.

The political-economic approach derives from national and international politics, and tends to view the international monetary system as merely one sphere for the contention of national rivalries. In this framework, the emergence of a major country's currency as the reserve currency for the international monetary system is viewed as an exercise in imperialism, and distrusted and resisted, even when such emergence is a natural consequence of economic size, wealth, efficiency, and superior financial organization, and can generally be explained by economic factors without the need for reference to any deliberate policies of "monetary imperialism." The central defect of this approach is that it provides, not analysis, but an emotive descriptive language in terms of which almost every important event or development can be rationalized and given intelligible meaning, even though the successive interpretations are logically inconsistent with one another. Thus one finds this school of thought, for example, attributing the rise of the pound sterling to reserve-currency status to the exercise of British imperial power, and its subsequent decline to the failure of Britain to exercise its imperial power fully and intelligently—whereas a contrary view would hold that the pound became a reserve currency as the inadvertent by-product of Britain's industrial leadership, and that the decline of British industrial leadership and imperial power was to a significant extent due to a mistaken British willingness to sacrifice domestic policy objectives for the sake of a mistakenly presumed obligation to the world economy as a whole to preserve the traditional gold standard. The same kind of illogic appears in the contemporary associated notions that the dollar standard gives the United States unwarranted imperialistic power, and that the 1971 crisis constituted a desperate attempt by the United States to reassert its waning imperial monetary power. Where this approach is useful is not in analysis, but in emphasizing the facts both that a lot of people, including some quite eminent economists, do think this way—though the trained economists are usually clever enough at concealing their emotions within the trappings of scientific analysis to pass for dispassionate experts—and that it often pays off in the understanding of events to recognize that governments both think and act this way in international monetary affairs.[3]

The scientific economic approach to the international monetary system, which goes back to David Hume's elaboration of the price-specie-flow mechanism, involves the basic concept of an automatic self-adjusting international monetary mechanism based on gold, in which national governments (more properly, their central banks) were simply automatons reacting blindly to the market pressures communicated to them through the balance of payments. This orientation of theory changed during the 1930s, under the circumstances of the time in which the balance of payments became a policy problem for governments involving choices between external and internal balance and between exchange rate adjustment and trade controls, and with the Keynesian revolution, which made full employment not a conclusion of economic analysis but a policy problem for governments. However, the post–World War II development of the theory of economic policy for an open economy by Meade, Tinbergen, and others restored the concept of an automatic system, on the basis of the assumption that once the theory had been clearly laid out governments could be relied on to apply it intelligently, and deflate and revalue or inflate and devalue in the appropriate combinations as circumstances required. The major virtue of this approach to international monetary problems is that it does concern itself with causal relationships, relationships moreover of a quantifiable kind. Its major defect is its assumption that governments have both the understanding and the power to follow its precepts, and that they will do so instead of using the understanding and the power to play international politics against their neighbors.

The problem of the international monetary expert at the present juncture is (and has been for many years) to understand the scientific logic of the international monetary system well enough to comprehend the system-wide implications of new developments, new policies, and policy alternatives, while understanding the political forces behind new developments, yet without committing himself to a particular judgment on the rights and wrongs of the politics derived either from his own nationality or from his own position in the left-right spectrum of politics.

Bretton Woods and Its Critics

A theme suggested earlier is that the international monetary system established at Bretton Woods and incorporated in the Charter of the International Monetary Fund represented an attempt to impose a fictitious equality on national currencies; that the actual system has drifted de facto away from its initial conception as a result of the economic dominance of the United States and the emergence and growth of the international dollar standard, to the point where the tensions involved became so severe as to precipitate the crisis of 1971; and that current concerns about the reform of the system through consolidation of reserve assets and the establishment of symmetry among currencies represent in essence an attempt to reestablish the original conception by institutional reform rather than to achieve genuine improvement in the light of the practical and political realities of the current crisis situation.

That the Bretton Woods Conference should have attempted to establish a sort of "rule of law" for international monetary behavior before which all currencies would be at least nominally equal, is perfectly understandable, as being necessary under the circumstances. First, there was the assumption of an atomistic competitive market ingrained in economic theorizing, already referred to. Second, it is impossible in any sort of negotiation among a group of individuals to incorporate in the final agreement the explicit assumption that one of them is expected to be a chronic bad actor, by comparison with the others. Third, the United States, which was generally agreed to have been the chronic bad actor of the 1940s,[4] was in the most powerful negotiating position, and could only be seduced into agreement by forms of words that did not insist on recognition of this fact.

Nevertheless, there were some vocal critics of the Bretton Woods agreements at the time, and it is instructive to look briefly at their criticisms for their insights and foresights into the problems that the International Monetary Fund system has encountered in its over-quarter-century of evolution.

First, there were the practical monetary experts experienced in the detailed developments of the 1930s, who saw the Tripartite Agreement of 1936 as having successfully terminated the international monetary chaos of the 1930s by agreement among the major currency countries to manage the pattern of exchange rates among their currencies by agreement among themselves, taking account of the implications for the whole system but letting the rest of the world adjust to their decisions. The academic reflection of this position was the "key currency" approach developed by John H. Williams of Harvard[5]; and while it made no intellectual headway at the time, it can fairly be said that the evolution of the International Monetary Fund system to date reflects the increasing dominance over the legal constitutional form of the realities of the power-play among the major currencies. The 1971 crisis may in a sense be said to have been the result of a breakdown of mutual understanding among the key currency countries; and this breakdown has led both to the emergence of political tensions within the system and to demands by lesser currency countries that they should have a share in the effective decision-making process.

Second, there was a mere handful of monetarists, centered on the University of Chicago and represented most lucidly by Henry Simons, who attributed the difficulties of the 1930s primarily to the failure of U.S. monetary policy to maintain price stability and prevent a collapse of the U.S. money supply and U.S. prices and employment.[6] This position was echoed, but inchoately and ineffectively, by large numbers elsewhere who realized, and asserted vociferously, that the United States was to blame for the mess, but had no economic explanation and blamed it instead on the evil propensities of the American national character.[7] For Simons, the key to a properly functioning postwar international monetary system was the successful pursuit in the United States of monetary policies designed to secure stability of the American price level, and trade policies aimed at freedom of international trade, both of which were in America's self-interest as well as being beneficial to the world economy as a whole.

Simons's analysis, in fundamentals, contains a great deal of insight into the conditions necessary for the successful working of an international monetary system composed of countries of vastly different sizes. Like subsequent Chicagoans (and many other American economists) he maintained that gold derived its value from the dollar and not vice versa—this of course is the crux of the contemporary debate over restoration of the convertibility of the dollar. His main point, however, can be put in terms of fundamental monetary theory: what countries are really after, in the shape of international reserve assets, is not really convertibility into gold (or some other non-national international asset) but stability of the value of the asset in terms of goods and services. Convertibility of currencies into gold (or, say, SDR's) is an indirect means of forcing countries to maintain price stability and so to stabilize the real purchasing power of international money. But, as both basic monetary theory and hard recent experience have shown, convertibility only guarantees price stability if the growth of the stock of the international reserve asset is proportioned to the growth of demand for international reserves at stable prices. Simons prescribed a direct policy of price stabilization in the United States, on the assumption that the economic size of the United States would guarantee that this would mean world price stability, and the subsidiary proposition that if other countries could not keep their prices in line with U.S. prices and had to make exchange rate adjustments against the dollar that would not matter too much to the system as a whole.

In an important and relevant sense, one can say that the international monetary system functioned satisfactorily for the world economy's prosperity and economic growth up until 1965 or so because the United States for one reason or another conformed to Simons's prescription and preserved a reasonable degree of price stability, thus providing other countries with an international asset of relatively stable real purchasing power superior to gold because it yielded enough interest to compensate for the effects on real purchasing power of the creeping inflationary trend. Moreover, other countries could pursue economic policies somewhat divergent from price stability in either direction, and correct occasionally for the effects of such divergent policies on their balances of payments by exchange rate changes, in the confidence that exchange rate changes against the dollar constituted a change in the real and not merely the nominal currency numeraire of their domestic money. In short, the exchange rate on the dollar was an index of the real purchasing power of a country's currency.

But with the emergency of inflation in the United States after 1965, the dollar ceased to have a stable purchasing power, and fixity of the exchange rate on the dollar guaranteed a depreciation of the real value of a country's currency sooner or later. In short, the dollar ceased to be a real purchasing power numeraire for other currencies. This changed the character of the fixed exchange rate system drastically: whereas previously exchange rate changes against the dollar were a matter of correcting for decreases or increases in the real purchasing power of domestic currency in the domestic market relative to its purchasing power in the world market at the current exchange rate, exchange rate changes had now to take account not only of the position of an individual country relative to the rest of the world, but of the position of the non-U.S. world relative to the U.S. world. There was no longer a reference point of money of stable real purchasing power to guide exchange rate adjustments. The difficulties created by this change lie behind both the efforts of other countries to devise institutional changes that will discipline the United States into maintaining price stability, and their efforts to develop a common European currency that can float against the dollar and so remove the inflationary influence of American inflation on their own prices. Simons was right in pointing to the maintenance of price stability in the United States as the key to a viable international monetary system, even though his fear was of a deflation of the U.S. price level of the 1930s variety, and he never anticipated the contrary case of a U.S. price inflation disrupting the system. (Fortunately, the economic costs of price inflation for the world economy are far less serious for the mass of humankind than the economic costs of the unemployment and lost output that follow pressure to deflate prices in the face of wage and price stickiness.)

A third group of critics of the Bretton Woods agreements consisted of the radical Keynesians and Marxo-Keynesians,[8] who developed the now-indefensible theory of the "deflationary bias" of the gold standard and interpreted the 1930s as a struggle among nations to maintain domestic employment at each other's expense through deflationary domestic policy stances in relation to their exchange rates or, the more popular example, "competitive devaluation" of their currencies. In the light of hindsight and more sophisticated monetary analysis, it is clear that the "deflationary bias" concept was largely a projection of the deflationary consequences for Britain of returning to gold at an overvalued parity at a time when Britain anyway had to shift resources out of her declining traditional export industries; that the collapse of the U.S. money supply permitted by the Federal Reserve triggered off an international liquidity shrinkage that required drastic world price deflation or a rise in the international price of gold to restore international monetary equilibrium; that the observed phenomena of "competitive depreciation" and "export of unemployment" were a painfully roundabout method of achieving a rise in the world price of gold; and that, as shown by recent experience, the gold exchange standard can equally well display an "inflationary bias"—it all depends on the behavior of the monetary policy of the reserve currency country.

The Bretton Woods agreements attempted to guard against a recurrence of these phenomena largely by providing additional liquidity on an international credit basis but also by permitting exchange rate adjustment (with depreciation the case in mind) only in cases of "fundamental disequilibrium" and through the incorporation of the "scarce currency" clause. (It may be noted in passing that there was considered to be no need for a "super-abundant currency" clause; and it is doubtful whether current European efforts to develop joint discrimination against capital imports from the United States could be as effective a disciplinary lever as the trade discrimination permitted under the scarce currency clause.) Presumably, they also relied on the assumption that, given an effective international monetary system and understanding of the fundamentals of Keynesian economic policy theory, countries would no longer find it advantageous to give away goods in order to import employment, any more than they would find it necessary to deflate employment and forego goods in order to correct deficits, rather than devalue.

The critics in question believed that no international monetary system could restrain the mercantilist propensities of nations to try to develop trade surpluses, and hence were critical both of the proposed new international monetary arrangements and of the associated agreements providing an international organization to promote the removal of tariff, quota, and other restrictions on international trade. Instead they wanted the maximum freedom for a nation (meaning Britain, the country where the vocal majority of these critics resided) to pursue domestic full employment and use trade and exchange interventions as necessary to protect its balance-of-payments position. (This stance reflected extreme scepticism about the efficacy of exchange rate adjustment in restoring equilibrium, based on what I believe to have been a misinterpretation of the 1930s experience derived from concentration on the real to the neglect of the monetary aspects of the problem, a scepticism which found its intellectual expression in the early postwar period in the emergence of the "elasticity pessimism" school.)

This group of critics was completely wrong in its forecast of the general characteristics of the postwar international economic system, which has not been characterized by the predicted mass unemployment and international struggle to create employment by beggar-my-neighbor balance-of-payments policies, but instead has been an unprecedented period of high employment, prosperity, and economic growth (even in Britain, despite the legacy of interventionist philosophy and policy left by the Marxo-Keynesians). The problem in recent years has been world inflation, not world deflation. However, these critics had an important element of truth on their side, in their emphasis on mercantilist motivations in the formation of national economic policies, even though they were wrong in casting their argument in the context of an assumed general tendency of the capitalist system to produce mass unemployment.

It is true, according to the now well-established Keynesian theory of economic policy, that a nation need not rely on a current account surplus created by undervaluation to maintain a high level of employment; and also that to do so, and to use the surplus either to accumulate international reserves yielding a low rate of return or to make relatively low-yield loans, investments, and aid donations abroad deprives the domestic population of resources that could be used to better domestic purpose. Hence rational economic policies would not be mercantilist in character. But this proposition ignores two important practical points. First, the political system may not be sophisticated enough, or the institutions of fiscal and monetary management flexible enough, to arrive at and carry out the appropriate fiscal, monetary, and exchange rate policies indicated by the policy theory. Second, it makes life easier for the politicians and their policymakers to have a current account surplus (or possibly a smaller deficit than would otherwise occur) buoying up effective demand and employment in the economy and facing them with a problem of restraining rather than stimulating the economy. (A fuller analysis would of course also have to take in the economic forces operating on the ordinary capital account of the balance of payments.)

In the 1930s such a comfortable position for the policymakers had to be created by a deliberate and politically distasteful act of currency depreciation. But in the U.S.-led inflationary circumstances that have prevailed since 1965, it could be created simply by inertia, stubbornness, the pleading of special circumstances and the uncertainty of the future, and other reasons for unwillingness to appreciate in order to offset the inflationary domestic impact of American inflation. It was even more comfortable to be able to blame the inflation on the United States, while taking credit for its domestic stimulative effects on employment, output, and economic growth. In an important sense, full employment and economic growth in Europe at least in recent years have ridden on the back of American inflation and the resulting loss of competitiveness of American goods in world markets, together with American willingness to tolerate the consequences in terms of a domestic unemployment problem, the domestic dislocations consequent on the loss of domestic and international competitiveness occurring for monetary and not "real" reasons, and the transfer of American enterprise capital to Europe in response to the artificially low costs of production there as compared with production in the U.S. for the European market created by European reluctance to appreciate against the dollar. (One must distinguish here between the real economic changes that would have occurred at equilibrium exchange rates, and the extra changes due to disequilibrium exchange rates.)

The United States could conceivably have reduced the unemployment and competitive adjustment costs of this situation by pursuing a policy of still greater monetary inflation directed solely at domestic employment objectives. This would have made the European and Japanese policies of undervaluation more expensive for them, and perhaps forced them to appreciate their currencies voluntarily; but the long-run consequences for American economic welfare and growth of an unsuccessful or only belatedly successful gamble on this strategy might have been seriously adverse, especially in terms of further artificial stimulation of the transfer of American enterprise capital to transitorily lower-cost foreign countries. Instead, however, the administration responded to the mercantilism of the Europeans and Japanese, expressed in their unwillingness to appreciate their currencies in face of the American inflation, by use of the mercantilist device of the import surcharge to force an appreciation of their exchange rates on the dollar. In responding in this way, the United States was motivated by a mixture of understanding of the monetary aspects of the situation—the effects on foreign trade and foreign investment of overvaluation of the dollar relative to the other major currencies—and mercantilist ambitions of its own—for there is no reason to expect that the United States is entitled by economic law to remain the technological leader of the world and to be entitled to an export surplus of technologically advanced goods, and every reason to expect that, like Britain before her, her large-scale foreign investments will entail both an erosion of her technological leadership and the necessity of developing a deficit on trade account to permit the servicing of her interest and dividend claims on investments in foreign countries.

Some Observations on the Theory of the International Monetary System

The "n-1" Problem

Many of the current problems of, and debates about, the international monetary system can be summarized simply in terms of the so-called "n-1" principle—that in a system of n commodities or n currencies, there can be only n-1 relative prices, with one commodity or currency serving as the numeraire. As applied to the international monetary system, we can contrast a system of n national currencies with one serving as the numeraire—the dollar standard—in which the position of the numeraire currency necessarily makes its position asymmetrical with those of the other currencies, because to fix the price of the other currencies in terms of the numeraire requires using the numeraire currency as an intervention currency, and also promotes its use as a medium of international exchange and a store of international value; and a system of n-1 national currencies and an international money, independent of the individual national currencies—such as gold, or "paper gold" in the form of some version of Special Drawing Rights at the I.M.F.—in which the international currency serves as the numeraire and the position of the individual national currencies in relation to it is symmetrical. (To dispel confusion, n in the first system has to be one less than n in the second for the same number of national currencies to exist.)

The crux of current reform proposals is to replace system I by system II. The basic problem, as Richard Cooper argues,[9] is that the emergence of one national currency as numeraire is the resultant of strong economic forces based on efficiency considerations, and that the replacement of a national currency numeraire by an international currency numeraire will require either or both of the sacrifice of the convenience and efficiency of the national currency numeraire and the endowment of the international currency numeraire with sufficiently attractive attributes to make it acceptable as a numeraire to both official and private holders. In this connection, it is important to note that the gradual replacement of gold (and silver) as international currency by a national currency (first the pound, then the dollar) through the evolution of the gold exchange standard was a direct consequence of the relative unattractiveness of the numeraire international currency, gold, with respect to performance of the concrete functions of money (i.e., as medium of exchange and store of value, due to its sterile, non-interest-bearing character). Hence the task of reestablishing an international currency numeraire to replace the dollar requires—as Cooper argues—a substantial effort to establish this currency as an actual money and not merely a unit of account, by making the yield on it sufficiently attractive by comparison with national money to encourage private use of it. This is a formidable task of institutional reform. (In this connection, I cannot understand the contention of a large number of international monetary experts that the rate of return on international money for official holdings should be kept below market rates of return in order to encourage the use of international reserves to meet balance-of-payments deficits. An initially given level of reserves, which may or may not be used according to discretion, is a completely arbitrary starting point for the analysis of international reserve-holding behavior, which is a problem in optimal inventory-holding theory; and that theory tells us, according to the theory of optimal money supply, that in the case of a zero resource-cost inventory such as money, optimum social behavior is achieved by imposing a zero private cost on holding of the inventory, which can be achieved by paying a competitive rate of interest on money.)

Formulation of the current problem of international monetary reform in terms of the "n-1" principle, however, is apt to be misleading because it ignores one of the fundamental points about money: that it derives its value from its purchasing power over goods and services; and that, given the probability of divergent movements in both national price levels and exchange rates, that national currency will be most attractive as numeraire which yields some optimum combination of domain over goods and services and stability in purchasing power over them. The *optimum optimorum* would occur if the largest and most economically diversified country also had the most stable price level—a condition, as suggested earlier, approximated by the United States from about 1950 to 1965. Otherwise, there is a three-sided conflict between domain of purchasing power, stability of purchasing power over that domain, and efficiency of financial services available through the holding of the numeraire currency. During the earlier phase of the postwar period when the United States maintained reasonable price stability, the U.S. dollar was the obvious choice for numeraire over all other contenders; but its advantages became problematical when the United Staets embarked on an inflationary course.

In the light of this observation, the proposal to establish a common European currency can be interpreted as an effort to establish a new numeraire that will be more stable in purchasing power over goods and services than the U.S. dollar, at the expense of sacrificing both the financial efficiency of the use of the dollar and the independence of national policy action for European countries permitted by the use of the dollar as the numeraire currency. Similarly, as already mentioned, the proposal to reestablish an international currency numeraire to replace the dollar can be regarded as an attempt to force the world in general, and the United States in particular, to pursue domestic economic policies consistent with world price stability and hence stability in the real purchasing power of international money. But that proposal contains an internal contradiction: if world price stability is ensured, the dollar will be again preferable to the international money (unless, contrary to all probability, the international money is made more attractive to hold than the dollar for private transactors).

It is necessary in conclusion to say something more precise about the problems posed for the other major countries in a dollar-exchange standard by inflation in the United States. Much has been made in recent literature of the "seigniorage" problem—the capacity of the reserve-currency–issuing country to impose a tax, through non-payment of interest on the reserve currency to foreign holders of it, on those foreign holders—and of the natural extension of this concept to the ability of the reserve-currency country to impose an inflationary tax on the holders of its currency by excessive issue of it resulting in domestic and foreign price inflation. But foreign holders of the reserve currency do not hold dollar bills yielding no interest; instead they hold treasury bills and other assets bearing interest— and to the extent that the interest rates involved are below rates of return on real capital they represent a liquidity yield and not a loss—and the interest rates afforded will be adjusted fairly quickly to reflect the expected rate of inflation. "Seigniorage," though a popular grievance, is therefore not the real issue.[10] The real issues are, on the one hand, the domestic disturbances for foreign countries involved in accepting an unwanted, U.S.-led, rate of inflation and, on the other hand, the sacrifice of real domestic resources involved in tardy adjustment to inflation expressed in an unwanted current surplus and the necessity of lending these resources out on capital account at relatively unprofitable rates of return.

The "Elasticity Approach" to Exchange Rate Theory

The prevalent approach to the theory of exchange rate adjustment developed by Meade, Tinbergen, and many others derives from Keynesian theory and the economic facts of the 1930s, in which mass unemployment combined with stickiness of wages and prices meant that exchange rate changes involved changes in real relative prices and therefore relative competitive positions in imperfectly competitive international markets.

The alternative contemporary "monetary" approach assumes both upward flexibility of wages and prices and a sufficient degree of international competition to ensure that in the long run domestic currency prices have to be aligned with the level of world prices. Hence an exchange rate adjustment, specifically a devaluation, has the same effect on the balance of payments and the acquisition of international reserves as a monetary deflation: in each case the improvement of the balance of payments is transitory, lasting only so long as the period of readjustment of actual to desired stocks of money demanded through net exports of goods or of securities. A continuing deficit-surplus situation in the world economy depends on either lags in the transmission of world inflation from the more inflationary to the less inflationary countries, or on the persistent failure of some countries to expand domestic credit as rapidly as the demand for money is expanding, thereby obliging the domestic population to acquire the money it needs by net exports of goods, securities, or both. In the context of this analysis, exchange rate adjustments are merely temporary palliatives of balance-of-payments disequilibria, and cannot remedy disequilibria created by national monetary policies that are excessively restrictive with respect to domestic credit expansion and hence create a structural need to acquire additional reserves through an overall balance-of-payments surplus, or alternatively are excessively expansionary in terms of domestic credit creation and hence create a structural need to get rid of international reserves through an overall balance-of-payments deficit. The remedy for such a situation, therefore, is not primarily greater exchange-rate flexibility, though this may be important for cushioning the effects of policy errors, but reforms of the conduct of domestic monetary policies designed to eliminate such structural propensities to accumulate or decumulate international reserves.

More accurately, in a dollar standard world the rest of the world must govern its monetary policies so as to accumulate international reserves at no faster a rate than it considers desirable, and the U.S. must expand its domestic credit at no faster a rate than is consistent with the growth of its own resident demand for domestic money and foreigners' demands for dollars as international reserves. This statement is ambiguous, however, because the absolute growth of foreign demand for dollars depends on the rate of inflation set by U.S. monetary policy, and even though inflation leads foreigners to demand the additional amounts of dollars supplied they may well resent the necessity of doing so; hence a rider stipulating a reasonable degree of price stability ensured by the appropriate rate of expansion of the overall dollar supply should be attached to the proposition. Similarly, equilibrium in a world monetary system based on "paper gold" requires that countries conduct their monetary policies in such a fashion that they acquire no more and no less reserves than they consider consistent with the requirements of their economic growth, and that the international monetary authority responsible for governing the rate of expansion of the supply of paper gold do so in conformance with the requirements of world price stability. (Stability, it should be noted, does not necessarily require a flat zero trend of world prices, if the appropriate index for such a trend could in fact be defined, but only a relatively small and predictable world price trend.)

Comments on the Problem of International Responsibility

As has been emphasized in this paper, the main problem of reform of the international monetary system is not institutional reform designed to replace the dollar standard by a paper gold standard in relation to which all currencies would be symmetrically treated—an objective which would be bound to founder on the immovable rock of American economic dominance of the world, and other countries' recognition of this fact—but a movement toward greater responsibility toward the system as a whole on the part of the major countries concerned. Such a movement would have to be based on reciprocal understanding both of the system and of the position of the nations in it, and on the abandonment of nationalistic rivalries expressed in the pursuit of mercantilistic policies within the framework of the system.

On the side of the United States, the obligation remains what it was generally assumed to be in the immediate postwar period—the pursuit of liberal policies of international trade, payments, and investment—but coupled with deliberate recognition of an obligation to maintain a reasonable degree of price stability in the United States economy, and corollary abnegation of the right to use inflation for domestic policy purposes. Such abnegation should incidentally make it easier to resist foreign insistence on any obligation of the United States to deflate its economy in case of balance-of-payments deficit, because then the United States could argue plausibly that the deficit was demand-determined by other countries. But it would require the American government and American public opinion getting used to the idea that in the long run the technological supremacy of the United States in the world economy must wane, as a natural result of the diffusion of capital and technology to lower-cost countries, and that the structure of the American economy must adjust to this diffusion process and to a change of comparative advantage from commodity to service production, just as the British economy has been changing in structure over a much longer period—though it is greatly to be hoped that American policy will avoid the errors into which British policy has been plunging over so long a period.

On the side of the European nations and Japan, the obligation is essentially to improve public and governmental understanding of the theory of economic policy, and the application of that theory in the design of fiscal, monetary, and exchange rate policy, as an alternative to reliance on undervalued exchange rates to create automatic buoyancy in the economy and so ease the task of the politicians in making hard choices among policy alternatives and explaining them to the public. An essential part of this change would be to induce European intellectuals and political leaders to mature past the naïve conception that Europe can only grow and prosper economically at the expense of the United States.[11] Both developments would, for reasons sketched earlier, be greatly facilitated if the United States could get itself back on a path of reasonable price stability. If it cannot or will not do so, we must envisage the ultimate results as a breaking-up of the international monetary system, currently a system of fixed exchange rates occasionally alterable with more or less concomitant international monetary crisis, into a system of currency blocs (the dollar bloc, the Europe bloc, possibly a yen bloc) with minor currencies either pegging onto one of the bloc currencies or fluctuating independently. This might—and I would argue that it probably would—be a better system than one of fixed exchange rates riddled with international political tensions; but the time for it is not yet ripe, and may never arrive.

18. Mercantilism: Past, Present, and Future

In the historical development of economic thought, the term *mercantilism* refers to a collection of ideas on economic policy characteristic of the period of preindustrial capitalism, a period whose termination in Britain may be dated—if indeed economic history can be divided into datable phases—sometime in the latter eighteenth century. This collection of ideas was thoroughly routed by Adam Smith in his *The Wealth of Nations* (whose bicentennary is fast approaching), though, as Jacob Viner records in his classic study of the commercial policy aspects of mercantilism,[1] it had already been in disarray for some considerable time. *The Wealth of Nations* was the starting point of modern economics, though Smith himself was neither as doctrinaire on the one hand nor as theoretically acute on the other in his criticisms of mercantilism as some of his successors. Nevertheless, despite its intellectual routing by *The Wealth of Nations*, carried on subsequently in the main body of economic theory, mercantilism has remained a potent force in popular and political thinking ever since.

That this should be so is scientifically and socially regrettable, but thoroughly understandable in terms of the nature of scientific inquiry and progress, particularly in the social sciences. Science starts from primitive man's concept of his environment and seeks to improve his knowledge of and control over it by the application of logical method and abstraction verified by experimentation and empirical testing. Since man is engaged with his natural environment in collaboration and conflict but not identified with it, and the environment is in a relevant sense immortal, the accretion of knowledge about it is demonstrably and permanently useful—until superseded by superior scientific knowledge, which gains its acceptance by proving its superior usefulness. But for the social sciences man is his own environment, and his brief mortality means that he is perpetually recreating his environment and with it his own prescientific primitive ideas about it. Hence while a layman or politician would be laughed out of court if he seriously suggested that space exploration should be guided by a pre-Copernican view of the universe, he can generally obtain a respectful hearing for pre-Smithian views on microeconomic policy and pre-Keynesian views on macroeconomic

Presidential Address to Section F of the British Association for the Advancement of Science, Canterbury, 20 August 1973.

267

policy. (To drive that point home, I would be prepared to argue that the much-touted inflation remedy of incomes policy basically expresses the premercantilist medieval and guild-economy philosophy of the "just price.") Worse, contemporary human societies may corner themselves by the pursuit of inconsistent policies into situations in which only primitive ideas have any chance of acceptance—and in which policies derived from such ideas may even have a chance of accomplishing something, failing all else. Worse still, in contrast to the natural scientists—who until the Second World War and its cold war aftermath debauched them with public prestige were content with the lonely rewards of acclaim among a handful of peers in the scientific community—social scientists (or at least, or particularly, economists) frequently derive their satisfaction from their social role as experts on their society and hence are prepared, in blunt terms, to sell out their science for a pot of political message. To put the point more politely and fairly, few if any contemporary economists have the social and scientific detachment of a Wicksell or a Walras, or a rate of psychological time preference low enough, for the thought of observing posterity prove them right from a safe seat in heaven to provide compensation for experiencing social unpopularity—or even tolerating mere social invisibility—at the height of their professional careers. To say this, I should emphasize, is not to blame my colleagues: every profession tends to attract the kind of personality that values most the rewards it offers in greatest abundance.

Like any other body of thought and group of thinkers important enough to merit being called an "-ism," mercantilism was a collection of often mutually contradictory ideas expressed with varying degrees of clarity by men of widely varying levels of intelligence and reasoning power. Reduced to its bare essentials, however, and doing far less than justice to the percipience of many of the writers concerned, it amounted to two propositions: that the wealth of a country consisted in the quantity of precious metals in circulation or in hoards within its borders, and that the way to increase that wealth was to secure a surplus on the balance of payments, usually identified with a balance on merchandise trade, by policies of import substitution and export promotion.

The first proposition involves a confusion between money and productive material capital so elementary as to appear incredible to modern economists. The most plausible defense of it is to reinterpret it into the proposition, appropriate to the historical circumstances of the stage of formation of nation-states, that a nation-state needs a war chest of foreign exchange reserves—a need borne in on British policy thinking in this century by the problems of financing two major wars in the early years of which the United States was not a belligerent ally, and reflected in the continuing policy of giving heavy protection to British agriculture allegedly on balance-of-payments grounds. But the war chest argument, as Viner rightly observes, does not lead to the recommendation of policies designed to ensure a continuing balance-of-payments surplus, since there must obviously be some limit to the size of the war chest it is rational to accumulate. (There is also the consideration that bringing money into the country does not necessarily bring it into the war chest; that requires taxation as well as or instead of mercantilist balance-of-payments policies, and to the rational-minded economist the argument should therefore concentrate on the desirability of building a war chest by taxation, a question which has little if any connection with commercial policy.)

The second proposition—that precious metals should be obtained by trade policies aimed at securing a balance-of-payments surplus—is by far the more interesting, both theoretically in itself and in terms of the development of modern economic theory. There are two answers to it. The first, and more fundamental, relies on the quantity theory of money, as extended to the international monetary system by David Hume in his famous price-specie flow mechanism. (Actually, a statement of the relevant monetary theory in some ways clearer than Hume's and published thirty years earlier is to be found in Isaac Gervaise's relatively obscure essay, *The System or Theory of the Trade of the World*, 1720.) To put the essential point in modern terminology, any attempt to achieve a perpetual balance-of-payments surplus, whether by mercantilist trade interventions or by the more orthodox method of currency devaluation, will prove self-defeating in the longer run, because the resulting inflow of international money will eventually satiate the economy's demand for money and, as it does so, expand the demand for imports and reduce the supply of exports (including in these terms for a modern economy imports and exports of securities) until the balance of payments is once more in balance. The second answer relies on Adam Smith's famous principle of specialization and division of labor, as extended by Ricardo in the principle of comparative advantage. What makes a nation rich is not money but the accumulation and efficient utilization of productive resources; and efficient utilization requires exploitation of the principle of comparative advantage through a policy of freedom of international trade, rather than mercantilist intervention.

One further point is worth noting in this connection. While the main concern of mercantilist writing was with the promotion of the opulence and economic development of the state, many were concerned with remedying the unemployment that was as endemic in the England of their times as in the less developed countries today[2]—though the "instrumental" attitude of the mercantilists toward the laboring class, held in common with the rest of the ruling class in a monarchical state, made this concern necessarily a minority view. The classical answer to this variant of the problem of development was expressed in Say's Law of Markets, that supply creates its own demand. This law was one of the focal points of criticism of the classical and neoclassical system of economic thought in Keynes's *General Theory of Employment, Interest and Money*. As a result of the controversy stirred up by the *General Theory*, it has come to be realized that the correct principle is what is known as Walras's Law (that any excess supply of goods must be matched by an equal excess demand for money); and that Say's Law holds and ensures full employment only in the long run when money wages and prices are so adapted as to secure equilibrium between the demand for and supply of money. In this framework of analysis, mercantilist trade policies can be successful in increasing employment, not for the superfically obvious reason that they direct aggregate demand toward domestic factors of production, but because they draw in the money required to support a higher level of domestic activity. (Moreover, they can be successful only insofar as they are effective in reducing real wages—in technical terms, only insofar as wage earners are subject to "money illusion.") Even in this rather special case, the associated balance-of-payments surplus will be not permanent but temporary, as the Hume-ian mechanism-of-adjustment analysis shows.

As was already mentioned in passing, the mercantilist system of thought developed in the formative period of the emerging nation-state, when social status and economic power rested on land ownership and government was by monarchy reinforced by "the divine right of kings." Its appeal was, therefore, partly an appeal on behalf of the emerging merchant class—which indeed provided virtually all its important spokesmen—for consideration by the monarchy and increasingly by the landowners who assumed power from the declining monarchy. With the onset of the industrial revolution and the associated transfer of power from the landowners to the bourgeosie and progressive democratization of the franchise, the laissez faire aspects of Adam Smith's economic thinking became a far more appealing general program for the rising merchant and industrial class, while at the same time democratization eroded the concept of the state as an entity over and above its citizens, and ultimately as the instrument of a ruling class over and above the masses. Thus the commercial policy aspects of mercantilism became gradually transformed into modern-period protectionism, and arguments for mercantilist policies had to address themselves to a concept of the general good rather than the good of the state, either by appealing to alleged economic considerations superior to the assumedly crass, myopic, and fumbling operations of the competitive market—contemporary (post–1930s) economics has responded to this intellectual market demand by producing countless hypothetical cases in which a comprehensive computer program could out-perform the market, without much serious attempt to verify the existence of these possibilities or to apply cost-benefit analysis to exploitation of them by governmental action—or by appealing to the vestiges of the concept of the state as an entity transcending individual interests but in some sense serving those interests better than they could serve themselves. In this latter connection, the survival of mercantilist habits of thought has been fostered by the late emergence of Germany as a nation-state, the establishment of a host of "new nations" naturally patterning themselves on the archaic imperial European concept of the nation-state, and the influence of two world wars in accentuating the identity of the nation in rivalry with other nations. The crucial point is that modern mercantilism has to justify itself by reference to the economic interests of the citizens of the state, somehow conceived, rather than to the economic and political interests of the rulers of the state in maximizing the wealth and power of the state that they command. (Even this point is subject to qualification, which may turn out to be important enough to invert the point itself in a longer historical perspective, since the numbers employed in running a modern nation and the power over their fellow citizens that they command are great enough to justify depicting the modern nation—and particularly the contemporary British nation—as one governed by a ruling class of politicians, civil servants, and communications-media personnel.)

Mercantilism as a system of thought identifying the growth of the wealth of the state, or in one version the growth of the gainfully employed or of the total population within its borders, with the achievement of a continuing inflow of money through policies designed to create a continuing balance-of-payments surplus, may be judged to have been disposed of by the emergence of the more sophisticated economic understanding of the English classical school, and particularly Smith's definitive dismissal of the mercantilist confusion between money and material capital, and his emphasis on the possession and efficient utilization of real factors of production as the fundamental source of the wealth of nations. Contemporary or twentieth-century mercantilism shares this more sophisticated concern with real income and wealth, but has in common with its original mercantilist ancestry the belief in the potentialities of commercial policy, particularly protection of domestic industry against competition from imports, as a means of increasing national income and wealth. It also shares with one stream of mercantilist thinking a concern about unemployment and a belief in the efficacy of trade intervention—here, both import restriction and export promotion—as an instrument for promoting employment. And it shares in a special sense the mercantilist concern with acquiring money through a balance-of-payments surplus, in the form of espousing import restriction, and with rather less emphasis export promotion, as means for remedying balance-of-payments deficits.

The revival of mercantilism can be traced to the slow and relatively mild erosion of the free trade movement—initiated by Britain roughly in the second quarter of the nineteenth century—that set in toward the end of the nineteenth century. But its proximate origins as a powerful policy movement can more appropriately be associated with the Great Depression and the

subsequent collapse of the international monetary system—the recently
restored gold-standard system—though for Britain it should be dated earlier
and associated with her difficulties in achieving economic recovery after the
First World War, which were greatly aggravated by the decision to return to
the prewar, overvalued, gold parity for the pound. Leaving aside Britain's
special (and self-imposed) problems, one may, in the light particularly of
recent theorizing and empirical research, reasonably attribute the depression
and subsequent international monetary collapse to a drastic and sudden
shrinkage of world liquidity, initiated by a major deflationary policy error on
the part of the Federal Reserve of the United States and communicated
rapidly to the rest of the world economy through the fixed-exchange-rate and
fractional-international-reserves characteristics of the gold standard. The
fundamental problem of shortage of the international liquidity necessary to
support the structure of national and international credit built on a
fractional reserve of gold on the basis of confidence in the gold-convertibility
of national currencies once that confidence began to crack, and hence to
support the existing level of world prices, could have been resolved relatively
painlessly—in the hindsight of post-World War II international monetary
developments—in either of two ways: by concerted action to raise the value
of existing gold stocks (that is, devaluation of all currencies against gold), or
by concerted action to provide an internationally acceptable credit substitute
for gold on a sufficiently large scale. But the capacity of national politicians,
central bankers, and other responsible officials to understand the basic
problem, as well as the international trust and good will required to solve it in
either of these ways, were conspicuously lacking. There remained two
alternatives open to the individual national members of the world system.
The first was to deflate their economies sufficiently to preserve balance in
their balances of payments. The results of all nations doing so together would
eventually have restored world liquidity by raising the purchasing power of
gold over goods. But in the meantime, given the downward stickiness of
money wages in the industrial economies, it would have meant prolonged
mass unemployment—which some nations (the "gold bloc") nevertheless
endured to the verge of political revolution. The second alternative was to
seek to maintain employment, consistently with balance-of-payments equilibrium, by means either of restrictions on international trade and payments
or of devaluation or (downward) flotation of the national currency. Both were
initially unthinkable in terms of the nineteenth-century tradition of a liberal
gold-standard world economy; but both were sooner or later chosen in
preference to still higher unemployment—Britain, largely as a result of her
uncharacteristic painful experience of mass unemployment in the 1920s,
being the first to move and therefore the least to suffer from the general
cataclysm.

Now, the modern theory of economic policy for an open economy, constructed on the basis of, but considerably subsequent to, Keynes's *General Theory*, has produced a number of propositions relevant to the situation of the early 1930s but not understood at that time. One is that if a country cannot or will not for one reason or another devalue its currency, it can achieve the same broad effect by imposing a general tax on imports and giving a general subsidy to exports at a uniform rate. Protection against imports alone is therefore a second best to a uniform import-tax export-subsidy policy, even though the latter superficially seems more discriminatory and therefore a worse offense against liberal principles; and if export subsidization is somehow ruled out, protection may be a better policy than free trade with an overvalued exchange rate—as Keynes proposed at the turn of the 1930s, to the consternation of his professional colleagues. But it is necessary to emphasize the constraints on policy that are assumed in reaching this conclusion. For a second point is that protection is definitely second-best to devaluation (or downward flotation), and devaluation removes the foregoing rationale for protection. Third, neither devaluation nor protection need be a "beggar-my-neighbor" policy for raising domestic employment at the expense of foreign employment; for either may—and should—be accompanied by a policy of expansion of domestic demand, which will compensate the foreigner for the otherwise adverse effects of devaluation or protection on his trade balance. But in the rudimentary state of understanding of economic policy theory that existed in the crucial years of the 1930s, it is not surprising that on the one hand the orthodox economists, steeped in the experience of the golden nineteenth-century age of free trade and an immutable but on the whole adaptive and stabilizing gold standard, should have continued to pin their faith to an inconsistent policy prescription of free trade plus the gold standard, and sought the explanation of the trouble in too high a level of money wages or in far-fetched theories of the satiation of wants for consumption goods and capital goods, instead of in international monetary disequilibrium; and that on the other hand the popular mind and the self-styled "radical" economists should have recommended, and the political process accepted, mercantilist policies as a means of increasing domestic employment and/or improving the balance of payments.

Thus mercantilist policies derived a new impetus from the international monetary collapse of the 1930s; and that shot-in-the-arm has had a lasting influence on policy thinking in the postwar period. The reason is partly the general one alluded to earlier, that mercantilism represents a primitive system of thought about the economic universe and a nation's (tribe's?) place in it, receptiveness to which is re-created every generation by the mortality of man, and restraint on the indulgence of which can be exercised only by more experienced and sophisticated rulers and then only under propitious circumstances—specifically, only if monetary disturbances and other types of economic change are sufficiently tolerable and the disadvantages of indulging in mercantilist policies, in terms either of domestic economic inefficiency or of provocation of foreign retaliation, sufficiently great. To the primitive mind, one case of magic's working (or seeming to work) is sufficiently impressive to confirm faith in magic against a long series of experienced failures. A second reason, or, more accurately, group of reasons, is to be found in the fact that in various ways in various countries self-imposed restraints on policymaking freedom have created circumstances in which there is at least a superficial case for mercantilist policies. In Britain the trauma of the interwar period and the euphoria generated by Keynes's theory of how to achieve full employment have generated chronic inflationary tendencies, while the historical tradition of sterling as a world currency plus the political taint of the devaluation (more correctly, gold-convertibility-suspension) of 1931 attached to the Labour Party, has meant a chronic propensity to allow the pound to become overvalued in consequence of inflation, thereby setting the stage for recommendation of mercantilist policies to improve the balance of payments or to remedy the unemployment necessitated by deflationary methods of defending the exchange rate.

In the United States, prolonged adherence to an overvalued dollar, out of reverence for the sanctity of $35 an ounce as the price of gold, has had similar effects in supporting mercantilist policies. In other countries, notably Germany and Japan, aversion to inflation, aversion to exchange rate appreciation, and weakness of the apparatus of fiscal policy or unwillingness to use it in the way indicated by the theory of economic policy combine to produce a de facto mercantilist policy of using currency undervaluation to generate domestic employment by means of a balance-of-payments surplus. (It is against mercantilism of this type, the mirror image of the "competitive currency devaluation" widely alleged to have been characteristic of the 1930s and not adequately provided for in the machinery of the International Monetary Fund, that the American "new economic policy" of 15 August 1971 was directed, though it should be noted that the emphasis of that policy on the United States' presumed natural right to run a balance-of-trade surplus in technologically-advanced industrial products itself reflects a mercantilist philosophy of a sort.)

While mercantilism of the 1930s type, concerned with employment and the balance of payments, survives and remains influential, it is more important to note the gradual emergence of a new and more sophisticated mercantilism, in response to new concepts of the objectives of economic policy—specifically, the promotion of economic growth on the basis of advanced technology—and new and more sophisticated concepts and techniques of intervention in international trade, made possible by the vast expansion of the relative economic size and power of the government in the national economy on the one hand, and the major exception to the rules of the

General Agreement on Tariffs and Trade allowed for customs unions and free trade areas or associations on the other.

The new growth and technology orientation of modern mercantilism represents a step forward in sophistication from the original style of mercantilism, in the specific sense of discriminating not merely in favor of domestic industry and commerce as against foreign, but also between categories of domestic industries according to their presumed growth potential. (The older style of mercantilism is, however, still represented academically in Britain and has exercised considerable influence on British economic policy in the person of Professor Nicholas Kaldor, who steadfastly continues to propound the naïve idea of the German nationalist tradition that all manufacturing is economically beneficial and all nonmanufacturing activity a second-class economic citizen.) It is also represented, though less directly, in the United States by special concern about the deterioration of the balance of payments on merchandise trade account that helped provoke the "new economic policy" of 1971. The new concept of growth potential, however, is heavily intermingled with older-style mercantilist ideas, notably the "infant industry argument" for protection (or more accurately, the identification of "infancy" with inability to compete unaided with imports) and the desirability of fostering potential export industries, in this instance on the assumption that high technology means comparative advantage. Unfortunately many British economists, intellectually drunk with the success of Keynes's demonstration that the country's interwar unemployment problem could be solved effortlessly by rejecting a misapplied orthodoxy and espousing in sophisticated form the popular and obvious idea that the way to create employment is to spend money, have responded to the country's apparent postwar problem of relatively slow economic growth (apparent, because there is no reason to think that the mass of the public, as distinct from the establishment, really wants more rapid growth) by recommending either the same Keynesian remedy of maintaining a high pressure of demand; or, on a slightly more sophisticated analytical level, incentives to new investment; or on a slightly still more sophisticated level, public and private spending on research and development. In so doing they reject classical and neoclassical orthodoxies to the effect that economic growth is the cumulated aggregate result of millions of microeconomic decisions taken by individuals who want to become richer and see opportunities to do so, and espouse, usually unwittingly, the British equivalent of the idea that what is good for General Motors is good for the country. Contrary to any number of plausible theories constructed to justify simple policy recommendations, there is no empirically validated simple theory of how to promote economic growth available—and many of those on offer do not even pass the tests of logical consistency necessarily prerequisite to empirical testing.

The new techniques of mercantilist policy, for their part, reflect recognition of two facts. One is that the protective tariff of traditional mercantilist philosophy is a very crude and blunt instrument for favoring domestic industry, by comparison with the techniques now available. In a modern economy, the government both imposes heavy taxation that can be remitted, or converted into a subsidy, conditionally on the beneficiary behaving in ways specified by the government—the tariff by contrast rests only on the hope of desired performance—and is itself the largest or one of the largest customers of private industry and, because it is subject neither to the test of profit-maximization nor to its own restrictive practices legislation, can use its spending power to discriminate in favor of domestic over foreign industry. It can even be argued—and indeed has been seriously suggested[3]—that the inferiority of the tariff as a protective device, rather than enthusiasm for the principle of free trade as such, has been largely responsible for the postwar movement toward trade liberalization by multilateral tariff-reducing negotiations under the General Agreement on Tariffs and Trade.

The second fact is that in the modern world of industries based on high technology and hence subject to important economies of scale and diminishing cost as overhead research-and-development investment is spread over a larger volume of output, protection of domestic producers in the domestic national market is no longer adequate or efficient. To be efficient, protection must extend to the export market. But since the rules of GATT frown on export subsidization, protection in the export market must be at least semidisguised in acceptable form. Techniques for achieving this include subsidization of export credit rather than of the exports themselves; tying of foreign development assistance and overseas military expenditure to purchases from domestic suppliers; and subsidization of research and development costs for potentially export-winning industries.

These devices, however, pale into insignificance by comparison with the opportunities for export subsidization on a reciprocal basis afforded by the exception allowed to the general principle of non-discrimination embodied in the rules of GATT for customs unions and free trade areas, under the fiction—subsequently exploded by Jacob Viner and more elegantly by James Meade—that such 100-percent discriminatory trading arrangements among groups of nations against outsiders can be automatically construed as entailing progress toward freer world trade. Economically speaking, such arrangements are on balance oriented toward free trade or protection according to the net balance of effects they produce as between trade creation and trade diversion—that is, between increasing total international trade by reducing protection of domestic producers, and diverting trade away from non-members toward partners in the arrangement. Politically speaking, the intention and probable effect can be inferred from whether the emphasis is on exclusiveness as embodied in membership eligibility requirements and "membership dues," or on the practical-minded freeing of internal trade and an "open-endedness" in receptivity toward admission of new members. In this respect there is a vast difference between the customs union of the Common Market type and the so-called free trade area of the Latin American type on the one hand, and the free trade association of the EFTA type, increasingly proposed as a model for the next step in negotiations for freer world trading arrangements, on the other.[4]

Seen in historical perspective, the European Economic Community represents the epitome of modernized mercantilism; and it seems at first sight surprising that Britain, the nation which produced the intellectual destruction of historical mercantilism, should have become so desperately anxious to participate in its contemporary manifestation. The matter is, however, easy enough to understand. Since Britain passed its industrial climacteric in the late nineteenth century, British economic policy has been seeking for a protectionist solution to its economic problems. Given the population's dependence on imported food and raw materials and hence on foreign markets for its manufactures, protection in the domestic market has clearly been an inadequate resort, although increasingly (and ineffectively) resorted to; some sort of protected position in overseas markets was necessary. Initially, the Empire and imperial preference seemed to offer the ideal solution; but as the Empire became transmogrified into the Commonwealth, and its overseas members became industrially ambitious and protectionist against British manufactured exports, its promise became increasingly hollow, while at the same time it was gradually recognized that trade between rival, industrially advanced countries, rather than complementary trade between manufacturing and agricultural countries, is the dominant pattern of contemporary international trade, so that attention shifted from the Commonwealth connection to the possibility of preferential trading relationships with other advanced countries. Britain was merely slower than the ex-imperial Continental powers to respond to the possibility, by virtue both of the amicable way in which its empire dissolved and of the "special relationship" with the United States.

Parallels between mercantilist motivations and the British motivations for joining the Common Market are indeed easy to discern. Just as mercantilism appealed to the monarch and landed gentry by the promise of augmenting the wealth and power of the state, so Common Market membership appealed to the politicians, civil service, press, and intellectual community of Britain by the promise of a wealthier nation and a supranational community to govern. And just as mercantilism appealed to the self-interest of the merchants by the promise of a protected home market, so Common Market membership appealed to the self-interest of British industry in a community home market protected against the most dangerous competitor, American industry. The major novel element concerns the interest of the working class, who in the circumstances of historical mercantilism had no say in the decision process but in contemporary democratic Britain do. Here the conventional British debate-stopper, "the issue is, after all, political, not economic," when properly interpreted, is highly relevant. The economic interests of British labor would have been best served by free trade, or by a free trade association with the United States; but the politics of such an association with the world's most powerful capitalist country would have been hard to sell at the best of times—though they might have been sold on a basis of Anglo-Saxon peoples' unity and a common interest in high wages and high consumption—and became impossible to contemplate once the United States became deeply involved in the increasingly unpopular war in Viet Nam. Unable to broach the fundamental political question—of Europe versus America—the Labour Party was forced into futile quibbling about the tactics of obtaining Common Market entry without being able to question the strategy, and the decision went by default in a carefully stage-managed non-debate over non-issues.

The two emerging characteristics of contemporary mercantilism just discussed—the use of the state's taxing and subsidizing, spending, and generally regulatory powers as more efficient protective substitutes for the crude tariff and quota instruments of the past, and the pursuit of protectionist aims through the formation of supranational trading blocs—promise to become the hallmarks of the mercantilism of the future. To them, as a third characteristic of future trade policy thinking already contemporarily emergent, must be added a new trade policy motivation, though one again with parallels in the original mercantilist period, which may for symmetry be described as "agriculturalism"—the protection of domestic agricultural production by a host of direct and indirect interferences with freedom of trade in agricultural products far transcending in complexity the protectionist measures applied to industrial trade. The underlying motives of agriculturalism are obscure in the extreme: the agricultural sector as a source both of soldier-fodder and of cannon-fodder no longer enjoys the military importance it had in an earlier age of primitive and labor-intensive military technology; farmers and farmworkers are a numerically insignificant component of the electorate in all industrially advanced countries; agricultural production is an expensive and inefficient way of keeping the countryside well manicured for the delectation of the weekending or vacationing urban dweller; and the typical methods of subsidizing domestic farm production are of very doubtful—and in Europe largely unknown—value in terms of promoting social objectives such as reduced income inequality, especially in these days of the stockbroker-landlord and the industrially employed part-time farmer.[5] Nevertheless, agriculturalism has acquired a tenacious hold on policymaking, especially in the Common Market, where the Common Agricultural Policy is regarded as the foundation of the community even though it is badly in disarray and its ultimate purposes and effects are profoundly obscure; and this is important, because any attempt to contain the forces of modern mercantilism by another round of GATT negotiations must cope in some nonineffectual fashion with the problems of liberalizing trade in agricultural products.

This brings me to the contemporary relevance of the theme of this essay, promised in its title. There is a serious danger to the world economic order of a retreat into mercantilist economic policies as a result of a cumulation of piecemeal decisions the full implications of which, and sometimes even the immediate and obvious implications of which, are never thought through.

It is important not to exaggerate the economic magnitude of the damage that might result, because to do so is to court dismissal of the genuine reasons for alarm. Certainly there is a temptation to conjure up visions of a return to the commercial policy chaos of the 1930s, just as in the international monetary field there is a temptation to conjure up visions of the exchange rate chaos of the 1930s in deploring the present regime of floating exchange rates, in both instances in disregard of the background of the 1930s experience in world depression and international monetary collapse and in spite of virtual certainty that nations will never again allow a massive world recession to develop—the politicians and central bankers may still be capable of the obstinate dogmatism required, but their publics would not let them get away with it and their economists would know better than to accept disaster as inevitable or inexplicable. There is also a temptation in some quarters to conjure up emotive visions of an entirely imaginary rapacious economic imperialism.

The real dangers are milder but nonetheless important: for the more advanced and powerful countries, preoccupation of their political and governmental processes with the snatching of petty advantages in international diplomacy, preoccupation of their industrialists with competition in winning political favors rather than in producing better products more cheaply, and a marginal but significant relative reduction of the standard of living, narrowing of economic opportunity, increase in inequality, and preoccupation with the politics of establishing claims to special consideration for their consumers generally; and for the less developed countries, a significant narrowing of opportunities for promoting their economic development through competition in a large, liberal, and impersonal international market.

It was one of the most commendable manifestations of cosmopolitan vision on the part of the postwar economic planners of Bretton Woods to attempt to cope simultaneously with world monetary, trade, and investment problems in an integrated fashion. Unfortunately, the institutionalization of the new rules of international citizenship in the Fund and Bank in Washington and the GATT in Geneva has meant the gradual separation of monetary and financial problems from trade problems, with the former

receiving most of the publicity and therefore attracting most of the intellectual and political talents of the major nations. Correspondingly, it was one
of the most perceptive facets of the U.S. administration's "new economic
policy" of August 1971 to call for an integrated approach to international
monetary and trade policy problems; and the response to that call has gone
some—but only some—of the way toward rehabilitation of the original
Bretton Woods concept.

Unfortunately again, however, European preoccupation on the one hand
with the details of British entry into the Common Market, and on the other
hand and more importantly with the rapidly evolving problems of the
international monetary system and the effort to warp plans for a reformed
international monetary system toward serving their own national interests
and subjugating those of the United States to discipline in their own favor,
have diverted European attention from problems of trade policy and made
professions of agreement with the United States on the objective of further
trade liberalization a matter of lip-service rather than of cooperative
conviction. The United States, for its part, still professes a determination to
press ahead with another round of negotiations for liberalization of world
trade; but the enabling legislation for this purpose is ominously designed to
be reversible into a move in the protectionist direction, and European policy
thinking seems unable to appreciate both the importance of the shift of the
American labor movement from a free trade position to protectionism, and
the crucial role of American agriculture as the last politically significant
supporter of a freer trade policy—provided that freer trade includes
significantly freer trade in agricultural products, and specifically a significant improvement of access to the European market for agricultural
products.

Under the circumstances, European insistence on the sacrosanctity of the
Common Agricultural Policy—whatever it may turn out to be when
reconstituted—will be a guarantee of failure of any new negotiations that
may be initiated; and so, in a more modest and typically British way, will be
the attitude apparently favored by British industry, of waiting for the
Americans to come up with some positive proposals and then deciding what
to think of them. What is required is a positive and enthusiastic European
response, such as greeted the Marshall Plan for European reconstruction.

An enthusiastic response, however, is only a necessary starting point. The
essential to success will be serious but generous-minded bargaining over
some extremely complex issues. These include the manifold barriers to
freedom of trade in agricultural products, especially temperate-zone
products; non-tariff barriers to industrial trade, a portmanteau term
including such items as discriminatory government purchasing policies and
safety standards; and the complementary problems of safeguards against
"market disruption" by rapid growth of imports and "adjustment assistance"

to domestic industries adversely affected by import competition—to mention but a few major topics.[6]

Unfortunately, it seems very unlikely that a positive European response to the American initiative will be forthcoming, and only too likely that the drift into modernized mercantilism will continue.

19. The Problem of Economic Development

I. Social, Political, and Economic Aspects of Development

There has been growing disillusionment in the past decade or so with the whole notion of promoting development by domestic planning efforts assisted by foreign aid. On the side of the aid-giving developed countries, there has been disillusionment with the results of foreign development assistance, and even a questioning whether aid has not done more harm than good to the recipient countries—especially in terms of supporting high-cost inward-looking industrialization programs and the neglect of traditional agriculture, but also in deeper terms of inhibiting the process of social and political modernization and stabilization. On the side of the would-be-developing countries, there has been growing recognition of and growing complaint about the fact that planned economic development, as executed in practice, has not achieved the hoped-for "take-off into self-sustaining economic growth"; has if anything been accompanied by increasing rather than decreasing inequalities of economic welfare, social position, and political power; has done relatively little for the rural as distinguished from the urban sector of the population; and has been accompanied by the socially and politically potentially disruptive growth of urban unemployment and urban slums and congestion.

This first section presents my own views on what has gone wrong with the grand objective of promoting the development of the poorer two-thirds of the world's population, and how this effort might be more effectively directed in the future. These views draw on my origins as a citizen of Canada—an ex-colonial country—and on my subsequent career as an international economist who has visited and lived in many countries, both "developed" and "developing." Basically, it is my belief that the problem was mis-conceived at the start, in two important ways. First, the problem was conceived of as far too narrowly an economic problem, in disregard that a society is an interwoven fabric of the economic, the political, and the social.

Two public lectures delivered at the University of Panama, August 1971. The second was published in *Economica* 19, no. 155 (August 1972): 269–75; reprinted with permission.

Second, within the economic sphere, the process of promoting development was also conceived far too narrowly as involving the manipulation by government of a few strategic economic variables, assumed to possess leverage over the rest of the system.

History is a continuing unfolding process, in which generations draw their beliefs and ideas from the experience of previous generations. I should like to begin my analysis by going back to the war years and particularly to the 1930s, when the basic ideas about development of contemporary society were formed. Several strands of experience and ideas—and particularly of European experience and ideas—combined in that formation.

The most important conditioning experience was the Great Depression of 1929–33 and the incomplete recovery thereafter. That depression had one side effect which has been especially important for Latin American thinking on development ever since: the collapse of the world prices of primary products. This gave rise to the historically unsupported belief that primary product prices are inherently unstable and inevitably declining, and hence to the emphasis, maintained ever since by Dr. Prebisch and his followers, on industrialization as the essential basic strategy of economic development. The belief in industrialization as an essential development strategy, incidentally, also has its origins in German thinking about the way to create a militarily powerful nation-state—ideas which were taken over by economists in other smaller central-European states and spread into the Anglo-Saxon tradition of economics by the Nazi-induced emigration of these scholars.

For many of the intellectuals of the period, the Great Depression proved the complete incapacity of the capitalist system to function as a system for organizing production and consumption, maintaining reasonably full employment, and providing economic growth. Ironically enough, experts on the period now attribute the breakdown, not to a failure of the system, but to a failure of its monetary managers (effectively, a branch of government) to prevent a monetary collapse that they could have averted by a resolute application of reasonably well-known principles. There were in fact two major failures: the failure of the Federal Reserve System to fight depression by monetary expansion, and, instead, its toleration of a sharp decline in the U.S. money supply; and the failure of the U.S. and European central banks to prevent an international liquidity crisis—something they have since learned how to do. In any case, the twenty-five years of prosperity and growth the world has enjoyed since the end of the Second World War effectively dispose of the belief that capitalism is doomed to go down in a general collapse—though there are still socialists who live by that hope.

If capitalism was a failure, what, then, was the alternative? The alternative answer was "planning." It was an attractive answer partly because it had no substantive intellectual and empirical content; it had never been tried in a Western country. But it derived strong support among many from the Fabian socialist tradition and its emphasis on social betterment through research; among some because of Nazi Germany's ability to obtain full employment by some version of it; and among others, more radical, because it was the proclaimed differentiating principle between the Russian communist and the capitalist systems of economic organization. Russian planning, incidentally, involved great emphasis on expanding so-called "heavy" industry, an emphasis which also became important in contemporary ideas on the promotion of development. It was only much later that three facts about Russian planning came to be appreciated: first, the emphasis on heavy industry derived more from preparation for the coming war with Germany than from a general desire to promote economic development; second, concentration on industrial inputs and investment goods achieves phenomenal growth figures without necessarily producing any commensurate growth of economic well-being; and third, much of Russia's success was due not to physical investment but to concentrated efforts to improve the skills of the population—"investment in human capital."

A fourth and very important contributor to the formation of contemporary ideas on development was the Keynesian revolution. The Keynesian revolution saved capitalism, in a sense, by demonstrating that full employment could be achieved by proper management of fiscal and monetary policy. However, the Keynesian emphasis on private investment as the unstable element in the system created the impression both that investment planning of some sort was required for proper economic management, and that investment was the key to the solution of almost all social problems. The use of Keynesian ideas as the basis for wartime financial planning, and their great success as contrasted with the techniques used in the First World War, also reinforced both the general idea of the need for planning and the specific idea that planning should be concerned with physical investment on the one hand and the extraction of the savings necessary to finance that investment on the other.

The emphasis on investment as the key strategic element in planning for development, derived from these various intellectual sources, happened to be strongly reinforced by the United States' first experiment with promoting development: the Marshall Plan for the economic reconstruction of Europe, which was tremendously successful on the basis of a relatively small injection of outside capital. As it happened, Europe had available the industrial and commercial organization, and the skilled people, required for modern industry; what it lacked was precisely capital for investment. The problem of promoting development in the less developed countries has proved quite different, however. What these countries lack is virtually everything necessary to a high standard of economic productivity, and the injection of only the one element was found to prove both wasteful and disappointing.

There are two other aspects of the background of the contemporary view of development that I should like to comment on as seeming to me highly relevant to understanding that view. The first is that, after a process of investment in the creation of viable nation-states extending over centuries in Europe, and in the United States over a shorter historical period but one characterized by a decisive civil war, it is only natural for thinkers in advanced Western countries to conceive of a nation as a political, social, and economic unit characterized by reasonable stability in all three respects, stability based on a social consensus and mutual understanding of some kind. The individual intellectual may want to change the society by revolutionary force, but even the lines of potential revolution run within the national society. It was natural to transfer this assumption of a national society, capable of changing and improving itself by peaceful political means, to the older and new nations of the developing world, and in so doing to overlook the problems of social and political integration necessary before a viable nation-state of the European—or for that matter American—variety could emerge. The assumption, alternatively put, was that the nation-state was all set and ready to go in political and social terms, so that the economic was the strategic aspect of development to promote.

The other point concerns the assumed nature of the raw material to be worked with; the material was not in fact of the assumed nature at all, in respects important for the results. While this is too large a subject to go into, it may be useful to draw one important line of distinction: that between populated territories acquired by military or political force and governed by a thin upper crust of imperial civil servants and educated natives, and colonial territories settled by immigration from an imperial motherland and other European countries.

In the former type there has often been great political instability, and even civil war, arising from the inability of the disparate groups to hold together in a peaceable political process once the threat of external force has been removed. These nations also have been prone to administrative disintegration, first as the result of the nationalization of civil service jobs and repatriation of Western administrators, second as the result of local resentment of the Westernized upper crust of natives and attempts to replace them by more trusted people. Further, the new political leaderships have generally sooner or later become either nationalistic or corrupt or both, making development in a real sense virtually impossible.

In the other type of underdeveloped country, the ex-colonial, there are different problems. Here I should make clear that I am drawing on certain themes in my Canadian background. First, as is well known, settlers have little use for indigenous peoples except as live sources of cheap labor or dead sources of cheap land. Secondly, the purpose of emigrating is to get rich if you possibly can, by virtue of wise investment of money you have brought with you, or farming of land you acquire somehow; and, once rich, to stay that way and if possible become richer. This is not a motivation that carries much social conscience with it. Instead it promotes use of the political process to maintain and increase one's existing wealth. A further relevant point is that the social structure of such countries has typically been formed in imitation of a considerably earlier period in European history, when ownership, especially of land and also of factories, was the basis of social status. The European countries, and the United States before them, have been growing out of that phase of social, political, and economic development, which is correlated with land being an important basis for economic activity and capital for building factories being scarce. In Galbraith's terminology, these countries are in the pre-affluent or pre-techno-structure phase of economic and social evolution. In both types of society, finally, the predominance of poverty makes those who have succeeded in escaping it callous and contemptuous toward those less fortunate than themselves.

So much by way of discussion of the historical origins and misconceptions of the prevailing views on the development process. In practical development planning, these views have led to a neglect of the social and political aspects of development, and especially of the consequences for the distribution of the benefits of economic development that will result in the absence of political and social modernization. Moreover, within the economic sphere, the concentration on industrialization through material capital investment has meant a concentration on the relatively small "modern" sector of the economy, to the neglect of the "traditional" or "subsistence" sector in which the bulk of the population is engaged.

It is relatively easy to construct a simple theoretical model of a development process based on governmental promotion, direct and indirect, of investment in the "modern" sector, that will generate many of the problems that have been concerning experts in development and making them despair.

First, and apart from the main model, suppose that we have a subsistence-agricultural sector, and that following Arthur Lewis's classic model of "economic development with unlimited supplies of labor," population in that sector breeds to the level of subsistence. Two things follow. First, better technology provided to that sector will be swallowed up by population increase, and its benefits go exclusively into higher rents for landlords, unless simultaneously some motivation is provided for population control. Second, assuming that population control is motivated and practiced outside the subsistence sector, a long-run solution to rural poverty is only possible if population can be pulled out of that sector, by expansion of the modern sector, faster than it reproduces itself by breeding. This is Dr. Prebisch's latest plan for solving Latin America's problems by crash industrialization; but it seems to me very unlikely to be feasible.

To turn to the main model, assume that the government attempts to promote development by stimulating the expansion of the industrial sector by tariffs, tax concessions, and so forth; and suppose that, as is invariably the case, wages in the industrial sector are well above subsistence-sector wages and wages in the service trades in the cities. Expansion of industry means expansion of the cities, with the associated social overhead costs of city life. The possibility of obtaining high-wage industrial jobs will attract workers to the cities in larger numbers than can find employment in such jobs, with resulting unemployment problems. Rather than remain looking for industrial work, many will resort to a hand-to-mouth existence in the service sector, transforming actual into disguised unemployment. Even though industrial jobs at high wages are known to be virtually impossible to obtain, people will move to the city from the subsistence sector because "that is where the action is." In technical economic terms, life in the city provides "externalities" or "public goods" in the shape of excitement, gossip, spectacles, free entertainment, and the ever-varying novelties encountered in crowds of people. The people involved prefer city life, at least in terms of choosing it instead of rural life. But they impose costs of housing, policing, medical care and so forth on the city's government; and they may constitute a politically unstable element in the population. There is also the consideration that starving in the city but with plenty of leisure time may be more attractive than slaving all day in the country for a barely adequate diet.

To look at the other side of the picture, if there is a scarcity of local entrepreneurial talent—and this may be either a fact of life or a result of monopolization of entrepreneurial opportunity by a few families through the use of their political power—industrialization will lead to the amassing of wealth by this limited group, and to growing inequality of wealth rather than decreasing social, political, and economic inequality. Alternatively, the shortage of local entrepreneurial talent may be so acute and the supply so inflexible that the government can only proceed by offering concessions to foreign enterprises—in which case the inequality is seen as the apparently undeserved superior economic affluence of foreigners as compared with natives and can become a potent source of political ill will and possibly instability.

In view of the problems created by the contemporary approach to development, what better approach might there be? It is comparatively easy to describe such an approach in terms of the kind of society that it should seek to establish. Politically, it is the old idea of democracy, a society in which rival political parties alternate in office on the basis of their success in convincing the electorate that they can manage the country's affairs better than can the rival party. But for such a democratic system to survive and be effective, there must be a consensus on what the purposes of the nation are, so that change of office from one party to another involves only marginal changes in the direction of policy. The forms of democracy will not long survive either if they are used simply to disguise control over the nation's destiny by a small oligarchy or if change of government through the electoral process means severe economic and social losses for the losing party. The formation of one-party governments in a number of less developed countries, at least for some periods of time, has been a means of containing violent divisions of opinion within a viable framework of decision-taking.

Socially, development should lead to a society in which people feel responsibility to one another, as fellow citizens, and are prepared to accept one another as such rather than to discriminate against one another on the basis of membership or non-membership in smaller groupings within the nation. This requires some definition of the identity of the nation, both with respect to the relation of the smaller groupings to the larger, and with respect to what differentiates the nation from other nations and defines its role in the world scene. These remarks raise the question of the functions of nationalism, which I shall deal with later.

Economically, development should establish an integrated economy in which the processes of competition work to equalize the returns to labor or entrepreneurship of a given degree of skill, wherever performed in the economy. This implies in particular a high degree of mobility of labor, especially between rural and urban activities. Economic development also entails establishing a framework within which individuals are both encouraged and helped to develop as much useful skill as they can, and rewarded fairly for the utilization of skills once developed.

These economic objectives of development may seem harmless enough, even mere platitudes. But in fact they rest on one very important presumption and have some strong implications for development policy. The important assumption is that people will respond to economic incentives for self-improvement, if these incentives are offered. Much development policy has been based on the contrary assumption that most people do not respond to incentives, so that, for example, agriculture can be safely taxed heavily to finance industrial development; and on the corollary assumption that the competitive market provides wrong or misleading signals of opportunity, so that much government intervention is needed, in the way of subsidies and other bribes, to respond to opportunities which the government believes are present but which the market does not seem to register. I believe that the mass of the evidence on economic development accumulated in the past twenty years shows both that people do respond sensitively to economic incentives and that market signals are generally better guides to economic opportunity than governmental judgments. One implication is that government should be careful about intervening extensively in the competitive process. But even if government is relatively good at it, it must be remembered both that the talents available to government are themselves scarce and should not be wasted by being spread too thin in deciding too many policies, and that the resources which the government can mobilize to implement policies of intervention by direct expenditures and subsidies are limited in quantity, by comparison with the resources the public might be induced to mobilize for itself given profitable opportunities for using them.

To repeat, one implication is that government should be careful to limit the range of its interventions to what it can manage, both administratively and economically. Another and less obvious implication concerns the question of encouraging people to develop their skills. In the contemporary developing world, as in the developed world, what is at stake here is the provision of greater equality of educational opportunity—and since education is largely a responsibility of the state, it becomes an important element of development policy—both for economic development and for social development more broadly conceived.

Almost inevitably, given the obvious differences between the problems of providing education in rural and urban districts, there is discrimination in education against rural children, in terms of quantity and quality provided. Furthermore, what education is provided is aimed at education for life on the farm, so that when a person who has been brought up in the country comes to the city, he is ill-equipped for any but the most menial jobs. This is still the case even in such a rich country as the United States and in more densely populated and culturally homogeneous countries like the United Kingdom. But the difference between rural and urban educational conditions differs by several orders of magnitude in the less developed countries. The consequence is a vicious circle which contributes to several of the contemporary problems of development policy. Because of lack of education, farmers are confined to backward and inefficient techniques, which they would otherwise improve on or replace. Because of poor technologies, life is hard in the country and young farm people try to escape to the cities; but their lot there is miserable too, due to lack of education. Because of the poverty of rural life and the lack of educational facilities, educated people, especially those with families to educate, are anxious to leave or reluctant to go to the country, even though in terms of money income their prospects might be better there. Hence the rural community is deprived of potential social and political leadership of adequate national standard and is accordingly condemned to political neglect.

In the long run, the aim of social and economic policy should be to raise educational standards in the country to a level such that (a) rural people can move to the cities and compete on equal terms with city-bred people; (b) those who stay in the country can command capital and technology on a sufficient scale to make them as productive as city workers; (c) with these higher incomes they will be able to own television sets and radios, automobiles and household equipment, and to enjoy leisure, to the extent required for them to participate in the national culture in the same way as city people. This would require a massive movement of people off the land, a project which unless carefully matched with expansion of economic activity in the cities and towns and carried out slowly would exacerbate the problems of the cities.

In the short run, however, a substantial increase in productivity in the agricultural sector would alleviate some of these problems. Such alleviation would require, I think, a three-pronged attack: improved rural education; development and propagation of improvements in agricultural technology simple to use and to teach and not too expensive to finance; and improved transportation to encourage the production of cash crops and give a farmer a larger share of the city price of his product. If rural life were made more attractive, not only would the farmers benefit but some of the pressure of rural immigration in the cities might be alleviated as well. I am informed that in parts of India the improved productivity made possible by the "Green Revolution" has attracted rural people back from the cities.

I should like to conclude this section with some remarks on the question of nationalism in economic development. I have necessarily been concerned fairly seriously with this question, as a citizen of a country that views itself as small and poor compared to its giant neighbor the United States, resents this, and expresses its resentment in periodic outbursts of anti-American nationalism. I have always had the gravest misgivings about nationalism, as it has manifested itself in Canada and in other countries where I have come across it. In principle it is intellectually conceivable that nationalism and the urge to demonstrate one's national competence in competition with other countries may serve as a potent force for breaking the crust of tradition and conservatism and making change accelerate. Even here there is a danger of attempting to achieve too much too fast, and also of setting the goals of national policy by inappropriate imitations of the outward symbols of development from a much larger and more developed country. Canada, with one-tenth the population and one-thirteenth the gross national product of the United States, is certainly a victim of this mistake; Panama, with a population of one–one-hundred-thirty-third of the U.S. population and with even more reason to be conscious of the American presence than Canada, is in even greater danger of making it. In practice, however, nationalism as I have observed it is typically concerned, not with developing and proving national competence, but with acquiring ownership of the symbols of accomplishment for nationals—ownership of executive positions for nationals regardless of competence (in Canada this now expresses itself also in a claim that only citizens should be allowed to hold tenure positions in universities) and ownership and control of industrial companies by national stockholders. This I view as an attempt to turn political power into undeserved economic rents for the minority at the expense of the majority of their fellow citizens; and I sincerely hope that Panamanian nationalism will not turn in this direction.

II.   Commercial Policy and Industrialization

In this section I propose to survey developments in the theory and practice of commercial policy, with general reference to the potential role of commercial policy in promoting economic development, and with special reference to the question of its potential service to this objective in small developing countries such as Panama. I claim no special, or even any, knowledge of the Panamanian economy; but I have both visited and studied a number of comparably small developing economies elsewhere.

I begin with a brief and impressionistic survey of the theory and history of tariffs. The mercantilist economists favored the use of interventions of various kinds in international trade primarily as a means of accumulating precious metals for the treasury of the state, but also as a means of building up a nation's population and therefore its political and military power as then conceived—and weakening the power of other nations. The classical economists reacted against and destroyed—at least intellectually—the mercantilist view of the world by developing two basic principles of economics. The first was David Hume's price-specie-flow mechanism, according to which in the long run a nation has no control over the quantity of the domestic money supply—which in those days was also its stock of precious metals—because the public can export or import money in exchange for imports or exports of domestic goods and services. (In the modern world, the same principle applies; but a nation can control the ratio of its international reserves to its domestic money supply, and therefore the amount of its international reserves, through the control its central bank can exercise over the volumes of domestic credit outstanding against its money supply. Also, the public can adjust actual to desired money supply through international transactions in securities as well as in goods and services.) The second was Adam Smith's principle of specialization and division of labor, which as applied to international trade clearly implied that free trade rather than governmental intervention in trade was the welfare-maximizing policy for a country to follow.

The subsequent development of the classical theory of international trade admitted only two important exceptions to the general optimality of a free trade policy. The first was the optimum-tariff argument: the possibility that by means of a tariff a country could exploit monopoly or monopsony power and turn its terms of trade in its favor at the expense of restricting its trade volume. The logic of this possibility had to be admitted, even though the writers in the classical tradition abhorred the narrowly national self-interest on which the argument rested and insisted firmly on the desirability of a cosmopolitan view. The second was the infant-industry argument for protection, a concession to the unorthodox views of Hamilton in the United States and later of List in Germany. In this connection the classical and neoclassical writers—who, it must be remembered, were at least as concerned with the dynamic growth-promoting consequences of international trade as with its static efficiency aspects—while accepting the theoretical possibility, advanced three negative counterarguments: that "infant-industry" possibilities could equally well exist in export industry as in import-competing industries; that a subsidy to infant industries was preferable to a tariff because its costs were more visible and hence more amenable to political decision and review; and that infant-industry tariffs were in practice never removed but remained as a source of continuing economic inefficiency. It may be noted in passing that the first counterargument remains valid, and has in fact gained greatly in strength in the modern world, wherein there exist many small countries whose major hope of economic success through "learning by doing" lies in the development of exports for the world market rather than in import substitution. The second counterargument—political visibility of the cost—has been replaced by a stronger argument involving the superior economic efficiency of a subsidy over a tariff in promoting domestic production, an argument resting on the fact that a production subsidy does not disturb consumer choices whereas a tariff on imports does. (That argument, however, raises the public finance question of the relative ease and efficiency of taxing the public indirectly through the extra-budgetary device of the tariff, or directly by income and other taxes to raise the revenue required to pay the subsidy.) The third counterargument—that infant-industry tariffs in fact are never removed—has been shown subsequently to be inconclusive, because it is possible for a nation to gain from the improved efficiency that an infant-industry tariff is supposed to promote and make possible, even though some marginal production of the protected good is carried on inefficiently in perpetuity.

In addition to these major exceptions—the optimum-tariff and infant-industry arguments for protection—classical and neoclassical theory recognized two other exceptions, viewed as of relatively minor importance. The first was that where an excise tax on domestic production existed, a compensating tax on imports was desirable to maintain fair competition between domestic and foreign producers. This exception has been shown by recent theorizing to be problematical, since the compensating tax on imports restores efficiency in production choices but introduces inefficiency in consumption choices. The second exception, recognized later and not investigated until after the Second World War, was that the beneficiality of free trade depended on money costs of production corresponding to real costs—otherwise, choices based on money costs would necessarily lead to inefficiency. The classical and neoclassical economists were prepared to assume this correspondence as an empirical approximation. But in the postwar literature of development economics the opposite assumption has become a major allegedly empirical foundation of the case for protection, the literature drawing slightly on the work of Manoilesco (the object of Viner's remark about real and money costs) but most importantly on the writings of Arthur Lewis and Everett Hagen on the rural–urban wage differential. Both exceptions involve the new theory of second best, which has developed as a result of the pioneering work of Jacob Viner, James Meade, and Lancaster and Lipsey, and has become the intellectual foundation of a mass of contemporary work on this sort of problem.

The classical and neoclassical literature increasingly took the protective tariff as the standard case of governmental intervention in international trade, and the analysis of government intervention in trade became the theory of tariffs. This was appropriate in the circumstances of the last two-thirds of the nineteenth century and first third of the twentieth, which witnessed initially the adoption by Britain of a free trade policy—derived intellectually from classical theory—and a general movement toward free trade on the basis of reciprocal negotiation for tariff-reduction, then a gradual drift back into protectionism, which was escalated by politico-military considerations after the First World War. The period before the First World War was also marked by the use of customs unions in Europe to create political nation-states, a development that escaped the attention or failed to attract the interest of international trade theorists.

The collapse of the international monetary system after 1929, however, evoked a massive escalation of protection, based essentially on the old mercantilist balance-of-payments argument for protection as a way of increasing or at least protecting international reserves and increasing domestic employment. The escalation took the new form of the use of quotas and exchange controls rather than tariffs, partly as a means of evading existing tariff agreements. The result was to pose a new theoretical problem, that of the relative merits of tariffs and quotas. Naturally, academic opinion was generally hostile to quotas and exchange controls.

The arrangements for postwar economic reconstruction thrashed out at Bretton Woods after the Second World War included among other things rules for national commercial policies, designed to subordinate these policies to the cosmopolitan interest as then conceived. The rules enshrined the principle that quotas and exchange controls are inferior to tariffs, though they had to be admitted as legitimate temporary devices for dealing with balance-of-payments problems. They also accepted the legitimacy of the infant-industry argument for protection, largely as a concession to the less developed countries. Finally, they accepted customs unions and free trade areas as exceptions to the general principle of nondiscrimination in the imposition of tariffs against foreigners, subject to certain safeguards, including no increase in the average tariff rate against outsiders, and application of the arrangements to most of the trade among partner countries, on the grounds that such arrangements involved, on balance, a movement toward free trade.

The evolution of the world economy under these rules has had a variety of implications, some good and some bad, for the less developed countries and their prospects of development. Consider first the evolution of trading arrangements among the developed countries, which evolution has been generalized by the principle of nondiscrimination to the less developed countries though with some important exceptions to be noted. First, the developed countries have gradually negotiated both the virtual elimination of quotas and exchange control restrictions on imports built up in the 1930s and the Second World War and the immediate postwar period, and a substantial reduction of tariff barriers to international trade in manufactures. These liberalizations of trade have benefited the less developed countries insofar as they have been, or have become, capable of supplying the goods on which trade barriers have been liberalized. On the other hand, because of the threat of "market disruption" due to the capacity of the less developed countries to supply certain kinds of low-technology labor-intensive goods in rapidly increasing quantities, the developed countries have imposed special "voluntary" quota barriers to imports of such goods, notably and on a multilateral and not bilateral basis in the long-term arrangements for cotton textiles. Secondly, as a result of agricultural protection problems in the United States, agricultural trade rules have been divorced—contrary to the original rules of the General Agreement on Tariffs and Trade—from those governing trade in manufactures. The result has been the chaos of the jungle as regards agricultural trade; and while this has been regarded as a problem affecting mainly the advanced agricultural exporting and importing countries in the temperate zone, it has in fact imposed severe uncertainties on and barriers to the export prospects of a number of less developed countries. Thirdly, the exception allowed by the GATT rules to the general principle of nondiscrimination, in the form of free trade areas and customs unions, has permitted the formation of the European Economic Community and the European Free Trade Association—which inherently discriminate against outside trade including the exports of developing countries—but also, for political rather than legal reasons, has permitted the development of the European Common Agricultural Policy, an economic nonsense that vastly aggravates the chaos of agricultural trading relationships. More important, the EEC is now far more important in world trade than the United States; and this means that the principle of nondiscrimination supported by the United States—and it is an important basic principle, no matter how far the

United States has dishonored it by discrimination in practice—is being increasingly undermined by the discriminatory trading arrangments with former colonies and with peripheral European countries favored by the "European Community" mentality. This is an important trend for Latin America, both because the EEC discriminates in general against its exports, and in particular against its agricultural (especially tropical) exports in favor of similar products from inside the Community and from former African colonies and the Mediterranean, and because such discrimination will inevitably force Latin America into still closer trading relationship with and dependence on the United States.

As regards the less developed countries, the principles of GATT—especially the condonation of quota and exchange control restriction of imports in case of balance-of-payments difficulties, and the explicit acceptance of the infant-industry argument for protection—together with what might be termed a "benign indifference" to violations of GATT principles when the violations are perpetrated by less developed countries, have sanctioned a proliferation of protectionism on the part of these countries. Moreover, to the armory of protectionist tools before the Second World War—tariffs, quotas and exchange restrictions—have been added potent new protectionist weapons: not merely complete import prohibition and the granting of monopolies of the domestic market to particular domestic producers, which are merely extremes of the older methods, but the fiscal devices of tax concessions, tax holidays, rights to repatriate profits, and the like.

The typical less developed country—perhaps I should say more fairly and accurately the typical large less developed country—has gone through a cycle of policymaking and policy problems that follows a logical pattern of sorts. It consists of protection for development reasons according to the infant-industry argument, combined with inflationary development finance; difficulties with traditional exports due to the taxation on them imposed by protection and cost inflation, combined with increasing demands for imports resulting from domestic cost inflation and from the demand for capital goods and imported components by protected industries, leading to more intensive and indiscriminate policies of import substitution; further inflationary balance-of-payments difficulties, and still more intensive resort to protectionist policies; gradually as the domestic price–cost level becomes sufficiently uncompetitive in world market terms, a shift from import-substituting policies to the promotion by subsidies, "export bonus" schemes, and so on, of exports of the products of manufactured goods industries but not of traditional exports; and eventually to devaluation of the currency—but not typically to any basic alteration in protectionist policies—at which point the process starts all over again. Naturally enough, the only possible solution to what seems an otherwise insoluble problem is to look to devices whereby other countries can be induced to buy the country's manufactured exports at prices above world market prices. There are two obvious possibilities—to induce the developed countries to give tariff preferences to the manufactured exports of the less developed countries, and to form customs unions, free trade areas, or weaker preferential arrangements among the less developed countries to encourage or force them to buy each other's high cost products. This was the logical development of policy and policy thinking that underlay Dr. Prebisch's report as secretary-general of the 1964 United Nations Conference on Trade and Development, *Towards a New Trade Policy for Development*. Both the idea of developed-country preferences for exports from less developed countries, and that of partial preferences among the less developed countries themselves, contradicted the GATT principles of nondiscrimination and reciprocity. Hence Prebisch's report necessarily had to place great emphasis on legalistic and logically fallacious semantic juggling, in which unilateral preferences extended by developed to less developed countries were claimed to represent true reciprocity, and both kinds of preferences were alleged to be justified by the infant-industry argument for protection. As is well known, the long-run consequence of the United Nations Conference on Trade and Development has been that the developed countries have agreed to grant the unilateral preferences, though in a form that is very likely to restrict and not accelerate the growth of less developed country exports of manufactures. On the other hand, preferential arrangements among less developed countries have had great difficulty in getting off the ground, precisely because they involve protecting one country's favored industries at another country's expense.

Let me turn now from this very brief and impressionistic account of the historical development of protectionism and the "classical" or "orthodox" theory of it before the Second World War, to developments of the theory of protection after the Second World War, developments which have largely been a response to the postwar evolution of policy. I shall not attempt to follow the chronological development of economic theory on this subject but instead summarize the theory relevant to the main questions.

The first question is the status and importance of the optimum-tariff theory. This has played a considerable role in theorizing about the possibilities of improving the lot of the poorer countries of the world, particularly in connection with their exports of primary products, especially tropical products such as coffee, cocoa, tea, sugar, and bananas, and mineral products such as oil, tin, and copper, in which they seem superficially to have considerable monopoly power, the demand for them of the advanced countries being of less than unit elasticity. Empirical and theoretical research, however, has done much to undermine the attractions of the theoretical possibility.

First, the degree of monopoly power depends on the elasticity of demand facing the monopolist. Here there are two relevant points: First, despite superficial appearances to the contrary, the elasticities of demand for many potentially promising products are in fact very high, when account is taken both of the fact that many of them are produced also in the developed countries and the fact that there are close substitutes for them producible by quite different technical processes. For example, there are eight different ways of producing edible oils and fats, the sources being animal, vegetable, and mineral—animal including livestock, whales, and fish. In addition, there are always synthetics. Secondly, elasticity of demand for the product may be low but that facing any individual country or combination of countries high, because of actual and potential competition from other less developed countries. Past efforts to exploit presumed monopoly power have led among other things to the migration of natural rubber production from Latin America to Southeast Asia, and of coffee production from Latin America to Africa—not to speak in both cases of the effects of attempted monopoly on the development in the one case of synthetic rubber and in the other of raw-material-saving soluble coffee.

Secondly, as I have shown in my own work, theorists have been grossly misled by the concentration of the theoretical analysis on the optimum tariff *rate*, rather than on the welfare gains achievable by imposing that tariff rate. A monopolist may have a very high rate of profit but so little volume that his net gains by comparison with competition are negligible. Specifically, if a country has no use itself for the oil it produces and cannot produce import substitutes, it can impose any tariff on imports it likes and will still export the same amount of oil and import the same amount of manufactured goods and edible foodstuffs.

The second question concerns the infant-industry argument. Modern theory leaves little, if any, of this argument still standing. In the first place, as has already been mentioned and will be explained more fully later, a tariff will always be less efficient than a subsidy in infant-industry cases. The conditions required for the optimum-tariff argument to apply are in fact the only conditions under which a tariff is the economically best method of increasing economic welfare. The reason is that only in these conditions is *restriction of trade*, rather than encouragement of domestic production or of the use of particular domestic factors of production, a sure means of increasing economic welfare.

Secondly, the argument has to demonstrate not only that there are long-run potential cost-savings accruing from a learning-by-doing process in the industry to be protected that are higher than the average potentialities existing in other industries (including export industries) but also that there is an excess of the social benefits from investment in this industry over the privately capturable benefits, such that (*a*) the social benefits are high enough to yield a return greater than the social alternative opportunity cost

of the resources absorbed in temporary protection of the industry, and
(b) the private benefits yield a return less than the alternative opportunity
cost of the capital invested. This is a severe restriction on the applicability of
the argument, since on the one hand while one can argue that there will be
privately uncapturable social benefits, these may not be great enough to
justify the investment, and on the other hand that, though private investors
may be unable to capture the "social spillovers" of their investment, that
investment may still be sufficiently profitable to attract them.

Thirdly, there is the question of the form the posited excess of social over
private benefit may reasonably be assumed to take. Here the argument has
been greatly clarified by Ronald Coase's classic article, "The Problem of
Social Cost," and Gary Becker's work on the economics of human capital. To
take the latter first, it is frequently argued that the "infant" entrepreneur
will get less than the social return on his capital investment because he will
have to train workers who will subsequently be able to move to a job with
another employer. Becker has shown that where the training is "general"
(i.e., transferable to another employer), the worker and not the employer will
pay the cost of it, through some sort of apprenticeship scheme; where the
training is specific to the employer's needs, it is a matter of indifference
whether the worker pays for it through apprenticeship or through later
receiving less than the value of the total marginal product of his labor plus
his training. Again, it is often argued that the "infant" firm generates new
knowledge about production and managerial methods that other firms can
use free of charge, so that they do not contribute their share to the cost of
investment in knowledge-creation and hence deprive the innovator of part or
all of his reward. Coase's general line of thought, and subsequent work by
Cheung and others on the theory of contract, suggest the obvious notions that
knowledge can be protected or copyrighted, and so privately appropriated
and charged for, and that where new knowledge results in cost reductions for
other firms using this firm's products, the cost-savings can be appropriated
by this firm through pricing policy or acquisitions. Apart from all these
qualifications, both contemporary theory and common sense suggest that, if
the argument for infant-industry protection is either labor training or
research and development, appropriate policy consists in subsidizing these
activities rather than mere production, since a production subsidy carries no
obligation to carry on either activity.

One further aspect of the infant-industry argument is worth commenting
on: the argument that protection is necessary because private entrepreneurs
either overestimate the risk and hence underestimate the return on their
investments, or have to pay a market rate of interest in excess of the social
opportunity cost of capital. In the former case, the proper policy would seem
to be to publicize the government's own (lower) estimates of the risk involved.
The latter case raises a tricky question in theory: if the government thinks the

social alternative opportunity cost of capital is less than the market interest rate, it should take steps to increase savings and lower market interest rates, not stimulate particular firms or industries by subsidizing their required rates of return down to the presumed social alternative opportunity cost of capital while leaving other firms to choose whether to invest or not on the basis of a market rate of interest higher than the presumed social alternative opportunity cost of capital.

The third question concerns the balance-of-payments argument for protection. It is obvious that the Hume-Smith argument on this score still stands. Protection for balance-of-payments reasons not only worsens the allocation of resources, but will be self-defeating as a balance-of-payments policy inasmuch as it will in the longer run lead simply to a counteracting increase in domestic wages and prices.

The fourth question concerns the relative efficiencies of production subsidies, tariffs, quotas and exchange controls, and other protective devices such as tax concessions. The fundamental economic principle here is that a subsidy, either on production itself or on some aspect of the overall productive activity yielding social externalities (e.g., labor training or research and development expenditure) is superior to the tariff. The old objection to subsidies—the problem of raising the revenue to finance them—is answered in the modern world by the fact that, due to the high taxation of income and production that now prevails, subsidies can be given implicitly by tax exemptions or deductions rather than by explicit subsidies. However, this procedure raises the old question of concealment from political scrutiny of the amount of the subsidy involved, and the new question of the appropriateness of the object of the subsidy (e.g., subsidization of capital investment through profits tax concessions) to the objective of the subsidy (e.g., labor training, research and development, or the importation of advanced technology).

Leaving aside the possibility of direct subsidies and the question of fiscal concessions, consider the choice between tariffs and quotas or exchange controls. The latter two alternatives are identical in principle, since one rations goods and the other the money allowed to be spent on them. This and other points are made in James Meade's classic analysis of the question, which argues that one can always find a tariff-equivalent of a quota. The difference is only that a tariff collects the revenue from artificially created scarcity for the state (as would auctioning of quotas, or of foreign exchange for purchasing the goods in question), whereas the distribution of quotas gives the implicit tax revenue to the recipients of the quotas. It also, incidentally, conceals from the public eye the amount of the subsidy being given to domestic producers; and where quotas are nontransferable, it may make importing less efficient that it otherwise would be, by favoring high-cost importing firms.

Since Meade's analysis, various economists, notably Corden and Bhagwati, have noted that the analysis holds only if the substitution of quotas for tariffs leaves the market structure still competitive. Where quotas foster domestic monopoly, there are potentially additional costs of protection.

The final question concerns the potentialities of customs unions and free trade areas. Subsequent to the drafting of the GATT the work of Viner, Meade, Lancaster and Lipsey, and others showed that the effects of joining a customs union or similar arrangement on the welfare of a participant depended on the balance of the gains from trade creation and the losses from trade diversion. Trade creation occurs when, because of the elimination of tariffs on imports from partner countries, the participating country shifts from buying a domestically produced good to buying either the same good at lower cost from a partner country, or a substitute from a partner that yields more satisfaction per unit of cost. Trade diversion occurs when, as a result of maintaining the tariff against imports from third parties but eliminating the tariff against imports from partners, the participating country shifts to importing a higher-cost substitute (either the same product at higher production cost, or a different product yielding less satisfaction per unit of net-of-tariff resource cost) from a partner country. The net balance of advantage involves weighing the amounts of trade creation and trade diversion by the average cost-saving or cost-increasing effect of each. This necessitates empirical study in each practical case.

How does this contemporary theory of tariffs apply to the case of a small country very open to the international economy, such as Panama?

First, it is evident that such countries offer no opportunity whatsoever for the application of the optimum-tariff argument, at least as applied to normal commercial trade. One possible exception occurs where the country happens to have a major export that is a depletable natural-resource product, as in the case of Chilean copper; but here the possibilities of increasing net export earnings by trade intervention are properly regarded as involving determination of the optimal tax on international trade. Another possible exception is where the country has a militarily valuable locational monopoly, as in the case of the Singapore Naval Base, the Malta Naval Base, Spain's contiguity to the Rock of Gibraltar, Egypt's envelopment of the Suez Canal and Panama's envelopment of the Panama Canal and Canal Zone, and can—or hopes it can—extract tribute by threats to take over or repossess the property. But this again is a question of rent rather than of international trade; and, moreover, recent experience has shown that the possibility of exploitation of such territorial monopolies is strictly limited by a high elasticity of substitution for the facilities in question.

Secondly, as regards the infant-industry argument for protection, recent theorizing and research have revealed a fundamental oversight in that augument—its dependence on the size of the market that can be monopolized for the favored industry by protection. The United Nations Conference on Trade and Development's demands for preferences of the two kinds referred to above reflect recognition of this oversight. In terms of the classical theory, infant-industry opportunities for government intervention are more likely to be in export than in import industries, the smaller the country and hence the smaller its home market. To be able to penetrate export markets, the infant industries need subsidies, and in particular subsidies directed at the source of their initial comparative disadvantage, rather than tariff protection. In this connection two points should be noted; they have special reference to Panama. First, "export industries" in the modern world do not necessarily export actual goods to consumers located in a foreign market. They may export services to such consumers, such as financial services, various kinds of designing work, and research and development activity. And the foundation of comparative advantage in such exports may be either liberal laws permitting free conduct of such activities (e.g., the absence of foreign exchange controls on external financial transactions) or a natural environment (e.g., regular warm sunshine) that makes such activities relatively easier and more pleasant to pursue than elsewhere. Or the exports in question may be services—generically described as "tourism"—provided on the spot to foreigners who have to come to the country to collect them.

The second point is that tax concessions in the modern world can serve as the equivalent of subsidies in the traditional theory. (I offer the thought that the Republic of Eire has recently offered tax-free status to all authors who choose residence there. Panama might offer the same to all artists in North America.) The central point, however, is that a country as small as Panama should probably concentrate its protective policies on potential exports rather than on import substitutes.

Thirdly the analysis of the balance-of-payments arguments for protection suggests that Panama would be well advised to maintain its present monetary arrangements, and not to go in for having its own central bank, because to do so might force it into the vicious circle of balance-of-payments problems and protection described earlier.

Fourthly, to the extent that the Panamanian government wishes to give protection to import-substituting industries, it should do so by means of a general tariff structure and not by quotas—particularly not by quotas that discriminate sharply among particular importing enterprises. The tariff collects actual revenue, while the quota gives potential revenue away to the favored few; and discriminatory quota-giving discriminates arbitrarily in favor of still fewer. In either case, the extent of the protection given to domestic production of various kinds is arbitrarily chosen and its amount concealed from the public.

Finally, it is unlikely in the extreme, given Panama's economic structure and the concentration of its trade both ways on the United States, that Panama has anything to gain from forming regional discriminatory trading relationships with any sub-group of its Latin American neighbors. The influence of the Canal and the Canal Zone is to make Panama a relatively high-wage Latin American country, unlikely to be able to compete in a free trade area with other Latin American countries not so favored. The trade created by substitution of somewhat lower-cost partner products for present very high-cost protected Panamanian products would be likely to be heavily out-weighed by the trade diverted from low-cost products (predominently from the United States) to relatively high-cost partner products. Panama's optimum policy would instead probably be to reduce the level and range of her protectionist policies and to concentrate her protective efforts on those products and potential products—including financial services and tourism— that promise to become competitive in the world market as a whole.

20. Direct Foreign Investment: A Survey of the Issues

Introduction

The purpose of this essay is to survey the issues involved in direct foreign investment. It should be noted at the outset that, technically speaking, direct foreign investment entails majority ownership or control of a domestic enterprise by foreigners, and such foreigners may be merely individuals and not necessarily a foreign-domiciled enterprise. However, foreign direct investment in the contemporary world is almost exclusively the preserve of foreign enterprises, and it is this type of direct investment that has recently been exciting political concern in such heavy recipients of it as Canada, Australia, and Western Europe, including the United Kingdom. Hence this paper will be confined to the issues raised by direct investment by the corporations of one country into the economies of others.

As has already been mentioned, there has been mounting concern in the advanced-country recipients of direct foreign investment (primarily from the United States) about its implications for their economies and national independence—in Canada since the mid-1950s, in Western Europe since the early 1960s, in Australia still more recently. This concern has frequently been based on ignorance or on faulty analysis of partial evidence. Moreover, in all probability it has concentrated far too heavily on the U.S. international corporation and on U.S. direct investment abroad, to the neglect of a more general trend toward worldwide operations by corporations of all countries.[1] On the other hand, the developing countries, which have traditionally been highly suspicious of the international corporation (especially the U.S.-based corporation), are being pressed by both the attenuation of the flow of official aid for economic development and the remarkable contributions of foreign enterprises to the promotion of economic development in various countries to a reconsideration of, and a more favorable attitude toward, the role of the corporation as an agency of economic change and growth. Meanwhile, economic theorists have begun to take an interest in the positive and normative analysis of the phenomenon of corporate direct foreign investment.

The growth of corporate direct foreign investment in the period since the Second World War raises issues at a variety of levels, both in economic

Reprinted with permission from *Direct Foreign Investment in Asia and the Pacific*, ed. Peter Drysdale (Canberra: Australian National University Press, 1972), pp. 1–14.

science and in policy formation. For the purposes of this survey, these issues are most conveniently arranged for discussion under the following headings: issues in economic theory, home country issues, host country issues, issues special to developing countries, and international policy issues. These constitute the remaining sections of the paper.

Issues in Economic Theory

It is evident at the outset that understanding of the economics of direct foreign investment requires a different orientation on the part of the economist than that of traditional trade theory (the so-called Heckscher-Ohlin-Samuelson model of international trade), with its assumption of international immobility of factors of production and complete mobility of technical knowledge. For the essence of direct foreign investment is the transmission to the "host" country of a "package" of capital, managerial skill, and technical knowledge. The major issues posed for theory are the reasons why the transmission of such a "package" of capital and knowledge is more profitable than the alternative of transmitting either the capital or the knowledge or both separately, and what the welfare implications are for the "home" and the "host" countries respectively. Along with the first issue goes the important empirical question of which industries are likely to be characterized by direct foreign investment and which are not. Economic theory offers two approaches to these questions, that of the theory of industrial organization and that of traditional trade theory. These approaches must be used as complements, since the former is microeconomic in character whereas the latter stresses the requirements of general macro-economic equilibrium.

The industrial organization approach to the problem was pioneered by Stephen Hymer, who emphasized the competition for market shares among oligopolists. The same sort of approach, but with an emphasis on the economics of new product development, characterizes the work of Raymond Vernon's group at Harvard. This approach has been elaborated in a forthcoming paper by R. E. Caves, which also surveys the empirical evidence and synthesizes the industrial organization and trade theory approaches.[2]

Caves's central theme is the parallelism between direct international investment, and horizontal and vertical integration of firms in a geographi-cally segregated market. In order to be able to invest successfully in production in a foreign market, the firm must possess some asset in the form of knowledge of a public-goods character (production technology, mana-gerial or marketing skills) which can be transferred to a new location at little cost. This is necessary for it to be able to surmount the excess costs of production in an alien location. For it to be induced to produce abroad rather than license its know-how, moreover, the rent it can obtain from its knowledge must be tied to the actual process of production and distribution, and the firm must be large enough to undertake the required investment. Thus Caves argues that direct foreign investment is associated with product-differentiated oligopoly, a hypothesis which is broadly consistent with Vernon's emphasis on new product development. In similar fashion, direct foreign investment of the "vertical" variety—that it, investment in the extraction of raw materials—is associated with oligopoly, differentiated or not, and the corresponding incentives to reduce uncertainty and to forestall potential competition. An important theoretical consequence of "horizontal" direct foreign investment is a tendency toward the equalization of profit rates in the same industry across nations, but not across industries within the national economy. Other implications are "cross-hauling" in investments by national corporations in each others' markets, and a tendency toward overcrowding of the smaller markets by an excessive number of relatively inefficient firms.[3]

Trade theory, as developed by Vernon, myself,[4] Caves, and others, contributes to this general picture the notion of national comparative advantages and disadvantages in the generation of new differentiated products, and in the attraction of direct foreign investment. It also raises the general equilibrium question of the effects of such investment on the distribution of income within the home and the host country and on their respective economic welfare. As regards distribution, a case can be constructed in which inward direct investment benefits domestic capital at the expense of labor; and R. W. Jones has developed an interesting model of international but not interindustrial mobility of capital, in which the attraction of foreign investment by a tariff benefits domestic labor.[5]

As regards welfare effects, it has been generally and rather uncritically assumed that the impact of a package of capital, technology, and managerial skill must be beneficial to the host country. Closer investigation of this issue, however, shows that the gains are not so obviously inevitable or significant.[6] To illustrate, if the foreign firm simply replaced imports by domestic output, charging the same price and paying the going wages for domestic labor, and remitting the interest on its capital and the rent on its superior knowledge as profits, the host country would gain nothing. (In fact, if the foreign investment were attracted by a tariff or by fiscal subsidies, the host country might well lose.)

However, under existing double-taxation agreements, the host country more or less preempts the right to tax the profits of the foreign enterprise, and thus captures a share of both the earnings of the foreign capital and the rents of the foreign knowledge. This is one source of gain from inward foreign investment, which may be particularly important for developing countries both because the foreign corporation affords for the tax collector a target easier to hit than most others, and because the corporation may need, or be forced to put up with, very little compensation for its taxes in the form of public expenditure on infrastructure and other public services.

Beyond this additional tax revenue, benefits to the host country depend on the inability of the investing corporation to capture all the social benefits from its investment, that is they depend on the generation of "spillovers" of various kinds. In theoretical terms, such spillovers involve a reduction of prices or improvement of product quality for consumers, or an increase in wages and prices of other local inputs into the production process. More concretely, Caves suggests two possible important sources of gain to the host country. The first is the training of labor which then becomes available to the economy generally. This will occur if the firm finances the training (rather than the workers financing it through an apprenticeship scheme), and if it overprovides training in relation to its actual needs for skills, as it is particularly likely to do if it is starting a new type of operation in a developing country. The second is productivity gains in domestic firms induced by the behavior of the foreign firm's subsidiary.

Such gains may result from the migration to domestic firms of executive talent developed in the foreign firm; efforts by the foreign firm to educate its suppliers in such matters as quality control and production flow management and its customers in the efficient use of its product; and the stimulus to better management of the domestic firms provided by the competition of the foreigner. (These points conflict with the frequent assertions that foreign firms enter the market in order to cartellize it, and that their entry somehow suppresses domestic entrepreneurship; the probabilities, however, seem to be on Caves's side.) Caves also argues, plausibly, that such training and industrial spillovers for the host country are unlikely to be matched by losses of spillovers to the home country from the investment's not having been made there; and that they are far less likely to accrue from "vertical" than from "horizontal" direct foreign investment, with the exception that "vertical" investment may have to pay abnormally high wages to attract local labor to inaccessible resource-extraction locations.

The foregoing arguments imply both that there are likely to be significant gains to a host country from direct foreign investment in it, and that these gains are secured at no cost to the country whose corporations are doing the investing—apart, of course, from the loss of profits tax revenue by the home to the host country. As regards this last, Caves notes that since profits tax rates are more or less the same in most countries, the allocation of capital is not distorted from a globally efficient pattern by the existence of profits taxes. (This means, however, that it will be distorted by fiscal attractions to direct foreign investment provided by tariffs or other fiscal incentives.) Caves also notes that any other way of handling conflicting national claims to the taxation of profits would probably produce chaos.

The analysis, however, rests on a marginal approach to the impact of direct foreign investment on the home and host countries. One would expect a significant and sustained inflow of foreign direct investment to have the end result of raising real wages and real incomes in the host countries, as a consequence on the one hand of the associated increase in the overall capital-to-labor ratio, and on the other hand of the fact that knowledge cannot be permanently monopolized but ultimately becomes a free good. (This expectation is subject to the proviso that potential increases in real income are not simply absorbed by a faster rate of increase of population.) One would also expect, again on a nonmarginal basis, that the outflow of capital and knowledge to the less advanced and less developed parts of the world would have adverse consequences for the real wages of labor in the advanced-country sources of direct foreign investment. There is thus a fairly solid theoretical basis for concern on the part of labor groups in the advanced countries about the implications for them of large-scale outflows of direct foreign investment, a basis which can be disputed only on the doubtful grounds either that the foreigners would otherwise have raised the capital and invested in the knowledge themselves, or that the direct foreign investment has such a powerful catalytic effect in energizing the indigenous potentialities for economic growth that the losses to home labor from relatively less capital per head and loss of monopoly in the exploitation of knowledge are more than compensated for.

The foregoing discussion of the issues of economic theory involved in direct foreign investment has been conducted in terms of the effects of such investment on "real" economic equilibrium. Much of the public discussion of it, however, has been conducted in terms of the balance-of-payments effects. The position taken here is that concern about balance-of-payments effects reflects the propensity on the part of both the major source-countries of direct foreign investment (specifically the United States, and the United Kingdom up to 1967), and many of the recipient countries (including Canada in the late 1950s and early 1960s, and many developing countries) to adhere stubbornly to an overvalued exchange rate. It also reflects the propensity of government economists to concern themselves with financial flows of investment and the remittance of earnings, without proper recognition of the real investment processes by which investments create the productive capacity to earn profits and pay dividends. It may be noted that adherence to an overvalued exchange rate itself creates artificial incentives both to invest abroad, for home country corporations, and to remit earnings rather than reinvest them, for corporations investing in countries with overvalued currencies.

Home Country Issues

As mentioned in the previous section, the most obvious economic problem for the home country involved in direct foreign investment by its corporations is the loss of revenue from profits tax on the earnings of their capital and know-how. This loss, however, has not been an issue in the United States, the major source of direct foreign investment, presumably because tax revenue is not a significant problem in the world's richest country and also because through most of the post–World War II period the United States has been anxious to encourage foreign investment by its corporations as a contribution to postwar economic reconstruction and to economic development. Nor has it been an important issue in the United Kingdom, which is both a recipient and a source of direct foreign investment, though the calculations of the Reddaway report[7] took it into account and in so doing aroused some criticism for failing to allow for the offsetting saving on the cost of public provision of overhead services for private industry.

In both countries the chief reason for concern about corporate direct foreign investment has been its contribution or asserted contribution to the country's balance-of-payments deficit. In the United Kingdom this concern led to changes in corporate profits tax legislation. In the United States it led first to "voluntary" and then to mandatory controls over corporate financial practices, designed to minimize the foreign exchange drain on the U.S. balance of payments. These controls evoked protests, particularly from Canada, about U.S. government interference with the operations of Canadian subsidiaries of U.S. corporations, the production of Canadian guidelines for good behavior on the part of foreign enterprises in Canada, and a continuing and mounting Canadian concern about U.S. subsidiaries in Canada. They also evoked protests from the American business community, and a series of controversial efforts to measure the immediate and longer-run impacts of direct foreign investment on the U.S. balance of payments, including the impact effect of the investment itself, the longer-run effects in stimulating and/or replacing U.S. exports, and the building up of earnings remittances over the course of time.

As argued in the previous section, concern about the balance-of-payments implications of direct foreign investment stemmed from the maintenance of an overvalued exchange rate, in the United Kingdom until November 1967 and in the United States to at least 1973. In terms of the pure theory of international monetary disequilibrium, it is very difficult to establish a case for the effectiveness of controls on foreign investment as a means of correcting a deficit associated with currency overvaluation, even if the controls are effective in restricting the particular financial transactions at which they are aimed. The only really persuasive argument for using them is that currency overvaluation stimulates foreign investments that would not appear profitable if the exchange rate were correctly valued. But in that case establishment of an appropriate currency valuation would be a superior policy to maintenance of an overvalued rate coupled with investment controls designed to prevent the inefficient allocation consequences of overvaluation.

In the heyday of the last historical era of massive private foreign investment, the era based on the export of British capital to the rest of the world through the London capital market, the view emerged in British socialist and labor circles that these capital exports were diverting capital from investment in British industry and hence from the improvement of the welfare of the British worker. This view gained ground in the conditions of mass unemployment of the interwar period, and was to some extent responsible for the imposition of capital issues control in the 1930s after the suspension of the gold standard. It continues to be an influence on left-wing British thinking about direct foreign investment by British corporations, and more generally the international role of the City of London.

In recent years, and to an important extent as a consequence of the overvaluation of the U.S. dollar, very similar criticisms of direct foreign investment by American corporations have come increasingly to be voiced by the American labor movement. The American unions' criticisms focus on two major issues. The first is the "export of jobs" implicit in direct foreign investment. In part this complaint reflects the overvaluation of the dollar and the absence of a firm governmental commitment to a full employment policy; in part, however, it reflects a more fundamental realization that unions in the United States have been enabled to raise wages to their present high levels by the relative abundance of capital in the United States and the country's leadership in advanced technology industries, both of which advantages, but especially the latter, are now being eroded by the process of direct foreign investment by American corporations in lower-wage countries. The second point of criticism concerns the implications for collective bargaining of the emerging world of "multinational production"; the argument is that multinational production enables employers to bring in "scab imports" to reduce the losses to themselves consequent on a domestic strike, and to threaten to expand production abroad and even close down domestic production facilities unless unions moderate their wage and other demands. The result of these criticisms has been a series of proposals, some quite unrealistic, for controlling and slowing down direct foreign investment by U.S. corporations.

By contrast, the unions in the United Kingdom, while also concerned about the operations of the multinational corporation, have tended to be content with pressing for more information about their activities and for the general desirability of surveillance and international control.

The issues just discussed are essentially economic in nature. It should be noted, however (somewhat in anticipation of the next section), that while much of the concern about direct foreign investment in host countries revolves around the infringement of national sovereignty through political intervention by the home country government in the affairs of its corporations' subsidiaries in the host countries, the home country itself suffers a gradual erosion of sovereignty through the evolution of its national corporations into international, transnational, or multinational corporations. This is not merely a matter of the difficulty of governmental policing of the manifold overseas operations of corporate subsidiaries; it is much more a matter of gradual change in the attitudes of corporation executives toward, and loss of their respect for, the politicians and officials of national governments— including their own—as their horizons expand to comprise the international economy as the sphere of their operations, and they become impatient of those whose vision and responsibilities are limited to the territorial domain of a particular nation-state.

Host Country Issues

The subsidiaries of foreign-based corporations tend to be viewed with considerable suspicion in host countries, just as the local branches of national corporations were viewed with considerable suspicion in an earlier era which witnessed the rise of the national corporation in competition with the local corporation or family business. Indeed, most of the contemporary criticisms of the economic behavior of the national subsidiaries of foreign corporations can be found in the historical records, novels, and plays about the economic and social consequences of the intrusion of a branch of a national corporation into a small but apparently prosperous and socially well-integrated local community. There are the same complaints that the local wealthy are not welcomed into partnership in management and profits, local talent is not preferred over rival aspirants to jobs, and potential local suppliers are not preferred over competitors elsewhere. The only difference, though it is an important one, is that the government to which the national firm was subservient was also the national government of the local community, however remote and however resented, whereas the international corporation owes allegiance to a government other than (and in addition to) the government of the nation in which the subsidiary operates. Even this difference was frequently, in the period of emergence of the national corporation, more a difference of degree than of kind. And there is some doubt as to how serious the conflicts between national sovereignties inherent in the dual responsibilities of international corporations to home and host governments really are. Nevertheless, it is necessary in discussing host country issues associated with corporate direct foreign investment to distinguish between issues concerning the economic behavior of foreign subsidiaries, and issues concerning the exercise of sovereignty by the home government over the foreign operations of subsidiaries of its national corporations.

Complaints about and criticisms of the presumed or potential economic behavior of the domestic subsidiaries of foreign corporations—the distinction between actual and potential is not usually drawn very carefully, though it is important for policy—may touch on any or all aspects of corporate activity, and tend to focus on behavior relevant to the current concerns of national policymakers. These concerns tend to be of two major types. The first is improvement in the balance of payments, which implies a policy emphasis on export promotion and import substitution. The second is growth and improved efficiency of the domestic economy, which implies policy emphasis on a variety of aspects of industrial activity that policymakers consider critical to the objective, such as participation by residents in ownership and top management, and the conduct of research and development activity domestically. It may be observed in passing that the fundamental theory of balance-of-payments adjustment does not suggest that microeconomic policies aimed at export promotion and import substitution will be effective by themselves in remedying a balance-of-payments deficit, since this typically requires some combination of deflation and devaluation; and also that political ideas of what it takes to make industry flourish are frequently derived by imitative magic rather than by economic analysis.

Concern about the performance of American subsidiaries in Canada has been active for a longer time, and has raised a broader range of issues, than parallel concern in other countries. An early interview study sponsored by the Canadian-American Committee[8] selected six aspects of subsidiaries' behavior that appeared to provoke the most irritation in Canada. The main points of criticism involved were: refusal to sell equity shares in the subsidiary to the Canadian public; insufficient "Canadianization" of personnel; publication of insufficient financial data; marketing and purchasing policies that discriminated against exports and in favor of imports from U.S. suppliers; insufficient domestic research; and centralization of philanthropic activities in the American parent's head office.

Some of these issues are specific to Canada, and reflect the opinions of particular vested interest groups. All raise issues of both empirical fact and theoretical interpretation too complex to enter into in this paper. It may be recorded, however, that Canadian radical opinion (partly in response to the findings of empirical research) has tended subsequently to narrow its specific criticisms down to the alleged failure of U.S. subsidiaries to purchase a sufficient proportion of its supplies locally, while broadening its general attack into the allegation that the presence of the subsidiaries has suppressed the development of indigenous Canadian entrepreneurship.[9] Meanwhile, Canadian policy has been developing along the lines of requiring more detailed information, establishing guidelines for foreign direct investment, and reserving certain sectors of Canadian economic activity (especially financial) for Canadian–owned or controlled enterprises.

While a detailed analysis of issues pertaining to the economic behavior of the subsidiaries of international corporations is beyond the scope of this paper,[10] casual observation of Canadian, British, and other public opinion suggests that public opinion is likely to be particularly aroused about four major issues. One is the issue of public disclosure of financial information, associated with the suspicion that subsidiaries make excess profits and/or evade their fair share of taxes by paying excessive transfer prices on purchases from their foreign affiliates or charging too little on sales to them.

A second issue is local research and development expenditure, which has come to be identified as vital to industrial competitiveness and supremacy. This issue raises the question of the character of knowledge as a public good, and the wastes involved in replicating its production or producing it on too small a scale. It also raises the question of efficient use of a country's scarce supplies of qualified scientists and engineers.

A third issue concerns foreign takeovers of domestic enterprises, which seem to excite public alarm. The facts that takeovers offer a capital gain to resident owners that they could not otherwise enjoy, and also that entry into the domestic market by a foreign competitor via takeover, rather than establishment of new production facilities, gives no indication of whether he intends to act competitively or monopolistically, are usually ignored.

A fourth issue derives from the widely held notion that there are "key sectors" or "commanding heights" in the economy that must be preserved, in whole or at least in part, for resident (national) firms. Unfortunately, economic analysis offers no guidance to the identification of such key sectors, if indeed they exist. Hence the "commanding heights" are likely to be defined by vested interests or by political symbolism.

Issues arising not from the economic behavior of subsidiaries but from the exercise of sovereignty by the government of the home country over the subsidiaries in conflict with the sovereign claims of the host country, have been most keenly felt in Canada. The main sources of resentment have been, on the one hand, the "extraterritorial" application of U.S. antitrust law, union law, and laws relating to exports to communist countries by U.S. subsidiaries in Canada, and on the other hand the application of U.S. balance-of-payments guidelines to the financial operations of such subsidiaries. Other countries do not seem to have been concerned about the extraterritoriality issue, especially as regards exports to communist countries, presumably because the presence of national firms capable of undertaking the business has made the issue an empty one. Nor have they objected strongly to the balance-of-payments guidelines, presumably because they have resented the U.S. deficit sufficiently strongly to tolerate infringements of their sovereignty by U.S. balance-of-payments policy.

Issues Special to Developing Countries

While all of the issues discussed in the previous section might arise in connection with direct foreign investment in the developing countries, certain special issues or versions of general issues are particularly likely to arise in that context.

For one thing, the typical developing country is small in relation to the international corporate giants mainly involved in direct foreign investment, and its expertise in negotiating with foreign corporations is likely to be extremely limited in comparison with what the corporation can bring to bear. Hence there is likely to be both suspicion on the part of government officials that they have been cozened into accepting a bargain too favorable to the corporation, with a resulting tendency to hector and harass the corporation subsequently, and suspicion on the part of public opinion that the government has "sold out" to the foreign capitalists. Misunderstanding, confusion, and acrimony on this score are likely to be enhanced by the popular failure to appreciate two facts about the corporation in the context of a developing country. The first is that the profits of the corporation are to a substantial degree a return on its past investments in the generation of productive knowledge, and should not be regarded simply as a return on the capital invested in the particular local production facility. The second is that the corporation is a competitive profit-seeking institution and not a government with the powers of taxation, and therefore cannot be expected to assume the responsibility for promoting development in the same way as a development plan undertakes that responsibility. As outlined in the second section of this essay, the contribution of direct foreign investment to development is incidental to the purpose of making profits—though it may nevertheless be important. In consequence, development by means of direct foreign investment is likely to be highly uneven and sector-specific—though there is the consolation that profits taxes on foreign capital and industrial knowledge will provide revenue for the development plan.[11]

The problems of negotiating with the international corporations are likely to be especially acute when, as is the case in many developing countries, the interest of the corporations is in the exploitation of natural resources rather than in the establishment of domestic manufacturing facilities. The problem here is to determine an appropriate rent, or an appropriate depletion allowance, in the face of a highly uncertain future market situation and under strong pressures to secure an immediate and large revenue for the government to devote to development programs. The typical outcome is a bargain that is repeatedly and acrimoniously renegotiated in favor of the government.

For fairly well-known reasons, developing countries are also likely to be particularly concerned with the balance-of-payments aspects of direct foreign investment. This particular concern stems largely from the official habit, already referred to, of concentrating on financial flows to the neglect of the real investment and production phenomena underlying them. If the exchange rate and the domestic economy are properly managed, the increase in output provided by the investment should provide the real resources for servicing it. (It has, in fact, frequently been pointed out that direct equity investment is superior to portfolio investment from a balance-of-payments point of view precisely because the servicing payments due are geared to the current profitability of the investment financed by the foreign capital.) However, where the foreign direct investment has been attracted by protection or fiscal incentives, the profits earned may not be matched by a genuine contribution to increased output, and the servicing drain on the balance of payments constitutes a real burden on the economy. Such a situation, though, should be ascribed to governmental error in providing socially undesirable incentives to foreign direct investment, rather than blamed on the foreign corporation per se.

International Policy Issues

The rapid growth of the operations of the international corporation and the conflicts of interest that have appeared on the one hand between national governments and foreign corporations operating in their territory and on the other hand between the claims of national sovereignty of the host and home governments have led a number of observers to remark on the fact that while there exists an established international agency—the General Agreement on Tariffs and Trade—for the policing of international trade practices and the arbitration of trade disputes between nations, no comparable international authority exists for the regulation of relations between corporations and governments and the arbitration of conflicts of sovereignty over the corporation among nations. Proposals have been put forward, both in business and in academic circles, that such an international authority should be established and properly empowered.[12] However, as C. P. Kindleberger has noted with some surprise, there seems to be little conviction of the need for such an agency among those most practically concerned with the problems involved— the international lawyers—at least one of whom has taken the view that conflicts of jurisdiction are in fact less common than is generally supposed and can be resolved within the framework of existing institutions.[13] There is also some question whether the rise of the international corporation and of international business is as powerful a challenge to the nation-state as both its enthusiasts and its critics have made it out to be.[14] Nevertheless, the growth of interest in and support for the idea, and the inauguration of research into the problem under a variety of auspices, suggest that it will eventually emerge as a practical issue in international economic policy.

Part 6   Economics
              and the
              Environment

21. Man and His Environment

Introduction

The possibility of harmful interaction of one sort or another between man and his environment has been a matter of concern, off and on, in popular economic thinking since the time of the English classical school of the early nineteenth century. Indeed, the crude economic analysis of the members of the classical school set the stage (i.e., the intellectual framework) for the expression of such concerns ever since. And it is a matter for dismay, for anyone concerned with the proper design of economic policy, that contemporary alarmists on the subjects of the population problem and the environment rarely reach the level of economic understanding achieved by the classical economists, let alone the level accomplished by professional economists after a century and a half of further intellectual work on the refinement, amendment, extension, and generalization of the crude framework of analysis adumbrated by the classical school.

The Population Problem

Thomas Robert Malthus, whose initial aim was to rebut the utopian socialist ideas of William Godwin, laid down the principle that population tends to breed to the level of subsistence. Consequently, any efforts to ameliorate the lot of the common man would simply be soaked up in an expansion of the population until the "positive checks" of mortality and starvation brought the process to a halt. Malthus attempted to prove these propositions on the basis of the empirical assertion that population could grow by geometrical progression, whereas agricultural production could increase only by absolute progression, so that the former must inevitably overtake the latter.[1] In fact, however, Malthus's argument was factually incorrect for his own time, since an immense improvement in agricultural productivity occurred, which laid the basis for the industrial revolution both by providing an agricultural surplus capable of sustaining large-scale industrial activity and by displacing workers from the land into industrial employment. Moreover, Mathus's argument was theoretically crude, since it did not allow for feedback from population growth into the development of superior food-producing techno-

Originally published as a pamphlet by the National Planning Association, Washington, D.C., 1973; reprinted with permission.

logy. Nevertheless, calculations of equal crudeness—although sometimes dressed up in high-powered statistical or econometric computations—remain characteristic of the literature on the "population problem" and a prospective "food crisis" and "ecological crisis."

In analyzing the prospective population problem, Malthus initially put his emphasis on the "positive checks" that increasing misery would impose on population growth. But, by the time of his second essay, he was de-emphasizing the inevitability of a population problem, stressing instead the "negative checks" of deferred marriage, continence in copulation after marriage, and other indirect methods of birth control that Christianity and the absence of a birth control technology suggested.[2] The result was to make the pressure of population on natural resources an analytical possibility arbitrarily and gloomily selected for theoretical emphasis, rather than a presumptive empirical fact. This characteristically plagued the efforts of Malthus's contemporaries and immediate successors (including Marx) to build their theories of distribution and growth on an assumed tendency of labor to breed to the level of subsistence (the so-called iron law of wages). The experience of steadily rising real wages in the Western world for at least the past three-quarters of a century, in spite of significant rates of population growth, strongly suggests that population does not blindly over-breed in relation to available natural resources (especially given the rapidly increasing availability of contraceptive information and techniques). People respond to the increasing availability of natural resources, and of economic opportunities generally, partly by raising their own standard of living and partly by raising more children. But—and this is a very important point—they raise their children to their own standards of education, living, and health, and do not simply cast them out eventually into the world as unskilled labor. This experience also suggests that, in due course, reproduction customs will become the same in the less developed countries as economic opportunities and knowledge of opportunities and birth control methods spread; and that, consequently, alarmist fears of population pressing on natural resources are unjustified, and the computations used to support these fears equally unjustified.[3] It is not logical to make projections of the future on the assumption that population behavior is completely independent of available resources and of human aspirations for improvement, when a wide range of human history—and not merely the recent history of a technologically advanced and highly educated Western world—points in the opposite direction.

On the other hand, however, there are some obvious cases in which the private costs of having children fall well short of the social costs, thus creating private incentives to excessive population growth. In the advanced countries, these cases typically involve the assumption by the public, through the state, of a large part of the cost of child-bearing and child-rearing in the form of free or subsidized medical care, free or subsidized nutrition, and free or subsidized education. This creates a problem, because these benefits are especially important to the poor, who could not otherwise afford the cost, and who also may lack the education and self-discipline required for rational family planning; hence, the tendency in developed countries to put increasing emphasis on the dissemination of contraceptive information as an integral part of antipoverty and social welfare programs. Similar factors are at work, to a smaller extent, in the less developed countries. Additionally, a large reason for the motivation for aid-giving by rich to poor countries is moral shock at the existence of poverty in those countries. But foreign development aid reduces the private cost of population growth in those countries, both by providing economic and medical support for children once born and by widening subsequent employment opportunities, and so may in whole or in part defeat its own aim of mitigating manifest poverty. The easiest way to eliminate manifest poverty is to prevent the poor from being born in the first place; the hardest way is to encourage them to be born and then try to remedy the results. Hence, the mounting concern of those involved in development assistance, and in development planning, for programs of population control.

Natural Resources

Malthus was concerned with the tendency of population to breed to the level of subsistence, and laid the foundations of the current concern about the population problem. David Ricardo, on the other hand, was concerned with the distribution of national income among the social classes of landlords, workers and capitalists, and with the effects of economic growth on this distribution. For this purpose, he accepted the "iron law of wages" (although he made the concept of subsistence wages a matter of social convention and therefore theoretically indeterminate) and made the determinant of the effects of economic growth on distribution, and especially on the rate of profit as the incentive for capitalists to save and accumulate capital, the assumed absolute fixity of "the original and indestructible properties of the soil." In modern terminology, man's capacity to enjoy a high standard of living is limited by the fixity of the natural resources available to him, and depends on the number of men relative to the available amount of natural resources.

One corollary of this proposition, discussed in the previous section, is the conclusion that man can destroy his economic well-being by over-breeding; coupled with the assumption that man will automatically tend to over-breed when left to his own devices, the proposition leads to the conclusion that avoidance of human disaster requires strong programs of population control.

The other corollary is the proposition that, if a fixed stock of natural resources sets the limit to man's potential economic welfare, *and* if the present generation of men has any concern for the economic welfare of its progeny, it is the obligation of the present generation to preserve the stock of natural resources intact for the use of future generations. (It should be noted here that the presumed obligation of the current generation to preserve the environment is an unsupported social judgment, not necessarily constituting rational self-interested economic behavior. One might well argue, instead, that "I had to cope with the environment my parents chose to leave me, let my children do the same.") This corollary has expressed itself in the past in the "conservation movement"—that is, the movement to prevent by legislation the depletion of existing natural resources such as (most typically) forests by lumbering, mineral deposits by mining, and agricultural land by cropping that destroys the fertility of the land. More recently, it has expressed itself in the "antipollution" and "environment-preservation" movements. In all of these movements, there are elements of the Ricardian assumption that there is something special about the environment that requires keeping it intact in its existing form.

The Ricardian assumption was doubtless convenient to Ricardo as a means of striking through the complexity of reality to the basic principles of resource allocation and the distribution of income. But, as a specification of economic reality, it is extremely naïve and misleading. Man's whole history has been one of transforming his environment rather than accepting its limitations. He has domesticated and raised animals for his own use rather than relying on hunting them, and previously he invented weapons for hunting them made from pieces of the environment rather than relying on his original physical powers. He has cleared ground for the planting of crops rather than relying on what he could collect from nature's rather niggardly abundance. And he has steadily shifted his economic activities from an overt and direct reliance on using products made available by nature to organizing those products, or those sophisticated by human ingenuity, into an industrial productive system which, directly at least, is completely independent of nature's bounty. It is true that we still have problems of local famine due to crop failures; but these are typically associated with lack of adequate local storage facilities and the difficulties of transporting food from areas of abundance to famine areas rather than to real, overall world shortages. Similarly, we still have earthquake and flood disasters; but, except in remote parts of the world, these disasters are usually the result of taking a calculated risk on how much of nature's potential depredations it is worthwhile ensuring against by investment in the reconstruction of the environment through such means as building earthquake-proof housing, shops, and factories, and constructing river-control and irrigation systems.

The crucial question, therefore, does not concern the transformation of the environment by man, and the presumptive undesirability of this transformation per se, but whether certain types of transformation have undesirable results, in the sense of worsening man's potential welfare. Analysis of this question raises much the same fundamental issues as analysis of the population question—specifically, whether the private costs and benefits of the environment-altering activity (in the population case, procreation) reflect social costs and benefits closely enough for private choices to approximate the choices that an all-wise, centralized social decision-taking process would make. However, there are some special aspects of the problem which economists have been particularly concerned with in recent years; these pertain to the definition and exercise of property rights in the environment, and will be discussed in the next section.

Some Elementary Economics of the Environment

The Environment as Capital

As already mentioned, Ricardian economics made the environment, in the form of "the original and indestructible properties of the soil," the basic capital that society had to work with, and the limiting factor in man's ability to improve his economic lot by accumulation of material capital in the form of factories and machines. This way of looking at the environment was natural enough for a society with what appeared to be a static technology of agricultural production and a static technology defining both what minerals and other natural resources were valuable enough to be worth extracting and the techniques for extracting them. But, in the context of contemporary society, natural resources derive their value from the available technology which is itself a variable alterable by investment in the creation of new technology itself, and from investment in transportation and distribution facilities. The environment, therefore, is a form of social capital which society must somehow manage if it is to maximize its welfare. From this point of view—the environment as a major part of society's capital—three crucial themes are apparent.

First, contrary to Ricardo, the environment is not "original and indestructible." On the contrary, it has built-in tendencies to self-destruction through such natural processes as the generation of forest fires by lightning, the erosion of soil by rainfall carrying it into the rivers and eventually the sea, and the gradual death of lakes through the sinking of sediment and the exhaustion of the oxygen content of the sub-surface water. More important, the economic value of the environment to man may be either augmented or destroyed by technical progress. Hence, wise social management of the environment may require *either* deliberate efforts to preserve and augment it, *or* deliberate efforts to transform the wealth that it represents into a more valuable form. Specifically, it may be in society's interests at one time to transform forest resources into cash, at another to preserve them as a form of future wealth; similarly, if a society possesses depletable mineral resources, it may or may not be advantageous to sell them or allow them to be used up in current production.

Second, but in the same vein, disinvestment in or depletion of the environment can generally (though not always) be corrected subsequently by investment. Forests can be replanted. Dead lakes can be revitalized by pumping oxygen into them, or the swimming and fishing facilities they formerly offered replaced by private or public swimming pools and commercial fish farms. Similarly, metals removed from the ground can be recaptured as scrap and reprocessed—a procedure already characteristic of the iron and steel industry—and stores of energy sources such as coal and oil could probably be reconstituted with enough ingenuity or, in any case, substituted for by other means—for example, by the use of nuclear or solar energy—if it became necessary to do so.

These considerations point to two of the main weaknesses of many conservationist and antipollutionist arguments: their failure to consider the costs and benefits of transforming the environment, and their failure to consider the possibility of reconstituting the environment (or constructing a new environment catering to man's environmental desires) at a cost in terms of investable resources. Many of the favorite examples of these social critics are characteristic of these failures. For instance, the early settlers of Ontario counted on cutting down a tall tree and floating it downstream for sale as a mast to the British navy as a means of providing cash with which to start farming; they also cut and stumped the other trees to make room for the growing of crops, thereby causing a soil erosion problem in the longer run. But the wealth they created in the process has enabled their modern successors to install tap water facilities, to plant trees and fertilize the soil they grow in, and to construct swimming pools to substitute more conveniently for the polluted rivers. This history makes a nonsense of alarmist views about the destruction of Canadian forest reserves. Similarly, Vance Packard's example of the using up of the world's iron resources in the manufacture of tin cans overlooks both the possibility of remelting scrap metal and the likelihood that if iron becomes scarce and expensive society will find some other way of packaging its preserved food (note that metal containers replaced glass containers because they were cheaper). Finally, while much has been written and said recently about pollution and congestion in the cities, no one who has read novels and histories or seen movies about cities in pre-modern times, with their narrow streets, their dumping of garbage and excrement in those streets to the peril of the passer-by, and their smog-creating methods of private heating, can doubt that the economic progress of humanity has been used in part to improve rather than to pollute the environment.

To say this is not to deny that problems of pollution exist. As will be argued in the next section, pollution is typically a by-product of production.

The real problems, however, are two: what social arrangements are necessary to achieve the optimal combination of pollution and production, and which kinds of pollution constitute really serious problems in the sense that they are difficult if not impossible to correct subsequently. The first problem requires reference to both the stage of affluence of society and the distribution of property rights in the environment, to be discussed below. The second, which will be discussed only briefly here, requires a great deal of scientific knowledge and economic analysis not available at present. Put very briefly and broadly, as mentioned earlier, forests can be replanted, soil refertilized, water de-polluted, and local air purified, although at a cost that may not be worthwhile, at least at current income levels. Alternatively, private individuals can plant their own trees, build their own swimming pools, and live in houses equipped with air purifiers and electrostatic dust precipitation, again if the cost is worth it. The crucial question is whether there are types of environment-destroying or pollutant activity that are not remediable within the bounds of present or foreseeable technology, economic resources, and governmental structure. It should be clear from the foregoing argument that most of the types of environment-destruction activity commonly complained of are remediable if this is desirable (which, it should be noted, it may not be). The types that come to mind as not being foreseeably remediable are those that have to do with common property resources of the world as a whole, where remedification might be too large a job to handle or where it might require an unprecedented degree of international cooperation. The specific examples are the pollution of the oceans (possibly also of lakes or seas on which several countries border) and the pollution of the upper atmosphere by jet aircraft. (It is difficult to envisage little men in space suits armed with large nets attempting to retrieve jet fuel ash, yet the accumulation of this waste in the upper atmosphere is gradually altering the planet's weather.) Various long-lived pollutants (e.g., heavy metals such as mercury and cadmium and synthetic organic chemicals such as DDT and PCB) that accumulate in the biosystem with unknown but possibly extremely hazardous effects also pose a serious problem. Society must decide whether the risks involved are worth the costs of forsaking use of these materials, considering the availability and costs of alternatives. Since the risks of using such materials will not be reflected in their price, the market cannot be expected necessarily to produce a socially optimal decision.

Pollution and Production as Joint Outputs

In a fundamental sense, pollution and production are joint products of man's efforts to transform his environment to his own use. ("Pollution" in this context is used for convenience to include destruction of the existing environment.) For it is rare that the process of satisfying man's wants by environment transformation can both leave intact the environment from which useful products are extracted and yield only useful products and no pollutant by-products. The production and consumption of goods inevitably involves the production and consumption of "bads."

This is true even at the most elementary biological level. The nourishment man requires to stay alive inevitably generates excrement. In primitive nomadic and agricultural societies, man merely returns the excrement to the environment, and conditions himself to ignore the resulting smells and unsightliness. In more advanced societies, the disposition of excrement is collectivized in the form of running water and sewage systems; then the pollution of the water by the sewage becomes a problem, actual or potential.[4] More important for contemporary concerns about pollution and the environment, however, is the fact that the production of goods to satisfy man's wants involves the production of "bads" as a by-product. As a rough classification, "bads" are produced at three stages of the process of transformation of the environment into useful consumption goods: transformation of the environment into new materials and energy sources (using up of natural resources); transformation of raw materials into consumption goods (involving two types of "bads"—waste products, and the atmospheric pollution resulting from the consumption of energy sources); and the consumption of the goods themselves (garbage, litter, excrement, and atmospheric pollution resulting from the combustion of energy sources).

As will be discussed in the next section, the central problem raised by the joint production of "goods" and "bads" concerns the extent to which the consumers of the "goods" are obliged to recognize the joint production of the "bads" and consume them as part of the cost of consuming the "goods." However, for purposes of the present argument, it is assumed that society collectively and not the individual consumer or producer of "goods" has to accept and put up with the joint production of "bads." To be more specific, it is assumed, for example, that production by a factory in a given location (e.g., a pulp mill or a coal electricity-generating plant) necessarily pollutes the air and the water (local river) supplies of the residents of the neighboring town. (In terms of the argument of the next section, the factory has the right to pollute the local environment.) Society then has a choice, which it may exercise in this example either by prohibiting or encouraging the establishment of the factory in an existing town or by moving into or out of a town with a factory, between accepting or rejecting the package of "goods" and "bads" that results from the productive process.

The main relevant point here is that, faced with such a "package" choice, society might choose either way. The factory provides either more employment or better paid employment than is otherwise available; and it also provides goods that raise people's standards of private living. On the other hand, to enjoy these benefits it is necessary to "consume" the "bads" that the factory creates in the way of environmental pollution. One would expect that in a generally poor economy—for instance, in a subsistence or a low-cash-crop-producing agricultural economy, in which people are used to their own private pollution of their own private environments as a natural by-product of their existence and subsistence—the choice would be in favor of the factory. The benefits from producing and consuming the "goods" would be seen as outweighing the inconvenience of having to consume the "bads" as well. Evidence of this can be found in the willingness of the average worker to accept the conditions of life—horrible by modern standards—in early post-industrialization cities, conditions well documented for England by a host of social critics and historians, and evident in contemporary times in the conditions of life in such cities as Tokyo. But one would also expect that as income-earning opportunities expanded, so that, on the one hand, as producers found it less and less urgent to earn the additional dollar per week, and, on the other, as consumers found it increasingly attractive to sacrifice marginal increments of consumption of material goods in return for enjoying a more pleasant environment, the choice would tend to go the other way. Either the establishment of the factory would be forbidden, or, if established, it would have to pay wages and salaries high enough to compensate its employees and those who earn their living by selling goods and services to its employees for the psychic cost of consuming the associated pollution or the material cost of offsetting the pollution.

The foregoing argument oversimplifies matters by positing an all-or-nothing choice between nothing and a fixed bundle of production of "goods" and "bads." Actually, in most and probably all cases, the mix of "goods" and "bads" produced is a matter of technological choice; and the most profitable choice as dictated by the market opportunities confronting the firm can be altered by legal control, providing society is prepared to pay the cost of such control. Thus, for example, society can require that factories and households use smokeless fuel, or that factories dispose of their waste products harmlessly at their own expense instead of dumping them into the nearest river to the discomfort of downstream residents. But the public may not be willing to pay the resulting sacrifice of consumption of "goods" for the sake of reducing its consumption of "bads." Again, its willingness to do so will depend on its average income level, and the effects of this on its willingness to trade off more "goods" against less "bads."

The preceding argument is also oversimplified by the implicit assumption that the public generally is aware of the nature of the "goods" and the "bads." This assumption is unrealistic for two reasons. First, man is a fairly flexible and adaptable organism, capable both of adjusting to considerable variations in environmental conditions on a permanent basis, and of tolerating considerable short-run variations of his environment about the accustomed norm. One can tolerate extreme heat or cold, extreme humidity or aridity, and extreme smog or dust in the air for short periods; and one also has biological mechanisms that will resist the penetration of germs and the communication of diseases. Hence, it is often extremely difficult to know when one's environment has become dangerous—that is, when "bads" are being produced along with "goods." For example, in some locations with strong prevailing winds, high enough chimneys can get rid of smoke pollution; in others with low cloud covers, high chimneys make no difference at all, except in the minds of the local authorities and their engineers. Second, knowledge of the "bads" is easy for a society to acquire only if its technology is static and it can learn by experience, and institutionalize, how to minimize the ill effects of the "bads." Primitive societies are characterized by an equilibrium in this respect: typically, certain parts of the environment are set aside for pollutant activities, and known by all to be polluted and therefore to be shunned except "on business." In a technologically advancing society, however, the pollutant by-products of new types or methods of productive activity are unpredictable in advance, either in nature or in quantity or in both, and man has to learn by trial and error. This involves costs of a kind that would be avoidable if no changes could be effected without absolutely exhaustive prior research into all the alternatives, or if no changes at all were permitted; but the first stipulation would involve tremendous costs and delays and the second would put an end to human progress and the prospect of the betterment of man's lot on earth. The relevant questions are whether the mistakes man makes in the process are remediable at all, and, if so, whether they are remediable in time to avoid human disaster. The first question was raised in the previous section, where it was suggested that most of the problems about the environment that conern alarmists are not problems in the sense of irretrievability of error, but that there may be some that are. However, to determine that issue would require far more scientific research into the potentialities of scientific research itself than is now available. The second question involves the economics of human response to error once recognized. Various arguments and empirical observations presented earlier in this essay suggest that there are strong grounds for optimism on this score. Mankind has steadily become better off—in terms of secular trend—since his origins on the planet, as measured by his capacity to support both increasing total numbers and a higher average standard of living for those numbers, in spite of the dangers implicit in the use of new and superior technologies for the transformation of his environment into more usable and gratifying means of self-support. There is no reason to think, in the light of millennia of human history and the consistent falsification of the prophesies of successive schools of doom predictors, that at the end of the third quarter of the twentieth century everything has suddenly changed, and man is doomed to be the victim of his incompetence to control and correct the consequences of his own ingenuity.

Property Rights in the Environment

The problems of pollution and environment destruction are ultimately bound up with the question of property rights, including both their definition and the costs of enforcing them. This subject has been explored in detail by economists in recent years, following two seminal studies by H. S. Gordon and R. H. Coase.[5]

Gordon's article, which had particular reference to fisheries, showed that in the case of a "common property resource" (specifically, the oceans) for which no rent is chargeable and to which everyone has free access, there will be overuse of the resource, since private users will carry the use of the resource up to the point where the average return, including the share of the uncharged rent on the resource collected by the user, is equal to the average cost of exploiting the resource paid by the user (which does not include the uncharged rent). In short, if everyone has the right to fish in any river or lake, and pays no fee for this right, the rivers and lakes will be overfished to the point where the catch available to any fisherman is just worth his while to catch. Similarly, if anyone can swim in any river or at any beach free of charge, there will be overcrowding of swimming holes and beaches; and if anyone can use a freeway without paying for the facility of using it instead of more congested and slow alternative routes, there will be congestion on the freeways. Coase's more fundamental contribution was to show that if property rights are clearly defined and transactions in such rights have negligible costs, the private competitive market will bring the problems of pollution and environment destruction under appropriate social control.

To illustrate these points concretely: first, if everyone has the right to graze his goats on the common land, or to cut down the trees on such land, it will pay everyone to use up the grass or the trees as long as the direct cost of so doing yields a net return, i.e., as long as there is enough grass left for a goat to survive and grow, or as long as there is enough timber standing to pay the costs of hiring loggers and their equipment. But it will never, or rarely ever, pay anyone to fertilize the soil and plant new grass for other people's animals to eat, or to replant timber for other people to cut. On the other hand, if one individual, or a collectivity of individuals, owned the land, it might or might not pay them to limit the number of goats being grazed, by either husbanding the goats themselves or changing a grazing fee for other people's goats, and to fertilize and seed the ground so as to maximize the profits they could make in the grazing business. Similarly, it might or might not pay them to replant the trees after they had been cut. In either case, the replanting decision would be taken only if the result were to increase the value of the property by more than the cost of the replanting; and the private decision would correspond to the socially optimal decision. By analogy, a private owner of the environment would permit pollution of it only to the extent that the price paid for the right to pollute it exceeded the reduction in the value of the property as a consequence of the pollution itself. This is what happens, for instance, on a private farm: the farmer may set aside a piece of his property on which to dump trash or burn rubbish, thereby reducing his farmable acreage, and he may rent out the right to grow crops on some of his acreage. But he will, if he is rational, do so only if the overall effect will increase his standard of living, in the one case by disposing conveniently of his waste products, and in the other by increasing his cash income above what he could obtain by his own efforts.

The relevance to the problem of the environment is as follows. Much of the environment—the air, the water supplies, the unpopulated forests and mineral-producing regions—is regarded by society as a common property resource. Everyone, whether poor or rich, is allowed to breath the air and swim and fish in the rivers—or to discharge wastes into them. The use of forests and minerals, on the other hand, is controlled in a more or less vague way by the state, and the state is entrusted with the responsibility for administering the property. In the former case, there are no clearly defined property rights, only social assumptions about how and to what extent other people will use the common property resource. In the latter case, the state's property rights may be used to obtain shortsighted political advantages for the party in power, in the two senses that rights in the common property resource may be exchanged for bribes for the politicians, and that these rights may be transferred at a price below market value in order to provide employment and the promise of economic development for the local citizens. In the former case, the absence of clearly defined property rights in the common property resource leads to what is regarded, on the one side of the argument, as pollution and, on the other, as a right of waste disposal necessary to efficient production. In the latter case, the willingness of government to dispose of natural resources at subsidized values leads to a loss of social capital, and the destruction of the environment in the genuine sense of a reduction of social wealth, instead of merely in the spurious sense of transformation of one specific kind of social wealth into another and more valuable kind.

Second, if property rights are clearly defined and transactions costs are negligble, the combined processes of private competition and legislation will arrive at the socially correct allocations of resources. Either my neighbor has the right to burn a fire whenever he wants and/or to pollute the local stream with the discharge of his wastes, in which case I must either live with the results (i.e., dry my laundry indoors or patronize a commercial laundry, or go dirty; fish at a commercial trout stream or fish farm and install my own swimming pool, or do without the pleasures of fishing and swimming), or bribe him not to exercise his rights of pollution. Or else I have the property rights in the environment, and either he has to pay the costs of preventing himself from polluting my environment, or he has to bribe me to accept the pollution he wants to impose in order to save himself the costs. (Note, in the light of the preceding argument, that I might be willing as a consumer to waive my property rights in consumption unpolluted by my neighbor in order to enjoy the benefits of high-paid employment in his productive but pollutant enterprises.)

With a clear and all-embracing definition of private property rights and an inexpensive system of litigation, there would therefore be no substantive problem of pollution and of environmental distribution. But property rights are not defined in such an all-embracing way; instead, they reflect past technologies which have made certain aspects of the environment valuable or otherwise. As an example, mineral rights in coal and solid metals are fairly clearly defined as coterminous with surface acreage. Mineral rights in petroleum are not, nor are fishing rights, the latter because the seas used to be regarded as an inexhaustible resource and the former because farm locations and boundaries are decided by surface and not sub-surface consider-ations of the distribution of natural resources. More important, the costs of property rights transactions—which include the costs of finding out with whom one needs to negotiate property rights—are extremely high in a technologically advanced economy. It is easy enough to discover—though still expensive to litigate about—who has been diverting water away from one's river in order to irrigate his own fields, and whether he is entitled to do it. It is much more difficult and expensive to determine who has been polluting one's atmosphere, and what his rights to do so are as compared with one's own rights not to have one's air polluted. (The noise caused by supersonic jets poses an even more difficult problem.)

In circumstances of either high transactions costs, or ill-defined or undefined property rights, or both, there will be, on the contrary, a tendency for pollution to reach a level beyond the socially optimum one, and correspondingly a case for government intervention of some sort to check it. More generally, whenever the total or social costs of some "good"—the private costs for labor, capital and materials that, say, a manufacturer pays in the market plus the costs that he does not pay for the uses of resources of, say, air and water to dispose of his residuals—exceed the private costs, there will be a tendency to overproduce that "good" and overuse the free resources. The result is not only a higher than optimal level of pollution but an inefficient allocation of resources among competing uses. Metal cans, for example, may result in water pollution as the ore is mined, air and water pollution in the smelting and fabrication, and solid waste disposal require-ments after use. If the costs of disposing of the residuals do not fall on the producer and user, too many metal cans will be made and subsequently dumped, too much acid mine waste will go into streams, and too much smelter exhaust into the air.

Assuming that the normal mechanisms of property rights and litigation cannot be efficiently applied, there may then be a case for the government to use its coercive powers of taxation and prohibition of activities to improve the situation, but not always so, because the use of these powers also involves enforcement costs. However—and this is a crucial point—the socially optimal government policy does not generally consist solely in taxing the polluters of the environment, let alone in prohibiting any form of pollution as specified by the currently available technology and the current preference system. The optimal policy involves determining the socially optimal amount of pollution, and implementing a system of taxes on the gainers from pollution *and* subsidies to the losers from it accordingly in the light of some determination of what the fair distribution of property rights should be. As one of many conceivable examples, if a river is being polluted by paper-pulp production, prohibition of such production or insistence that pulp manu-facturers use a non-polluting technology (a form of tax on them) might well be socially less efficient than a smaller tax on pulp mills used to provide free communal parking, swimming pools, and fish ponds, since the former remedy might well benefit the aesthetically sensitive rich while depriving the poor of employment opportunities, while the latter would compensate the poor for pollution by providing equivalent free facilities for recreation.

As in the case of the farmer who sets aside part of his land for rubbish disposal, society will, if it is rational, incur costs for pollution abatement (whether in the form of higher taxes, higher prices, or loss of jobs and income) only to the extent that it improves its standard of living by eliminating "bads" whose value is at least as great as the costs of getting rid of them.

Society achieves a socially optimal amount of pollution when it is not willing to give up any further "goods" to achieve a further reduction of "bads." In this situation, intelligent public policy confronts two difficult tasks: determining the value society places on the "bads" inevitably asso-ciated with the production of "goods," and finding means to achieve the reduction of "bads" at the least cost in foregone "goods." Much of the debate over environmental policy revolves around the varying assessments of different individuals and groups of the values of the "bads" resulting from economic activity and the differing mechanisms prescribed for reducing these "bads."

Economic Growth and the Environment

As mentioned in the introduction, there have been flurries of popular concern about the effects of man, and specifically the expansion of man's numbers and the increase in his per capita production and consumption, on his environment and hence on his future prospects for well-being. This concern has arisen at various times in the contemporary (post–World War II) period.

Population Growth and Food Shortage

Early in the postwar period there was widespread concern along very orthodox Malthusian lines about a prospective shortage of food resulting from rapid rates of population growth in most parts of the world. As mentioned, this concern confused starvation with general poverty, rapid population growth helping to perpetuate the latter (where it exists) but not necessarily the former. Of greater practical importance, the "food alarmists" failed to take account of the possibilities of increasing agricultural production by developing and applying improved agricultural technology. These possibilities have been amply demonstrated since by the so-called green revolution, which has led to the appearance of embarrassing food surpluses in some regions or countries formerly regarded as famine prone. In any case, a prospective food shortage that actually began to manifest itself would do so through a general rise in food prices, which would call into play a wide variety of mechanisms that would tend to correct the situation. These would include, on the consumer side, a variety of substitutions of alternatives to food as a source of warmth (heating, warm clothing, etc.), more care in minimizing waste in the use of food (the "leftover" meal would come back, as would "potluck," and food would be increasingly prepared in the household instead of in the factory), and substitutions toward the cheaper types of nourishment. On the producer side, there would be, in addition to the profitability-induced investment in superior agricultural technology just mentioned, a profitability-induced expansion of agricultural output in the two forms discussed by the classical economists—taking new and fertile land into cultivation, and working existing farmland more intensively.

It is important in this connection to note that in the developed countries there has been a general tendency toward withdrawing farmland from cultivation, as rising real wages made possible by economic growth have made farming unprofitable except on the most fertile lands using the most productive methods, and that this land could always be returned to cultivation if food prices became high enough. It should also be pointed out that much cultivation is devoted to the production of crops other than foodstuffs, and that if food became sufficiently high-priced, land would be diverted from those other crops to food production. Finally, it should be noted that while an increase in food prices hits the poor and the lower-income groups hard, it touches the rich and the high-income groups very lightly, since the proportion of the budget spent on food falls as income rises ("Engel's Law"). Hence, it is nonsense to conjure up, as some of the population problem extremists have done, a vision of the world's population all starving to death simultaneously.

Economic Growth

More recently, concern has shifted from population growth to general economic growth as a source of alarm. Such concerns have varied in nature. A good many, in this writer's somewhat biased judgment, tend to reflect a conservative and aristocratic hankering after an earlier and simpler period of social organization in which people knew and kept to their place and upstarts could not become as affluent as oneself (or worse, destroy one's affluence) by making intelligent use of new resources and new technologies. In addition, some of this thinking is marked by strong undertones of anti-Americanism, both in general and reflecting the dislike of the rest of the world for and the disillusionment of American opinion with the war in Viet Nam. One may cite John Kenneth Galbraith's olympian disdain for the failure of the United States to use its private affluence for public purposes (both to construct a nobler physical environment and to transfer income to the poor) and to make work more interesting to the worker; E. J. Mishan's obvious dislike of the fact that affluence allows the hoi polloi to enjoy the good things of life (the wonders of nature, privacy, and so on) formerly reserved for the few wealthier members of society, and hence to impair his own enjoyment of them by intruding on them; and the recently popularized idea that economic growth will destroy the ecology of the planet, which obviously involves a certain amount of covert anti-Americanism and a large amount of political conservatism. The extreme policy recommendation of no (further) growth, which presumably would freeze everyone into his current position in the economic system, and among other things keep the rich countries rich and the poor countries poor, can hardly be interpreted as the voice of liberalism and democracy speaking.

A full discussion of all the issues raised by the critics of economic growth would require a book. Two issues seem worth detailed discussion here: the effects of economic growth on the quality of life, and the effects of growth on the "ecosystem" (the so-called coming ecological crisis). In each case, it is assumed for simplicity that the population problem can be ignored, and that economic growth is synonymous with rising income per head.

Growth and the Quality of Life. It must be recognized at the outset that the Gross Domestic Product (GDP) is a statistical measurement of a clearly specified and internationally standardized kind, and as such is not, and is not intended to be, a measure of national welfare; nor is GDP per head a measure of average individual welfare, nor the rate of growth of GDP per head a measure of improvement of average welfare over time. The GDP measures the market value of final goods and services produced by the economy (for growth calculations, the prices used are standardized on some base year, to isolate "real" growth of quantities from the effects on money prices of inflation or deflation and the effects of changes in relative prices). There are many things which affect the quality of life that do not pass through the market, for example, the by-product "bads" resulting from the production of "goods," and some of those that do pass through the market, such as the costs of police forces, social workers, and regulating departments of government of various kinds, should more properly be regarded as costs of the production of goods and services rather than as the production of goods and services themselves, though by stretching the imagination one might regard them as contributing to human welfare by reducing the production of "bads."

It must also be recognized that economic growth, especially in the contemporary form of large-scale industrial production and urbanization of the population, tends to increase the production of "bads" as well as of "goods." Examples include the emergence of problems of fresh water supplies and of sewage and garbage disposal as cities grow in size and their residents wax more affluent, and of atmospheric and water pollution as factory production per head rises. These are objective "bads"; but there are also subjective "bads" resulting from the fact that both people and their increasing affluence get in each other's way. An automobile is a great asset if I live in a modest-sized town where few other people have them, and I can use it to get quickly to and from work and to take myself and my family to isolated spots of natural beauty. It becomes less of an asset, perhaps even a liability, if I live in a large city where a lot of other people have one, I have to make my way to work through traffic jams and at considerable risk of accidents, and when I drive out to the country I have to find a parking place among the other sightseers and listen to their bawling children and their portable radios while I seek to commune with nature. Similarly, the occasional countryside shack representing rural poverty is not too much of an eyesore, and may even have a certain charm; a ghetto of people living the same way (though at what for them constitutes an improved standard of living) affronts my eyes and social conscience and may involve considerable danger to my life or my property.

That much being said, the opinion may be ventured that those who complain most about the adverse effects of economic growth on the quality of life tend to start their complaints implicitly from an extremely egocentric view of society. This comes in two forms, one considerably more admirable than the other. The more admirable one consists of imaginatively putting oneself in the place of the lower and less affluent orders, and saying "I would not like to work in a factory turning bolts in an assembly line all day; and I would not like to spend all my evenings watching television in a tiny apartment or little suburban house. A society that makes people live that way is a very low-quality society, and if that is what economic growth produces I am against it." The egocentricity consists in assuming that because the way they live is unattractive compared with the way you live, it is less attractive to them than the way they would have to live if it were not for affluence and growth—which way would necessarily not be yours. But the argument has an admirable side, in stressing that there is culture and there are higher standards of taste. What it overlooks is something that is reflected in many nineteenth-century novels about the *nouveaux riches*: they are as aware of their cultural poverty as are their social critics, but they have to learn for themselves how to improve their tastes and spending habits.[6] It betrays a great deal of unjustified pessimism about man as a social animal to assume that as he becomes more and more affluent he will become more and more of a pig. After all, our existing standards of culture, taste and the good life were built up by a discriminating use of their affluence by kings and nobles. If they could learn to use their money to support the arts rather than gluttony, drunkenness and lechery, why should the common man be different? And, in any case, why should he be deprived of the opportunity to try, by a forcible cessation of the economic growth that gives him that opportunity?

There is a further aspect to this subject. Some social critics, while pessimistic about the capacity of the lower-income groups to learn how to spend the rising income that economic growth brings them, would be quite happy and indeed anxious to transfer income to them provided that the ways in which it was spent were carefully supervised by the state. It is a fact that economic growth per se does very little to change the distribution of income in a more egalitarian direction, though it does accomplish something in this direction over time, largely by increasing the productive value of labor skills. Hence, economic growth is not an engine for producing economic equality, and there has been considerable despondency recently in less developed countries about this fact. On the other hand, there are fairly strict political limits as to how far the high-income groups in an economically static society will tolerate fiscal redistribution of their incomes toward lower-income groups. And there is a fairly firmly established view among politicians in various countries that it is much easier to redistribute *increments* of income, which the nominal recipients will not miss, than *existing* income, which will force them to reduce their existing standards of living rather than merely their potential increase in standard of living. This may, of course, merely be a political myth, and it is clearly not a strong argument for government policies to raise the rate of economic growth by all available means, regardless of consequences for the environment and for the quality of life. But it is a serious qualification to the assertion that stopping or slowing down the rate of economic growth that the economy would otherwise produce would improve the quality of life, if "quality" is defined to include social justice in the personal distribution of income.

The less admirable form of egocentricity involves the complaint that other people's affluence reduces the value of one's own claim to the use of the environment ("public goods") and of one's own income. Well-paid jobs for them mean pollution of the rivers and the air for me, too many cars on the road for me to drive with the ease, speed and safety I would like, too many people on the top of a mountain I would like to stand on in splendid isolation. High incomes for them mean too many people competing with me for cheap personal service, and for tenancy of my cheap little flat in the center of London, or out-doing me in the kind of housing and household equipment I can afford. If I could just stop economic growth, I could preserve the public goods for the unrestrained enjoyment of people of taste like myself, and prevent these economic upstarts from competing away my comforts and my sense of social superiority.

Clearly, the argument that economic growth should be stopped in order to preserve the quality of my private life in terms of purchasing power over goods and services is too self-seeking to be given serious consideration. The argument about public goods, however, does have a kind of economic truth in it, if one divorces it from the argument that growth should be stopped in order to prevent others from causing congestion of facilities that I could previously enjoy in privacy. There is undoubtedly a tendency, as economic growth proceeds and affluence rises, for public goods to become overused and hence less enjoyable. But the proper remedy is not to stop growth and quash the possibility of affluence for those who have not yet enjoyed it, but to impose a charge for the use of the public good. If there are too many people climbing to the mountain top for those who get there to enjoy the view, ration access by charging a high enough fee to keep the numbers down. If water is being polluted by the by-product "bads" of goods production, tax production enough to make consumers pay for the damage their consumption of "goods" imposes on the unwilling consumers of "bads." Similarly, if the roads get overcrowded, congested and dangerous, tax the owners of motor vehicles enough to achieve a combination of road provision and road usage that is socially optimal. (One can also throw in a system of establishing minimum safety standards for vehicles and their drivers and testing them regularly.)

The central points here are that the "quality of life" in a growing society should not be left for evaluation to the self-interest of the already affluent in monopolized amenities, cheap labor service, and ostentatious charity, but should be judged by the quality of life for the not-yet-affluent. As general affluence increases, people gradually acquire higher standards both for their own private consumption and for the control of the use of public goods. A poor society can afford to let a few habitual drunkards drive around in fast cars. As it gets more affluent, other people who can afford to buy cheap and unsafe cars are allowed the same privileges. As it becomes still more affluent, people become more and more conscious of the need for their own well-being of well constructed roads and the imposition of more stringent standards of driver and vehicle safety. Far from economic growth deteriorating the quality of life for the average man, it tends to improve that quality; but the process is one of learning better ways of doing things, and it frequently takes considerable time to appreciate what is vulgar, dangerous or antisocial about the old ways, and what new ways will be more effective.

Growth and Resources. Concern about the effects of economic growth on the quality of life is a matter of taste and preference, and subject to argument on the grounds of whose taste, whose preferences and what time perspective is being asserted. Concern about the effects of economic growth on the ecology of the planet purports, at least, to be a matter of objective economic analysis. As such, it is essentially a more sophisticated version of Malthusianism, sophisticated by the recognition that the totality of natural resources, and not merely agricultural land, constitute the environmental capital with which man has to work, and that unlike agricultural land in the classical model many of these resources are depletable and will disappear in their original form as they are extracted from nature and employed in the productive process. But the assertion of a coming "ecological crisis" is as crude and unsophisticated in its economic analysis as the crudest form of Malthusianism, in neglecting the fact that manifest scarcities will give rise to price changes which, in turn, will promote substitutions in favor of cheap as opposed to expensive materials, products and forms of consumption, and the exploration of new technologies for transforming the environment into useful goods and services.

It should be noted that there are two crucial fallacies in the usual practice (which may be either statistically naive or statistically sophisticated) of projecting current rates of increase of usage of materials and energy sources provided by the environment into the future and comparing the results with presently known available supplies of these inputs. First, current rates of usage and rate of increase of usage reflect the current abundance and cheapness of the inputs in question. This, in turn, reflects current market conditions and expectations of future market conditions on the part of both private producers and users of these inputs, and the governments which frequently control access to these inputs. Consumption of oil, for example, has been rising rapidly because oil has been a relatively cheap fuel; and it has been cheap partly because the governments of countries with proven oil supplies have been anxious to sell the fuel quickly, in order to cash in on their good fortune.[7] If it were known with certainty that oil would become extremely scarce in one or two decades, it would be advantageous for either the governments to keep their oil underground and borrow on the value of the asset, or for oil companies to buy up oil rights but keep the oil itself underground until the future had produced an increase in its value. It is economic nonsense to project rates of oil consumption on the basis of the effects of current low prices into a future when it is predicted that oil will become scarce. As it becomes scarce (assuming it does), oil prices will rise, oil reserves will be held for future profit rather than exploited immediately, substitutes for oil will be found, and the rate of increase of oil consumption, and perhaps even the absolute amount of oil consumption, will drop as a result.

Second, estimates of the availability of natural resources such as oil and other minerals are not made on a total, once-for-all, global inventory basis. Instead, they are largely the result of investments in exploration by private companies that wish to ensure themselves adequate supplies to meet future demand over a commercially reasonable period ahead, on the basis of existing technology and costs of production. Even where the exploration is undertaken by governments, the estimates are made in the light of existing technology and cost configurations. About twenty years ahead is the limit of worthwhile exploration of existing supplies, though the explorations some-times turn up resources that might be commercially profitable with a sufficient increase in price or improvement of technology. Estimates of this kind provide no basis for predictions that in twenty years' time the world will run out of oil, or iron, or whatever. By the time the twenty years have passed, either further exploration will have discovered a further twenty years' supply exploitable at the then prevailing prices and technology, or the price will have risen so much that other materials became dominant in the production process.

These remarks simply illustrate the fallacies of applying arithmetic, whether crude of sophisticated, to an economic system in which the available factual information is itself generated by the economic processes of competi-tion and growth, and hence represents no inevitability in the relationship between man and his environment. If man's economic system currently depends on an unsustainable rate of increase of production of oil, iron, hydroelectric power, or anything else, this does not mean that man is doomed to ecological disaster. It means only that the unsustainability of his present productive system will gradually communicate itself to him via the market system of changing prices reflecting changing relative scarcities, and that he will react both by developing new technologies for more efficient production of old inputs from the environment and by substituting new types of inputs, perhaps involving new technologies, for the old. The process will definitely not be smooth, efficient and error-free; but there is no reason whatsoever to think that it will inevitably fail, and still less to think that it is imperative to avoid any possible risk by stopping economic growth in its tracks. In fact, one could argue the contrary: if man were compelled to live by his present technologies and their corollary definitions of the usable part of the environment, he might well run into disaster, because present technologies do involve the using up of certain depletable resources made available by the environment. It is only by switching to new technologies and the use of new resources from the environment that he can hope to maintain his present standard of living, let alone keep increasing it and improving his welfare. There is also the consideration that only as his standard of living rises can he afford to devote larger amounts of his resources to the preservation and improvement of that part of his environment that he considers valuable. It is the rich countries and not the poor ones that can afford to turn potentially valuable hunting, fishing and farming areas into game preserves and national parks, insist on industrial safety devices and the control of air pollution by smoke from factories, homes and automobiles, build safe roads and insist on safety in driving practices and automobile construction, and provide good housing, schooling and medical care to their poorer citizens.

To maintain that economic growth, and not the impediment or prohibition of it, is the way to betterment of the quality of life and the avoidance of ecological disaster, however, is not to deny that economic growth involves ecological problems. New technologies often have considerable side effects that might have been foreseeable if more time and effort had been put into studying them before the new technologies were introduced. This is one of the major defects of the private enterprise system (although this term should be interpreted to include the entrepreneurial activities of governments as well)— that it emphasizes immediate benefits to the neglect of longer-run costs. Perhaps it is a defect attributable more fundamentally to the shortness of human life, and the even more abbreviated period during which human beings are entrusted by their fellow men with powers of economic and social decision making. Thus far, man has on the whole succeeded in remedying his errors in time, using the powers of public opinion and government to correct failures of the private competitive system to take account of all the relevant social considerations, especially as regards adverse effects of private competitive activity on the environment. But, as mentioned in an earlier section, the most advanced technologies, and specifically those that involve using the common property resources of the oceans and the atmosphere, may be perpetrating damage that is irretrievable.

We can replant forests, de-pollute water, rebuild our city centers, and re-landscape our suburbs and the scenery around our highways. What we cannot yet do is re-create extinct species of animals, birds and fish by laboratory methods, let alone reproduce valuable mental and physical characteristics of man himself. Nor is it yet established that we have the scientific capacity to remedy the damage we may be doing to our oceans and our upper atmosphere by treating both as a costless medium for the transport of people and goods, and the oceans as an inexhaustible source of fish and crustaceans for human nourishment.

It is in this direction, rather than in the direction of the conventional problems of population pressure and the destruction of the environment as conventionally conceived, that one must look for the genuine and difficult problems of the potentially adverse effects of man's activities on his environment.

Notes

Chapter 2

1. Lionel Robbins, *An Essay on the Nature and Significance of Economic Science* (New York, 1935), p. 16.

2. Robbins's work, ibid., was an important stimulus in this direction at its time; the *locus classicus* of the positive philosophy for the postwar generations of economists is Milton Friedman's "The Mehodology of Positive Economics," in his *Essays in Positive Economics* (Chicago: University of Chicago Press, 1953), pp. 3–43.

3. Much of this work was done at the London School of Economics and Political Science by G. C. Archibald and Kelvin Lancaster as part of their important work on the content of qualitative maximization models; see in particular G. C. Archibald, "Chamberlin versus Chicago," *Review of Economic Studies* 29 (1961): 1–28.

4. Armen Alchian, "Uncertainty, Evolution, and Economic Theory," *Journal of Political Economy* 58 (1950): 211–21.

5. G. S. Becker, "Irrational Behavior and Economic Theory," *Journal of Political Economy* 70 (1962): 1–13. The present writer anticipated Becker in reaching this conclusion, but failed to develop its implications: see appendix to R. L. Marris, "Professor Hicks' Index Number Theorem," *Review of Economic Studies* 25 (1957): 25–40.

6. J. E. Meade, *The Theory of International Economic Policy,* vol. 2, *Trade and Welfare* (Oxford, 1955); R. G. Lipsey and K. Lancaster, "The General Theory of Second Best," *Review of Economic Studies* 24 (1956): 11–32.

7. For a compendium of approaches to a variety of economic problems in terms of the human capital concept, see T. W. Schultz, ed., "Investment in Human Beings," *Journal of Political Economy* 70 (October 1962), Suppl. The most detailed exposition of the concept as it applies to labor is to be found in G. S. Becker, *Human Capital: A Theoretical and Empirical Analysis, with Special Reference to Education* (New York, 1964).

8. G. S. Becker, "A Theory of the Allocation of Time," *Economic Journal* 75 (1965): 493–517.

9. Saburo Okita, *Causes and Problems of Rapid Growth in Postwar Japan and their Implications for Newly Developing Economies,* Japan Economic Research Center, Center Paper No. 6, March 1967, p. 36.

10. As an example, see George J. Stigler, "The Economics of Information," *Journal of Political Economy* 69 (1961): 213–25.

11. See especially Anthony Downs, *An Economic Theory of Democracy* (New York, 1957).

12. J. K. Galbraith, *The Affluent Society* (New York, 1958).

13. J. M. Buchanan, "Simple Majority Voting, Game Theory, and Resource Use," *Canadian Journal of Economics and Political Science* 27 (1961): 337–48.

14. Brinley Thomas, "The International Circulation of Human Capital," published in *Minerva* 5 (1967): 479–506.

15. For a convenient collection of extended statements of this and other points of view on the problem of "brain drain," see Walter Adams, ed., *The Brain Drain* (New York, 1968).

16. See G. S. Becker, *Human Capital,* chap. 2, section 1.

17. A further line of attack, that might be considered by those concerned about "brain drain"

but unwilling to contemplate fundamental changes in pricing policies for brains, would be to increase the proportion of the returns to education received in the years immediately after completion of formal training, since it is at this stage of life that individuals are most mobile and the attractions of higher income to meet the cost of establishing a comfortable household most pressing.

18. For a more extended treatment of this subject, see Harry G. Johnson, "Advertising in Today's Economy," in *The Canadian Quandary*, chaps. 17 and 18.

19. For a discussion of poverty in the context of the American "War on Poverty," see Harry G. Johnson, "Unemployment and Poverty," chap. 9, pp. 182–99 in Leo Fishman, ed., *Poverty Amid Affluence* (New Haven, 1966). Other contributions to this volume illustrate the contributions economic analysis can make to the understanding of this problem and possible solutions to it.

20. I am grateful to my sometimes colleague, Professor T. W. Schultz, for stressing the importance of this factor in the long run explanation of the persistence of poverty.

Chapter 3

1. Lionel Robbins, *An Essay on the Nature and Significance of Economic Science*, 2d ed. (London, 1935), p. 16.

2. An abridged version, under the title "Rostow on Economic Growth," may be found in the *Economist* 192, no. 6051 (August 1959): 409–16.

3. Cf., e.g., Alfred Marshall, *Principles of Economics*, 8th ed. (London, 1920).

4. See his *Ethics of Competition* (London, 1935), esp. "Ethics and the Economic Interpretation," 19–40.

5. R. F. Kahn, "Some Notes on Ideal Output," *Economic Journal* 45, no. 177 (March 1935): 1–35, esp. 24 ff.

6. For a more extended discussion of the problems raised for both normative and positive economics by the creation of wants, with particular reference to advertising, see my "The Consumer and Madison Avenue," *Current Economic Comment* 22, no. 3 (August 1960): 3–10.

7. See Vance Packard, *The Hidden Persuaders* (New York, 1957).

8. See W. H. Whyte, *The Organization Man* (New York, 1956).

9. K. E. Boulding, *A Reconstruction of Economics* (New York, 1950), esp. chap. 8, pp. 135–54.

10. Marshall, in a letter to Edgeworth dated 26 April 1892, explains that he "deliberately decided that temporary demand curves . . . would not be of any practical use."

11. For a fuller analysis of the theory of demand for consumer durables, see, e.g., J. S. Cramer, "A Dynamic Approach to the Theory of Consumer Demand," *Review of Economic Studies* 24 (2), no. 64 (February 1957): 73–86; Richard Stone and D. A. Rowe, "The Market Demand for Durable Goods," *Econometrica* 25, no. 3 (July 1957): 423–43; Hans Neisser, "The Pricing of Consumers' Durables," *Econometrica* 27, no. 4 (October 1959): 547–74; Arnold C. Harberger, ed., *The Demand for Durable Goods* (Chicago, 1960).

12. I am indebted for this notion to G. A. Elliott, "The Impersonal Market," *Canadian Journal of Economics and Political Science* 24, no. 4 (November 1958): 453–64, esp. 461–62.

13. One of the embarrassments of a long scholarly life is that one forgets significant articles that have shaped one's own subsequent thinking; I am grateful to James Tobin for reminding me of Talcott Parsons's two articles on Marshall: "Wants and Activities in Marshall," *Quarterly Journal of Economics* 46 (November 1931): 101–40, and "Economics and Sociology: Marshall in Relation to the Thought of His Time," *Quarterly Journal of Economics* 46 (February 1932): 316–47. Parsons stresses the interaction in Marshall's thought of "economic theory proper" and a theory of the progressive development of human character and activities in relation to economic want-satisfaction. While the late nineteenth-century British form of "free industry and enterprise" that Marshall regarded as the apotheosis of the latter development has proved to be a transient historical phase, I still find the more general notion of increasing rationality in the selection and cultivation of wants a persuasive view of the nature of capitalism.

14. E. H. Chamberlin, *The Theory of Monopolistic Competition* (Cambridge, Mass., 1933).

15. Marshall, *Principles of Economics*, pp. 315-17.

16. Cf. A. G. Papandreou, "Some Basic Problems in the Theory of the Firm" in B. F. Haley, ed., *A Survey of Contemporary Economics* (Homewood, Ill., 1952), vol. 2, chap. 5.

17. New York, 1959, chap. 10, pp. 88-100, esp. sec. 4, pp. 93-95.

18. For a critique of modern theory stressing this aspect of the Ricardian system, see M. H. Dobb, *Political Economy and Capitalism* (New York, 1945).

19. Marshall, *Principles of Economics*, bk. 5, chaps. 8-12.

20. Irving Fisher, *The Nature of Capital and Income* (New York and London, 1906).

21. J. Schumpeter, *The Theory of Economic Development*, trans. Redvers Opie (Cambridge, Mass., 1934); F. H. Knight, *Risk, Uncertainty and Profit* (Boston and New York, 1921). For an interesting reformulation of the theory of profit on Schumpeterian lines, see R. Triffin, *Monopolistic Competition and General Equilibrium Theory* (Cambridge, Mass., 1940), esp. chap. 5, pp. 158-87.

22. David Ricardo, *On the Principles of Political Economy and Taxation*, in P. Sraffa, ed., *The Works and Correspondence of David Ricardo* (Cambridge, 1951), 1:67.

23. Cf. Joan Robinson, *The Economics of Imperfect Competition* (London, 1933), chap. 8, pp. 102-19.

24. E.g., R. F. Harrod, *Towards a Dynamic Economics* (London, 1948), and the voluminous journal literature which has grown from it; W. J. Fellner, *Trends and Cycles in Economic Activity* (New York, 1956); Joan Robinson, *The Accumulation of Capital* (London, 1956).

25. See M. Kalecki, "The Determinants of Distribution of National Income," *Econometrica* 6, no. 2 (April 1938): 97-112; also N. Kaldor, "Alternative Theories of Distribution," *Review of Economic Studies* 23 (2), no. 61 (February 1956): 83-100. Whether the share is constant enough to pose a problem is a matter for legitimate scepticism: cf. J. T. Dunlop, *Wage Determination under Trade Unions* (New York, 1944), chap. 8, 149-91, and R. M. Solow, "A Skeptical Note on the Constancy of Relative Shares," *American Economic Review* 48, no. 4 (September 1958): 618-31.

26. This remark is not inconsistent with the fact that interest in both problems is an outgrowth of the Keynesian revolution, since Keynes was extraordinarily classical in his treatment of production, as evidenced by his use of the wage unit.

27. This point has been mentioned in connection with the constant share problem by Solow ("Skeptical Note," p. 630).

28. The identification of development with capital accumulation permeates the folklore of development planning, with its emphasis on investment programming, capital: output ratios, "infra-structure," industrialization, "balanced growth," and the like.

29. James Burnham, *The Managerial Revolution* (New York, 1941); David Riesman, *The Lonely Crowd* (New Haven, Conn., 1950); Michael Young, *The Rise of the Meritocracy, 1870-2033* (London, 1958); see also Vance Packard, *The Status Seekers* (New York, 1959).

30. The argument is that ownership of capital in these two forms, and also in the form of financial assets, promotes the independence necessary for effective democratic citizenship; also that participation in the capitalist system is pluralist. It can, however, be argued on the other side that wealth breeds indifference and self-indulgence, exemplified in the opulent society by the problems of alcoholism, obesity, divorce, and automobile accidents: cf. the pessimistic views of Dennis Gabor, "Inventing the Future," *Encounter* 14, no. 5 (May 1960): 3-16, esp. 14 ff.

Chapter 4

1. Sir William Beveridge, *Social Insurance and Allied Services* (London, 1942), part 1, pp. 5-20.

2. Burton Weisbrod, "The Valuation of Human Capital," *Journal of Political Economy* 69, no. 5 (October 1961): 425-36.

3. T. W. Schultz, "Education and Economic Growth," chap. 3, pp. 46–88, in *Social Forces Influencing American Education 1961*, Sixtieth Yearbook of the National Society for the Study of Education, part 2.

4. Gary S. Becker, "Underinvestment in College Education?" *American Economic Review* 50, no. 2 (May 1960): 346–54.

5. Schultz, "Education and Economic Growth," pp. 82–84.

6. Cf. M. Friedman and S. Kuznets, *Income from Independent Professional Practice* (New York: National Bureau of Economic Research, 1945), chap. 4, pp. 95–173, and chap. 9, sec. 3, pp. 393–95. These authors found, on the basis of prewar data for the United States, that the average income of doctors was 32 percent higher than that of dentists; of this difference, 17 percent could be accounted for by the cost of the three years additional education required of doctors; the remainder is attributed to the greater difficulty of entry into medicine.

7. See Reuben Kessel, "Price Discrimination in Medicine," *Journal of Law and Economics* 1 (October 1958): 20–53. For an analysis of the influence of the Canadian medical profession on Canadian public policy regarding health and related matters, see Malcolm G. Taylor, "The Medical Profession and Public Policy," *Canadian Journal of Economics and Political Science* 26, no. 1 (February 1960): 108–27.

Chapter 7

1. S. G. Checkland, "The Propagation of Ricardian Economics in England," *Economica*, n.s. 16, no. 61 (February 1949): 40–52.

2. See Harry G. Johnson, "Monetary Theory and Monetary Policy," *Euromoney* 2 (December 1970): 16–20.

3. Axel Leijonhufvud, *On Keynesian Economics and the Economics of Keynes* (New York, 1968).

4. Alvin Hansen, "Economic Progress and Declining Population Growth," *American Economic Review* 29 (March 1939): 1–15.

5. Milton Friedman, "The Quantity Theory of Money—A Restatement," in M. Friedman, ed., *Studies in the Quantity Theory of Money* (Chicago, 1956), pp. 3–21.

6. Don Patinkin, "The Chicago Tradition, the Quantity Theory, and Friedman," *Journal of Money, Credit and Banking* 1 (February 1969): 46–70.

7. Harry G. Johnson, "Recent Developments in Monetary Theory—A Commentary," in David R. Croome and Harry G. Johnson, eds., *Money in Britain, 1959–1969* (London, 1970), pp. 83–114.

8. See Milton Friedman, "A Theoretical Framework for Monetary Analysis," *Journal of Political Economy* 78, no. 2 (March–April 1970): 193–238.

Chapter 8

1. Seymour Harris (whom I was to know but learn little from later at Harvard) got into the act very quickly with a denunciation of this; and that set off a whole wave of books on the permanent dollar shortage. The most unfortunate economist in that respect was Donald MacDougall, who managed to produce a very scholarly 400-odd page book, full of regression analyses of everything you could think of, demonstrating conclusively that there *was* a permanent dollar shortage. He had taken so long over the regressions that by the time the book came out there was clearly a dollar surplus, and the book had to be remaindered. And there has been a dollar glut virtually ever since, in more or less the same basic and mistaken sense.

Well, Keynes was right. In fact, we are suffering now in the American economy from an over-shooting of the mechanism he talked about, though the mechanism failed to grab hold for long enough for all those people to get their tenure and full professorships on the basis of "the permanent dollar shortage."

2. The description "secret seminar," incidentally, was a violent misnomer: its existence was known to all, and non-invitation to attend was deliberately used to snub those who lacked the

correct Keynesian qualifications and/or political orientation, even though their theoretical abilities were indisputably at least equal to the group's average. "Included out" in this way were both the Cambridge economist P. T. Bauer and the American visitor Milton Friedman.

3. Cambridge (U.S.A.), out of a misplaced sense of rivalry, an underestimation of its own intellectual capacity, and an abnegation of its own common sense, chose to engage with Cambridge (England) in debate about these allegedly fundamental issues in theory, and so kept Cambridge (England) in the zombie business. It is a sucker's game for Cambridge (U.S.A.). Nonsense is nonsense, no matter how prestigiously pronounced; so why take it seriously and reconstruct it to the point where you make mistakes yourself?

Chapter 10

1. For a fuller comparative treatment of the profession in different countries, see my "National Styles in Economic Research: The United States, The United Kingdom, Canada, and Various European Countries," chapter 9 in this volume.

2. This applies also to political science, though it has a longer history as a subject of scholarly study, because the great historical figures were concerned with explaining the need for the existence of government and in particular reconciling the medieval "divine right of kings" with the fact of successful revolutions.

3. To explain this distinction very briefly, "real" theory is concerned with what determines the price of potatoes relative to the price of ham, shoes and other things. If we can assume the prices of these other things to remain roughly constant on the average, we can take the short-cut of using the money (dollars and cents) price of potatoes to represent the value of potatoes in terms of their purchasing power over goods in general. But we cannot do this if all money prices on average are falling (deflation) or rising (inflation), because in a deflation a fall in the money price of potatoes is consistent with an increase in their purchasing power over other things, and in an inflation a rise in the money prices of potatoes is consistent with a decrease in their purchasing power over other things. "Monetary" theory, by contrast with "real" theory, is concerned with the causes and consequences of general movements up or down in the average money prices of goods and services, and finds the explanation of such movements in one formulation or another of the balance between the demand for and the supply of money. The problem for economists, and still more for policymakers, is to distinguish between cases in which "real" theory is approximately adequate and cases in which it is not. A case in point is inflation, with respect to which even many professional economists persist in seeking for "real" causes such as union monopoly power.

4. For an analysis of the reasons for the scientific success of the Keynesian revolution and the speed of that success, see "The Keynesian Revolution and the Monetarist Counterrevolution," chapter 7 of this volume.

5. The author can remember, as an instructor at Toronto in 1946–47, being assailed by a pamphlet attacking a new textbook by an eminent Keynesian in a midwestern university as being subversive. As a graduate student at Harvard, he overheard a telephone conversation in which the anti-Keynesian chairman at Harvard assured a chairman elsewhere that the man he was recommending for appointment was definitely not a Keynesian.

6. When the author was a professor of economic theory in Manchester, virtually no one in the communications media, let alone the civil service or the Parliament, solicited his views on any public policy issue. When, after an interval perhaps significant in terms of the increasing emphasis of the British political process on economic growth as the panacea for the country's problems, he became the professor of political economy at the London School of Economics, he found himself deluged with such solicitations from all quarters of the "establishment."

7. There is a strong disagreement among economists over whether the full employment of the past quarter-century has been due to the transformation of the Keynesian revolution into economic policy, or to "natural forces" independent of policies of governments.

8. See Harry G. Johnson, "Individual and Social Choice," in William Robson, ed., *Man and*

the Social Sciences (London: Allen & Unwin, 1972), pp. 1–22 for a more detailed discussion of the development of economic theory in these terms.

9. The most obvious exception to this generalization in American economics is the rivalry between Milton Friedman of the University of Chicago and Paul Samuelson of M.I.T.; but even this is largely confined to monetary theory, and there is little but peripheral disagreement between them on issues in "real" economic theory. Similarly, though Friedman as leader of the "Chicago School" of monetarists and James Tobin as the leader of the "Yale School" of post-Keynesians are sharp adversaries in monetary theory, both when confronted with the question of the best way of dealing with the poverty problem came up independently with the proposal for a negative income tax.

10. These remarks are not meant to be condescending. The author's experience of economics outside the United States is that much of the practice, as distinct from the science, of economics is, deplorably, of exactly the same description.

Chapter 11

1. It might be noted in passing that the contemporary large business firm, to which economists would like conceptually to assimilate the university, has a problem very similar in kind, with some pressure groups demanding safer and at the same time cheaper products, others demanding higher wages and more concern for employees, others demanding the non-pollution of the environment, and still others demanding more charitable contributions to worthy causes; fortunately the corporation still has to make a profit, whereas the government-subsidized university does not.

2. This has been well described by James M. Buchanan and Nicos E. Devletoglou, *Academia in Anarchy* (New York and London: Basic Books Inc., 1970).

3. It might be best to cut off the educational process at the university admissions stage, except for genuinely professional training, and announce the results of the preliminary filter to prospective employers. They could then carry out their own training programs immediately—but this is a mischievous speculation.

4. It is relevant to observe, however, that where the university is forced to admit students whose qualifications for entry are determined by the secondary education system, it has a choice between deliberately enforcing a high first-year (or first- and second-year) failure rate—which choice simply shifts its admission procedure one or two years on—and watering down its courses to the level of comprehension of its student intake. The choice is largely one of political acceptability: American state universities have traditionally adopted the first alternative; recently, "black studies" and product adulteration have furnished a way out of the political demand for "open admission policies" in the better American universities.

5. This is one reason why academics are often avid to become university administrators—to obtain offices commensurate with their own opinion of their social importance.

Chapter 12

1. Economics at this level has been brilliantly written by John Kenneth Galbraith in *The Affluent Society* (Boston: Houghton Mifflin, 1957) and *The New Industrial State* (Boston: Houghton Mifflin, 1967). From another point of view, Galbraith is the only leading contemporary economist to apply Marx's method seriously to modern society, as contrasted with interpreting modern society in outdated emotive language, by analyzing the contemporary system of production.

2. Joan Robinson, *The Accumulation of Capital* (London: Macmillan, 1956). For a Cambridge-oriented view of the controversy, see G. C. Harcourt, "Some Cambridge Controversies in the Theory of Capital," *Journal of Economic Literature* 7, no. 2 (June 1969): 369–405.

3. Paul H. Douglas, *Theory of Wages* (New York: Macmillan, 1934); J. R. Hicks, *The Theory of Wages*, 2d ed. (London: Macmillan, 1963).

4. Piero Sraffa, *Production of Commodities by Means of Commodities* (Cambridge: Cambridge University Press, 1960).

5. Nicholas Kaldor, "Alternative Theories of Distribution," *Review of Economic Studies* 23 (1956): 83–100.

6. Milton Friedman, "The Methodology of Positive Economics," part 1, pp. 3–43, in his *Essays in Positive Economics* (Chicago: University of Chicago Press, 1953).

7. Michael Kalecki, *Selected Essays on the Dynamics of the Capitalist Economy* (Cambridge: Cambridge University Press, 1971), chaps. 1–3.

Chapter 13

1. See, for example, R. C. O Matthews, "Why Has Britain Had Full Employment since the War?" *Economic Journal* 78, no. 311 (September 1968): 555–69.

2. Nicholas Kaldor, "The Sea-Change of the Dollar," "The New Era of Floating Rates," and "Reserves on a Commodity Standard," *The Times*, London, 6, 7, and 8 September 1971.

3. M. W. Reder, "The Theoretical Problems of a National Wage-Price Policy," *Canadian Journal of Economics and Political Science* 14, no. 1 (February 1948): 46–61.

4. J. R. Hicks, "Economic Foundations of Wage Policy," *Economic Journal* 66, no. 259 (September 1955): 388–404.

5. For a refutation of this hypothesis in the context of Chilean experience, see Tom E. Davis, "Eight Decades of Inflation in Chile: A Political Interpretation," *Journal of Political Economy* 71, no. 4, (August 1963): 389–97.

6. See my "Government and the Corporation: A Fallacious Analogy," in *Approaches to Greater Flexibility of Exchange Rates: The Burgenstock Papers*, ed. George N. Halm (Princeton: Princeton University Press, 1970).

7. Anthony Downs, *An Economic Theory of Democracy* (New York: Harper and Row, 1957).

8. See particularly James Tobin, "Money and Economic Growth," *Econometrica* 33, no. 4 (October 1965): 671–84; Harry G. Johnson, "Money in a Neo-classical One-sector Growth Model", chapter 4 in *Essays in Monetary Economics* (London: Allen & Unwin, 1967); James Tobin, "Notes on Optimal Monetary Growth," *Journal of Political Economy* 76, no. 4, supplement (August 1968): 833–59; A. L. Marty, "The Optimal Rate of Growth of Money," ibid., pp. 860–73; Harry G. Johnson, "Inside Money, Outside Money, Income, Wealth, and Welfare in Monetary Theory," *Journal of Money, Credit and Banking* 1, no. 1 (February 1969): 30–45; Miguel Sidrauski, "Inflation and Economic Growth," *Journal of Political Economy* 76, no. 6 (December 1967): 796–810; D. Levhari and D. Patinkin, "The Role of Money in a Simple Growth Model," *American Economic Review* 58 no. 4 (September 1968): 713–53.

Chapter 14

1. An important signpost is the tendency for western governments to be pressed increasingly toward the use of incomes policy as a means of controlling the inflation otherwise virtually inevitably consequent on state assumption of responsibility for providing full employment as a matter of achieving the two presumed social objectives of economic efficiency and economic equality. What is initially intended as a macroeconomic policy for eliminating a socially undesirable side effect of pursuit of these objectives immediately and inevitably becomes a range of microeconomic policy interventions in the freedom of individual economic decisions.

2. For further discussion see my *Theory of Income Distribution* (London: Gray-Mills Publishing, 1973), especially the final two chapters, one of which constitutes chapter 15 below.

3. In place of resenting those people whose life style involves high and conspicuous consumption of material goods, one might well pity them for the poverty of personal and cultural resources that makes this life style their optimal choice. Some radicals, of course, manage to meld resentment and contempt to a high pitch of moral indignation about those who live more richly and ostentatiously than themselves.

4. The author has encountered complaints in Sweden that the younger generation is unwilling to adopt careers requiring responsibility and hard work, and in the United Kingdom that it is impossible to do the private saving required to attain a modicum of independence; while in the United States there is mounting complaint that "welfare" makes it preferable for inordinately large numbers of people to opt out of work entirely.

Chapter 17

1. Richara N. Cooper, "Eurodollars, Reserve Dollars, and Asymmetries in the International Monetary System," *Journal of International Economics* 2, no. 4 (September 1972): 325–44.

2. It may be noted as a theoretical point that while the unit of account function does not necessarily entail the standard for deferred payments function, the medium of exchange function necessarily requires money to be a store of value at least for the period between sales and purchases of goods, services, and assets. Hence, instead of distinguishing sharply, as many writers do, between these two functions of the dollar as such, it might be more acurate to say that the international function of the dollar as a medium of exchange promotes the use of assets dominated in dollars as the unit of account, as a store of value.

3. The points of view described in this paragraph may seem bizarre to many readers; so much so that some readers have asked for references. Unfortunately, useful references are hard to provide, since this approach was most prominent in the early years after the Second World War, when the writer was a graduate student, among other things strongly flavoring the contemporary writings of Thomas Balogh, and has tended to be suppressed since then by the rise to dominance of a more scientific-theoretical approach to international monetary relations. It tends to survive among certain European economists and among some Japanese economists. Readers will have to be satisfied by the writer's assurance that there is such a tradition, though much of it is oral.

4. A "bad actor" in the sense of running a chronic balance-of-payments surplus and draining both gold and employment from the rest of the world. A study, *The United States in the World Economy*, prepared by Hal B. Lary for the U.S. Department of Commerce, published in 1943 and republished by H.M.S.O. in the United Kingdom, gave apparent official U.S. support for this view, and was only the first of a series of scholarly volumes designed to provide theoretical and empirical underpinnings for the concept of "chronic dollar shortage" (eminent authors included C. P. Kindleberger, Thomas Balogh, and G. D. A. MacDougall). The journal literature was immense, the most distinguished item being J. R. Hicks's Inaugural Lecture of 1954, which stimulated many others to delve into the theoretical relation between economic growth and international trade.

5. John H. Williams, *Postwar Monetary Plans* (New York: Alfred A. Knopf, 1944).

6. See Henry C. Simons, "International Monetary and Credit Arrangements: Discussion," *American Economic Review* 35, no. 2, supplement (May 1945): 289–96, reprinted in his *Economic Policy for a Free Society*, ed. Arron Director (Chicago: University of Chicago Press, 1948), for the analysis summarized in this and the following paragraph.

7. As before, the propensity of the Americans to run a chronic balance-of-payments surplus at the expense of other nations' reserves and employment.

8. See the contemporary writings of Joan Robinson and various others associated with the Oxford Institute of Statistics; this point of view still dominates Joan Robinson's opinions on the international monetary system, as expressed in the relevant parts of her recent *Economics: A Narrow Corner* (London: Allen & Unwin, 1967).

9. Cooper, "Eurodollars, Reserve Dollars, and Asymmetries in the International Monetary System."

10. Some readers have objected that the argument is correct only if there is no "involuntary" holding of dollars by foreign central banks. Since countries could always resist dollar inflows by appropriately expansionary monetary policy on a fixed exchange rate, or by appreciation against the dollar, not to speak of investing them in non-dollar foreign earning

assets, the term "involuntary" in this context is a word essentially disguising the failure of those central banks to understand the elementary theory of economic policy and to assist them in their efforts to blame their shortcomings on the United States. About the only grain of sense in it is that the United States did use a variety of political pressure to dissuade them from attempts to turn their dollars into gold. But to have disregarded this pressure would in all likelihood have been an even worse bargain for them, as the events of 1971 showed.

11. One of the major international political and economic problems of the world is that it is currently populated by rival kinds of Europeans: the resident Europeans who never left home and bask in their assumedly superior civilization; the emigrant Europeans in North and South America and other regions of recent settlement who are uneasy about having left home but consider themselves economically and culturally superior to the resident Europeans by virtue of economic success and a more democratic way of life, and also superior to each other on an appropriate choice of economic success versus loyalty to European culture; the would-be Europeans of the ex-colonial–conquered non-white parts of the world; and the communist countries, which have espoused a minority European intellectual alternative to European capitalism in the form of Marxism or ("true") socialism.

Chapter 18

1. Jacob Viner, *Studies in the Theory of International Trade* (Chicago: University of Chicago Press, 1937), chaps. 1 and 2. This essay draws heavily on Viner's summary and more generally on Eli Heckscher's superlative two-volume work, *Mercantilism*, first published in Swedish in 1931; authorized translation by Mendel Shapiro, rev. ed. edited by E. F. Söderlund (London: Allen & Unwin; New York: Macmillan, 1955).

2. I am indebted for emphasis on this point to a paper by J. M. Letiche presented at the Conference on the History of Economic Thought, held in Chicago in May 1973; it draws the parallel between the problem of unemployment in mercantilist times and in the less developed countries at the present time.

3. By Goran Ohlin, in a paper presented to the 1968 (Montreal) World Congress of the International Economic Association; see his "Trade in a Non–Laissez-Faire World," pp. 157–75 in P. A. Samuelson, ed., *International Economic Relations* (London: Macmillan, 1969).

4. Latin American free trade associations are primarily intended to provide markets for new high-cost import substitution industries rather than rationalization of existing industries through internal competition. On EFTA, see Dr. Victoria Curzon, *Essentials of Integration: The E.F.T.A. Experience* (London: Macmillan, for the Trade Policy Research Centre, 1973).

5. On this point see D. Gale Johnson, "Government and Agricultural Adjustment," Office of Agricultural Economics Research, University of Chicago, Paper No. 73:16, 2 July 1973; mimeographed.

6. For a concrete agenda for trade policy action, developed from a European point of view, see McFadzean et al., *Towards an Open Economy: The Next Phase*, a report of the Trade Policy Research Centre (London: Macmillan, for the Trade Policy Research Centre, 1972).

Chapter 20

1. Stephen Hymer and Robert Rowthorn present an empirical refutation of the Servan-Schreiber thesis, and argue that the European corporations will in their turn become multinational and competitive with the American international corporations, in "Multinational Corporations and International Oligopoly: The Non-American Challenge," chap. 3, pp. 57–91, in Charles P. Kindleberger, ed., *The International Corporation: A Symposium* (Cambridge: M.I.T. Press, 1970).

2. S. H. Hymer, "The International Operations of National Firms: A Study of Direct Investment" (Ph.D. diss., Massachusetts Institute of Technology, 1960). For Vernon's work, see especially Raymond Vernon, "International Investment and International Trade in the Product

Cycle," *Quarterly Journal of Economics* 80, no. 2 (May 1966): 190-207. R. E. Caves, "International Corporations: The Industrial Economics of Foreign Investment," *Economica* 38, no. 149 (February 1971): 1-27.

3. An alternative theory of direct foreign investment in terms of exchange risk, according to which investors in the strongest-currency country have an advantage over investors elsewhere because their investment converts local into internationally desirable assets, has been offered by R. Z. Aliber in "A Theory of Direct Foreign Investment," chap. 1, pp. 17-34, in C. P. Kindleberger, *International Corporation.*

4. Harry G. Johnson, *Comparative Cost and Commercial Policy Theory for a Developing World Economy*, the Wicksell Lectures (Stockholm: Almqvist & Wiksell, 1968). See also "The Efficiency and Welfare Implications of the International Corporation," chap. 2, pp. 35-56 in Kindleberger, *International Corporation.*

5. Kindleberger, *International Corporation*, pp. 45-47. R. W. Jones, "A Three-Factor Model in Theory, Trade and History," in *Trade, Balance of Payments, and Growth: Essays in Honor of C. P. Kindleberger*, ed. J. Bhagwati et al. (Amsterdam: North-Holland Publishing Co., 1971), pp. 3-21.

6. See Johnson, "Efficiency and Welfare Implications of the International Corporation"; also Caves, "International Corporations." The following paragraphs draw extensively on Caves's formulation of the analysis.

7. W. B. Reddaway et al., *Effects of U. K. Direct Investment Overseas: Final Report*, University of Cambridge, Department of Applied Economics, Occasional Paper No. 15 (Cambridge: Cambridge University Press, 1968).

8. John Lindeman and Donald Armstrong, *Policies and Practices of U.S. Subsidiaries in Canada* (Washington and Montreal: The Canadian-American Committee of the National Planning Association and the Private Planning Association of Canada, 1960).

9. See, for example, C. W. Gonick, "Foreign Ownership and Political Decay," pp. 43-74 in Ian Lumsden, ed., *Close the 49th Parallel, etc.: The Americanization of Canada* (Toronto: University of Toronto Press, 1970).

10. A useful and carefully dispassionate discussion of the issues raised by American investment in the United Kingdom is presented in M. D. Steuer, *American Capital and Free Trade: Effects of Integration* (London: Trade Policy Research Centre, 1969).

11. For a fuller discussion, see my "The Multinational Corporation as A Development Agent," *Columbia Journal of World Business* 5, no. 3 (May-June 1970): 25-30.

12. For example, C. P. Kindleberger, *American Business Abroad* (New Haven and London: Yale University Press, 1969), pp. 206-7.

13. C. P. Kindleberger, *International Corporation*, pp. 5-7, in reference to Seymour J. Rubin, "The International Firm and the National Jurisdiction," chapter 7, pp. 179-204 in the volume.

14. Kenneth N. Waltz, "The Myth of National Interdependence," chap. 8, pp. 205-23 in Kindleberger, *International Corporation.*

Chapter 21

1. That is, population grows according to the series:
$$1, 1+p, (1+p)^2, (1+p)^3, (1+p)^4, \ldots (1+p)^n$$
whereas agricultural output grows according to the series:
$$1, 1+a, 1+2a, 1+3a, 1+4a, \ldots 1+na$$
It is obvious that regardless of the sizes of p and a, provided both are positive, $(1+p)^n$ must exceed $1+na$ for large enough n.

2. This, in fact, gave rise to the first birth control movement, which consisted of efforts to persuade the working class to exercise family limitation in order to improve their economic lot and standard of living. The second birth control movement was aimed at teaching middle-class women to liberate themselves from childbearing for economic activities by using newly developed contraceptive devices, and has culminated in the widespread use of oral contraception

in our time. The third birth control movement, of recent origin, has been aimed at poor people in less developed countries, and has encountered serious difficulties, on the one hand, with social motivations for procreation deriving from considerations of social status and economic security, and on the other, with the expense of contraceptive devices and the absence of the sophistication required to use them effectively.

It may be noted that contraceptive techniques have been known and used among upper-class women at least since Roman times. The problem has been to devise and popularize techniques for the masses, not the classes.

3. It is necessary here to distinguish between the alleged prospective pressure of population on food supply, and the prospective pressure of population on resources in general. The classical analysis rested on an assumed absolute limitation in the amount and fertility of available land, and a consequent pressure of increasing population on the producible food supply. This assumption that food is the limitational factor has been repeatedly falsified by the development of new technologies of food production and of substitution of other items for food, such as better warm clothing, central heating, and more indoor and sedentary occupations. Technological developments have also, in effect, added to the amount of agricultural land available to feed people. Introduction of the internal combustion engine released vast quantities of land and agricultural output previously used to feed animals. On the other hand, expansion of population at a constant standard of living, given technology, usually requires a more or less proportionate expansion of the stock of capital (exception being made for the possibility of switching to less capital-intensive types of products), and hence uses up savings that could otherwise be available for increasing capital intensity, or educational levels, on the level of technology. Thus, rapid population growth increases the dificulty of alleviating poverty. But the reason is not shortage of food or of nonagricultural natural resources per head, but shortage per head of resources in general.

4. In the early nineteenth century in England, there was a keen debate over whether the city sewage problem should be dealt with by the installation of running water systems or by provision of a service of house-to-house slop-pail collection. Running water won, and its victory led eventually to the problems of water supply and water pollution we now confront. The reader is invited to speculate on how different our society would be if sewage were handled the same way as garbage, by household collection. He should note, however, that most if not all of contemporary problems concerning water are attributable to subsidized pricing of its use, and/or to charging a flat rate overhead cost for access to water supplies rather than (or without) a charge based on volume used.

5. H. S. Gordon, "The Economic Theory of a Common-Property Resource: The Fishery," *Journal of Political Economy* 62 (April 1954): 124–42; and R. H. Coase, "The Problem of Social Cost," *Journal of Law and Economics* 3 (October 1960): 1–44.

6. In this connection, television in the United Kingdom particularly has been a powerful civilizing force; not only has it made the working-class home inhabitable by the family in the evening and virtually ended the pattern of the old man boozing at the pub in order to stay out of the presence of his wife and therefore an inevitable argument, but it has given the working class an insight (through both advertisements and films) into how more cultured people spend their money.

7. The reader should note and consider the fact that even late in the nineteenth century approximately 80 percent of U.S. energy consumption was provided by burning firewood.

Index

A.B.D. status, 179
Adjustment: asymmetry of, 248 ff.; auto-
maticity of, 250
Administration and universities, 169 ff.
Advertising, 10, 27, 36
"Agriculturalism," 278
Aggregate production function, 121, 122, 123,
189
Åkerman, J., 117
Anthropomorphism and inequality, 212
Anti-Americanism, 192; and environmen-
talism, 332
Apostles, the, 111
Arrow, K. J., 156

"Bads," production of, 324, 333
Bagehot, W., 119
Balogh, T., 121
Baumol, W. J., 41
Becker, G. S., 53, 228, 298
Belling the cat, 250–51
Bentham, *Book of Fallacies*, 227
Beveridge Report, 46
Boulding, K. E., 37
Brain drain, 26
Bretton Woods, 255
Brittan, Samuel, 87
Brunner, K., 91
Burnham, J., 44
Business and universities, 162

Cambridge: examining, 113–14; lecturing,
108–9; methodology, 190; teaching, 107
Cambridge vs. Cambridge, 188 ff., 191; and
anti-Americanism, 192
Canadian universities, slackness of, 137
Capital, consumer, 37
Capital, human. *See* Human capital
Capital theory in *General Theory*, 65, 67
Capitalism and rationality, 10, 11
Cash vs. kind, 231 ff.

Caves, R. E., 304, 305
Central banking, 75
Chamberlin, E. H., 40
Cheung, S. N., 298
Chicago oral tradition, 103
Choice, 3, 17, 18; and pollution, 324
Coase, R. H., 298, 327
Cohen, R. L., 188
Common Agricultural Policy, 280
Common Market, British case for joining,
277
Common property resources, 327; environ-
ment as, 328
Conservation movement, 320
Consume, propensity to, 71
Cooper, R. N., 250–51, 261
Cooperation, international, 252
Corporation, the, 7, 40 ff.; and research, 41
Cost-push, 75, 240
Counterrevolution in economics, 92; mon-
etarist, 92; monetarist, and petering out,
104–5; and past orthodoxy, 102
Crime, 11

Demand-pull, 75, 240
Democracy, economic theory of, 24
Devaluations, 1969, 198
Development, economic, 43, 282 ff.; and
direct foreign investment, 312–13; model
of, 286; political and social, 287–90
Direct foreign investment, 303 ff.; developing
country issues, 312–13; home country
issues, 307–10, host country issues, 310–
312; international policy issues, 314;
labor objections to, 306; theory of, 304 ff.
Discrimination, 30, 226; compensation for,
228
Disequilibrium, fundamental, 258
Disruption, trade, 294
Distribution theory, 41, 123
Dobb, M. H., 108–9

Dollar as reserve currency, 246, 264

Economic science, Keynes's theory of, 85
Economic theory: definition, 3; evolution, 106, 143 ff.
Economics, British, 134; domination by left, 87, 135; 1920s failure of, 83, 94
Economics, as English-language subject, 138; of information, 23; "positive" and "normative," 17; prospects of, 192 ff.
Education: economics of, 26, 55; free, 18; loans for, 56; and restriction, 13
Egocentricity and environmentalism, 334
Elasticity approach, 263
Employment theory, 70 ff., 97
Engels' Law, 332
England, Bank of, 83
Entrepreneurship, shortage of, 287
Environment, 54; as capital, 321; reinvestment in, 322; transformation of, 320
"Equal pay" and poverty, 229
Equilibrium, monetary, 82, 118; of poverty, 234
Eugenics, 218–19
Externalities, 4, 13, 50, 232–33, 234, 319

Family, the, 28; as automated utility factory, 39, 47–48, 224; and inequality, 218 ff.; and inflation, 207; and poverty, 223
Firm, Marshallian, 40
Fisher, I., 41, 209
Fixed rates, preference for, 251
Foundations and universities, 161
Friedman, M., 91, 242 ff.
Full employment: and affluence, 89; and Keynesian policy, 88, 199; naiveté of goal of, 88, 201; and social security, 89

Galbraith, J. K., 7, 25, 32 ff., 45, 218, 286, 322
G.D.P., limitations of as index, 332–33
General Theory, The: and bias against monetary policy, 74; capital theory in, 65; contribution of, 77; distinguished from Keynesian economics, 65; as distraction from British problems, 80; as economic literature, 62 ff.; employment theory vs. monetary theory in, 66; order of analysis in, 64; policy implications of, 73; sterile controversy, 66; and testing, 73
Gervaise, I., 269
Gold, return to in 1925, 79
Gorden. H. S., 12, 327

Government: and economics, 177 ff.; and inflation, 202; and pollution, 330; and population growth, 5; and universities, 161
Government, expansion of, 5; financing of by property, 57; and size, 25
Government, public's transactions with, 203
Growth: and environment, 330 ff.; and public goods, 335; and resources, 336
Growth models, 43; and money, 210 ff.; and poverty, 223
Gurley, O., and Shaw, 70

Hagen, E., 293
Hansen, A., 113, 198
Harris, S. E., 113
Harrod, R. F., 85
Hayek, F., 82, 118, 121
Hicks, J. R., 85, 96, 121, 123, 189, 201
Hoarding, 119
Human capital, 8, 20, 52; investment in, 49; and life quality, 9; obsolescence of, 29; and political stability, 9; and poverty, 223, 226; and rationality, 11; and universities, 155

Ideology and economics, 186 ff.
Imagination, growth of, 333
Inadequacy, human, 29
Incentives and poverty, 229
Income, lifetime, 21
Income redistribution: and growth, 334; and inflation, 206; and universities, 159
Incomes policy, 75, 89, 202, 241, 268
Inequality: and lifecycle, 215; of opportunity, 216 ff.; and preferences, 215; and risk, 216; and self-fulfillment, 213; and tastes, 214
Inflation, 74, 97, 197 ff., 239 ff.; economic costs of, 207 ff., 240; and immorality, 201; presumed irrationality of, 204 ff.; revealed preference for, 204 ff.; world, 243, 245
Inflation tax, 119, 208, 239
Information, economics of, 23; need for, 48, 326
Inside and outside money, 69
Insurance, 50, 55; reversal of, 55
Insurance principle, 46
Instalment buying, 8, 38
Integration in goods market and capital market, 244
Interest, 115
Interest-bearing money, 211
Interest groups in universities: external, 160

ff.; internal, 166 ff.
International Monetary Fund, 80, 244
International monetary theory, two traditions of, 253

Johnson, E. S., 88
Jones, R. W., 304, 305

Kahn, R. F., 113, 119
Kaldor, N., 86, 113, 122, 123, 190, 199, 275
Kalecki, M., 115, 190
Keynes, J. M., 16, 82; character of, 83–84; as end of era, 85; as speaker, 110–12
Keynes, J. N., 151
Keynesianism vs. monetarism, 199, 239
Keynesian revolution, 92 ff., 145, 177, 210, 240, 270
Knight, F. H., 36, 41, 219
Koopmans, J. J., 82

Labor as unique factor, 42
Lewis, A., 286, 293
Libraries, university, 172 ff.
Lifestyles, scholarly, 183–84, 185
Liquidity preference vs. loanable funds, 66–67, 110

Macroeconomics, 6
Malthus, T. R., 222, 317–18
Mannheim, K., 150
Markup theory, 122
Marshall, A., 15, 35, 38, 41, 78, 83, 96
Marx, K., 44
Marxo-Keynesianism, 115, 258
Maturation Hypothesis, 155
McCarthy era, 150
Meade, J. E., 85, 254, 299–300
Mercantilism, 258–60, 267 ff., 291 ff.; cost of, 279; new, 270 ff.; sophisticated, 274 ff.
Microeconomics, 7, 148
Mishan, E. J., 332
M.I.T., 191
Modigliani, F., 69
Monetary approach to balance of payments, 263
Monetary management, perversity of in 1930s, 80
Money, neutrality of, 81, 117, 210
Monument-building, and universities, 171
Mundell, R. A., 247
Myrdal, G., 150

Nation, as stable unit, 285
National Bureau of Economic Research, 134
National Institute for Economic and Social Research, 136
Nationalism: Canadian, 180; and development, 290
Negative income tax, 231
Neutrality of money. See Money, neutrality of
"n–1 problem," 261

Optimality, 4; and price stability, 211
Optimum optimorum, 262
"Optimum quantity of money," 210
Optimum tariff argument, 291; defects of, 296–97
"Orthodoxy," 16, 94; Keynesian, 97, 147
Output vs. prices, 82

Panama, 300–302
Partisanship, 142
Patinkin, D. 70, 103
Phillips curve, 241; world, 245
Ph.D., employer skepticism of, 179
Pigou, A. C., 83
Planning, Russian, 115, 284
Polarization, 9, 12
Policy, economic: and science, 141; social, 54
Policy research, 180
Political Economy Club, 111
Political economy of opulence, 32 ff., 35
Politicization of British economics, 87, 135
Politics: academic, 182 ff.; economics of, 5
Pollution: and government, 330; possibility of irrevocable, 338–39
Popper, K., 150
Population, growth of, 13, 317; and food shortage, 331
Portfolio balance theory, 68, 120
Positive economics, 101, 151
Poverty: and discrimination, 30; and inequality, 27, 220; theory of, 28 ff.
Prebisch, R., 283, 286, 296
Price expectations, 68
Price-fixing and poverty, 230
Price stability and fixed rates, 256
Private vs. public sector, 9
Production, joint, of goods and bads, 323
Professional associations and universities, 162
Professionalization, 99, 132, 151
Property, rights of, 5; in environment, 327 ff.
"Publish or perish," 185–86
Pursuit curve, 117

Quality of life, 332–33, 335 ff.
Quantity theory: and Cambridge, 117; and inflation, 239; in interwar period, 81

Reder, M. W., 201
Research, outer-directed, 133; revolution in (see Revolution, research)
Research institutes, 174
Resources, natural, 319; Ricardo misleading on, 320
Responsibility, international, 264–65
Revolution, in economics, 91, 92, 187 ff.; and absorption, 95, 100; difficulty yet ease of theory of, 95, 101; and empirical testing, 96, 101; and need for social problem, 95, 98–100; new methodology in, 96, 101; reversal of propositions in, 95, 100; speed of propagation of, 93–94, 146
Revolution, research, 129, 182; probable transience of, 139, 186; U.S. dominance in, 131–33
Ricardo, D., 41, 319
Riesman, D., 44
Robbins, L., 19, 32, 149
Robertson, D. H., 82, 84, 86, 108, 111, 112, 114–15, 116, 118, 120, 121, 210
Robinson, J., 85, 86, 109–10, 113, 116, 121, 122, 188, 190
Rostow, W. W., 35
Rowe, J. W. F., 109
Rowntree studies, 221

Samuelson, P. A., 96, 120
Saving and investment, 118
Scholarship: individual and community, 141; and society, 176
Schultz, T. W., 53, 223, 234
Schumpeter, J., 41
Scott, A. D., 116, 186
"Second-best," economics of, 20, 293
Seigniorage, 263
Service staff and universities, 173
Shive, G. F., 108
Simons, H. C. 256
Smith, A., 291
Smithsonian agreement, 249
Snow, C. P., 113
Social security and incentives, 57
Social science, problem of, 267
Special Drawing Rights, 247
"Spillovers," 306
Sraffa, P., 190

Statistical fallacies in environmental projections, 336 ff.
Students and universities, 165 ff., 183
Substitution between production and pollution, 325; for food, 331; within technologies, 338
Suburbanization, 39

Tariffs, theory of, 272 ff.
Teaching staff and universities, 166 ff.
Technological improvement, effects of, 4
Time as cost, 22, 39
Tinbergen, J., 254
Tobin, J., 68, 91, 100
Trade-off, 242
Training, specific and general, 26
Transactions costs and resources, 328 ff.
Transfers vs. investment as poverty relief, 233
Treatise, The, 64, 114, 118
Two-sector model, 124

UNCTAD, 296
Underemployment equilibrium, 72
Unemployment and mercantilism, 269
Unemployment: natural rate of, 242; and poverty, 29, 225
Unidirectional causation in General Theory, 64
"Union militancy," 202
Unions and poverty, 229
University: as competitive firm, 153 ff.; as consumption, 105, 168, 171; expansion, 182; functions of, 153 ff.; obstacles to efficiency in, 158 ff.
Urbanization, 50

Value judgments, 19, 149
Vernon, R., 304, 305

Walras, 268
Walras' Law, 121, 270
Wants, creation of, 35–36
Wealth, myth of British, 79
Wealth effect, 69, 72
Weisbrod, B., 53
Welfare economics, new, 149
Whyte, W. F., 44
Wicksell, K., 117, 209, 268
Williams, J. H., 256
World economy, 243
Women, emancipation of, 8

Young, M. 44